THE FALL OF THE SOUTHERN SHAOLIN TEMPLE

AND RISE OF THE

TEN TIGERS OF CANTON

Paul Burkinshaw

authorHOUSE

AuthorHouse™ UK
1663 Liberty Drive
Bloomington, IN 47403 USA
www.authorhouse.co.uk
Phone: UK TFN: 0800 0148641 (Toll Free inside the UK)
*   UK Local: (02) 0369 56322 (+44 20 3695 6322 from outside the UK)*

Published by AuthorHouse 09/24/2024

ISBN: 978-1-7283-8250-0 (sc)
ISBN: 978-1-7283-8520-4 (e)

Contents

Preface

The founder of our style of Kung Fu [少林功夫] [2] (referring to Chinese martial arts [中國武術] [2a]) was So Hak Fu / Su Heihu [蘇黑虎] who was famed for being one of the Ten Tigers of Canton / Kwong Tung Sap Fu [廣東十虎]. At the onset of trying to research, not only him, but also the other Tigers, I was amazed at how scarce and fragmented documentary information existed about them. I therefore started to gather any information relating to the Ten Tigers [廣東十虎] so that I could compile a detailed history of these outstanding Kung Fu masters [功夫大師]. The only possible way to do this was to research them on an individual basis as opposed to a collective group. Even this proved very difficult for several of these renowned Kung Fu masters [功夫大師] as extremely little has been recorded about them or has survived the passage of time. Besides the general lack of documentary information, I also encountered other obstacles during my study into the history of Chinese martial arts [中國武術] in the Canton [廣州] region of China.

There are several stumbling blocks in researching any information about Chinese history. One of these is the complexity of the Chinese language and, more precisely, the use of characters in writing rather than an alphabet to represent the spoken word. Due to the different dialects used in China and the use of tones (four in Mandarin and nine in Cantonese), the same word can be pronounced and then written in several different ways. For example, Cantonese speaking Chinese will pronounce and write a name one way, which is very different from Mandarin speaking Chinese in Beijing (Pinyin). Even if Cantonese is considered in isolation, similar sounding words can be represented by several different characters that bear no relationship to each other. Therefore the written word will vary due to accents and tones. I have included several Chinese individuals in this book and then continued using the more common Cantonese written character for their detailed histories thereafter. Some of the Ten Tigers were also known more by their nicknames than their real family names which also initially complicated things.

*The **Cantonese** language originated in the area of Canton (i.e. now Guangzhou) in southern China and is spoken by approximately 70 million people around the world.* [1]

Pinyin *is the phonetic method for writing down the Mandarin pronunciations of Chinese characters into the Latin alphabet in the People's Republic of China. The Hanyu Pinyin system was developed in the 1950s. It was published by the Chinese government in 1958 and has been revised several times since.* [1a]

The other factor that makes research difficult into much of Chinese martial arts [中國武術] history is that most of it was passed on orally from one generation to the next.

This was because many of these groups (especially Hung Kuen [洪拳]) were rebels whose aim it was to overthrow the Ch'ing / Qing [清朝] government. Therefore it was much safer to pass information on orally, as any written documents could be judged as treasonous and lead to the execution of the authors by beheading. Some of the historical facts then get embellished with stories or myths which when passed on orally makes it very complicated to distinguish several generations later, fact from fiction. Any written information was most likely destroyed during the many conflicts of the nineteenth and twentieth centuries in the Cantonese region of China. The Southern Siu Lum/Shaolin Temples [南少林寺], for instance, were attacked and burnt so completely that no buildings remained. All documents not removed by the monks would have been destroyed and lost forever. Some documents may also have been destroyed because they could incriminate certain Kung Fu masters [功夫大師] who were in hiding as well as proving them to be regarded as rebels and traitors by the Ch'ing / Qing [清朝] government. The Ch'ing / Qing [清朝] officials at the time may also have destroyed any documents to erase all trace of what they believed was the traitors' existence. Even during China's Cultural Revolution (1966-1976) [無產階級文化大革命], many historical relics and artefacts were destroyed in an attempt to purge "old ideas and old thought". Cultural and religious sites were ransacked and many books burnt in large public bonfires.

During the reign of the Qianlong Emperor [乾隆皇帝] (25th September 1711 to 7th February 1799), many books were either burned or the text altered and modified. It is likely that this practice may also have occurred during the reigns of the following emperors.

Over 2,000 works were listed for total suppression and another 350 for partial suppression. The aim was to destroy all writings that were anti-Qing or rebellious. The full editing of Siku Quanshu was completed in about ten years and during this time, over 3100 titles (or works), approxiamately 150,000 copies of books were either burnt or banned. The works that had been categorized into Siku Quanshu, were either deleted or modified. Books issued during the Ming dynasty suffered the greatest damage.

During the reign of Qianlong, there were 53 cases of literary inquisition which resulted in the victims being either beheaded, or victims being sliced into pieces until death (Lingchi). [1c]

An example of this is one of the source books I have used entitled, "The Qianlong Emperor Inspects Southern China / Kin Loong har Kwong Nam / Qianlong Xia Jiangnan [乾隆下江南]". [50b] It is stated that this story has been released under a variety of other titles over the years such as, "The sacred dynasty's tripods flourish, verdant for ten thousand years / Shengchao ding sheng wannian qing," and "The new tale of the marvellous hero of the everlasting Qing / Wannian qing qicai xinzhuan." These novels were first released around 1893. [50c]

Although the book provides certain information and details, it must be remembered that it was written in the prerspective of the Ch'ing Dynasty / Qing Dynasty [清朝] (1644–1912). The Southern Siu Lum / Shaolin Temples / 南少林寺, including all subsidiary temples located throughout Fukien / Fujian Province [福建省] and Guangdong Province [廣東省] and their Siu Lum / Shaolin martial artists [少林武術家] were regarded as rebels. Therefore the book was slanted to portray them in an adverse manner and to also discourage any other Siu Lum / Shaolin followers [少林追隨者]. It also emphasized how any revolutionary or rebellious people would be violently and lethally dealt with by the Ch'ing Dynasty / Qing Dynasty [清朝].

Another matter to bear in mind is that because the book was written many years after the events, some of the dates quoted are questionable. This could be a genuine mistake or possibly a deliberate intention to lessen the influence the Southern Siu Lum / Shaolin Temples [南少林寺] had in this region and how long it actually took for the Ch'ing / Qing Dynasty [清朝] to defeat them. The book states, for example, that the Siu Lum / Shaolin Abbot [少林方丈] Gee Seen [至善禪師] died at the Quanzhou Temple [泉州少林寺], but it is known that he escaped the destruction of this temple and re-established himself later at the Putian Temple [莆田寺] where several other sources state that he died many years later. I believe that the destruction of the Southern Siu Lum / Shaolin Temples [南少林寺] in Fukien / Fujian Province [福建省] actually took nearly one hundred years. This could possibly be due to not openly using the Siu Lum / Shaolin [少林] name so as to keep their presence and activities hidden from the Ch'ing / Qing Dynasty [清朝] authorities. This was most definitely the case with the temples in Canton [廣州] that were part of the Siu Lum / Shaolin [少林] order.

A third factor is that many of the sources for this period are the actual histories of the various Kung Fu [功夫] styles of today. These tend to focus on the details and persons applicable to their own style and only give part of the facts. These accounts differ from style to style and at times even contradict each other. Over time and due to the lack of concrete information, dates and stories have often been embellished to fit certain known facts. During my research, this has often been evident with the events of the early Ch'ing / Qing [清朝] period from 1650 through to the early 1800s. The discrepancies become obvious when comparing names, dates and histories of several individuals together with recorded known facts dated to the early 1800s. I have stated within this book these discrepancies and then written my assumptions and suggestions when comparing the available information.

I found that many of the notable individuals of this period sometimes differ in their accounts of the historical events that occurred. Some of these recorded versions agree in many of their facts but also differ in several important events and facts. I have tried to tie them together as much as possible to give a fuller account and thus enable the reader to draw their own conclusions.

I do not claim to be an expert on the place of the Ten Tigers in Chinese history but have used my judgement in writing as detailed a history as possible from the limited information available. It must be borne in mind that this information is only as reliable as the sources the facts come from. I have quoted the sources (internet sites, books, magazines etc) used where applicable. In this twenty-first century of open access to many documents that would otherwise have been unobtainable and the endless information on the internet, it is probably reasonable to assume that all the information we now have is all that is available. Therefore these stories and facts are all that we will ever know unless some further undiscovered documentation is unearthed.

Acknowledgements

I do not speak or read Chinese and have therefore relied on my Sifu, Low Shiu Lun [盧紹麟] (Alan Low) for Chinese translations. Low Shiu Lun [盧紹麟] (Alan Low) is the Head Coach of Hak Fu Mun [黑虎門] in Hong Kong and Vice President of the Siu Lum Hak Fu Mun Wong Cheung Martial Arts Association [少林黑虎門益群堂黃祥體育會]. Therefore I would like to thank my Sifu, Low Shiu Lun [盧紹麟] for all his help and patience with me in translating over the last several years.

I would also like to thank my friend's father Brian Wilson (a published author) who proof read this book for me, and a thank you for the final proof read by Alice James.

Historical Events Leading Up To The Ten Tigers

It is understood that the majority of Han Chinese [漢族] always had thoughts of hostility towards the ruling Manchurians [滿洲] during the Ch'ing / Qing [清朝] Dynasty (1644–1912), who were often resented for being foreign and barbaric. The Ch'ing / Qing [清朝] rulers were accused of destroying traditional Chinese culture by banning traditional Chinese clothes (the hanfu [漢服]) [3] and forcing Chinese to wear their hair in a queue [辮子 / 頭鬃尾] as was the Manchu style. (The queue was a specific male hairstyle worn by the Manchus from central Manchuria and later imposed on the Han Chinese [漢族] during the Ch'ing / Qing[清朝] dynasty.) The hairstyle consisted of the hair on the front of the head being shaved off above the temples every ten days and the rest of the hair braided into a long ponytail. This hairstyle was compulsory on all males, the penalty for not conforming being execution as it was considered treason. [4]) The Ch'ing / Qing [清朝] rulers were also blamed for suppressing Chinese science, causing China to be transformed from the world's premiere power to a poor, backwards nation. [5]

During the late 17th and throughout the 18th century, many European countries were establishing trade with other nations around the world. By the early 1800's Europeans had acquired a huge appetite for Chinese silk, tea and ceramics and trading companies channelled their wealth of silver into China to meet demand. The British and French governments in particular became increasingly alarmed at their dwindling stockpiles of precious metals and sought a different means of trading with China. This led to the opium trade which involved the export of British cotton goods to India, the transfer of opium [鴉片] from India to China and the transfer of silk, tea and ceramics to Britain. When the Ch'ing/ Qing [清朝] rulers attempted to ban the opium trade in 1838, Great Britain later retaliated by declaring war on China.

British forces advancing on Chuenpee, Kwangtung, 1841

This was the First Opium War, which lasted four years until 1842, (although actual fighting was only from June 1840 until August 1842). The British forces with their modern equipment and tactics easily defeated the outdated Ch'ing / Qing troops on both land and water. The Qing rulers were forced to sign the Treaty of Nanjing [南京條約] which allowed British ships access to Chinese ports, and ceded the area of Hong Kong with payments of compensation to Great Britain.[6]

Nemesis Steamer (British Gunship)
firing on war junks in Canton River, 1842

The general Chinese populace felt betrayed by their Ch'ing / Qing [清朝] rulers and the government officials that acted on their country's behalf. This general feeling of resentment grew into a very strong loathing of the Ch'ing / Qing [清朝], their handling of the whole affair and the humiliation this entailed. This resentment was much stronger in southern China far away from the capital in Beijing and slowly built until by the mid 1800's, many decided they had suffered enough.

Signing of the Treaty of Nanking on board HMS Cornwallis

In 1850 the Taiping Rebellion broke out in southern China with the rebels establishing the Taiping Heavenly Kingdom [太平天國], basing their capital at Nanking / Nanjing [南京], northwest of Shanghai, approximately 1120kms northeast of Guangzhou [廣州]. The Taiping Heavenly Kingdom's army is said to have been 30 million people strong at its height and controlled large parts of southern China. During the rebellion, the Heavenly Kingdom introduced many social reforms in the lands they controlled, but they were besieged by Ch'ing / Qing [清朝] troops throughout. [7] [8]

During this rebellion an incident occurred in Canton [廣州] in 1856 on a British ship called the Arrow that sparked the so called Second Opium War. [9] British and French forces occupied Canton [廣州] and the Shameen Island [沙面島] (now known as Shamian) was ceded to them for business and residential purposes as part of the peace treaty thereafter. Shameen Island [沙面島] was connected to Canton [廣州] by two bridges. This island had many fine buildings with gardens and pleasant wide avenues drastically differing from the rest on Canton [廣州] with its very crowded narrow streets. [10] The Ch'ing / Qing [清朝] rulers were eventually able to crush the Taiping Rebellion in 1864 with the aid of French and British forces but were weakened by the rebellion and the unfair trading schemes forced on them by many Western powers. Revolts also broke out in the southwest of China with the Panthay Rebellion in Yunnan Province [雲南省] (1856-1873)[11] and then later the Dungan revolt in the northwest of China, (1862-1877).[11a]

Chinese officers tearing down the British flag and arresting the crew of the British ship the 'Arrow.

Viceroy of Liangguang Governor-general of Guangdong and Guangxi

Liangguang (simplified Chinese: 两广; traditional Chinese: 兩廣; pinyin: translates to: "Two Guangs"/ "Two Kwangs") which refers to the province of Guangdong and Guangxi on the southern coast of China. The province also includes the former leased territories of British Hong Kong, French Kouang-Tchéou-Wan, and Portuguese Macau.

The names of the two entities form a pair, as they literally mean "Guang-East" and "Guang-West". "Guang" itself means "expanse" or "vast", and has been associated with the region since the creation of Guang Prefecture (Guangzhou) in AD 226. During the Qing dynasty, the office of the Governor-General of Liangguang existed from 1735 to 1911 to oversee both provinces. [12]

The full title of the Viceroy of Liangguang (Two Guangs) (Chinese: 兩廣總督), was the "Governor-general of Liangguang and surrounding areas responsibility for supervising Military Affairs, Food Production; Manager of Waterways; Director of Civil Affairs". (總督兩廣等處地方, 提督軍務、糧餉、管理河道兼巡撫事). There were eight viceroys in China during the Qing dynasty. This Viceroy had jurisdiction over the provinces of Guangdong and Guangxi.

Time period	Viceroy of Liangguang / Governor-general of Guangdong and Guangxi
1844–1848	Kiyeng / Qiying (耆英)
1848–1852	Xu Guangjin (徐廣縉)
1852–1858	Ye Mingchen (葉名琛)
1858–1859	Huang Zonghan (黃宗漢)
May 1859 – October 1859	Wang Qingyun
1859–1862	Lao Chongguang
1862–1863	Liu Changyou (劉長佑)
February – July 1863	Yan Duanshu (晏端書)
1863–1865	Mao Hongbin (毛鴻賓)
1865–1874	Ruilin (瑞麟)

***Kiyeng / Qiying** (耆英) conducted the settlement of the First Opium War with the British and other western powers between 1843 and 1847. He was sent to negotiate once again in 1858 to settle the Arrow War, but the settlement was repudiated by the Daoguang Emperor and he was forced to commit suicide.*

***Xu Guangjin** (徐廣縉) – no information.*

Yeh Ming-ch'en / Ye Mingchen (葉名琛) *As the governor of Guangdong, Yeh was faced with both internal and external problems. British merchants claimed the right to reside in the city of Canton which had been guaranteed by the Treaty of Nanking. In fact, the treaty read differently in its English and Chinese versions, with the latter only permitting foreigners to reside temporarily in the harbours of the newly opened treaty ports. Yeh stood strong and refused the British demands.*

As a reward for his ostensible success in keeping the British out of Canton, Yeh was promoted to Viceroy of Liangguang as well as Imperial Commissioner in 1852, which made him the highest-ranking official in relations with the West. [12a]

The City of Canton [廣州] Provincial Capital [省城] of Kwantung / Guangdong [廣東]

Like many of the great cities in China, Canton [廣州] had a substantially large wall surrounding it. The city walls were of brick construction, on a foundation of sandstone and granite. These walls were between 25 to 40 feet high and 20 thick running close to six miles in circumference. The city inside was divided between the larger older city area and the new city area that bordered the Pearl River [珠江]. Within the city walls were the central districts which served different purposes. The official's headquarters were located in the northern central area of the city facing south so that they overlooked their subjects. The residential areas called wards were separated by wide avenues which often had gates between them. The majority of the buildings within the city were two or three stories high. The two exceptions being the pagoda and five-story watchtower located at the northern area of the city. Market places were located throughout the city, but the majority of commercial trade took place outside the city between the walls and the Pearl River [珠江].

Many of the poorer districts for housing the general populace were also located outside the walls in the surrounding districts. Including these outer suburbs, the city had a circumference of approximately ten miles. Foreigners lived in a separate quarter outside the city walls lined up along the waterfront. Their buildings were called factories which included residential buildings, warehouses and offices. The buildings along the riverbanks stretched for about four miles. These riverbanks were crowded with boats ranging in design and size from small sampans to large junks [船]. It is recorded that as many as a 100,000 people lived on these boats that were moored against the river banks of the provincial capital city [省會城市] of Canton [廣州] and the island of Honam [河南島] (Honan). There were so many boats hustled together that the clear river channel between the two banks was only about twenty feet wide. [12b] [12g]

A detailed description of Canton [廣州] from around this period can be found at the following link :-http://www.1902encyclopedia.com/C/CAN/canton.html [12c]

The Battle of Canton

During the early part of the Second Opium War (October 1856 to January 1858), many military and governmental areas of the city were destroyed by heavy naval bombardment from British and French gunships on the Pearl River [珠江]. This war was due to the incident with the "Arrow" and the trade restrictions imposed by the Chinese officials in the Canton [廣州] area. The British wanted the same free access allowed to all foreigners by the Chinese in Canton [廣州] as was allowed at the other four ports under the treaty of Nanking. Because Yeh Ming-ch'en [葉名琛], the Viceroy of Liangguang / Governor-general of Guangdong and Guangxi would not honour this treaty or negotiate any terms, hostilities ensued. The British fully appreciated the hostile attitude the general populace had towards their Ch'ing / Qing [清朝] rulers and so issued proclamations to the inhabitants of Canton [廣州] stating that their quarrel was with the government and not its people. Strict written orders were also issued to the British soldiers stating that they were not to molest the persons or property of the general inhabitants during these hostilities.

Initial encounters involved attacking and seizing several of the Chinese forts that guarded the city of Canton [廣州]. The British also secured the site of the British factory and seized the surrounding area in an attempt to protect it better. At 1.00pm on the 27th October 1856 the British steam sloop, HMS Encounter opened fire on the Govenor- general's compound with its ten inch pivot gun and continued to fire until sunset at intervals of five to ten minutes. At the same time, HMS Barracouta, (a Steam paddle sloop) fired on Chinese soldiers near Grough's Fort from its position at the head of Sulphur Creek. Before the bombardment, the British had given due notice to the local inhabitants and only targeted government buildings. It is stated that the Viceroy of Liangguang / Governor-general of Guangdong and Guangxi, Yeh Ming-ch'en / Ye Mingchen [葉名琛] retaliated to this attack by publicly offering a reward of 30 Taels [兩] [12cc] of silver for the head of every Englishman. The bombardment on the Governor-general's compound in the new city area is believed to have destroyed much of this property.

HMS Barracouta and the boats of HMS Calcutta engaging
Mandarin junks in the Canton River on 6 November 1856.

On the 28th and 29th October, the shelling was then focused on a section of the city walls in the vicinity of the Dutch Folly in order to create a breach. On the 29th a detachment of marines and soldiers under the command of the Rear-Admiral, Sir Michael Seymour, formed a storming-party which landed on the shore of the Pearl River [珠江]. The space between the landing-place and the breach was approximately 300 yards which before the bombardment had been occupied by houses, but was now a heap of ruins. The marines and soldiers quickly covered this ground and occupied the walls. A nearby gate in the walls on the right was blown to pieces and the archway above it was partially destroyed. A detachment, including the Rear-Admiral, Commodore Elliot and Mr. Parkes, entered the city going to the Governor-general Yeh's [葉名琛] mansion before then returning at sunset. The object of this being to demonstrate their power to enter the city at will. Over the next several days all the houses between the factories and the city were demolished to prevent the Chinese using them to attack the British and the allies.

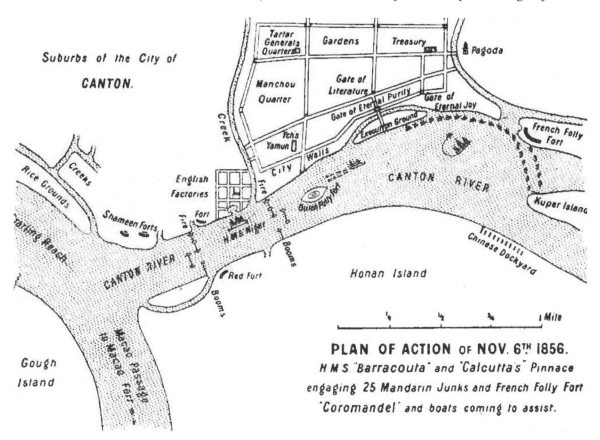

Suburbs of the City of CANTON.

PLAN OF ACTION OF NOV. 6TH 1856.
H M S "Barracouta" and "Calcutta's" Pinnace
engaging 25 Mandarin Junks and French Folly Fort
"Coromandel" and boats coming to assist.

From the 30th October to the 5th November, HMS Encounter and HMS Samson aided by the guns stationed at the Dutch-folly bombarded government buildings in the old city of Canton [廣州] known as the Tartar Quarter and the nearby fortifications at the rear north end of the city. Over the next couple of months most of the military action involved subduing the various forts along the river or dealing with various attacks by junks [船] on the British and allied ships. One night in the middle of December, the Chinese managed to set fire to an area of the factories with the loss of the British Consulate building. In retaliation the British sent several detachments to the city to set fires at several locations. The Chinese authorities were now offering 500 Taels [兩] of silver for the capture of an Englishman, dead or alive. Several had been caught and their heads were placed on view on the city walls for all to see.

During most of 1857, very little offensive action was taken by the British. This was due to them awaiting reinforcements, but these were delayed in India dealing with the Indian Mutiny. The little fighting that did take place during the summer was mainly naval battles dealing with the Chinese junks [船] on the various rivers and creeks within the region.

The advance of Royal Navy boats on Chinese war junks during the
battle at Fatshan Creek (by Oswald Walter Brierly)

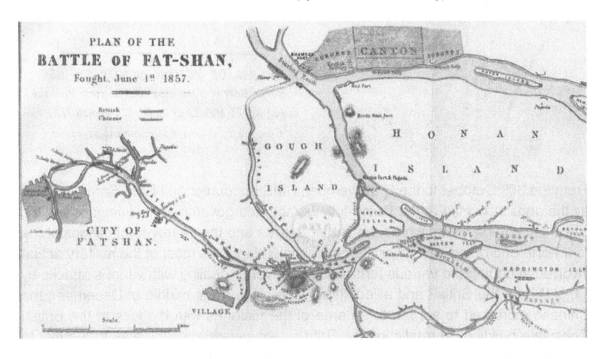

The plan of the Battle of Fat-Shan / Foshan [佛山] (Fat-Shan / Foshan [佛山] literally translates to mean Buddha Mountain) shows how close the two cities of Fat Shan / Foshan [佛山] and Canton [廣州] were. This plan also shows some of the surrounding area. The scale on this plan shows that the distance between these two cities during the mid 1850s was only approximately six miles. Therefore I think that it is fair to assume that travelling between these two cities would have been reasonably common.

On 15th December 1857, British and French forces combined and landed on Honam Island / [河南島] unopposed. Before the landing, a proclamation written in Chinese had been distributed around the suburbs of Canton [廣州] by the British stating that the Imperial Commissioner, Yeh [葉名琛] had been given ten days to comply with the allied forces. During this time the Allies would occupy Honam Island [河南島] awaiting Yeh's

[葉名琛] reply. They would not attack or damage property unless it was in self defence or if Yeh [葉名琛] did not yield. The proclamation advised that all non-belligerents use this period to take appropriate measures to remove themselves and their property. Preparations were then made for an attack on Canton [廣州] if Governor-general Yeh [葉名琛] did not concede to the demands of the British. The troops occupied many of the warehouse buildings that lined the shore of Honam Island [河南島] as their superiors conducted reconnaissance missions around Canton [廣州].

On Thursday 24th December, the British once again distributed proclamations along the Canton [廣州] shore warning the inhabitants that Yeh [葉名琛] had rejected terms offered by them and if the city had not surrendered within forty-eight hours it would be bombarded. This warning gave the population plenty of time to leave the area and so avoid being caught in the crossfire. As these demands were not met, hostilities began on the morning of Monday, 28th December 1857 with a general bombardment of military targets in and around the city of Canton [廣州], conducted by 32 ships of the Anglo-French contingent supported by artillery batteries located at the Dutch Folly and other nearby islands. Orders clearly stated that the general inhabitants and civilian areas were to be avoided.

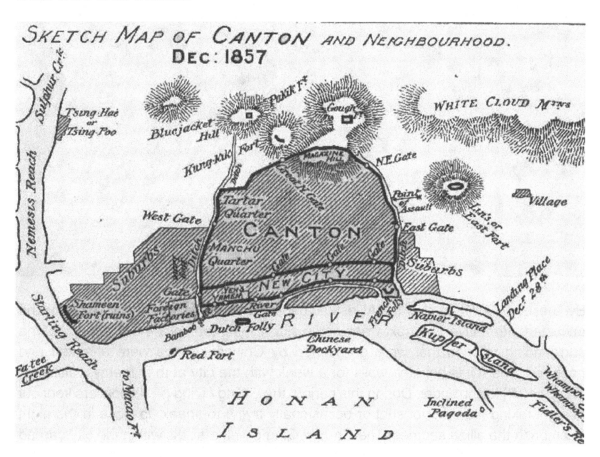

Allied forces consisted of 800 men from the Indian Royal Sappers and Miners and the British 59th (2nd Nottinghamshire) Regiment of Foot, 2,100 Royal Marines, plus a 1,829-man naval brigade from the crews of British ships. The British were aided by a 950-man force from the French Navy. The allies faced a Chinese garrison of 30,000 men. The battle started with a bombardment from the ships guns on 28th December and the capture of Lin's Fort one mile inland. The following day allied troops landed by Kupar Creek to the south-east of the city. The Chinese believed that the allied forces would try to capture Magazine Hill before moving onto the city walls, but they were mistaken. On the 29th December, after a naval bombardment which ended at 9am, the French troops climbed the city walls with very little resistance. Due to French arriving half an hour early at the walls, they had initially faced fire from their own guns. Over 4700 British and Indian troops and 950 French troops scaled the city walls. The allies maned the walls for a week, before on the morning of 5th January, they moved into the streets of the city. [12f]

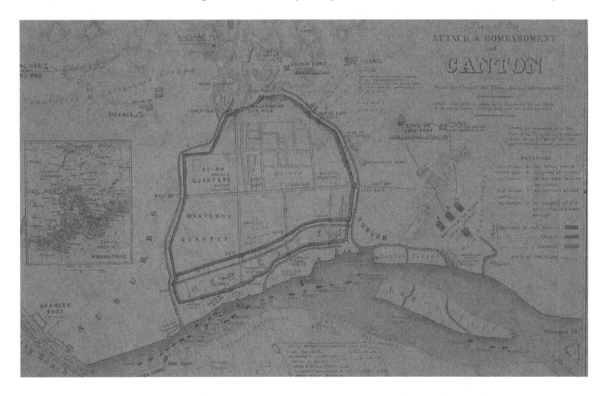

By Tuesday 29th December the Allies had captured the walls surrounding the city and occupied them. Over the next week some skirmishing took place and several of the surrounding villages that were garrisoned by Chinese troops were attacked and captured. The Allies held the walls for a week with the city at their mercy waiting for Yeh [葉名琛] to surrender. During this period, the Ch'ing / Qing [清朝] soldiers kept out of sight taking the odd pot shot or occasionally trying to sneak up close in the night to ambush the allied sentries. The Ch'ing / Qing [清朝] officials within the city carried on as if nothing had occurred, seeming to ignore the presence of the allied troops, and possibly hoping that they would just get bored and go away. Yeh [葉名琛] also had four hundred Chinese prisoners executed by cutting off their heads in this week. The allies therefore devised a decisive plan to help bring a conclusion to this whole episode.

Early on the 5th January 1858, one French and two British detachments entered the city with the objective of capturing pre-arranged targets. The French detachment arrested Muh Ki Tenar [廣州將軍穆克德納], the Ch'ing / Qing [清朝] general hiding in a closet at his vast decaying and empty yamun located near the West gate; British marines captured Peh-Kwei [柏貴] the governor of Canton [廣州] at breakfast in his large yamun located at Benevolence and Love Street / Wai Oi Street [惠愛街]; and the third seized Yeh Ming-ch'en [葉名琛], the Viceroy of Liangguang / Governor-general of Guangdong and Guangxi. Yeh [葉名琛] was eventually found three hours later in the south-west corner of Canton [廣州] at a small yamun belonging to one of the lieutenant-governors.

This picture shows allied troops enter a yuman in search of the Viceroy, Yeh Ming-ch'en, from the London Illustrated Times which reported this incident, printed on the 20th March 1858.

When the troops arrived at this yamun and forced open the doors, the place was full of hastily packed baggage with Mandarins running everywhere. When apprehended, Yeh [葉名琛] was found at the rear of this residence at a boundary wall considering his escape.

It is interesting to note that during the allies' search of the city for these men, that they were not hindered or attacked in any manner by the local population. In fact during this whole episode, the local inhabitants helped them, working for them and before the attack on the city sailed out in their boats to the allied ships selling fruit and other produce to them. Just over a week later on Saturday 14th January, the general, Muh Ki Tenar / [廣州將軍穆克德納] and the governor, Peh-Kwei [柏貴] were released and allowed back into the city to enable them to carry out their duties and maintain order, but under the close supervision of an international commission. [12g]

Yeh's capture by the rear boundary wall.

Yeh Ming-ch'en being escorted by
allied troops after his capture.

Yeh Ming-ch'en [葉名琛], the Viceroy of Liangguang / Governor-general of Guangdong and Guangxi was later taken by the British to Calcutta where he was held under open house arrest in a villa at Tolly Gunge. During his voyage to this location, he freely admitted to executing at least 100,000 Chinese who he stated were rebels. [12g]

Detailed accounts of the Battle of Canton can be found in the following books :-

The Royal Navy: "A History from the Earliest Times to 1900" written by Sir William Laird Clowes ISBN-13: 978-1861760166 [12k]

China: Being "The Times" Special Correspondence from China in the Years 1857-58 by George Wingrove Cooke ISBN-13: 978-1241161996 [12g]

or at the following :- http://www.pbenyon.plus. com/Hurrah/Chap_05.htm [12d]
http://www.pdavis.nl/China2.htm [12e]

Yeh Ming-ch'en [葉名琛]

After January 1858, much of the city of Canton [廣州] had to be rebuilt. This plan of Canton [廣州] was drawn after the restoration works had been completed and shows various areas of the city. Location 4 on the plan shows the site of the Viceroy's / Governor-General's mansion before it was destroyed during this battle. The Cathedral of the Sacred Heart of Jesus was then built on this site in 1860. [12h] Location 5 shows the site of the Viceroy's / Governor-General's mansion after 1860.

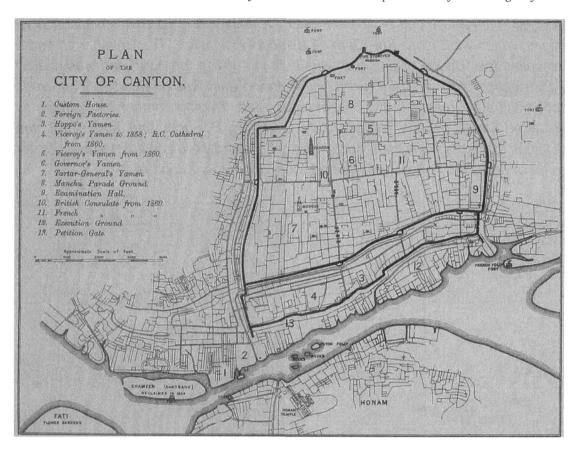

The British factory was in ruins following the first battle of October 1856. After much consideration a new location was chosen for a permanent British settlement. This new site was a large mudflat / sand bank called Shameen which was close to the original site. This mudflat was a filthy stagnant swamp area covered with long low decrepit wooden sheds and hovels built upon wooden stilts. In the midst of this swamp were two forts built on patches of solid land. In 1859, masonry embankments were constructed around the perimeter and the land inbetween filled in. A canal was dug out on the north side to separate Shameen [沙面島] from the rest of the city. The buildings on this island followed British designs and were separated by wide avenues lined with trees. This whole project was completed within two years.

Shamian Island */ 沙面島, is a sandbank island in the Liwan District of Guangzhou city, Guangdong province, China. Shamian translates to "sandy surface" in Chinese.*

Shamian Island was the port for Canton's foreign trade. From the 18th to the mid 19th century, foreigners lived and conducted their business in a row of buildings known as the Thirteen Factories. This was on the banks of the Pearl River just to the east of the present Shamian, which was at that time an anchorage area for thousands of boat people. During the First and Second Opium Wars, Shamian became a strategic point for city defence. In 1859, Shamian was partitioned in two concessions of which 3/5 belonged to the British and 2/5 to the French). It was connected to the mainland by two bridges, which were closed at 10pm as a security measure. The British arch bridge, also called the "Bridge of England" was built in 1861 to the north and was guarded by Sikh police officers. The French bridge to the east was guarded by Vietnamese (Cochinchina) recruits with the Troupes colonials. Trading companies from Britain, the United States, France, Holland, Italy, Germany, Portugal, and Japan built stone mansions along the waterfront. Buildings on the island were constructed in a Western design of detached houses with hipped roofs and large verandas. [12i]

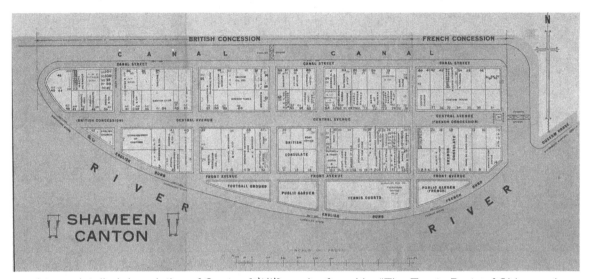

A very detailed description of Canton [廣州] can be found in, "The Treaty Ports of China and Japan: A Complete Guide to the Open Ports of those Countries, together with Peking, Yedo, Hongkong and Macao." (Pgs 116-201, written in 1867) **ISBN-13:** 978-1108045902 [12i]

Rise of the Kung Fu Master and the spread of Martial Arts

The Ch'ing / Qing [清朝] government and army had been fighting enemies on all fronts for many years. Taking into consideration the size of the country and the vast distances between the various rebellions and wars, this had put an immense burden on their resources. Administration had always been slow due to the immense size of the country and so many matters were left to be dealt with locally by the viceroys / Governor-Generals of each region. They in turn had their subordinates which left the whole system wide open to corruption.

With the Ch'ing / Qing [清朝] forces weakened and spread so thinly dealing with these issues, it left many parts of the countryside almost lawless with few troops to maintain order. All these conflicts with the massive loss of life created a harsh environment. This, coupled with the persecution by the Ch'ing / Qing [清朝] government, became a precarious time for Siu Lum / Shaolin martial artists [少林武術家]. This was a time of refinement of their styles to produce more powerful and effective methods. They ensured that they honed their skills not knowing when their life might depend on it. They would train to inflict either serious or life threatening damage to an opponent and were willing to die to preserve their art. The general populace in these lawless times therefore looked to hiring Kung Fu masters [功夫大師] to help them learn self-defence and create militias to protect their villages and local communities. As well as protecting their interests, the general population also appreciated that by studying martial arts [武術] they would be stronger and healthier like these revered masters [功夫大師]. [13]

One of the major influences for the spread of martial arts [武術] was the formation of the secret societies during the mid 1700s. The objective of many of these societies was rebellion against the Ch'ing / Qing [清朝] authorities to bring about their downfall and reinstate the former Ming [明] government. One of the biggest groups was the Heaven and Earth Society (also known as the Hong Men) whose motto was "Overthrow the Qing, restore the Ming." Members therefore learnt martial arts [武術] so that they could achieve their goal. [14]

(For a more detailed account please see :- Tian Di Hui (天地會 / Heaven and Earth Society) & Hong Men and Shaolin. [14]
or
"The Origins of the Tiandihui", by Dian H. Murray In Collaboration with Qin Baoqi.
ISBN-13: 978-0804723244 [36c]

Massive changes occurred in Southern China with the opening of several ports in that region. Due to the authorities dealing with the various wars and rebellions, rural areas became lawless. Many of the ordinary people therefore moved to the cities not only to find work but also to avoid the troubles that were sweeping the countryside. These ordinary people felt that they were not being protected by the laws and authorities and so had to find a way to safeguard themselves. This resulted in many people wanting to learn martial arts [武術] which created a huge demand for good Kung Fu masters [功夫大師]. The study of martial arts [武術] began to be very popular and it became common practice to establish martial arts schools [武術學校] in Guangdong Province [廣東省].

As Canton [廣州] was the capital city of this province and the biggest city port in Southern China, many martial artists [武術家] gathered there to seek employment and teach their arts. This resulted in many masters [功夫大師] vying with each other in trying to build reputations as to who taught the most effective style or who was the best fighter. An esteemed reputation was gained in one of two ways, firstly for their virtue and secondly, for their fighting prowess. Fighting ability was gained through the experience of real life encounters. These abilities were then proven through duels [決鬥] which were often conducted on a public stage called a Lei tai [擂臺].

*The **lèi tái** (Traditional: 擂臺 Simplified: 擂台 translating to "striking platform") is an raised fighting arena, without railings, for martial arts tournaments which were fought either bare-knuckle or with weapons. "Sanctioned" matches were supervised by a referee on the platform and judges on the sides. Fighters lost if they surrendered, were incapacitated, were thrown or otherwise forced from the platform. The winner would remain on the platform unless ousted by a stronger or more skilled opponent until there were no more challengers, then they would become the champion. Private duels on the platform often had no rules and could sometimes be fought to the death.*

"Historically, if a new fighter wanted to announce themselves in a town or village, they built a lei tai, stood on it, and invited all comers to try beat them from it." Some issued challenges in the form of a hand written letter to on opponent they wished to duel. This type of challenge was illustrated in Jet Li's movie Fearless, when his character challenges another warrior to a fight. The book Ultimate Sparring: Principles & Practices states, "martial artists conducted 'Challenge matches' [on the lei tai] to test one another's skills, because of either a personal dispute, or to prove one martial system's superiority over another system." If a fighter lost the match, was forced off the platform or was knocked to the floor then he would lose credibility. As a result, no one would want to learn boxing from him. The winner of the bout became the "owner of the platform" and

remained on stage untill there were no more challengers. He became the champion and or established the dominance of his style in that area. Another way was to defeat an already established master on the lei tai and then take over his school. [15]

Keen competition between the different schools [武術學校] often resulted in duels [決鬥] and challenges with the losing master [功夫大師] often being run out of town and his school [武術學校] either closed or taken over by the victor. Therefore the weakest fighters were eliminated from the martial arts community leaving only the strongest and most able surviving. These surviving masters [功夫大師] became notable characters who the public and their peers would rate on not only their prowess as a fighter but also their reputation of honour and integrity. The ten most outstanding Kung Fu masters [功夫大師] at this time became known as the Ten Tigers of Guangdong / Kwong Tung Sap Fu [廣東十虎] (Canton [廣州]).

The Siu Lum / Shaolin Temples [少林寺]

Author, Paul Burkinshaw & students at entrance to the Henan Shaolin Temple in 2005

It appears that outwardly, Siu Lum / Shaolin [少林] only publically advertised the fact that they had the temple in Henan Province [河南省] at Dengfeng [登封] which is located at the foot of the Mount Song (Song Shan [嵩山]) near Zhengzhou [鄭州] City. As Siu Lum / Shaolin [少林] grew it expanded having sister temples at various locations around China. These were often kept secret so that if it was to fall out of favour with the reigning emperor or government, then only this one site would be persecuted.

Presentation with head monks at Henan Shaolin Temple in 2005.

Several sources including the histories of many Kung Fu [功夫] styles and other documents including the Shaolin Grandmaster's Text [16] state that the Siu Lum / Shaolin Order had sister temples at :-

Author, Paul Burkinshaw & students at entrance to the Henan Shaolin Temple in 2006.

Author, Paul Burkinshaw with head monk
during club trip to O Mei Shan Temple in 2006

O Mei Shan / Emei [峨眉山] (translates to Great White Mountain), located in Szechuan Province [四川省]. This temple was also a library and a medical, learning and research site as well as maintaining its normal monastic role. The O Mei temple accepted Siu Lum / Shaolin monks [少林僧] in 945AD, and then became completely Siu Lum / Shaolin in 1500AD.

The Wu-tang / Wudang [武當山] Temple, known as the Tiger Temple, is located on a small mountain range in the north-western part of Hubei Province / [湖北省]. This temple was established in 980AD by Taoists.

Paul & students with head monks during
club trip to Wudang Temple in 2006

(Some sources also believe that Siu Lum / Shaolin established a temple or had a presence at Hua Shan [華山] which is located in Shaanxi Province [陝西省].)

Hsu K'o / Xu Ke [徐珂] (1869-1928) was a Chinese scholar who compiled various stories, anecdotes and fables from the Ch'ing / Qing Dynasty [清朝], and published these volumes in 1917 under the title of "Ch'ing-pai lei-ch'ao / Qingbao leichao [清稗類鈔]". Information about the Heaven and Earth Society / Tian Di Hui [天地會] is contained within this book which states that the Southern Siu Lum / Shaolin Temple [南少林寺] was located in Fukien Province / Fujian Province [福建省] in the area of P'u-t'ien-hsien / Putian [莆田] and Fu-chou-fu / Fuzhou [福州]. This area would therefore cover the sites of both the Putian Siu Lum / Shaolin Temple [莆田少林寺] and the Fuqing Siu Lum / Shaolin Temple [福清少林寺].

The book, "The Qianlong Emperor Inspects Southern China / Kin Loong har Kwong Nam / Qianlong Xia Jiangnan [乾隆下江南]" [50b], mentions a Southern Siu Lum / Shaolin Temple [南少林寺] which was located in Fukien Province / Fujian Province [福建省] in the area of Quanzhou [泉州].

It is generally believed and now accepted that the Fukien Temple / Fujian si [福建寺] had three main sites during its existence in this province. It is also possible that in Fukien / Fujian Province [福建省], Siu Lum / Shaolin had other temple sites which may also have been used from time to time to avoid attention from the Ch'ing / Qing [清朝] authorities. The three main temples sites in Fukien / Fujian Province [福建省] were located at Fuqing]福清], at Quanzhou [泉州] and near Putian [莆田]. It is not known with any certainty whether these temples operated at the same time as each other, but it is believed that after the destruction of one temple then another site was used. According to the Shaolin Grandmaster's Text, the first Siu Lum / Shaolin Temple [少林寺] in Fukien / Fujian Province [福建省] was established around 683AD and then later, around 1399AD the Fukien Temple / Fujian si [福建寺] was rebuilt and expanded. [16] [17] [18][19] [20] [21] [22]

Fuqing Shaolin Temple [福清少林寺]

The Fuqing Siu Lum / Shaolin Temple [福清少林寺] was located near the village of Dongzhangzhen [東張鎮] approximately 22kms west of Fuqing [福清]. It is believed that this temple became part of the Siu Lum / Shaolin Order sometime during the Song Dynasty (960-1279AD). This site was excavated from 1995 to late 1996 and covered a large area of over 5000 sq meters making it possibly one of the biggest temple sites in China. From this excavation, archaeologists found various ruins and artefacts which they stated confirmed its Siu Lum / Shaolin [少林寺] affiliation. To date, only the middle section of this temple has been rebuilt with the ruins of other parts of the original temple still visible. [19] [21] [22]

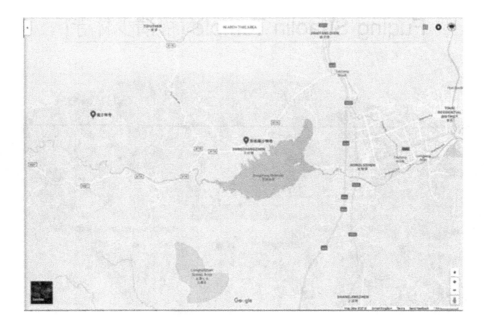

photos showing archaeological digs & old books.

I visited the Fuqing Siu Lum / Shaolin Temple [福清少林寺] in November 2015 and found it to be a quiet and remote site. The temple was reached by travelling along a minor road from the town of Dongzhangzhen [東張鎮] for approximately 9kms. Just before the temple we had to turn off the minor road and complete the last several hundred meters along a dirt track. The Fuqing Siu Lum / Shaolin Temple [福清少林寺] has a grand entrance before passing through the front gate house into the temple grounds. From the front gate house, there was a room off to the right-hand side of the main buildings which contained various photos, documents and information from the archaeological digs. These included the various ruins and artefacts retrieved from these digs. In this room were several old books which stated that a Southern Siu Lum / Shaolin Temple [南少林寺] existed in this area. To the left of the main temple buildings there were two main areas where the ruins of several buildings were visible as shown in the photos below. At the time of our group's visit, the temple was very quiet with no other tourists or visitors.

Aerial view of the temple site

The ruins of various temple buildings

Quanzhou Shaolin Temple [泉州少林寺]

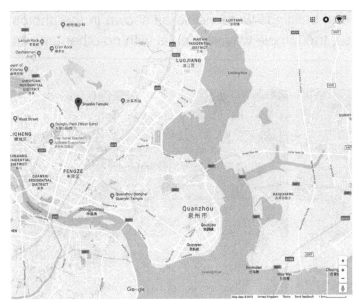

The Quanzhou Siu Lum / Shaolin Temple [泉州少林寺] was located on the Dongyue [東岳] hillside near the city of Quanzhou [泉州] at the foot of Mount Qingyuan [清源山]. (Quanzhou [泉州] was formerly called Zayton / Chinchew and is called Ch'uan-chou in Cantonese.) Originally this temple was not easily accessible, but during recent times due to the expansion of Quanzhou [泉州], it is now surrounded by urban development just off Dongqiu Front Street / Dong Qiu Qian Jie. A sign at the temple states that it was originally founded in the early Tang Dynasty [唐朝] (618-907) by the Siu Lum / Shaolin Monk [少林僧], Master Zhi kong [智空], who was one of the Thirteen Guarding Monks from the Northern Henan Siu Lum / Shaolin Temple [河南少林寺]. He came to Fukien / Fujian Province [福建省] about 620 and built thirteen buildings at the foot of Qingyuan Mountain [清源山]. Chi Hom / Zhi Kong [智空] put much time and effort into collecting alms in order to build his new temple. It is stated that much of this funding came from the Wan Lang / Wen Ling people[溫陵百姓] who greatly supported Chi Hom /Zhi Kong [智空]. They were good Buddhists and the money was raised without too much difficulty. [30a]

Presentation to monks at the Quanzhou Temple, 2006.

Author, Paul Burkinshaw & students at entrance to the Quanzhou Shaolin Temple, 2006

The temple was formerly known as Zhenguo Eastern Dhyana (Chan) Shaolin Temple / Zhenguo Dong Chan Shaolin Si [鎮國東禪少林寺]. A history sign near the entrance states that the Quanzhou Siu Lum / Shaolin Temple [泉州少林寺] covered an area of approximately one hundred hectares (250 acres). The temple was surrounded by high walls with thirteen gates and at its height was home to more than one thousand monks. At this time, much of the temple grounds were hidden and enclosed by the surrounding forest. Over the years the temple has been destroyed and rebuilt several times.

The temple was attacked at the end of the Song Dynasty [宋朝] (960-1279) by an army of thirty thousand men of the Yuen Dynasty [元朝] (1279-1368). Although the Siu Lum / Shaolin Monks [少林僧] fought bravely killing many soldiers, they were eventually overcome and their temple destroyed. Two Siu Lum / Shaolin monks [少林僧] called Fat Bu / Fa Ben [法本] and Fat Wan / Fa Hua [法華] escaped to Daiyun Mountain [戴云山] in Dehua [德化] where they continued to practice Siu Lum / Shaolin Kung Fu [少林功夫]. The Quanzhou Siu Lum / Shaolin Temple [泉州少林寺] was restored around the 1370s during the reign of the Ming emperor, Hong Wu [明洪武皇帝]. [30a] Its last total destruction was in 1763 (although some sources state 1768 [22a]) and after excavation in the 1980s, reconstruction work began in 1992.[19] [21] [22] [22b]

This photo, taken during our club trip in 2006 shows how close the suburbs of the city of Quanzhou [泉州] are in relation to the temple grounds. The rebuilding work was still continuing but was delayed due to lack of funds. The temple was relying on raising the money itself and donations from either visitors or other interested parties.

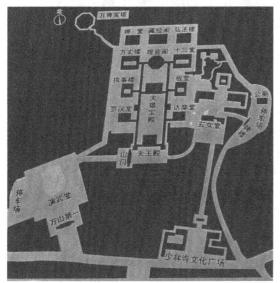

Map of Quanzhou Shaolin Temple.

Entrance to the Quanzhou Shaolin Temple, 2015.

Since my first visit in April 2006, the Quanzhou Siu Lum / Shaolin Temple [泉州少林寺] has been greatly expanded to include several new buildings with surrounding grounds. Some of these areas still look unfinished. Several areas within the complex needed generally tidying up and pathways completing. To the left side of the main temple area there was a large plot of land for growing vegetables and a grassed training area with the plum flower posts. During our recent visit in November 2015, we had the privilege to have a meeting with the Abbot [方丈], Chang Ding [常定] who has been in this position since 2007.

| Looking up towards the rear of the temple from the left of the Hall of Mahavira. | Looking upto the Goddess of Mercy Pavillion (Avalokitesvara Buddhisatrava) |

Uppermost buildings at the
Quanzhou Shaolin Temple site

Bottom left gate of the Quanzhou
Shaolin Temple

Looking down from near the top of the Quanzhou Shaolin Temple site towards the city below.

Putian Shaolin Temple [莆田少林寺]

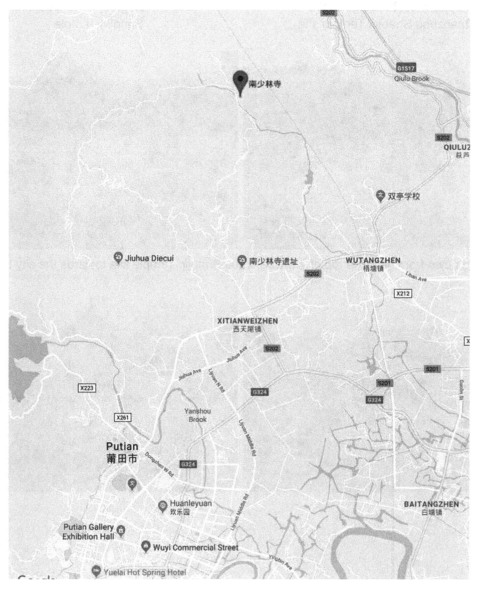

The Putian Siu Lum / Shaolin Temple [莆田少林寺] was located at a remote site approximately 30 kms from the city of Putian. Some legends state that the temple was surrounded by the Nine Lotus Mountains / Jiu lian shan [九蓮山]. This temple had first been built around 557AD and was originally called Lin Quan Yuan Temple [林泉院]. During the reign of the second Tang Emperor T'ang T'ai-tsung / Taizong [唐太宗] (626-649AD) a force of 500 monks had been sent to the coastal area of Fukien / Fujian Province [福建省] to deal with pirates that were plaguing this region.

After defeating these pirates the Siu Lum / Shaolin monks [少林僧] were granted permission to build a branch of the order at Putian [莆田]. It is stated that this site was eventually chosen because the landscape was very similar to that of the Henan temple [河南寺] at Dengfeng [登封]. It is believed that this temple was totally destroyed in the early 1800s.

The Chinese National Culture Bureau [中華人民共和國文化部] located some temple ruins around 1986 and subsequently carried out an archaeological investigation. In September 1991, their findings prompted a conference which included more than thirty experts in martial arts, history, religion and archaeology which declared that this was the site of a Southern Siu Lum / Shaolin Temple [南少林寺]. On the 25th April 1992, a news conference was held in the Beijing People's Conference Hall [北京人民大會堂] by the People's Government of Fujian Province [福建省人民政府] who formally announced to the outside world, that they had discovered the ruins and would rebuild the Southern Siu Lum / Shaolin Temple [南少林寺]. [19] [21a] [21b] [22]

Author, Paul Burkinshaw & students at entrance to the Putian Shaolin Temple, 2006.

When I first visited the Putian Siu Lum / Shaolin Temple [莆田少林寺] in April 2006, there were no monks there and very few visitors. The temple was already beginning to look a littile tired with paint flaking off some of the walls. On the right of the Four Heavenly Kings Hall and after the Bell House was a room that had several artefacts with photos and information about the archaeological digs. To the left of side of the temple there was a small shop selling various gifts and souvenirs.

As we approached the Putian Siu Lum / Shaolin Temple [莆田少林寺] on a more recent visit in November 2015, I noticed a large residential complex had been built close to the right hand side and several shops had opened next to the car park. A martial arts school had also been constructed to the left of the temple. The temple now had many more visitors and in the grounds were several monks who were aided by numerous volunteers. Some of these volunteers were manning a food area under the corridor after the Patriarch Hall and to the left of the Main Hall.

Hak Fu Mun group line up in front of main entrance to the Putian Shaolin Temple, 2015

Looking towards the rear of the temple from the left of the Four Heavenly Kings Hall.

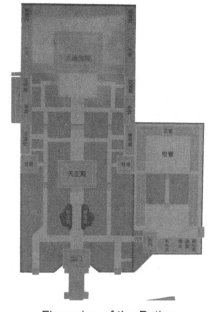

Floor plan of the Putian Shaolin Temple [莆田少林寺]

Looking towards the Four Heavenly
Kings Hall from the Lotus pond.

Looking back at the front gate
from the Lotus pond.

During the visit we were fortunate to have a meeting with one of the Siu Lum / Shaolin Monks [少林僧], who was called Yin Yan [延因]. He informed us that he believed that at one time there were ten Southern Siu Lum / Shaolin Temples [南少林寺] in China. Six of these were in Fukien / Fujian Province [福建省] and four were in Canton [廣州]. The Siu Lum / Shaolin Monk [少林僧], Yin Yan [延因] understood that four of the six temples in Fukien / Fujian Province [福建省] were located at Putian [莆田], Fuqing [福清], Quanzhou [泉州], and Xianyou [仙游縣] but he could not recall the locations of the other two.

Interview with Shaolin Monk Yin Yan [延因].
Alan Low (Low Shiu Lun),
Franco Lok (Lok Wah Fai),
Paul Burkinshaw,
Andrew Shenton,
Ho Wai Man,
Maggie Leung,
& standing Yuen Chap Man,
Lee Wai & Tse Lai Fun.

Group photo with Shaolin Monk Yin Yan [延因]

Xianyou [仙游縣] is a town and county that borders the south-west of the city of Putian [莆田].

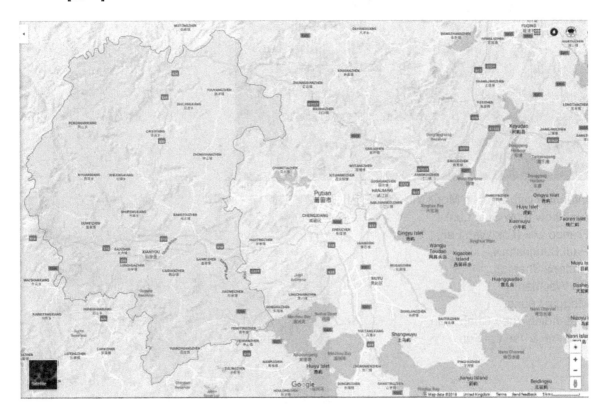

It was also interesting to note that the Siu Lum / Shaolin Monk [少林僧] Yin Yan [延因] stated that there were four Siu Lum / Shaolin Temple [少林寺] sites in Canton [廣州]. In the next chapter I have listed the main Buddhist Temples [佛寺] in Canton [廣州] (Guangzhou) during the period and explained which temples I believe may have been part of the Siu Lum / Shaolin Order.

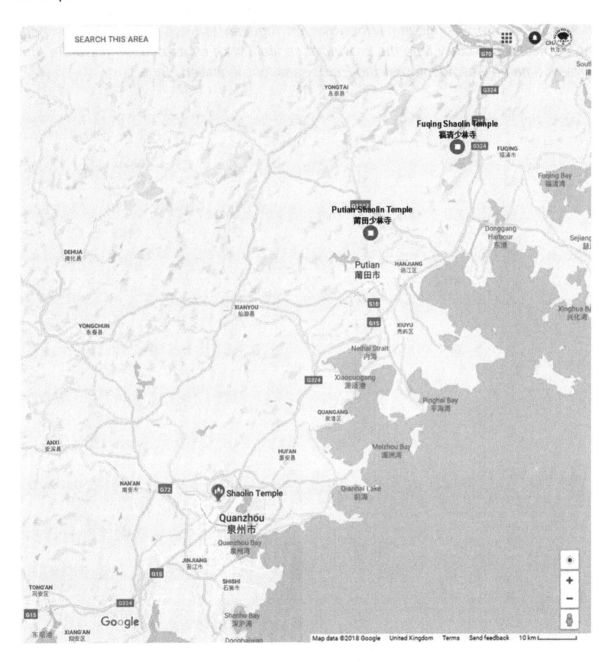

This map shows the three Siu Lum / Shaolin temples [少林寺] in Fukien / Fujian Province [福建省]. The distance from the Fuqing Temple [福清寺] to the Putian Temple [莆田寺] is approximately 25 kms and then the distance from Putian Temple [莆田寺] to the Quanzhou Temple [泉州少林寺] is approximately 81 kms. Further south of Fukien /

Fujian [福建] was another temple known as the Kwangtung Siu Lum / Shaolin Temple [廣東少林寺]. This temple was located in the province of Kwangtung (Guangdong [廣東省]) in or near the City of Canton [廣州] and was established in 970AD. [16]. The city of Canton [廣州] is now called Guangzhou [廣州].

It is believed that "Canton" originated from the Portuguese: Cantão, which was transcribed from Guangdong. When the Portuguese arrived, the capital city had no particular title other than the provincial capital [省城] by its people, therefore the province name was adopted by the Europeans for the walled city. [23]

The Siu Lum / Shaolin Temple Order

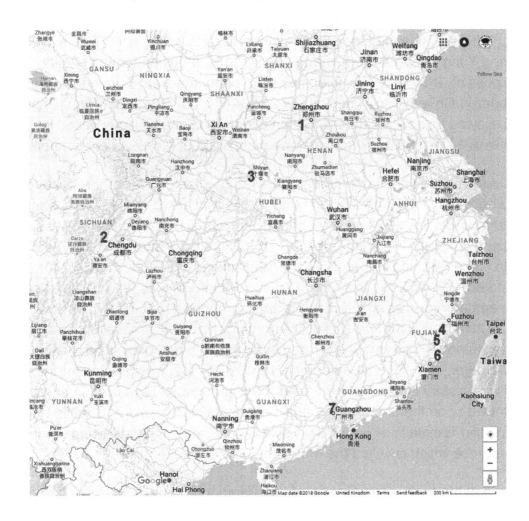

1. Henan Siu Lum / Shaolin Temple (Dengfeng [登封], Henan Province [河南省])

2. O'Mei Shan Temple (Mount Emei [峨眉山], Sichuan Province [四川省])

3. Wudang Temple (Mount Wudang [武當山], Hubei Province [湖北省])

4. Fuqing Siu Lum / Shaolin Temple (Fuqing [福清], Fujian Province [福建省])

5. Putian Siu Lum / Shaolin Temple (Putian [莆田], Fujian Province [福建省])

6. Quanzhou Siu Lum / Shaolin Temple (Quanzhou [泉州], Fujian Province [福建省])

7. Kwangtung Siu Lum / Shaolin Temple (Guangzhou [廣州], Guangdong Province [廣東省])

8. Hua Shan Temple (Mount Hua [華山], Shaanxi Province [陝西省])

Paul Burkinshaw

Due to the monks fighting prowess and the belief that rebels were training at the Siu Lum / Shaolin Temples [少林寺], the order became unpopular with the Ch'ing / Qing [清朝] government. The third Ch'ing / Qing [清朝] emperor, Yung Cheng / Yongzheng [雍正帝] (1723-1735) banned the practice of martial arts [武術] in 1727. [16] It is believed that during Yung Cheng's / Yongzheng [雍正帝] rule, a Fukien temple / Fujian si [福建寺] and possibly the Henan Temple, may have been attacked. During the reign of the next emperor, Ch'ien Lung / Qianlong [乾隆皇帝] (1735-1796), Siu Lum / Shaolin [少林] was allowed to rebuild. Emperor Ch'ien Lung / Qianlong [乾隆帝] visited the Henan temple [河南寺] in 1750 and wrote several poems about his experiences there. [16] [24]

Many sources state various conflicting dates during the 1700s for the destruction of the Southern Siu Lum / Shaolin Temples [南少林寺]. Due to these discrepancies it is almost impossible to prove with any certainty the actual historic dates of these events. It is accepted that the Henan Temple [河南寺] was attacked around 1647, but during the reign of the following emperor, K'ang His / Kangxi [康熙帝] (1661-1722), this temple was restored. It is recorded that 128 Siu Lum / Shaolin Monks [少林僧] volunteered to help the emperor's forces against bandits and marauders (Xi Lu [西魯]), on the Western border of China during the late 1600s. Many sources state that these monks came from the Fukien temple / Fujian si [福建寺], and that they were responsible for gaining victory for the emperor. [24] [25] [36c] The emperor K'ang Hsi [康熙帝] was grateful for the monks' support and history states that he visited the Henan temple in 1704. During this visit he bestowed upon the order his imperial seal and a sign entitled, "Shaolin Ssu," (Siu Lum / Shaolin Temple [少林寺]). [16] This sign is now located at the Henan Temple's [河南寺] entrance which is called the Mountain Gate and was built in 1735. [26]

It is stated in the book, "The Origins of the Tiandihui: Chinese Triads in Legend and History", which was written by Dian H. Murray in collaboration with Qin Baoqi, that the Heaven and Earth Society / Tian Di Hui [天地會] was formed at Gaoxi township [高溪鄉], Zhangpu county [漳浦縣], Zhangzhou [漳州] prefecture, Fukien / Fujian [福建]. In this book, seven Tiandihui (Heaven and Earth Society [天地會]) manuscripts are referenced that tell accounts of the Xi Lu [西魯] legend. These differ in their versions of what happened and contain instances of divine intervention. It is understood that these manuscripts were written at different times between the early 1800s and early 1900s, with the later accounts being far more detailed. Unfortunately, they cannot be relied on factually due to their discrepancies in the stories and the errors of certain dates. However, they are consistent in that Siu Lum / Shaolin monks [少林僧] came to the aid of the emperor, K'ang His / Kangxi [康熙帝] (1661-1722), in defeating Xi Lu [西魯] invaders. Sometime later, treacherous officials convinced the emperor that these monks were a threat to his rule or that they were plotting rebellion. 110 monks died during an attack on the temple and 18 monks escaped. During the pursuit that followed, a further 13 monks died leaving five survivors. The accounts of their later

38

travels vary but all refer to a Gaoxi temple [高溪寺] and most mention various locations in and around Huizhou [惠州] prefecture in Guangdong Province [廣東省]. [36c]

We have different accounts for the destruction of a Southern Siu Lum / Shaolin Temple [南少林寺]. I have therefore concluded that these differing accounts could possibly be for the various Southern Siu Lum / Shaolin Temples [南少林寺]. One account could be for the attack on the Fuqing temple [福清寺], one for the Quanzhou temple [泉州寺] and the other may possibly be for the Putian temple [莆田寺]. I have assumed that Gee Seen [至善禪師] died in duel [決鬥] with Bak Mei [白眉] at the destruction of the Putian temple [莆田寺]. Despite the slight differences in the accounts, they do also share some similarities. I can only conclude that over the years, the stories have possibly been interwoven somehow, which has caused this confusion. It is not certain when the Siu Lum / Shaolin Temples at Putian [莆田少林寺] and Fuqing [福清少林寺] were destroyed. It is understood that a Southern Siu Lum / Shaolin Temple [南少林寺] in Fukien / Fujian Province [福建省] did survive until sometime between the late 1700s and the early 1800s, but again there is no surviving documentary evidence to prove the dates, only oral histories and legend. I have written the following accounts for the destruction of the Southern Siu Lum / Shaolin Temples [南少林寺]:-

One account for the destruction of a Southern Siu Lum / Shaolin Temple [南少林寺] states that the attack was assigned to Cheung Gin Cau / Zhang Jianqiu [張建秋], the High Commissioner of Fukien / Fujian province [福建省]. He led an army of 3000 troops and with the aid of a local magistrate [知縣], Chan Man Jiu / Chen Wenyao [陳文耀] from the neighbouring Putian District [莆田], surrounded the temple. In this story, there is no mention of the Siu Lum / Shaolin abbot [少林方丈], Gee Seen [至善禪師], so I have concluded that this attack may possibly have been against the Fuqing temple [福清寺]. [19] [49] Some sources tie in with the above account but dates do not match and some details differ. After reading so many different accounts of the Southern Siu Lum / Shaolin Temple's [南少林寺] destruction it is clear that all these various stories have some similar details. I can only conclude that some facts may possibly have been used to fit one temple's destruction, which may have actually occurred at another site.

Sometime later, the Quanzhou temple [泉州少林寺] was totally destroyed by the local Ch'ing / Qing [清朝] authorities because rebels were training at this site. I have found several sources which state this occurred in 1760s. [25a] (I found two dates of 1763 and 1768.) [21] [27] The Venerable Gee Seen Sim See / Zhi Zhan Chan Shi [至善禪師] who was the abbot [方丈] of the Quanzhou temple [泉州少林寺], managed to escape with four other masters [功夫大師] when the temple was destroyed by the Ch'ing / Qing army [清朝軍隊]. They became known as the "Five Elders" [少林五祖]. Sometime later Gee Seen [至善禪師] made his way to another Southern Siu Lum / Shaolin Temple [南少林寺] not far from Putian [莆田] and re-established himself there. Several histories state this was in the area of Nine Lotus Mountains / Jiu lian shan [九蓮山]. [28] [29] [30] [31]

Several sources state that Gee Seen [至善禪師] died in a fight with one of the other Shaolin Five Elders / Sui Lum Ng Cho [少林五祖] known as Bak Mei [白眉] during the attack on the Putian Temple [莆田寺]. Lineages of the Bak Mei [白眉] style state that Bak Mei [白眉] had trained a force to fight the Ch'ing / Qing [清朝], but were unfortunately captured before they were ready. To prevent his followers from being tortured or killed he was forced to lead government troops on a second destruction of the Southern Siu Lum / Shaolin Temple [南少林寺]. During the attack Bak Mei [白眉] and Gee Seen [至善禪師] fought in single combat, and unfortunately the Siu Lum / Shaolin abbot [少林方丈] was killed. It is stated that Bak Mei [白眉] eventually gained victory and killed Gee Seen [至善禪師] by breaking his neck. [29] [31] [32] [32a]

Some sources also state that a temple was betrayed by Ma Ling Yee [馬寧兒] (a.k.a. Ma Chut. Wong Kiew Kit spells it Ma Ling Yi) and that he revealed the temple's escape tunnels to Ch'ing / Qing [清朝] forces who packed them with explosives and the monks were given three days to surrender. It is believed that the duel [決鬥] between Gee Seen [至善禪師] and Bak Mei [白眉] took place during these three days. After the death of Gee Seen [至善禪師], the Green Grass Monk / Ching Cho [青草] took over as the abbot [方丈] of the Putian Siu Lum / Shaolin Temple [莆田少林寺]. The temple had a fighting force of just over one hundred monks and novices who were then split into five groups to attack the besieging army [清朝軍隊]. The hardest fighting took place near the main road with over a hundred of the Ch'ing / Qing [清朝] soldiers killed by the Siu Lum / Shaolin forces who then withdrew back into the temple. [33] [34]

The besieging army [清朝軍隊] was making little progress and so decided to burn the monks out. The soldiers were commanded to set the temple on fire which soon turned into an inferno. The surviving monks had little choice but to try and escape down the tunnel. As Ch'ing / Qing [清朝] forces realised this they exploded the tunnel killing many of these monks. The Green Grass Monk Ching Cho [青草] and several others survived. One story tells of a large heavy curtain falling on these monks as they prayed in the main hall. This curtain protected them from the majority of the flames as the temple collapsed around them. Once the fire had subsided and the besiegers believing everyone dead, the eighteen survivors managed to escape using the smoke as cover. It is stated that from the eighteen that escaped the temple, only five survived as the others died of wounds and smoke inhalation. They agreed to use their names instead of Siu Lum / Shaolin and to promote their Kung Fu [少林功夫] in an effort to overthrow the Ch'ing / Qing [清朝] authorities. [33] [49]

One source concurs with the above account but states that the Green Grass Monk Ching Cho [青草], took command as the abbot [方丈], and that Gee Seen [至善禪師], made his escape from the temple and went into hiding. The five survivors were Choi Dak Jung / Chua Teck Tiong [蔡德忠], Fong Daai Hung / Hong Dai Ang [方大洪], Mah Chiu Hing / Ma Chew Heng [馬超興], Wu Dak Dai / Ho Teck Deh [胡德帝] and Lei Sik

Hoi / Lee Si Kai [李式開]. It is stated that these five monks were known as the Ng Jing Wo Seung / Five Book Monks [五書僧] who are also known as the five Heaven and Earth Society / Tian Di Hui [天地會] elders. [36] [36a]

If this account is correct then the destruction of this temple could be before 1762 (possibly the Fuqing temple [福清寺]) which is the date the Heaven and Earth Society / Tian Di Hui [天地會] was formed by the Ng Jing Wo Seung / Five Book Monks [方大洪] and Ming / 明 loyalists. [36a] [36c] Several sources state that the Green Grass Monk, / Ching Cho's [青草] real name was Fong Daai Hung [方大洪]. [36] [36b] Another possible explanation is that these five monks were aready founding members who would meet with other Ming [明] loyalists at the Red Flower Pavillion / Hung Fa Ting [红花亭] located at the Putian Siu Lum / Shaolin Temple [莆田少林寺]. It was for this reason that the Ch'ing / Qing [清朝] authorities attacked and destroyed the Putian Siu Lum / Shaolin Temple [莆田少林寺]. About thirty monks and unshaved lay disciples [俗家弟子] [111] [111a] are believed to have survived and escaped the destruction of the Putian temple [莆田寺].[[33a] Sal Canzonieri in his article, *The Story of Traditional Chinese Martial Arts: Southern Styles During the Qing Dynasty",* for the Han Wei Wushu Newsletter (February 1997 issues #28, Article #14) also states that about thirty escaped the destruction of the Fukien temple / Fujian si [福建寺]. Unfortunately, he does not state which temple this was but only that it was a Fukien temple / Fujian si [福建寺] and that the survivors then scattered further south. [66]

The Green Grass Monk / Ching Cho [青草] retreated to Eight Row Mountain / Pak Pai Mountain / Bapaishan [八排山] which is located in Kwangsi / Guangxi Province [廣西省]. In 1841, Jeong Ah Yim [張炎] sought out Ching Cho / [青草] (the Green Grass Monk) at the Zhajian Temple on Pak Pai Mountain / Bapaishan [八排山] and studied the style which is now called Fut Ga Kuen [佛家拳] under him for eight years. [33] [34] [35] [36] So if we do the maths, we know that Jeong Yim [張炎] studied under Ching Cho [青草] (the Green Grass Monk) on Pak Pai Mountain from around 1841. Therefore it is reasonable to assume that the Siu Lum / Shaolin Temple at Putian [莆田少林寺] could have been attacked and destroyed sometime into the early 1800s. [25a] To me this time scale would fit and would also coincide with the histories of all the notable characters that came from Siu Lum / Shaolin [少林] in and around this period.

The more I read these accounts it is easy to wonder if all of these incidents have been confused and mixed up into one story? What is generally agreed is that after the destruction of the Southern Siu Lum / Shaolin Temple [南少林寺] in Fukien / Fujian Province [福建省], many of the monks and unshaved lay disciples [俗家弟子] [111] [111a] who escaped this attack fled south into Guangdong Province [廣東省]. Most went into hiding at other Buddhist temples [佛教徒寺] in this region, particularly in the provincial capital [省會城市] of Canton [廣州] (Guangzhou [廣州]) and this may have possibly been at the Kwangtung Siu Lum / Shaolin temple [廣東少林寺]. It must also be remembered that there were many Siu Lum / Shaolin monks [少林僧] and unshaved lay disciples [俗家弟子][111] [111a] who were already in different parts of southern China performing various duties or on personal errands when their temple was destroyed. It must be concluded that the majority of these would probably also have sought sanctuary at other temples. [16] [84]

The actual location of the Kwangtung temple [廣東少林寺] is not recorded, but stated as in or near the city of Canton [廣州]. As it didn't publically advertise the fact it was a Siu Lum / Shaolin temple [少林寺], it was never attacked and so had the most peaceful existence within the Siu Lum / Shaolin Order. [16] This makes sense because of the turbulent times the Henan / 河南 and Fukien temples / Fujian si [福建寺] both experienced during the early and middle part of the Ch'ing / Qing [清朝] Dynasty. Another possibility is that with the attacks on the Fukien temples / Fujian si [福建寺] and their total destructions, the Siu Lum / Shaolin Monks [少林僧] at Kwangtung [廣東] may have moved around between several of the other Buddhist temples [佛寺] within Canton [廣州] to safeguard their order and their heritage. Using several temples would obviously make it harder for the Ch'ing / Qing [清朝] authorities to establish which were which and so reduce the possibility of the temples been attacked or destroyed.

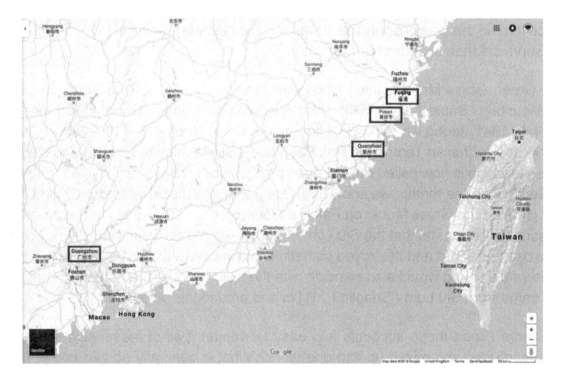

The distance of the Fuqing temple [福清寺] from Canton [廣州] (Guangzhou [廣州]) was approximately 680 kms following the coast line in a south-west direction. Slightly closer was the Putian temple [莆田寺] which was approximately 640 kms and then the Quanzhou temple [泉州寺] at approximately 578 kms from Canton [廣州] on the same coast line.

There were several main Buddhist temples [佛教徒寺] in Canton [廣州], all of which were located within a five kilometre area of the city. [38] It is possible that one or more of them may have been at times used by Siu Lum / Shaolin [少林]. It is known that several prominent Siu Lum / Shaolin monks [少林僧] and their unshaved lay disciples [俗家弟子] went to these temples after the destruction of the Putian [莆田少林寺] and Quanzhou temples [泉州少林寺]. These Siu Lum / Shaolin monks [少林僧] would have continued their teachings at these sites, or sometimes moved around keeping a low profile ensuring that they did not attract the attention of the Ch'ing / Qing [清朝] authorities. This they mainly achieved, because only one of the temples was ever attacked by the Ch'ing army / Qing army / 清朝軍隊 during this period. In my research, I discovered that most of these temples played a role in the various histories of the Siu Lum / Shaolin monks [少林僧], Siu Lum / Shaolin Ten Best [少林十傑] and the Ten Tigers of Canton / Kwong Tung Sap Fu [廣東十虎]. In the next section I have listed these temples and marked them on a map to show their proximity to one another.

Buddhist Temples in Canton (Guangzhou)

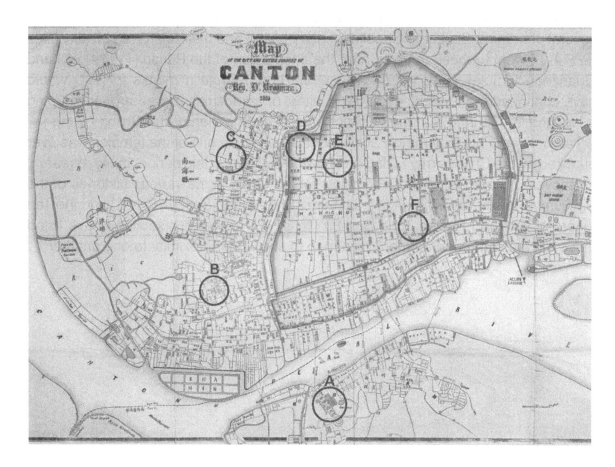

Temples marked on 1860 Canton map

A = Honam Temple [河南寺]
B = Haulin Temple [華林寺]
C = West Zen Temple [西禪寺]
D = Guangxiao Temple [光孝寺]
E = Temple of the Six Banyan Trees [六榕寺]
F = Dafo Temple / Big Buddha Temple [大佛寺]

Honam Temple [河南寺] or The Haizhuang Temple [海幢寺]

(can also be spelt and known as :- Haitong, Hoi Tong, Hoy Tung, Haichung or Sea Monastery [海幢寺].

This temple is located on the island district of Haizhu [海珠區] and was built around 1662. In the nineteenth century it was one of Canton's [廣州] largest monasteries and was more commonly known as the Honam Temple [河南寺] as it was located on Honam Island [河南島]. In Cantonese, Honam means south of the river. The Temple buildings are located on the Tong Fu Xi Lu [同福中路], which translates to Tongfu Middle Road (337 Tongfu Road), and covers an area of seven acres. [39] [40] This temple was very prominent during the 1800s and is mentioned in the histories of several of the Tigers of Canton. During this period, the temple grounds covered three times the size of the present day's site. To give an idea of what the Honam Temple [河南寺] was like in the mid 1800s, I have included the following description of the temple by John Thomson, a pioneering Scottish photographer, geographer and traveller. He was one of the first photographers to travel to the Far East, documenting the people, landscapes and artefacts of eastern cultures. [41]

"HONAM TEMPLE, one of the largest Buddhist establishments in the south of China, stands on the southern bank of the Pearl River at Canton. Passing along the broad granite pavement which conducts from the water-side, and entering the outer porch, beneath the shade of venerable trees, the visitor finds himself within a spacious outer compartment, having gigantic gateways in front and to the rear. Two colossal statues, deities of Indian mythology, and armed and equipped as warriors present themselves next to his gaze. These are the adopted guardians of Buddha, and in temples even greater than that of Honam these panoptical champions are increased to four. We next ascend by a flight of broad steps to an inner causeway, and the vista shown in the photograph comes there upon into view. Beyond, in a central court, is the adytum or innermost shrine, where

three images of Buddha glisten with a coating of polished gold. Here the air is laden heavily with the fumes of incense, rising in spiral columns from the altar in front of the gods. A priest tends the burning tapers that from generation to generation have been kept alight ; and all round are bowls of bronze, and vases filled with ashes, embers of incense sticks, and the relics of a thousand votive gifts. The candles which burn upon the altar cast a lurid flare over the mystic images and amid the silken hangings of the roof. The constant tinkling of a bell, or the solemn monotonous chant of some aged priest, the surrounding darkness of the dim interior, combined with the worship of a strange god, induce a sense of depression, which is speedily dissipated by a stroll in the wonderful garden beyond. Here the priests delight to tend and rear rare and beautiful plants, dwarf trees, growing marvels in the form of tiny boats and bird-cages, and plants, whose stems are trained into a hundred curious devices. Here, too, is a pen full of fortunate pigs, guaranteed immunity from slaughter, as under the protecting roof of Buddha, the mighty saviour of life." [42]

Another detailed description of this temple can be found in, <u>The Treaty Ports of China and Japan: A Complete Guide to the Open Ports of those Countries, together with Peking, Yedo, Hongkong and Macao</u>. (The following account is from pages 160-162) [12i]

"A short distance above the island called Dutch Folly will be noticed, on the South bank of the river, the dense mass of foliage marking the avenue of banyans in front of the portals of this fine monastic establishment, which is named in Chinese Hai Chwang Sze (海幢寺) or The Temple of the Ocean Banner. Immediately on landing from the river and passing through an unpretending door-way, the avenue bordering a pathway paved with granite is entered, leading to a square building forming a double gate with two colossal figures standing within the porch and representing certain deified warriors who keep watch and ward over the sanctuaries of Buddha. Another small court and a third gateway are still to be passed before the great inner quadrangle is reached; where in the centre of the grassy enclosure dotted with magnificent trees, rises a platform supporting the great hall of worship, some hundred feet square, in the midst of which tower tranquil images of the past, present and the future Buddha. In front of these gilded figures is an altar of richly carved wood, upon which huge candlesticks of white metal support a galaxy of tapers, whilst in the centre is displayed a massive bowl of similar material, filled with the fine, impalpable powder of the fragrant incense kept constantly burning before the shrine. From the roof, streamers of red cloth bordered with black velvet and inscribed in velvet characters with the invocation "NAN-MO O-M1-TO-F61" hang in dense array, adding materially to the dimness of the "religious light," the soft mysteriousness of which is enhanced by the light blue clouds of scented smoke arising from the slow combustion of a block of sandalwood and of the incense-sticks. On both sides of the hall are arranged the images of the Eighteen Lo-Han, or Apostles of Buddha and small tables covered with embroidered cloths serve as lecterns to the priests who perform daily mass. This spectacle may usually be witnessed about four

o'clock in the afternoon, when ten to twenty priests may be seen, attired in the gowns of crimson, yellow or ash-gray silk (according to their rank and functions) chanting the Pa-li words, quite unintelligible to themselves, of the mass-book, whilst one of their number beats time on the "wooden fish," a hollowed block of wood, carved in the resemblance of a potbellied fish, which gives forth a booming sound when struck – whilst the duty of another is to strike a small hand-bell from time to time. The alternate risings and genuflections, the droning hum of the chanters, the silvery interruption of the bell, the investments, incense, decorations, flowers, images, combine to invest this scene with a striking resemblance to the ceremonies of the Romish Church and the mummeries, still more unmeaning, of the so-called "Anglican" imitators of Romanism.

Another large hall, in the rear of the first, contains an image of Kwan-yin (Koon-yum), the Goddess Hearer of Prayers and still further on, in the midst of a gloomy sanctuary, stands a pagoda sculptured in white marble, about thirty feet in height, which was presented to the temple by one of the emperors of the present dynasty. On both sides of the great quadrangle are long ranges of buildings, intersected by courts and corridors, which constitute the apartments of the priests. On the right hand are a range of pens where pigs are kept at the expense of the temple, in fulfilment of the command of Buddha that each man shall do what in him lies to prevent the destruction of a single living creature. Passing through an apparently endless range of corridors on the left hand and after viewing the large hall, filled with benches and tables, which is set aside as the refectory for the priests, a small paved yard is reached which gives admission to a spacious garden, covering some four or five acres of ground, where flowers, fruit and vegetables are cultivated for sale. At the extremity of the garden are two ponds where fish are allowed to breed undisturbed, in obedience to the same law of Buddha which has been above referred to. Besides the fish ponds is a mausoleum in which ashes of deceased priests are deposited, after the process of cremation by which the bodies are consumed. The number of priests or monks inhabiting this temple is upwards of one hundred, who are subject to the authority of an abbot, periodically elected. Large revenues are derived from lands belonging to the monastery. The present buildings date only from the latter half of the seventeenth century, when they were founded by the son-in law of the Emperor K'ang Hi, by whom the subjugation of the Province of Kwang-tung was completed. A temple had, however, existed on this spot for fully fifteen hundred years." [12]

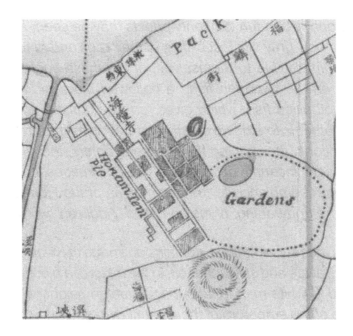

The Honam Temple's [河南寺] grounds covered an area of about seven acres which were surrounded by a wall, and divided into courts, gardens, and a burial-ground. The priests who died were cremated and their ashes placed in the burial ground. During the mid 1800s, there were about 175 priests residing at this temple. [12c]

Thomas Allom, a British architect and illustrator, engraved a number of scenes that were published in four volumes in London in 1843. These engravings were accompanied by detailed commentaries written by G.H Wright, a Protestant missionary, who had spent a significant time in China. [43] [44]

Front riverbank entrance of the Honam Temple. Victorian print dated 1843 by Thomas Allom

Victorian print dated 1843 by Thomas Allom

Consecration of the Abbot at Honam Temple, printed in the
Illustrated London News, Dec 11th 1858.

The Hualin Temple [華南寺]

The Hualin temple [華南寺] was constructed during the Southern Dynasties [南朝] around 526AD, shortly after the arrival in China of the Indian monk, Bodhidharma [達摩]. It was originally named the Xilai Temple [西来寺] meaning "the visitor from the west", after Bodhidharma [達摩] who founded Chan / Zen Buddhism [禪] in China. This temple is located on Kangwang South Road [康王南路], in the Liwan district [荔灣區] (originally called Xiguan / West Gate / Sai Kwan [西關]) of Guangzhou [廣州]. It was expanded in 1655 and then renamed the Hualin Temple [華南寺]. According to John Thomson (a Scottish photographer, geographer and traveller, 1837-1921), who was one of the first photographers to travel to the Far East, documenting the people, landscapes and artefacts of eastern cultures. [48a]), the temple was again rebuilt in 1755, under the direction of the Emperor Ch'ien Lung / Qianlong [乾隆皇帝] making it one of the five largest Buddhist temples [佛教徒寺] in Guangzhou [廣州], with a large team of monks in residence. The Five-Hundred-Arhat Hall [五百羅漢堂] which contains the golden painted statues of 500 different monks was added and completed about 1851. [45] [46] [57a] The following write up is by John Thomson.

"This celebrated shrine, which the Chinese call "Hua-lin-szu," "Magnificent Forest Temple," is situated in the western suburbs of Canton, and was erected by Bodhidharama, a Buddhist missionary from India, who landed in Canton about the year 520 A. D. and who is frequently pictured on Chinese tea-cups ascending the Yangtsze on his bamboo raft. The temple was rebuilt in 1755, under the auspices of the Emperor Kien-lung, and with its courts, halls, and dwellings for the priests, covers a very large space of ground. It is the Lo-Han-T'ang, or Hall of Saints, partly shown in the photograph, that forms the chief attraction of the place.

This Hall contains 500 gilded effigies of saints out of the Buddhist calendar, representing men of different Eastern nationalities. Colonel Yule, in his new edition of "Marco Polo," says that one of these is an image of the Venetian traveller ; but careful inquiry proves this statement incorrect, as there is no statue presenting the European type of face, and all the records connected with them are of prior antiquity. The aged figure shown in the next picture is that of the abbot, OR Chief Priest of this temple. About three years ago, when I paid my first visit to this establishment, in company with a native gentleman from the Canton Customs

Office, I was introduced to this Abbot. He received us with great courtesy, conducted us to his private apartments, and there refreshed us with tea-cakes and fruit. The rooms he occupied were enclosed by a high wall, and approached through a granite-paved

inner quadrangle, adorned with a variety of rare and beautiful flowers. Conspicuous among the latter was a splendid specimen of the Sacred Lotus, in full bloom, and growing in an ornamental tank, on whose surface floated many other brilliantly green aquatic plants. The old gentleman had spent half his lifetime in this secluded place, and was greatly devoted to his flowers, discoursing on their beauty with an eloquent fondness, and expressing his delight to discover in a foreigner kindred sentiments of admiration. The furniture of the apartments consisted of chairs of skilfully carved black wood, one or two tables, and a

shrine of the same material ; while a number of well-executed drawings, hung about the white walls, displayed a simple taste and refinement in keeping with the surroundings of their proprietor's secluded life. Two years afterwards I visited the temple again, and executed the photograph here represented. On the second occasion I met with the same kind hospitality at the hands of the Abbot and the priests in his care. [42]

Photographing an interior like this was no easy task as the emulsions were much less receptive to light. As a result you can see how the light from the windows has bled into the photograph due to Thomson's long exposure. [41] [47] [48]

These photographs of the Hualin Temple [華南寺] were taken by John Thomson sometime around 1872. This photograph shows an interior view of 'hall of gods' in the Buddhist 'Temple of the 500 Gods'. Nowadays this temple is more often referred to as the Hualin Temple [華南寺].

51

广州华林寺和尚抽水烟下围棋 1869 Canton(Guangzhou), Monk Playing Go with Chinese Hookah in Hualin Temple

Sai Sim Ji / Xi Chan Temple / West Zen Temple [西禪寺]

Several histories including our own Hak Fu Mun [黑虎門] tell of a West Zen Temple [西禪寺] in Canton [廣州]. [50] [50a] [51] This temple was also known as the Lingfeng Temple [靈峰寺]because of the turtle shaped stone within its grounds. The West Zen Temple / Sai Sim Ji / Xi Chan Si [西禪寺] was built around 1176 in an area near Canton [廣州] known as Fan Hill / Fan Shan [番山]. This was outside the West Gate / Sai Kwan / Xiguan [西關] of the city walls located on West China Road / Wai See Lou / Xi Hua Lu [西華路]. During its history it was destroyed several times around 1440, 1530 and again at the start of the Ch'ing / Qing [清朝] dynasty in the1640s. It was last rebuilt in 1658. This area was mainly farming land until the late 1700s to early 1800s, when Canton [廣州] experienced rapid development which encroached on lands in the surrounding area. The Canton weaving industry [廣州紡織業] developed in this region.

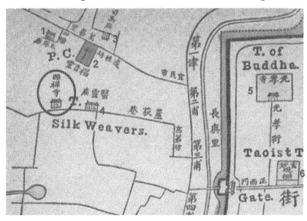

Much of the land between the city walls and area near this temple was utilised to build several factories and provide housing for the workers. [52]

This basic map shows the land around the West Zen Temple / Sai Sim Ji / Xi Chan Si [西禪寺] (circled) and the area occupied by the expanding silk weaving industry of Canton [廣州].

1. Tai Po Temple / Taibao Miao [太保廟]
2. Evangelical Christian Church / Fuyin Tang [福音堂]
3. See Ma Temple / Sima Miao [司馬廟]
4. Medical Ling Temple / Yi Ling Miao [醫靈廟]
5. Kwong Hau Temple / Guangxiao Si [光孝寺]
6. Yuen Miu Kwun / Xuanmiao Guan [玄妙觀]

The area out side the west gate of Guangdong (Canton) is referred to as Xiguan. Historically this was the name for the west outskirts of the ancient city of Canton.

Originally, Canton (Guangzhou) had three city gates situated at the east, south and west. These are called the East Gate / Dongguan[東關], South Gate / Nanguan [南關] and West Gate / Xiguan [西關]. Due to the mountains in

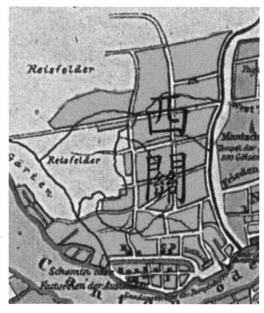

the north of the city, there was no North Gate / Beiguan [北關]. The Chinese name for gate is Guan [關]. Thus, Xiguan refers to the area outside the west gate of Guangzhou. The former name for Xiguan is Sai Kwan which is the Cantonese Romanisation. [140]

Initially, due to the temple being located outside the city walls, it was not as convenient as some of the other main temples, such as the Guangxiao Temple [光孝寺] and the Temple of the Six Banyan Trees [六榕寺], for the general public to use. But, its location also ensured that it was not too noticeable to the Ch'ing / Qing [清朝] authorities. History records that Gee Seen Sim See [至善禪師] established martial arts [武術] training at the temple, for which it became renowned, during the late 1700s and early 1800s. Some of his disciples [武術弟子] here included Hung Hei-Kwun (Hong Xiguan [洪熙官]), Fong Sai-Yuk [方世玉] and Wu Wai-Kin [胡惠乾] (members of Gee Seen's Siu Lum / Shaolin Ten Best [少林十傑]). Gee Seen [至善禪師] later returned to the Putian [莆田少林寺] Siu Lum / Shaolin Temple [少林寺] in Fukien / Fujian Province [福建省]. One of his best students at the Putian Siu Lum / Shaolin Temple [莆田少林寺] was a monk called Sam Dak / San De [三德].

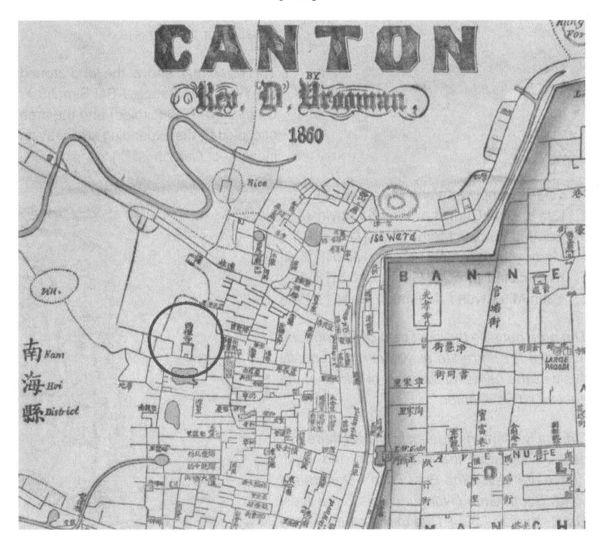

Sometime in the early 1800s, Gee Seen [至善禪師] sent Sam Dak / San De [三德] to the West Zen Temple / Sai Sim Ji / Xi Chan Si [西禪寺] to teach martial arts [武術]. He was born and raised in Canton [廣州] so he knew the area well. [50b]

It is not known whether Sam Dak / San De [三德] became the abbot [方丈] of the temple on his arrival, or sometime later. For several years Sam Dak / San De [三德] would travel between the Southern Siu Lum / Shaolin Temple [南少林寺] at Putian [莆田] and the West Zen Temple / Sai Sim Ji / Xi Chan Si [西禪寺]. Sometime after he had become the abbot [方丈] of the West Zen Temple / Sai Sim Ji / Xi Chan Si [西禪寺], the Southern Siu Lum / Shaolin Temple [南少林寺] at Putian [莆田] was attacked and destroyed by the Ch'ing / Qing [清朝] authorities. It is stated that during this time, many Southern Siu Lum / Shaolin heroes then gathered at the Sai Sim Ji / Xi Chan Si / West Zen Temple [西禪寺]. [65] In his position as abbot [方丈] of the temple, Sam Dak / San De [三德] attracted both martial artists [武術家] and ordinary people to study under him. Unfortunately, Sam Dak / San De [三德] was killed and the temple looted by Ch'ing / Qing [清朝] soldiers sometime after the early 1840s. It is stated that the Ch'ing / Qing [清朝] authorities then selected monks to run the temple which is shown on Rev. Daniel Vrooman's map of Canton, dated 1860. (The Rev. Daniel Vrooman was sent to Canton by the American Board of Commissioners for Foreign Missions in 1852. He remained their missionary in Canton until 1866).

General Chan Chai Tong [陳濟棠將軍], a local warlord, built the 51st primary school from the ruins of the former West Zen Temple / Sai Sim Ji / Xi Chan Si [西禪寺] in 1933. When the Japanese army occupied Guangzhou [廣州] during the Second World War, the school closed and became a shelter for many of the poor. After the war, the school reopened and was later renamed the 4th Secondary School under the reforms of the People's Republic of China. (Guangzhou City 4th Secondary School, Xi Hua Lu & Tai Bao Zhi Jie, Yuexiu Qu, Guangzhou Shi, Guangdong [西华路太保直街廣州市第四中学]) [52]

Guangxiao Temple [光孝寺]

This photo dated 1860 shows the temple's main hall from the side. In the background can be seen the Flower Tower of the Six Banyan Trees Temple.

(Spelt Kwong Hau in Cantonese which translates to mean Bright Filial Piety Temple) The original structure was built as a mansion for a local prince, before it was converted into a temple around the 4th century AD. It is therefore reputed to be the oldest and also the largest temple of Buddhism [佛教] in Guangzhou [廣州]. During the Zhenguan years [貞觀年間] (the reign of the Emperor T'ang T'ai-tsung / Tang Taizong [唐太宗] from 627 to 649AD), the temple area expanded and become an important Buddhist / [佛教徒] centre in the Lingnan region [嶺南] (Southern China).

Lingnan [嶺南]; refers to a region to the south of China's Nan Mountains : Tayu, Qitian, Dupang, Mengzhu, and Yuecheng. This large area covers the modern Chinese provinces ofJiangxi, Hunan, Guangdong, Guangxi and Hainan as well as modern northern Vietnam. [53b]

Front view of the Guangxiao Temple's main hall.

Two of the Four Kings which were destroyed during the Cultural Revolution.

Part of the importance of the temple was because it became a translation centre for Buddhist [佛教徒] scriptures in Southern China. In addition, because of its geographical position, it became a stopover point for the many Buddhist monks [和尚] who were travelling around Southern Asia (especially from India). During the following centuries the temple continued to grow, with other buildings and structures being erected. Some of these included a pagoda where Huineng's hair was buried, the Sakyamuni Hall, the Samgharama Hall, the King of Heaven Hall, and two iron towers.

The temple has had various names during its early history and was renamed the Guangxiao Temple [光孝寺] in 1482 by the Ming [明朝] Emperor Xianzong [明憲宗], (Chenghua [成化]1447–1487AD). On the 24th November 1650, Ch'ing / Qing [清朝軍隊] forces led by Shang Ko-hsi / Shang Kexi [尚可喜] captured Canton [廣州] and massacred the city's population, killing as many as 70,000 people. [53c] Many parts of this temple were engulfed in flames during the capturing and sacking of the city and for a time after, it was used as temporary army barracks before being rebuilt as the Guangxiao Temple [光孝寺].

Various views of the Guangxiao Temple's main hall.

The Garan Temple

The Iron Tower

Patriarch Temple

The Drum Tower

The Guangxiao Temple [光孝寺] is located on Guangxiao Road [光孝路] in what is now the Yuexiu district [越秀區]. It is only about 400 metres west of the Temple of the Six Banyan Trees / Liu Rong Si [六榕寺]. There is an old saying that; "Guangxiao [光孝寺] is famous for its trees and Jinghui is famous for its tower." Jinghui is another name for the Liurong Temple [六榕寺] [53] [53a] [54] [57a]

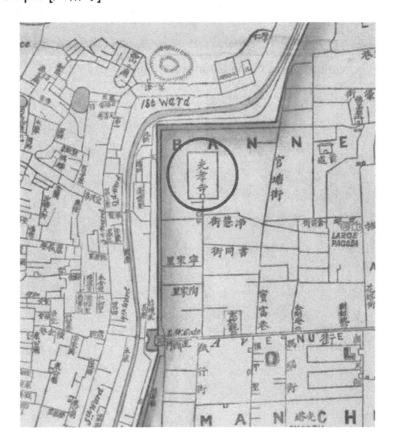

A more detailed history of this temple can be found in Chinese at:-
http://zh.wikipedia.org/wiki/光孝寺(广州) [53a]

The Temple of the Six Banyan Trees [六榕寺]
(which is known as the Liurong Temple in Mandarin)

This photo from 1863 shows the temple and tower damaged. This was caused by a typoon in 1856 and the British attack on the city in 1857.

These photos from 1880 show the rebuilt temple and tower which had been completed in around 1875.

This Temple was originally built in 537AD and called the Baozhuangyan Temple (Baozhi) [寶莊嚴寺] (which translates to Po Yan Temple), but during its history, it has also been called various names like the Cheung Sui Chee / Changshou Temple [長壽寺] (which translates to mean Longevity Temple) and the Jinghui Temple / Net Hui Si [净慧寺]. Its current name of the Six Banyan Trees, was due to a famous writer, Sik / Su Shi [蘇軾], who wrote the inscription *Liu Rong* (Six Banyan Trees) because of the six banyan trees that were there during his visit. This was during the Song Dynasty / [宋朝] (approx 1110AD), and the temple was later officially renamed the Six Banyan Trees / Liu Rong Si [六榕寺] by the Yongle Emperor [永樂帝] around 1411AD.

The temple is located in Liurong Road / Six Banyan Trees Road in the Yuexiu district [越秀區]. It has a very impressive 17 story pagoda, which is 58 metres (190ft) high, called the Hua Ta [花塔] which translates to Flower Tower (more commonly known as the Flower Pagoda). The wooden pagoda was originally built in the 11th century and features beautiful carvings and balconies. Over the years the temple was rebuilt and enlarged several times. The Flower Pagoda was last rebuilt in 1931 when the interior was reinforced with concrete. [55] [56]

A more detailed history of this temple can be found in Chinese at:- [55a] *http://zh.wikipedia.org/wiki/六榕寺*

Dafo Temple / Big Buddha Temple [大佛寺]

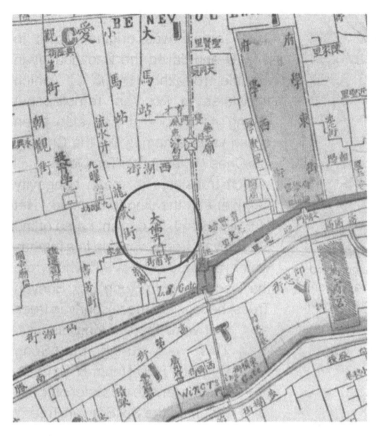

Dafo translates to the Big Buddha Temple. The Dafo Temple was built around 950AD, during the Five Dynasties and Ten Kingdoms [五代十國] period. With the decline of Buddhism [佛教] during the late Ming Dynasty [明朝] the temple became offices for the Emperor's Representative Censor Office [巡按御史公署]. Shortly after the start of the Ch'ing / Qing Dynasty [清朝] these buildings were destroyed by fire. The temple was rebuilt and flourished during the reign of the emperor, Ch'ien Lung / Qianlong [乾隆皇帝] (1735-1796), becoming one of the most famous Buddhist temples [佛教寺院] in southern China. During its heyday, this temple covered a vast area of 30,000 square metres and was home to over a hundred monks.

Entrance to Dafo Temple   Original main hall   New building work, Oct 2014

Unfortunately, during China's Cultural Revolution [文化大革命](1966-1976), this temple as well as all the other remaining temples were ransacked. All the monks here were expelled, and most of the temple was destroyed. Buildings and statues were smashed, with many of the priceless or symbolic artefacts lost, damaged or stolen. Some of these temples have since been repaired or rebuilt, but are not the size they once were and are unable to match their former glory in this expanding city, surrounded by colossal modern buildings. The only exception seems to be the Dafo Temple / Big Buddha Temple [大佛寺]. It is currently subject to major renovation work, involving the construction of an enormous building. This temple is located in the heart of the city next to the main shopping area.

Before recent renovation work began, only the main hall remained, representing a fifth of the original complex. During my visit in October 2014, a major renovation scheme was underway to expand the temple. The temple is located at 21 Huixin Zhong Street / 21 New Middle Street [新中街21号] and just off Huifu Dong Road [惠福東路] in the Yuexiu district / [越秀區]. [57] [57a] [58]

Assumption about the Kwantung Siu Lum / Shaolin Temple [廣東少林寺]

In our interview of the Siu Lum / Shaolin Monk [少林僧], Yin Yan [延因], at the Putian Temple [莆田寺] in November 2015, he stated that there were four Siu Lum / Shaolin Temple [少林寺] sites in Canton [廣州]. After visiting the remaining five temples and examining the facts and stories regarding them, I have come to the conclusion that the Kwangtung Siu Lum / Shaolin Temple [廣東少林寺] could possibly be one of four Buddhist temples [佛教徒寺] in Canton / Guangzhou [廣州] that existed during the period of the 1700 and 1800s. It is possible that all four of them could have been part of the Siu Lum / Shaolin Order. We now know that in the late 1700s, and after the destruction of the Southern Siu Lum / Shaolin Temples [南少林寺] at Quanzhou / 泉州 and at Putian [莆田], many Siu Lum / Shaolin monks [少林僧] and unshaved lay disciples [俗家弟子][111] [111a] stayed at some of these temples.

The Hualin Temple [華南寺] was built in honour of Bodhidharma [達摩] and consequently shares many similarities with Henan Siu Lum / Shaolin Temple. The Shaolin Grandmasters' text states that the Kwangtung Temple [廣東少林寺] was established about 970AD so this may be when it came under Siu Lum / Shaolin's authority or influence.

Hualin Temple [華南寺]

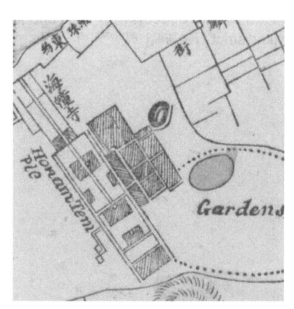
Honam Temple [河南寺] (Hoi Tong Temple [海幢寺])

The second possible temple that could formerly have been known as the Kwangtung Siu Lum / Shaolin Temple [廣東少林寺] is the Haitong / Honam temple [河南寺]. The Southern 5 Chinese Boxing Academy states that the Hoi Tong [海幢寺] (Honam [河南寺]) monastery later became the Siu Lum / Shaolin Temple [少林寺] in Guangdong.

[59] It is recorded that Gee Seen Sim See [至善禪師], who was the last abbot [方丈] of the Southern Siu Lum / Shaolin temples [南少林寺] initially at Quanzhou [泉州] and then Putian [莆田], visited the Hoi Tong [海幢寺] monastery (also known as the Honam temple [河南寺]), when he was in Canton [廣州]. [50b] It is also recorded that many Siu Lum / Shaolin monks [少林僧] gathered at this temple after the destruction of the Fukien temple / Fujian si [福建寺]. [84]

I also believe that the West Zen Temple / Sai Sim Ji / Xi Chan Si [西禪寺] fell under the influence of the Siu Lum / Shaolin order. It is recorded that Gee Seen Sim See [至善禪師], the renowned great master [功夫大師] and abbot [方丈], visited the West Zen Temple / Sai Sim Ji / Xi Chan Si [西禪寺] when he was in Canton [廣州]. He later sent one of his best students to this temple to replace the head monks and teach Siu Lum / Shaolin martial arts [少林武術]. In order to do this, Siu Lum / Shaolin [少林] must have had some degree of authority over the West Zen Temple / Sai Sim Ji / Xi Chan Si [西禪寺]. Unfortunately, this temple was destroyed by Ch'ing / Qing [清朝] soldiers when they discovered that the Siu Lum / Shaolin Monk [少林僧人], Sam Dak / San De [三德], was training lay-persons with revolutionary intentions. [50b]

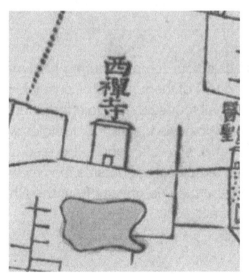
Guangxiao Temple [光孝寺]

West Zen Temple [西禪寺]

It is stated that Gee Seen Sim See [至善禪師] also spent time at this temple when he was in Canton [廣州]. He later sent some of his students to teach Siu Lum / Shaolin Martial Arts at the Kwong Hau Temple, the Cantonese name for the Guangxiao Temple [光孝寺]. [50b]

West Zen Temple / 西禪寺   **Guangxiao Temple / 光孝寺**

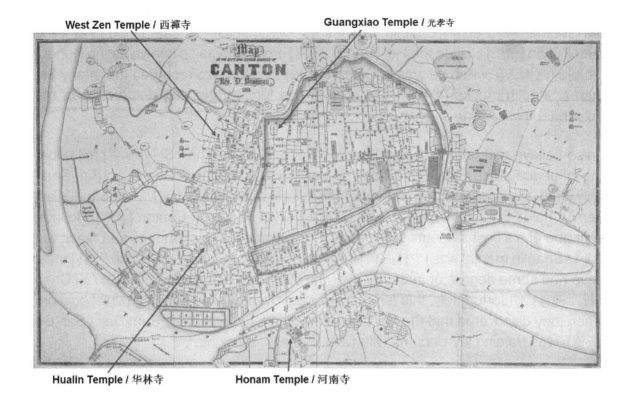

Hualin Temple / 华林寺   **Honam Temple / 河南寺**

Gee Seen Sim See [至善禪師] may have visited all four temples during his time in Canton / [廣州], but he is only recorded as visiting two of them. It is also possible that the Siu Lum / Shaolin order moved around, using all four sites to avoid the attention of the Ch'ing / Qing [清朝] authorities. It is therefore possible that all four temples were subsidiary temples of the Siu Lum / Shaolin Order during this period. It is also clear to see from the old 1860s map that three of these temples were outside the city walls of Canton [廣州], and their locations would allow them some privacy from the Ch'ing / Qing [清朝] authorities stationed within the city walls.

The Region of Guangdong Province [廣東省]

Guangdong [廣東] is a province in Southern China which has a large river system and coastline on the South China Sea [南海]. Until the introduction of Hanyu Pinyin it was also known under the alternative English name of Kwangtung Province [廣東省]. Canton [廣州], was derived from a Portuguese transliteration of "Guangdong", but really only refers to the provincial capital [省會城市] instead of the whole province, as documented by authoritative English dictionaries. The local people of the city of Guangzhou [廣州] (Canton [廣州]) and their language are still commonly referred to as Cantonese in English. Because of the prestige of Canton and its accent, Cantonese can also be used for related residents and Chinese dialects outside the provincial capital [省會城市]. This province is covered by several rivers and hundreds of canals known as the Pearl River Delta [珠江三角洲]. [60]

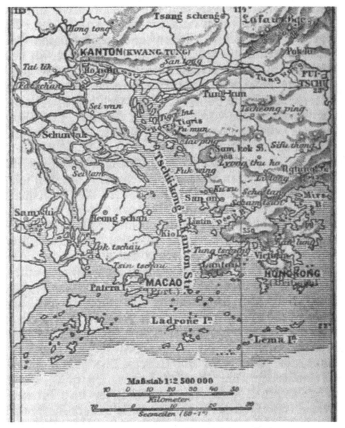
Old map showing the Pearl River Delta

Wikipedia states :- *The Pearl River or "Guangdong River" or "Canton River", is a very large river network in southern China which is actually made up of three rivers. These there rivers are, the West River / Xi Jiang, the North River / Bei Jiang and the East River / Dong Jiang. The flat lands of this delta region are criss-crossed by a network of tributaries and distributaries of the Pearl River. Some of the main cities that are connected by this river system include Guangzhou, Shenzen, Zhuhai, Dongguan, Zhongshan, Foshan, Huizhou, Jiangmen, Zhaoqing and also Hong Kong and Macau.*

Historically, the Pearl River acquired its name because of all the pearl coloured shells that lie at the bottom of the river bed in the area that flows through the city of Guangzhou. [60a]

During the 1800s, the majority of trade and travel was conducted on the waterways that covered this region. Many people lived on the waterways around the major towns and cities, and therefore due to the amount of constantly moving vessels on the rivers and canals, it made it almost impossible for the Ch'ing / Qing [清朝] authorities to control them.

These photos show Canton's many waterways

To give some idea of what Canton [廣州] was like during the late 1800s, I have included the following extract from a book entitled, "Chambers's Concise Gazetteer Of The World", by David Patrick. This book was first published in 1907. [62]

<u>Canton</u>

Canton, a large commercial city and port in the south of China, and capital of the province of Kwang-tung (of which the name Canton is merely a corruption), is situated in 23° 7' 10" N. lat., and 113° 14' 30" E. long., on the north or left side of the Shu-kiang, or Pearl River, in a rich alluvial plain, 70 miles N. of Macao, at the mouth of the estuary of the Canton River, and 90 NW. of Hong-kong. The city is surrounded by walls 25 to 40 feet high and 20 thick, with an esplanade inside, six miles in circumference; and it is divided by a partition wall running east and west into two unequal parts, the north or old city, much the larger, and the south or new city. There are twelve outer gates, four gates in partition wall, and two water gates; shut and guarded by night. The entire circuit, including suburbs, is nearly 10 miles. At the south-west corner of the suburbs, south of the river, are the Hongs or European quarter, divided from the river by a quay, 100 yards wide, called Respondentia Walk. The streets, more than 600, are in general less than 8 feet wide, and very crooked.

The houses along the water-side are built on piles, and subject to inundations. There are two pagodas, the 'Plain Pagoda,' erected ten centuries ago, 160 feet high, and an octagonal nine-storied pagoda, 175 feet high, erected more than 1300 years ago; and 124 temples or Joss-houses. The Honam temple covers, with its grounds, 7 acres, and has 175 priests attached. The 'Temple of Filial Duty' has 200 priests, supported by

3500 acres of glebe-lands. The priests and nuns in Canton number more than 2000, nine-tenths of them Buddhists. The 'Temple of Five Hundred Genii' has 500 statues of various sizes in honour of Buddha and his disciples. Examination Hall, in the old city, is 1330 feet by 583 feet, covers 16 acres, and has 8653 cells. Nearly half the craft on the river are fixed residences, and the population on land and water can hardly be less than a million and a half. The climate of Canton may be pronounced healthy. The average temperature ranges from 42° to 96° F.; though falls of snow occurred in 1835 and 1861. The average rainfall is 70 inches. Pop. 1,800,000.

The admirable situation of Canton, with a safe and commodious anchorage for the largest vessels, explains how, from an early period, it was a favourite port with foreign merchants. The earliest notices date back to two centuries b.c.; and the Arabs made regular voyages hither as early as the 9th century a.d. The Portuguese found their way to it in 1517, and were followed by the Dutch a hundred years later. These in turn were supplanted by the English before the close of the 17th century, and an immense trade was carried on by the agents of the East India Company, whose monopoly ceased in April 1834. In 1842 Canton became one of the five 'treaty ports' open to foreign commerce. The city was captured by the allied French and English forces in December 1857, and continued to be garrisoned by them till October 1861. The chief exports from Canton are tea, silk, sugar, and cassia; the chief imports, cotton, woollen, and metal goods, foodstuffs, opium, kerosene, etc. [62]

If the reader wishes to know more of Canton [廣州] in the late 1800s, I recommend further reading of the Presbyterian Archives Research Centre, "A Tour of Old Canton" [63]

More old photos of Canton [廣州] can also be found at the following :-
https://www.flickr.com/photos/keepmyword/sets/72157615035703233
http://commons.wikimedia.org/wiki/Category:Historical_images_of_Guangzhou?uselang=zh-hans

The Great Masters from Siu Lum / Shaolin

Wing Lam [64] records three branches of Hung Gar Kuen [洪家拳] from the survivors of the Southern Siu Lum / Shaolin Temple [南少林寺]:-
1. The first branch is from the monk Gee Seen [至善禪師], then his ten best students, with Hung Hei Kwun [洪熙官] and Luk Ah-Choi [陸阿采].
2. The second branch is from the monk Gwok Yan [覺因] (Kwok Yan / Guo Yen), then Leung Kwan / Liang Kun [梁坤] (Tit Kiu Sam).
3. The third branch is from the monk Sam Dak / San De [三德]. [64]

During my research I found that the venerable Sam Dak / San De [三德] was also tutored by the Siu Lum / Shaolin abbot [少林方丈], Gee Seen Sim See [至善禪師] and that the venerable Gwok Yan [覺因] was also tutored by both Gee Seen Sim See [至善禪師] and Sam Dak / San De [三德]. Several of the Ten Tigers of Canton / Kwong Tung Sap Fu [廣東十虎] were trained by one or more of these monks or their students.

The Venerable Gee Seen Sim See

(can also be spelt as Jee Sin / Ji Sin Sim Si / Zhi Shan Chan Shi [至善禅师]) [29]

Approximately early 1700s-1800s

Gee Seen Sim See [至善禪師] means Most Kindness or Perfection Chan / Zen [禪] teacher or master and is the Buddhist [佛教徒] name that Chi Thien Su [趙天壽] was more commonly known by. Little is known of his early life or when he came to the Siu Lum / Shaolin Temple [少林寺]. Records state that when the previous abbot [方丈] known by the Buddhist [佛教徒] name of Hung Mei (which means Red Eyebrow [红眉]) passed away, Gee Seen Sim See [至善禪師] was then chosen to take his place and become the abbot [少林方丈]. [32] [32a] [32b] Gee Seen [至善禪師] is stated as being an exceptional Kung Fu master [功夫大師] without equal in Siu Lum / Shaolin martial arts [少林武術], particularly of the Tiger style [虎拳]. It is understood that he taught several styles which included Chi Kung / Qigong [氣功], Hakka Kuen [客家拳], (also known as Southern Praying Mantis [南派螳螂]), Eagle Claw / Jing Jar [鷹爪] in addition to the Tiger [虎] style which later developed into what is known today as Hung Gar Kuen [洪家拳]. It is also stated that he was an outstanding master [功夫大師] in the various Siu Lum / Shaolin arts of conditioning [少林內息調理功], such as Iron Shirt / Tee Po Sam / Tie bu shan [鐵布衫] and Iron Head / Tee Tau Kun / Tie tou gong [鐵頭功], as well as many Siu Lum / Shaolin weapons. [22] [64] [69] [70] [71] [73]

Several accounts state that Gee Seen [至善禪師] had escaped the attack in 1647 on the Northern Siu Lum / Shaolin Temple [北少林寺] in Henan Province [河南省] by the Ch'ing / Qing [清朝] authorities. After the attack he travelled south to the Southern Siu Lum / Shaolin Temple [南少林寺] at Quanzhou [泉州] where he became the head abbot [方丈] at this temple.

70

(This is clearly not possible due to the time scale and dates of future events. I believe that before the finding of the Southern Siu Lum / Shaolin Temples [南少林寺] ruins, certain sources had implied this to make the events fit the story. Another possible and, in my opinion, more likely scenario is that Gee Seen [至善禪師] did not flee the Northern Siu Lum / Shaolin Temple [北少林寺] but was always at the Southern Siu Lum / Shaolin Temple [南少林寺] at Quanzhou [泉州]. When this temple was attacked and destroyed, the Shaolin Five Elders / Sui Lum Ng Cho [少林五祖] escaped from here and not the northern temple at Henan [河南]. This would be more plausible with time scales, the outcome of future events and stories of the Shaolin Five Elders / Sui Lum Ng Cho [少林五祖] which are prolific in Southern Chinese folklore. The Shaolin Grandmasters Text also states that these Shaolin Five Elders / Sui Lam Ng Cho [少林五祖] escaped from the Fukien temple / Fujian si [福建寺] in the 1700s and Wong Kiew Kit also came to this conclusion. [16] [29] [31] [65] When the Henan [河南] temple was attacked and burnt there was considerable damage. When the Southern Siu Lum / Shaolin Temples [南少林寺] were attacked at Fuqing [福清], Quanzhou [泉州] and later Putian [莆田], they were totally destroyed, so much so that the sites were completely levelled and nothing remained. It is only with modern day archaeology (1980s-1990s) that these sites have been located once again.)

If Gee Seen [至善禪師] did escape an attack on the Northern Siu Lum / Shaolin Temple [北少林寺] in Henan Province [河南省], however this surely must have been in the early to mid 1700s, although no definite attack is recorded against the Henan temple [河南寺] during this period. Some sources state that it is rumoured that an un-named temple may have been attacked during this period. I would assume that this may have been the Fuqing Temple [福清寺].) Several sources state that the Southern Siu Lum / Shaolin Temple [南少林寺] was attacked by a large Ch'ing army / Qing army [清朝軍隊] during either the 1720s or 1730s. We know that during this period the Ch'ing / Qing [清朝] emperor, Yung Cheng / Yongzheng [雍正帝], (1723-1735) who banned the practice of martial arts [武術] in 1727 [16] or 1728 [19], had no liking for Siu Lum / Shaolin [少林]. Sometime during his reign he may have given the order to attack the Southern Siu Lum / Shaolin Temple [南少林寺]. [16] [19] [37] [37a] [66] Salvatore Canzonieri [19] states that the destruction of this temple was assigned to Cheung Gin Cau / Zhang Jianqiu [張建秋], the high commissioner of Fukien / Fujian province [福建省] with the aid of a local magistrate [知縣], Chan Man Jiu / Chen Wenyao [陳文耀] who was from the neighbouring Putian District [莆田].

Several sources, including Wong Kiew Kit, state that this was the Southern Siu Lum / Shaolin Temple [南少林寺] at Quanzhou [泉州], but this would create a problem with timescales and future known events such as Gee Seen [至善禪師] teaching Luk Ah Choi / Lu A Cai [陸阿采]. I believe that if a Southern Siu Lum / Shaolin Temple [南少林寺] was destroyed during this period it may have been the site at Fuqing [福清] as other sources quite clearly state that the Quanzhou temple [泉州少林寺] was believed to been destroyed in the 1760s; and that after Gee Seen [至善禪師] later established himself at the Putian temple [莆田寺].

It is understood that due to the attacks by the Ch'ing / Qing [清朝] authorities on the Siu Lum / Shaolin temples [少林寺], their oppressive attitude towards the Han Chinese [漢族], and their ban of practicing martial arts [武術], Gee Seen [至善禪師] had developed a strong hatred for them. Due to his own anti-Ch'ing / anti-Qing [反清清朝] sympathies he was willing to allow rebels to train at the Quanzhou temple [泉州少林寺]. This enabled high quality fighters to be trained up in an effort to one day overthrow the Ch'ing / Qing [清朝] rulers. The Southern Siu Lum / Shaolin Temple [南少林寺] then became regarded as a haven for rebels and a site for underground revolutionary activities, which may have included the Hung men (known as the Heaven and Earth Society / Tian Di Hui [天地會]. The Heaven and Earth Society / Tian Di Hui [天地會] was a political group that included many martial artists [武術家] who plotted the downfall of the Ch'ing / Qing [清朝] dynasty in order to restore the previous Ming dynasty [明朝]).

The following is a description of the Southern Siu Lum / Shaolin Monastery [南少林寺] and the martial arts students' daily training regime at the temple, by William C. Hu [61d] -

The Southern Siu Lum / Shaolin Monastery [南少林寺] was situated on a remote part of the mountain surrounded by a large forest. Access to the monastery was difficult as the roads were very poor and sometimes bad weather conditions made them impassable. Although the buildings were very old, they were extremely strong being constructed from stone. The grounds were divided into the religious area for the monks and the martial arts training area. The most important building in the religious area was the main hall which had a very high ceiling that housed a large statue of the Lord Buddha. This was surrounded by other golden figures of Bodhisattvas and Buddhist deities. The holy areas were for solitude and silent meditation. They were magnificently furnished with numerous treasures and relics that had been gifted to the monastery over the centuries from various nobles, princes and even emperors.

The Southern Siu Lum / Shaolin Monastery [南少林寺] had become renowned for its martial arts [武術] and the buildings used for this training were separated from the holy buildings. Students of the martial arts [武術] were kept isolated so that people or news of the outside world did not interfere with their training. Also, the Siu Lum / Shaolin Monks [少林僧] kept their Kung Fu [少林功夫] secret so as to avoid spies and prying eyes. The martial arts training buildings were particularly secure almost like a prison with locked doors and barred windows. The whole complex was surrounded by a thick and high stone wall, giving it the appearance of a fortress. The martial arts students who were novice trainees were only allowed into the main hall on special occasions for worship and only when they were escorted, whereas the graduates that had proven themselves were allowed the privilege to roam around freely.

A students schedule was strictly organised. They were woken early in the morning around 5.00am as the night watchmen came off duty. They would then perform Chi Kung / Qigong [氣功] (breathing exercises) for two hours until 7.00am, before attending morning services. Here they would meditate while the monks chanted the holy Sutras to Buddha. At 9.00am they would have a morning meal before then stance training and the education of fighting techniques until noon. For mid-day lunch they would have two rice cakes and water before then performing three hours of menial manual labour duties around the grounds which were all part of the general maintenance of daily temple life. This was followed by two hours of exercises using various equipment and sand bag training. Evening supper was at 5.00pm and what followed depended on the level of the student. Novices would resume stance training and practice fighting techniques, intermediate students would be trained in the use of various weapons and advanced students would study martial arts theory. After this they would go to the lecture hall where they were educated in the codes, morals and virtues of chivalry and righteousness. This was followed by half an hour of meditation until 10.00pm when they would go to bed. [61d]

Another important event that occurred during the 1760s is that martial arts [武術] training at Siu Lum / Shaolin [少林寺] which, until about 1765 had been optional, was implemented into all Siu Lum / Shaolin training. [16] Unfortunately the Ch'ing / Qing [清朝] authorities became aware of rebels training at the temple in the early 1760s and the Southern Siu Lum / Shaolin Temple [南少林寺] at Quanzhou [泉州] was destroyed in 1763. *(Some sources differ, stating it was 1768.)* Many of the monks and other inhabitants were killed during the prolonged assault on the temple.

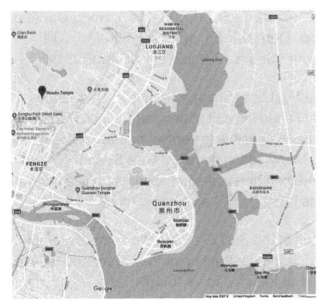

These time scales lead me to believe that the Shaolin Five Elders / Sui Lum Ng Cho [少林五祖] possibly escaped from the destruction of the Quanzhou temple [泉州少林寺] in the 1760s. Accounts state that only eighteen fought their way out of the temple and inflicted heavy casualties on the attacking army [清朝軍隊]. Forces pursued these eighteen who eventually reduced to only five that survived and escaped. These became known as the Shaolin Five Elders / Sui Lum Ng Cho [少林五祖]" who were:- the Buddhist

Monk [和尚], Gee Seen [至善禪師], the Buddhist nun [尼姑], Wu Mei Da Shi / Ng Mui Daai Si [五梅大師], the Buddhist monk [和尚] Bak Mei / Bai Mei Dao Ren [白眉道人] (who one source states that his real name was Chu Long Tuyen [32a]), the Taoist [道家] Fung Do-Duk / Feng Daode [馮道德] and the unshaved lay disciple [俗家弟子][111] [111a], Miu Hin / Miao Xian [苗顯]. [31a] [32] [32b] [33a]

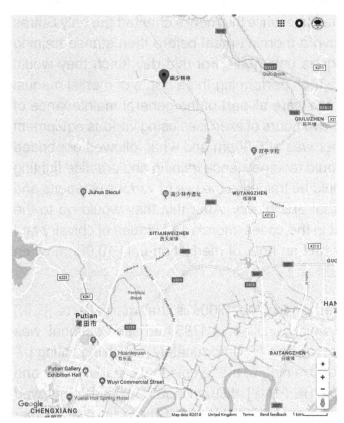

My research has identified a discrepancy in the lists of the Shaolin Five Elders / Sui Lum Ng Cho [少林五祖]. Some sources such as Wing Lam [64] state that Fong Do-Duk and Bak-Mei were the same person, and that the fifth elder was Lei Ba-Saan / Li Bashan [李巴山].

There are many similarities with this story and that of the Five Book Monks / Ng Jing Wo Seung [方大洪] who are also known as the five Heaven and Earth Society / Tian Di Hui [天地會] elders. [36] [36a] In both accounts there are eighteen who initially escape the temple's destruction but due to injuries etc, only five survive. Is this a coincidence, or over the years have the facts and details of these two stories been mixed up and confused? Jie Kon Sieuw / Yu Guanxiu [余官秀] [33a] states that the Five Book Monks / Ng Jing Wo Seung [方大洪] (Chua Teck Tiong [蔡德忠], Hong Dai Ang [方大洪], Ma Chew Heng [馬超興], Ho Teck Deh [胡德帝], and Lee Si Kai [李式開] [36a] [19]) escaped the destruction of the Siu Lum / Shaolin Temple at Putian [莆田少林寺].

It is known that after the destruction of the Siu Lum / Shaolin Temple at Quanzhou [泉州少林寺], Gee Seen [至善禪師] later established himself at another Siu Lum / Shaolin Temple at Putian [莆田少林寺]. It has not been possible to verify whether this occured shortly afterwards or several years later. Many accounts tell of Gee Seen [至善禪師] escaping the destruction of the temple and then heading south disguised as a beggar before hiding out on the Red Opera boats [紅船粵劇團] as a cook. [64]

Sometime later he then established himself at the Siu Lum / Shaolin Temple at Putian [莆田少林寺]. Wong Kiew Kit states that after the destruction of the Quanzhou temple [泉州少林寺], Gee Seen [至善禪師] stayed at the Hoi Tong Temple [海幢寺] (Honam

Temple [河南寺]) before establishing himself at the Putian Temple [莆田寺]. [75] I believe that there are two possiblilties; either Gee Seen [至善禪師] did escape south disguised as a beggar or he went to the Putian temple [莆田寺] and that while he was the abbot

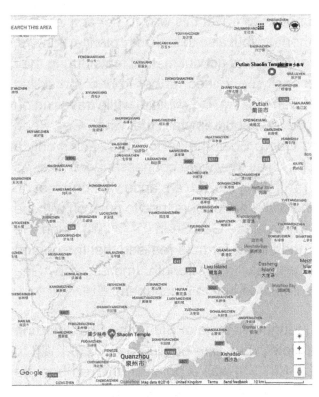

[少林方丈] of the Putian Temple [莆田寺], he travelled from time to time to Canton [廣州] to meet people, collect alms for the temple and recruit new students. It is stated that Gee Seen [至善禪師] made three trips to Canton [廣州] and that during these journeys, he observed the different fighting styles. From these observations he altered his style, increasing the attacking range of the strikes and widening some stances. [64] [66] It is possible that on one or more of these trips, Gee Seen [至善禪師] disguised himself as a beggar.

The book, "<u>The Qianlong Emperor Inspects Southern China / Kin Loong har Kwong Nam / Qianlong Xia Jiangnan</u> [乾隆下江南]" [50b], states that Gee Seen [至善禪師] would travel between the Southern Siu Lum / Shaolin Temple [南少林寺] and Canton [廣州]. Unfortunately the book states that these trips and events occurred from the Siu Lum / Shaolin Temple at Quanzhou [泉州少林寺] and not the Siu Lum / Shaolin Temple at Putian [莆田少林寺].

(I have written a possible explanation for this in the Preface, on page vii).

This book, as do both Wing Lam [64] and Salvatore Canzonieri [66] all state that Gee Seen [至善禪師] made three trips to Canton [廣州] while he was abbot [方丈] of the Southern Siu Lum / Shaolin Temple [南少林寺].

Cantonese Red Boat Opera troupes *[紅船粵劇團]*
During the Ming dynasty and the reign of Ch'ien Lung / Qianlong 1735-1796, Foshan had become home to most of the Cantonese opera troupes and the Qionghua Guild Hall was built in the Dajiwei region of the city. This hall was also used for training performers as well as a base for the opera troupe management. Near the hall was a waterfront area reserved for the red boats to anchor. The opera troupes used wooden boats called Junks which were painted red, as a means of transporting people and equipment such as props and costumes, around the Pearl River Delta region. According to the Foshan museum, there were over thirty opera centres in the Foshan

area alone at one time. Due to the amount of time the troupes would spend touring around on these boats, they would also use them as their home living on these red boats. [67]

Gee Seen [至善禪師] is reputed to have chosen to travel this way to not only escape the attention of the Ch'ing / Qing [清朝] authorities, but also to look for potential fighters. As the opera performers trained from an early age to act out martial feats during their shows, he surmised that they could more easily be trained further to become skilled fighters. There are several stories of Gee Seen's [至善禪師] exploits while travelling on these Red Junk Opera Boats [紅船粵劇]. Several sources state that when Gee Seen [至善禪師] tried to gain passage on a Red Opera Boat, the performers seeing only a scruffy beggar, told him to walk to Canton [廣州] as they were not passenger boats. As the boat was about to cast off, Gee Seen [至善禪師] took up a stance with one foot on the boat and the other on the pier. When one of the performers tried to push off with the pole, they were unable to move the boat, which made Gee Seen [至善禪師] laugh. He then started to rock the boat with his foot and the performers realised that the person dressed as a beggar was really a man of great skill and strength. Impressed by Gee Seen's [至善禪師] abilities, the performers implored him to teach them. [68] [69] [70]

On these red boats Gee Seen [至善禪師] taught his style of Siu Lum / Shaolin Kung Fu [少林功夫] and the "Six and Half Point Pole", (Luk Dim Boon Gwan [六點半棍]) to the performers. Leung Yee-Tai / Liang Erti [梁二娣] was a poler on the red boat (ie he used a pole to steer the Red Boat away from rocks and shoals) and was therefore chosen by Gee Seen [至善禪師] to learn the Six and Half Point Pole. [70a] Wing Chun [詠春拳] history states that as well as Leung Yee-Tai, Wong Wa Bo / Huang Hua Bao [黃華寶] and Dai Fa Min Kam / Da Hua Mian Jin [大花面錦] also trained under Gee Seen [至善禪師] while he travelled on the boats [紅船粵劇]. [71] Gee Seen [至善禪師] realised that travelling on the boats [紅船粵劇團] gave him a great opportunity to teach his martial arts [武術] not only to the actors but also other militant patriots that he came into contact with. The main martial style in the region at this time was Hakka Kuen [客家拳], also known as Southern Praying Mantis [南派螳螂]. Many of the people that Gee Seen [至善禪師] came into contact with and trained during his time on the boats, were practitioners of the Hakka style [客家拳]. Several of these martial artists [武術家] combined Gee Seen's [至善禪師] Siu Lum / Shaolin teachings with their Hakka style [客家拳] and it is believed that Gee Seen's [至善禪師] style had some influence in the development of the Hakka style [客家拳] during this period. [139]

In the book, "The Qianlong Emperor Inspects Southern China / Kin Loong har Kwong Nam / Qianlong Xia Jiangnan [乾隆下江南]" [50b], it is understood that Gee Seen [至善禪師] sheltered at various Buddhist temples [佛教徒寺] within the provincial capital [省會城市] during this time. Miu Tsui Fa [苗翠花] (who many sources state was the daughter of the unshaved lay disciple [俗家弟子][111] [111a], Miu Hin / Miao Xian [苗顯] known as one of the Shaolin Five Elders / Sui Lum Ng Cho [少林五祖] [112] [112a]) took her three sons Fong How Yuk / 方孝玉, Fong Mei Yuk / 方美玉 and Fong Sai Yuk [方世玉] to Canton [廣州] to be trained by Gee Seen [至善禪師]. It is stated in the book that she first went to the Kwong Hau Temple / Guangxiao [光孝寺], but the abbot there told her that Gee Seen [至善禪師] was now at the West Zen Temple / Sai Sim Ji / Xi Chan Si [西禪寺].

Gee Seen [至善禪師] had set up a gym at the West Zen Temple / Sai Sim Ji / Xi Chan Si / [西禪寺] and started to teach martial arts [武術家] there. He had furnished this gym with various apparatus and equipment to enhance his students' martial arts [武術家] training, including various types of wooden dummies, wooden horse, sand bags, throwing disk and the Siu Lum / Shaolin eighteen weapons. [卻言至善在西禪寺開設武場, 擺列著埋樁木馬、 沙袋飛陀及十八般兵器, 件件齊備]. After accepting Fong How Yuk [方孝玉], Fong Mei Yuk [方美玉] and Fong Sai Yuk [方世玉], Gee Seen [至善禪師] had nine students at this site. It is stated that his other students included Lee Kam Lun [李錦倫], Tse Ah Fok [謝亞福], Lee Ah Chun [李亞松], Hung Hei Kwun [洪熙官], Tong Chin Kan [童千斤] and Wu Wei Kin [胡惠乾]. After six months of teaching here, Gee Seen [至善禪師] told his students that he needed to return to the Southern Siu Lum / Shaolin Temple [南少林寺] as he had been gone a year. They all returned with him.

"The Qianlong Emperor Inspects Southern China / Kin Loong har Kwong Nam / Qianlong Xia Jiangnan [乾隆下江南]", [50b] also states that a student's training was for a least ten years. This training was very hard and when they had completed it, a final test involved passing through the corridor of wooden men. The Southern Siu Lum / Shaolin Temple [南少林寺] had an outstanding reputation for the skill and expertise of the martial artists [武術家] it produced. Unfortunately, some students started to leave the temple before they had completed their training. Many of these therefore had a lower level of skill, but boasted that they had trained at Siu Lum / Shaolin [少林]. Before the reputation of the temple began to erode, Gee Seen [至善禪師] is reputed to have altered the training structure to counter this. This involved the creation of the Thirty-Six Chambers, which was a step by step method of training. A student had to master each chamber's skill before they could advance onto the next level, and they were required to complete all the chambers before they were allowed to leave the temple.

The Thirty-Six Chambers covered a multitude of skills ranging from unarmed combat and weapons training, to physical and psychological concept training. Different methods were used to improve and strengthen the skills and capabilities of the students. Some of the methods were conducted outside the temple, such as lifting heavy water barrels up the hill to the temple. These practical methods and skills were intended to enhance the student's chance of survival in the cruel and harsh world outside. As the abbot [少林方丈] of the temple, Gee Seen [至善禪師] had many other duties to perform and therefore he decreed that the monk, Hung Yan Sim See [洪恩和尚] was to oversee the day to day running of the Chambers. [27] [31] [33]

Gee Seen [至善禪師] is credited with this new training method of the the various chambers, but this may have originally only been thirty-five as some sources state that his exceptional student Sam Dak / San De [三德] created the thirty-sixth Chamber. This idea is also acknowledged in the famous movie, The 36th Chamber of Shaolin / Siu Lam Saam Sap Luk Fong / Shaolin San Shi Liu Fang [少林三十六房]. This tells the story of Sam Dak's / San De [三德] training at the Southern Siu Lum / Shaolin Temple [南少林寺] advancing through these Chambers, and with him eventually establishing the thirty-sixth Chamber to teach martial arts [武術] to laypeople. [81a] [81b] [81c] It does not state that this thirty-sixth Chamber was first established at the Southern Siu Lum / Shaolin Temple [南少林寺], but it is known that Sam Dak / San De [三德] was eventually sent to the West Zen Temple / Sai Sim Ji / Xi Chan Si [西禪寺] in Canton [廣州] to teach martial arts [武術] to laypeople in the provincial capital [省會城市]. [50b] (Some details of the thirty-six chambers can be found at : http://practicalhungkyun.com/wp-content/uploads/2015/01/36th-chamber-of-shaolin.pdf [81d])

Gee Seen [至善禪師] is acknowledged for revolutionising the students' training at this Southern Siu Lum / Shaolin Temple [南少林寺]. Martial arts [武術] training had originally been conducted over ten years to cover the required discipline, but this was condensed to produce competent, skilful and proficient fighters in a much shorter time scale. Some sources state that he was also responsible for devising the "wooden dummy hall", which was called the Lohan Tung or Buddha Hall [佛殿]. The purpose of this hall was to test the Kung Fu [功夫] (martial arts [武術]) skill of potential graduates before they left the temple. [31] [33] [33b] [33c] [33d]

Quanzhou Eighteen Wooden Men Trial. The Renfeng community of Quanzhou East Street used to be where the Eighteen Wooden Men were located. During the reign of Emperors Yonzheng and Qianlong, the abbot of Shaolin Monastery Master Zhishan / Gee Seen Sim See [至善禪師] was proficient in both internal and external Kung Fu and noted for helping the poor. When a disciple had attained sufficient accomplishments in Kung Fu he would normally bid farewell to his master and leave through the Hall of Vajras. This Hall was designed by Master Zhishan with a large interior space and 18 wooden men the size of real people. They all held weapons and would attack whoever tried to pass through the hall. After this test, the disciple had to pass through a long gallery named Bags Trial. If he stepped on one of the gears, the bags would attack him from different directions. This was the final and supreme test of the disciples' skill, endurance and will power. Only those with extraordinary Kung Fu skills could safely pass the trial and be allowed to leave the Monastery.

After the Shaolin Monastery was burned down, the basement of this gallery was filled with water and then named Bags Pool. There used to be an alley outside the Bajra Hall connecting the Dongchan Shaolin and Renfeng Street. After the Vajra Hall was destroyed, the alley was still called Eighteen Wooden Men Alley. ***Written by Gregory Brundage*** [22]

Wing Lam tells a story about this hall with the wooden men. He states that after being trained in the style of Ba-Chi Kuen / Baji quan [八極拳] a young man called Wu Jon / Wu Zhong [吳鐘], travelled to the Siu Lum / Shaolin Temple [少林寺] in Fukien / Fujian [福建省] Province. While at the temple, he attempted the Lohan Hall of Wooden Men. This hall was equipped with mechanised wooden dummies that were capable of striking and throwing objects, to test a person's skill as they fought their way through the chamber. This test was very intensive, and only the highest level of martial artists [武術家] managed to complete it. Many students were injured, sometimes seriously or even fatally, but Wu Jon / Wu Zhong [吳鐘] is reputed to have fought his way through this hall three times without any injuries. Wing Lam also states that a talented female student of Gee Seen [至善禪師] called Lei Choi-Ping [李翠屏], who he taught the style of Eagle Claw / Jing Jar [鷹爪] to and became famed as one of the Siu Lum / Shaolin Ten Best [少林十傑], also completed the passage through this hall at the age of only fourteen. [64]

Several sources state that this hall was also known as the Priest-Scholar Hall [牧師,傳道大堂] or the Den of the Wooden Men. These sources differ on the number of dummies within this hall with some stating 18 and others 108. They do however, all agree that these dummies were activated by the person's movement through the hall, and that the dummies were armed with not only wooden clubs but also knives and spears. [33c] [33d] [72]

Sometime around the 1790s to early 1800s, Gee Seen [至善禪師] arrived at Canton [廣州] (Guangzhou [廣州]) and stayed at a Buddhist monastery [佛教寺院] in the city known as the Hoi Tong [海幢寺] (Honam [河南寺]) Monastery. As he was in hiding from the authorities he maintained a low profile at this temple, with only a select few of trusted students knowing his location. Wing Lam [64] states that Luk Ah-Choi [陸阿采] first trained under Gee Seen [至善禪師] at the Hoi Tong [海幢寺] (Honam [河南寺]) Temple. This was after meeting Tong Chin-Goon (also spelt Tung Chin Kan / Tong Qian Jin [童千斤]) who later introduced him to Lei Choi-Ping [李翠屏] who were former students of Gee Seen [至善禪師]. Lei Choi-Ping [李翠屏] wrote a letter to Gee Seen [至善禪師] requesting that he accept Luk Ah-Choi / Lu A Cai [陸阿采] as a student. Once this was agreed, Lei Choi-Ping [李翠屏] took Luk Ah-Choi [陸阿采] to the Hoi Tong [海幢寺] (Honam Temple [河南寺]) and introduced him to her teacher. While at this temple, Luk Ah-Choi [陸阿采] was taught by Gee Seen [至善禪師] his style of Tiger Kung Fu [少林虎功夫] (Hung Kuen [洪拳]) which included the Taming the Tiger / Kung Gee Fook Fu Kuen [伏虎拳] routine and the Five Animal routine / Ng Ying Kuen [五形拳]. [64]

Gee Seen [至善禪師] taught many students in his time and would constantly monitor and test them to enable him to identify areas for improvement. Some of his students were from the Southern Siu Lum / Shaolin Temples [南少林寺] in Quanzhou [泉州], and later Putian [莆田], some were from his travels south to Canton [廣州], and some were from his time at the various temples in Canton [廣州]. Many of his students were fellow sympathisers and therefore possibly members of the Hung secret society (known as the Heaven and Earth Society / Tian Di Hui [天地會]), who would keep in touch with each other through this underground group. During many years of testing his students, he chose the leading ten who he considered as exceptional and would be known as members of his Siu Lum / Shaolin Ten Best [少林十傑]. [64] Wong Kiew Kit states that while Gee Seen [至善禪師] was abbot [方丈] of the Southern Siu Lum / Shaolin Temple [南少林寺], he would organise an annual free sparring contest. The ten best were chosen by their performance in this competition rather than their seniority in mastering skills or time spent training with their teacher.

The Siu Lum / Shaolin Ten Best [少林十傑] were:-

Wing Lam source [64]
Hung Hei-Goon [洪熙官]
Tong Chin-Goon [童千斤]
Wun Lung-Yuk [溫良玉]
Lei Choi-Ping [李翠屏]
Wu Wei-Kin [胡惠乾]
Lei Ba-Fu [黎伯符]
Fong How-Yuk [方孝玉]
Fong Mai-Yuk [方美玉]
Fong Sai Yuk [方世玉]
Luk Ah-Choi [陸阿采]

Wong Kiew Kit source [65]
Venerable Harng Yien *(monk)*
Venerable Sam Dak [三德] *(monk)*
Hoong Hei Khoon [洪熙官]
Luk Ah Choy [陸阿采]
Miu Choi Fa [苗翠花] (mother of Sai, How & Mai Yuk)
Thoong Chein Kern [童千斤]
Lin Swee Hin
Fong Sai Yoke [方世玉]
Li Choi Ping [李翠屏]
Ma Ling Yi

3ʳᵈ Source [73]
Hung Hei Goon [洪熙官]
Tong Chin-Goon [童千斤]
Wun Lung-Yuk [溫良玉]
Lei Choi-Ping [李翠屏]
Wu Wei-Kin [胡惠乾]
Lei Ban-Chu [黎伯符]
Fong How-Yuk [方孝玉]
Fong Sai-Yuk [方世玉]
Luk Ah-Choi [陸阿采]
Fong Mai-Yuk [方美玉]

4ᵗʰ Source [74]
Hung Hei Gun [洪熙官]
Tung Chin Gan [童千斤]
Wan Leung Yuk [溫良玉]
Lei Cheui Ping [李翠屏]
Wu Wai Kin [胡惠乾]
Lei Baak Fu [黎伯符]
Fong Haau Yuk [方孝玉]
Fong Mei Yuk [方美玉]
Fong Sai Yuk [方世玉]
Luk Ah Choi [陸阿采]

These four groups have been reproduced in the same order that the sources listed them as. Notice that there are slightly different spellings for the same person's name. The Wing Lam and the Wong Kiew Kit lists agree on five of the ten names but differ on the remaining five. According to the Wong Kiew Kit source, it states that Wu Wei-Kin [胡惠乾] was a good fighter but left the temple before completing his training and so was not included in the ten. (The 3rd and 4th sources have the same ten as Wing Lam but in different orders with some different spellings.)

Another source for the Siu Lum / Shaolin Ten Best [少林十傑] has been taken from the book entitled, The Qianlong Emperor Inspects Southern China / Kin Loong har Kwong Nam / Qianlong Xia Jiangnan [乾隆下江南]. [50b]

	Cantonese	Pinyin
洪熙官	Hung Hei-Kwun	Hong Xiguan
方世玉	Fong Sai Yuk	Fang Shiyu
劉裕德	Lau Tak Yue	Liu Yude (later known as the Monk Sam Dak / San De)
胡惠乾	Wu Wei Kin	Hu Hui Gan
童千斤	Tung Chin Kan	Tong Qian Jin
李錦倫	Lee Kam Lun	Li Jinlun
谢亞福	Tse Ah Fok	Xieya Fu
方孝玉	Fong How Yuk	Fang Xiaoyu
方美玉	Fong Mei Yuk	Fang Meiyu
陸阿采	Luk Ah-Choi	Lu Acai

This book includes seven of the Wing Lam list and also includes Lau Tak-Yue / Liu Yude [劉裕德], who was later more commonly known by his Buddhist [佛教徒] name as the Monk Sam Dak / San De [三德], who is named in Wong Kiew Kit's list. My assumption is that Gee Seen [至善禪師] compiled this list later on in his life looking back at who his ten best students had been. The main difference is that three lists are purely of Gee Seen's [至善禪師] laymen disciples [俗家弟子] whereas Wong Kiew Kit's list includes two monks.

Wong Kiew Kit states that the Putian temple [莆田寺] was betrayed by one of Gee Seen's [至善禪師] disciples [俗家弟子] and a member of his Siu Lum / Shaolin Ten Best [少林十傑], Ma Ling Yee [馬寧兒] (Ma Ling Yi), who informed Ko Chun Chong. Ko Chun Chong was the military governor of the two neighbouring provinces of Kwangtung [廣東省] and Kwangsi [廣西省]. He led an army against the temple and was also aided by Bak Mei [白眉]. [65] Frank McCarthy gives a similar account but states that Cheung Gin Cau / Zhang Jianqiu [張建秋], the high commissioner of Fukien / Fujian province [福建省], and a local magistrate called Chan Man Jiu / Chen Wenyao [陳文耀], led the attack on the temple. [49]

Reading the various histories it is hard to know if this betrayal was at the Fuqing temple [福清寺] Quanzhou temple [泉州寺] or the Putian temple [莆田寺]. According to Jie Kon Sieuw / Yu Guanxiu [余官秀] this betrayal occurred during the reign of the emperor, Yung Cheng / Yongzheng [雍正帝] (1723-1735). [33a] Unfortunately, several sources state the date as 1723, which as I have previously commented on, seems too early to then correspond with other known facts. I can only assume that the dates of the possible destructions of the three known Southern Siu Lum / Shaolin Temples [南少林寺] of Fuqing [福清], Quanzhou [泉州] and Putian [莆田], may have been mixed up, confused with one another or just regarded as the one temple, for there to be so many stories and discrepancies.

A fact that many sources do agree on is that the Siu Lum / Shaolin abbot [少林方丈] Gee Seen [至善禪師] died in a fight with one of the other Shaolin Five Elders / Sui Lum Ng Cho [少林五祖], known as Bak Mei [白眉], during the attack on the Putian Temple [莆田寺]. Lineages of the Bak Mei [白眉] style state that his betrayal of Siu Lum / Shaolin [少林] was due to one of two reasons. The first account states that he had trained a force to fight the Ch'ing / Qing [清朝] authorities, but they were unfortunately captured before they were ready. To prevent his followers from being tortured or killed, he was forced to lead government troops on a second destruction of the Southern Siu Lum / Shaolin Temple [南少林寺]. The other account states that Bak Mei [白眉] came to accept that their efforts to overthrow the Ch'ing / Qing [清朝] were pointless, and that the Ming [明] who he had once wished to replace them, had now become corrupt. [29] [31] [32] [32a] [33a]

It is stated that during the attack on the Putian [莆田] Southern Siu Lum / Shaolin Temple [南少林寺], Bak Mei [白眉] and Gee Seen [至善禪師] (Chi Thien Su [趙天壽]) fought in a duel [決鬥], but the Siu Lum / Shaolin abbot [少林方丈] was eventually killed by Bak Mei [白眉] breaking his neck. [29] [31] [32] [32a]

All the sources state that this fight was a duel [決鬥] or single combat.
A duel is an organised fighting contest between two opponents, that could be either hand to hand combat or with prescribed weapons with agreed rules.
The duel was regarded as a match of honour and was usually fought to demonstrate a willingness to risk one's life for it. [75a]

Chinese martial arts [武術] histories are littered with stories of duels [決鬥] and challenges to settle various issues or feuds. Both Bak Mei [白眉] and the Venerable Siu Lum / Shaolin abbot [少林方丈] Gee Seen [至善禪師] were esteemed Kung Fu masters [功夫大師] with renowned reputations for their fighting prowess; it is therefore very plausible that this event did take place. I can only assume that although these two masters were now on opposite sides fighting for their different beliefs, there could have been a mutual respect for each other's skill and abilities, having for many years been Siu Lum / Shaolin brothers [少林兄弟] before this.

A detailed account of this duel is stated in the book, "The Qianlong Emperor Inspects Southern China / Kin Loong har Kwong Nam / Qianlong Xia Jiangnan [乾隆下江南]". [50b]

The book states that after trouble in Canton [廣州] with persons who had been trained at the Southern Siu Lum / Shaolin Temple [南少林寺], the Ch'ing / Qing [清朝] authorities had decided to put an end to this place. To aid their army, they had enlisted the help of other renowned Kung Fu masters [功夫大師] to fight against Siu Lum / Shaolin [少林]. The Ch'ing / Qing [清朝] authorities had gathered together Wu Mei Nun [五枚師太] (Abbot of Yunnan White Crane Temple [雲南白鶴寺]), Fung Do-Duk / Feng Daode [馮道德] of Wu Dang Style [武當拳] and White Eyebrow / Bak Mei / Bai Mei Dao Ren [清朝軍隊] of White Eyebrow style / Bak Mei Kuen [白眉拳] and several of their disciples including Ma Hung / Ma xiong [馬雄], Ko Chun Chung / Gao Jin Zhong [高進忠], Pun Lung / Bao Long [鮑龍], Hung Fook / Hong Fu [洪福] and Fung Fue / Fang Fey [方魁]. These martial artists [武術家] joined the Ch'ing army / Qing army [清朝軍隊] close to the Southern Siu Lum / Shaolin Temple [南少林寺].

The Southern Siu Lum / Shaolin Temple [南少林寺] was surrounded by the Ch'ing army / Qing army [清朝軍隊] under the command of the governor of Fukien Province / Fujian Province [福建省]. It is stated that Bak Mei [白眉] was aiding the Ch'ing army / Qing army [清朝軍隊] because of the trouble in Canton [廣州] caused by Wu Wei Kin [胡惠乾] which had resulted in the death of the three best disciples of Fung Do-Duk / Feng Daode [馮道德].

Because Wu Wei Kin [胡惠乾] was a student of the Siu Lum / Shaolin abbot [少林方丈] Gee Seen [至善禪師], both Bak Mei / Bai Mei Dao Ren [白眉道人] and Fung Do-Duk / Feng Daode [馮道德] had come to seek their revenge against Gee Seen [至善禪師] and Siu Lum / Shaolin [少林]. Bak Mei [白眉] called out to Gee Seen [至善禪師] demanding a duel. Bak Mei [白眉] was allowed inside the temple with several of his followers where the duel was held. Intially the duel started with both Bak Mei [白眉] and Gee Seen [至善禪師] fighting with a long handled broadsword called a Pudoa [樸刀].

The duel with weapons went on for a very long time, and after each fighter lost their pudoa [樸刀], it continued with unarmed combat, with both men using their Kung Fu [功夫] skills. Gee Seen [至善禪師] utilised his external strength of the Siu Lum / Shaolin arts of conditioning [少林內息調理功], such as Iron Shirt / Tee Po Sam / Tie bu shan [鐵布衫] and Iron Head / Tee Tau Kun / Tie Tou Gong [鐵頭功], while Bak Mei [白眉] relied on his internal skills. In a bid to defeat Bak Mei [白眉], Gee Seen [至善禪師] finally used his Iron Head [鐵頭功] conditioning and attacked his opponent's stomach. Bak Mei [白眉] countered this technique by concentrating all his internal force in his abdomen. He sucked the head of Gee Seen [至善禪師] into his belly as he moved backwards before he then suddenly expanded his belly which threw Gee Seen [至善禪師] to the floor ten feet away. This technique had broken Gee Seen's [至善禪師] neck. Bak Mei [白眉] then jumped forward and killed Gee Seen [至善禪師] with another punch.

After the death of Gee Seen [至善禪師], fights broke out between his students and Bak Mei's [白眉] followers who had accompied him into the temple for the duel. When the governor of Fukien Province / Fujian Province [福建省] realised what was happening, he ordered the Ch'ing army / Qing army [清朝軍隊] to attack and the temple was finally destroyed by fire.[30a]

One source states that about thirty monks and unshaven lay disciples [俗家弟子] [111] [111a] escaped the destruction of the Putian temple [莆田寺]. [33a] These survivors dispersed around the province and went into hiding. It is understood that many of them fled south where they eventually ended up in and around Canton [廣州]. Here, it is believed that they sought sanctuary intermingling with other monks at the Buddhist temples [佛教徒寺] within the provincial capital [省會城市]. [84]

The Venerable Sam Dak [三德]

(Sometimes spelt as Sam Tak / Tuck / Duck / San De
or Te which means "three virtues" [三德])
(Orignal name was Lau Tak Yue / Liu Yude or Yu-te [劉裕德])

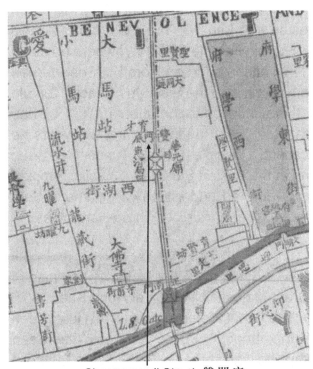

Shuangmendi Street 雙門底

Sam Dak / San De [三德] was originally named Lau Tak Yue / Liu Yude [劉裕德] and was the son of a tea merchant who lived in Shuangmendi Lu (Street) [雙門底], which was located within the old walled city of Canton [廣州]. This area is now in the Yuexiu district [越秀區].

(Since 1966, Shuangmendi Lu has been renamed Beijing Road. Now as in the past this is a pedestrian street area with no vehicles allowed. This was because it was a bureaucratic area with many government officials and their families living and working there. [76a]*)*

His father had a shop in this district which had a large population of Manchurians [滿族]. He had grown up learning martial arts [武術] and had become skilled by the time he was a young man. At the age of sixteen, it is stated that Lau Tak Yue / Liu Yude [劉裕德] was studying Kung Fu [功夫] under a Shaolin Monk [少林僧] called Lam Ti Quai / Lin Tie Guai [林鐵拐]. In his training, he would use the iron rings / Tien Wan [鐵環] which had helped him to develop tremendous strength, and it is stated that he was able to lift a weight of 400 Jin [斤]. Due to his strength, he was known as Iron arms (Tien Bay / Tie bi [鐵臂]) Lau Tak Yue / Liu Yude [劉裕德].

When he was a young man his father passed away and sometime after, he got into a fight with a Ch'ing / Qing [清朝] officer. It is stated that the Ch'ing / Qing [清朝] officer was a deputy commander who during the fight, Lau Tak Yue / Liu Yude [劉裕德] accidently killed in self-defence. To escape execution by the Ch'ing / Qing [清朝] authorities, he fled into Fukien / Fujian province [福建省] where his father's business partner, Lam Pak Ping / Lin Bo Ping [林伯平] lived. He stayed here for three months until Lam Pak Ping / Lin Bo Ping [林伯平] saw a wanted poster for Lau Tak Yue / Liu Yude [劉裕德]. To avoid trouble with the authorities, Lam Pak Ping / Lin Bo Ping [林伯平] gave him 500 Taels [兩] of silver to leave. While wandering around, he came across a Shaolin Monk [少林僧] who he befriended. During their conversation, the monk [少林僧] noticed Lau Tak Yue's / Liu Yude's [劉裕德] strong physique and so asked who his Sifu [師父] was. When he told him it was Lam Ti Quai / Lin Tie Guai [林鐵拐], the monk [少林僧] told him that he knew his Sifu [師父], as they were both from the same Fukien Siu Lum / Shaolin Temple [福建少林寺].

The monk [少林僧] was called Yuen Hom Fat See / Yuan Kong Fa Shi [圓空法師] which means Perfect and Empty and he suggested that Lau Tak Yue / Liu Yude [劉裕德] return with him to the Southern Siu Lum / Shaolin Temple [南少林寺] where he could seek refuge. Lau Tak Yue / Liu Yude [劉裕德] accepted Yuen Hom Fat See's / Yuan Kong Fa Shi's [圓空法師] invitation and went with him to the Siu Lum / Shaolin Temple [少林寺]. When they arrived they explained the situation to the abbot [少林方丈]. Lau Tak Yue / Liu Yude [劉裕德] was given sanctuary, and during his first two years he performed labouring tasks before later becaming a disciple [俗家弟子] under Gee Seen [至善禪師], the abbot [方丈]. Whilst training at the Fukien Siu Lum / Shaolin Temple [福建少林寺] he became a monk, and was given the Buddhist [佛教徒] name of Sam Dak / San De [三德] which translates to mean Three Virtues or Three Harmonies. [76] [81] [81a] [82]

Sam Dak / San De [三德] was a master [功夫大師] of the Tiger [虎] style and also of the internal force method known as the Great Majestic Kuen / Tai Hung Kuen [大雄拳] (also known as the Triple-Stretch Set). The Great Majestic Kuen / Tai Hung Kuen [大雄拳] (Triple-Stretch Set) was taught by the abbot [方丈], the venerable Gee Seen [至善禪師], to Sam Dak / San De [三德] while he was at the Putian Siu Lum / Shaolin Temple [莆田少林寺]. It is stated that this routine [套路] was taught and named after the grand hall at the temple called the Great Majestic Hall / Tai Hung Po Deen [大雄寶殿]. *(Wong Kiew Kit spells it, Cantonese; "Tai Hoong Kuen", Mandarin; "Da Hung Quan".)* It is reputed that Sam Dak / San De [三德] and Hung Hei-Kwun [洪熙官] were both highly skilled in this set.

The Triple Stretch Set is a name more commonly used by Wong Kiew Kit and his Shaolin Wahnam Institute. Wong Kiew Kit states that because he learnt two different Great Majestic Sets / Tai Hung Kuen [大雄拳] from two teachers [功夫老師], he renamed the one by Uncle Righteous lineage and called it the Triple Stretch set. This method came from the Putian Siu Lum / Shaolin Temple [莆田少林寺] via Gee Seen [至善禪師] to Sam Dak / San De [三德] who then taught it to both Gwok Yan [覺因] and Chan Fook [陳福]. The other Great Majestic set / Tai Hung Po Deen [大雄寶殿] originated from the Quanzhou Siu Lum / Shaolin Temple [泉州少林寺]. [78a] [78b] [78c]

Wong Kiew Kit's description of the Triple Stretch:-
The Triple Stretch is a very long set comprising of three sections.

The first section, called "ta chong" or "force training while on stance", is focused on developing internal force using the triple-stretch approach. This approach is derived from Sinew Metamorphosis.

The second section is called "lin chip" or "continuation", which links the first section of force training to the third section of combat application. Some intriguing applications are found in this linking section.

The third section is called "ta sei moon" or "striking four gates". Four combat sequences are found here, and they are repeated in four directions in the set. The patterns for internal force training in Triple Stretch are similar to those in the Flower Set, but they are "harder". It uses the form-force-flow approach, or the force method. It employs the Dragon-Hand Form, or Two-Finger Zen, and is "harder" and less fluid than One-Finger Shooting Zen. [78a]

The monk referred to as the "Three Virtues" (Saam Dak Wo Seung), was also known as the Venerable master "Iron Arms" (Tien Bay / Tie bi [鐵臂]), another popular name given to him due to his skill and also his strength using the iron rings / Tien Wan [鐵環]. [77] Sam Dak / San De [三德] also conditioned his arms while at Siu Lum / Shaolin and practiced the Skill of the Iron Arm /Tein Bak Kuen / Tie Bi Gong [鐵臂功]. Training starts initially by striking against a smooth pole swinging the arms to contact with both the inner and outer forearms. Over time the practitioner will increase in both power and number of strikes to gradually strengthen both the inner and outer forearms. Once the arms have toughened up and become stronger, the smooth pole is changed for a rougher more uneven surface such as the course bark on a tree. This skill can be mastered within three years with dedicated training and is one of the famed 72 arts of Siu Lum / Shaolin. [114]

The following information comes from practicalhungkyun.com:-
The following twenty-eight character mnemonic poem is citing the Venerable Master "Iron Arms" (Tit Bei Sim Si) in his endorsement of this technique:

*Four Fingers Supporting Heaven is heavenly indeed
(Sei Ji Chaang Tin Tin Seung Tin),
Sink the elbows in line with the shoulders are true words
(Cham Jaang Deui Bok Si Jan Yin);
One cannot say Hung's boxing lacks extraordinary methods
(Mok Wa Hung Kyun Mou Miu Faat),
As the Venerable Master Iron Arms himself once said
(Tit Bei Sim Si Ya Si Yin).* [77]

The famous movie, "The 36th Chamber of Shaolin / Siu Lam Saam Sap Luk Fong / Shaolin San Shi Liu Fang [少林三十六房]", tells the story of Sam Dak's / San De [三德] training at the Southern Siu Lum / Shaolin Temple [南少林寺], under the altered training structure of the various chambers devised by the Siu Lum / Shaolin abbot [少林方丈], Gee Seen [至善禪師]. This condensed training system drastically reduced the time to achieve proficient martial artists [武術家] and capable fighters. Sam Dak / San De [三德] advanced through the thirty five chambers to become one of the Siu Lum / Shaolin Ten Best [少林十傑] students of Gee Seen [至善禪師]. [81a] [81b] [81c]

Sam Dak / San De [三德] was also renowned for his skill with the staff / Gwun [棍], in particular, the "Six and Half Point Pole" (Luk Dim Boon Gwun [六點半棍]) which again he had studied under his teacher [功夫老師], Gee Seen [至善禪師]. [78]

Pavel Macek Sifu, Practical Hung Kyun :-

It is stated that the "Six and Half Point Long Pole" comes from the time when the Venerable Gee Seen (Ji Sin), hid from his Ch'ing pursuers on the "Red Junks of the Chinese Opera".

He is connected to the "Six and Half Point Long Pole" in most Southern Chinese legends. Wing Chun also utilises this routine from their lineage with the Red Junks of the Chinese Opera. It is therefore probable that due to this common link, both Hung Kuen and Wing Chun have similar long pole techniques.

The pole (staff) is generally a standard size of seven feet and two inches (just over two metres). Due to the length and weight of the pole, it helps the practitioner to develop strength, balance, accuracy and posture. It is performed with an orthodox guard with the left leg leading. The various applications of this routine can be practised through drills which lead onto combat fighting with the weapon. The principal philosophy behind the long pole is that only one sound should be heard, meaning that weapons should clash only once then the next technique should be a strike to the opponent. [78d]

Several sources state that Sam Dak / San De [三德] also taught Hung Hei-Kwun [洪熙官] while he was at the Southern Siu Lum / Shaolin Temple [南少林寺] in the style of Short Fist known as Duan Kuen / Duan Quan [短拳]. [100] [100a] Sam Dak / San De [三德] therefore must have been taught this style during his initial training at the Putian temple [莆田寺]. [66]

Duan Quan, is also known as Short-Range Boxing and is a style of kung fu practiced mainly in the Hebei Province of China. This style was developed over four hundred years ago for close-range combat.

Duan Quan focuses on low stances with quick vigorous movements for combat. Practitioners are trained to constantly be on the move, making it very difficult for an opponent to strike at them. Moves are kept swift and simple, with an emphasis on not wasting energy. A Duan Quan fighter will move to avoid an opponent's attack then close in to counter attack with numerous techniques. [79]

Some sources state that another one of Sam Dak's / San De [三德] students was a fellow monk called the Venerable Gwok Yan [覺因]. [77] [83] If these sources are correct and Sam Dak / San De [三德] did teach both Hung Hei-Kwun [洪熙官] and Gwok Yan [覺因], I have concluded that he would have been much younger than them for this to have actually taken place at the Southern Siu Lum / Shaolin Temple [南少林寺].

The following is a story about Sam Dak / San De [三德] which was told by Wong Kiew Kit who spells his name as Sam Tuck and Tak.

"Sam Tuck's Kung Fu was fantastic. He specialized in the Tiger Style. In a deadly public duel with Foong Tou Tuck, one of the five Shaolin Grandmasters and a junior classmate of Chee Seen, Sam Tak defeated Foong Tou Tuck with a tiger-tail kick. One of Foong Tou Tuck's disciples (I can't remember his name, but he could be Lin Swee Hin), fearing for his master's life, sent a flying dart at Sam Tuck, who kicked it away, thus giving time for Foong Tou Tuck to escape. (Lin Swee Hin later discovered that his father was the great Manchurian general, Lin Kang Yiew, whom the emperor killed out of fear and jealousy. Discovering that Foong Tou Tuck sided with the Manchurian government, Lin Swee Hin was disappointed and joined the Shaolin side, but he remained faithful to his master, Foong Tou Tuck, and considered saving his life with a flying dart one of the best things he ever did in his life. Lin Swee Hin was also one of Chee Seen's Ten Great Shaolin Disciples. He and Lok Ah Choy (the sigung of Wong Fei Hoong) were the two Manchurians of the ten disciples." [80]

Years later after the Venerable Sam Dak / San De [三德] had completed his training and proved himself a very good and capable teacher [功夫老師], he left the Putian Siu Lum / Shaolin Temple [莆田少林寺], moving back to Canton [廣州]. Here he settled at another Buddhist temple [佛教徒寺] called the Sai Sim Monastery / West Zen Temple / Xi Chan [西禪寺]. This temple was located in an area outside the West Gate / Sai Kwan / Xiguan [西關] of the city walls on West China Road / Wai See Lou / Xi Hua Lu [西華路]. This location had once been farming land until Canton's growing weaving industry / 廣州紡織業 had recently started to expand in this area. Wong Kiew Kit also confirmed that Sam Dak / San De [三德] was at the West Zen Temple / Sai Sim Ji / Xi Chan Si [西禪寺] and that in time became its abbot [方丈]. [65]

It is stated that Gee Seen [至善禪師] and Sam Dak / San De [三德] had agreed a plan for him to take charge of the West Zen Temple / Sai Sim Ji / Xi Chan Si [西禪寺] in the West Gate / Sai Kwan / Xiguan [西關] (now called Liwan district [荔灣區]). Gee Seen [至善禪師] had become aware that two of the head monks at this temple had gone astray from their Buddhist [佛教徒] practices and so needed to be replaced. He therefore decided that Sam Dak / San De [三德] should take over this temple and in doing so would also fulfil another purpose. The Ch'ing / Qing [清朝] authorities had attacked and destroyed the previous two Southern Siu Lum / Shaolin Temples [南少林寺] at Fuqing [福清] and Quanzhou [泉州]. Therefore, Gee Seen [至善禪師] and Sam Dak / San De [三德] realised that it was only a matter of time before the authorities found out about the Putian temple [莆田寺] and attacked it. Such an attack could mean the demise of their Siu Lum / Shaolin martial arts [少林功夫], and in an attempt to preserve and spread these arts they decided to teach more laypersons / Or Hong Yan [外行人] from the general population. Due to their resentment of the Ch'ing / Qing [清朝] for their hostilities towards Siu Lum / Shaolin [少林] and the general Han Chinese [漢族] they decided to teach Kung Fu [功夫] to the general public who had anti-Ch'ing / anti-Qing [反清清朝] sentiments. [100] It is believed that this resulted in the establishment of the thirty sixth chamber to teach martial arts [武術] to laypeople by Sam Dak / San De [三德] as portrayed in the famous movie, The 36th Chamber of Shaolin / Siu Lam Saam Sap Luk Fong / Shaolin San Shi Liu Fang [少林三十六房]. [81a] [81b] [81c]

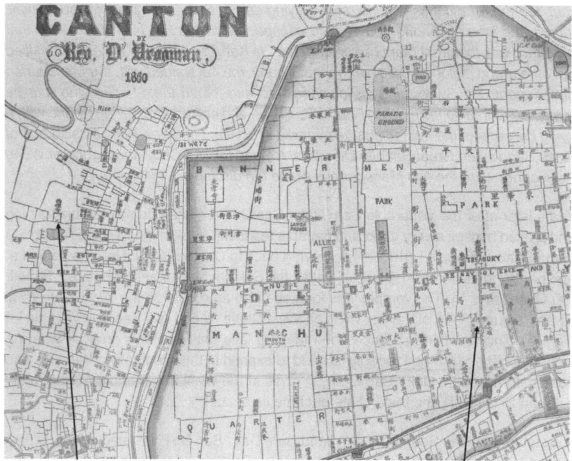

West Zen Temple / 西禪寺　　　　　　　　　Shuangmendi Street / 雙門底

All sources state that Sam Dak / San De [三德] was a highly skilled and talented Kung Fu master [功夫大師], who had excelled during his training at the Southern Siu Lum /

Shaolin Temple [南少林寺]. His proficiency and dedication made him an ideal teacher [功夫老師] of Siu Lum / Shaolin martial arts [少林功夫] in the Canton [廣州] area. Sam Dak / San De [三德] had lived nearby in Shuangmendi Lu (Street) [雙門底] in the neighbouring district of Yuexiu [越秀區] before he had gone into hiding at the Fukien temple / Fujian si [福建寺]. That had been many years previously, and now that he was older, with a shaven head and had become the Buddhist monk Three Virtues [三德和尚], no one would recognise him as Lau Yude / Liu Yu-te [劉裕德], the wanted man. Because he had grown up nearby he therefore knew the area very well. During this period when he was teaching at the West Zen Temple / Sai Sim Ji / Xi Chan Si [西禪寺], Sam Dak / San De [三德] gained a great reputation with the general public for sharing his Kung Fu [少林功夫] skills with laymen. Sam Dak / San De [三德] would return to the Putian Siu Lum / Shaolin Temple [莆田少林寺] several times as part of his duties.

During this period, a story is told of one of Sam Dak's / San De [三德] younger Kung Fu brothers / Si Dai [師弟] from Siu Lum / Shaolin [少林], called Wu Wei Kin / Hu Hui Gan [胡惠乾], who had also returned to Canton [廣州]. Wu's [胡惠乾] father had been killed and he, himself, had been badly beaten by the local Weavers Guild before he went to the Southern Siu Lum / Shaolin Temple [南少林寺]. He had learned Kung Fu [少林功夫] to enable him to one day seek his revenge on these weavers, but had left the Putian temple [莆田寺] before completing his training. Shortly after his return, Wu [胡惠乾] got into a fight with the weavers and during it, he killed thirteen of them. The weavers then hired a Kung Fu master [功夫大師] who had studied the Wu-tang / Wudang style [武當拳] under one of the Shaolin Five Elders / Sui Lum Ng Cho [少林五祖], called Fung Dou Dak / Feng Dao de [馮道德]. Wu Wei Kin [胡惠乾] was challenged to a duel [決鬥] on the Lei tai [擂臺] by a disciple [武術弟子] of Fung Dou Dak / Feng Dao de [馮道德]. Wu Wei Kin [胡惠乾] defeated and killed him in this staged fight on a Lei tai [擂臺]. When Fung Dou Dak / Feng Dao de [馮道德] heard this news of the death of his student, he was outraged, and sought revenge. In some accounts the situation was resolved by another one of the Shaolin Five Elders / Sui Lum Ng Cho [少林五祖] called Wu Mei / Ng Mui [五梅] who intervened. [64] [80a]

(This is a popular story and for a more detailed account it can be can be found in several books including Black Belt magazine, Jan 1966 pages 15-21, 52-53 [61e]*, Feb 1966 pages 30-35.* [61f] *Several films have also told this story including the 1978 Hong Kong movie called, "Showdown at the Cotton Mill." (Chinese title: 胡惠乾血戰西禪寺; Mandarin: Hu Hui Chien xie zhan xi chan si), also released as Cold Face, Heart and Blood.* [80b]
Sam Dak / San De [三德] is mentioned in both of these accounts.)

At the time of destruction of the Putian Temple [莆田少林寺], Sam Dak / San De [三德] was still at the West Zen Temple / Sai Sim Ji / Xi Chan Si [西禪寺] in Canton [廣

州]. Wong Kiew Kit states that after the destruction of the Putian Siu Lum / Shaolin Temple [莆田少林寺], other "Southern Siu Lum / Shaolin Heroes" joined him at this temple. [65] It is understood that Sam Dak / San De [三德] as the abbot [方丈] of this temple, granted sanctuary to his fellow Siu Lum / Shaolin brothers [少林兄弟] who had escaped the Fukien temple's / Fujian si [福建寺] destruction.

It is understood that Sam Dak / San De [三德] like a great many of the general Han Chinese [漢族] population, had anti-Ch'ing / anti-Qing [反清清朝] (anti-Manchurian) sentiments. He was forced to leave his home and seek sanctuary at the Southern Siu Lum / Shaolin Temple [南少林寺] after killing a Ch'ing / Qing [清朝] soldier in self-defence. His teacher [功夫老師], the Siu Lum / Shaolin abbot [少林方丈], Gee Seen Sim See [至善禪師] and many of his brothers at the temple, also had anti-Ch'ing / anti-Qing [反清清朝] feelings and attitudes which influenced him. Gee Seen [至善禪師] sent him back to Canton [廣州] to teach the general public martial arts [武術] so that more skilled fighters could take up the cause and become insurgents. These people would then go out to spread more unrest and ferment uprisings. It is understood that Sam Dak / San De [三德] used the West Zen Temple / Sai Sim Ji / Xi Chan Si [西禪寺] to not only teach Buddhism [佛教] and martial arts [武術] but also as a meeting place for other anti-Ch'ing / anti-Qing [反清清朝] sympathisers. From time to time, Sam Dak / San De [三德] would also leave the temple to travel around the neighbouring districts, to collect alms and meet associates. Although he did collect alms while on these journeys, they were also a cover for his meetings with other fellow anti-Ch'ing / anti-Qing [反清清朝] sympathisers. This gave him the opportunity to meet different people and recruit new students.

In Buddhism, the giving of alms is a sign of respect given by a lay Buddhist to a Buddhist monk or nun. This is not charity, but Buddists believe they are making a symbolic link to the spiritual realm to show their humbleness and respect in the presence of the wordly society. The act of alms giving assists in linking the human to the monk or nun and what he / she represents. [80a]

Our Hak Fu Mun [黑虎門] tradition states that our founder, So [蘇] more commonly known by his nickname of So Hak Fu / Su Heihu [蘇黑虎] was taught by a Siu Lum / Shaolin monk [少林僧] called Siu Dak / Zhaode [兆德] (which translates to mean Fortune Virtue). This information was passed down from our last Grandmaster, Wong Cheung [黃祥宗師] (alias Gat Seun [吉旋]) who passed away in 1989. We believe that Siu Dak / Zhaode [兆德] and Sam Dak / San De [三德] are the same person due to several identical facts regarding their lives and positions as abbot [方丈] of the West Zen Temple / Sai Sim Monastery / Xi Chan Si [西禪寺]. We understand that the name Siu Dak / Zhaode [兆德] was another alias for Sam Dak / San De [三德], that he would use sometimes to escape the attention of the Ch'ing / Qing [清朝] authorities. Many of Sam Dak's / San De [三德] students at the West Zen Temple / Sai Sim Ji / Xi Chan Si

[西禪寺] were rebels who then went on to promote anti-Ch'ing / anti-Qing [反清清朝] activities. It appears that during these times it was very common for certain people to either change their names or have several aliases to try to avoid being known or detected by the authorities. This would account for the several aliases that Sam Dak / San De [三德] was also known by, such as Siu Dak / Zhaode [兆德] and Iron Arms / Tien Bay / Tie bi [鐵臂].

Sometime around 1830, Sam / Siu Dak / San De / [三德] was in a village close to Pek Ho Town (what is now Beijiaozhen [北滘镇], translates to North Kau town) in the district of Shunde [順德區], near the town of Fat Shan / Foshan [佛山], under the pretence of collecting alms for the temple. He observed a teenager training each morning whilst he was stopping with a local business man called Mr So [蘇]. He considered that the young man had potential, and after finding out he was Mr So's [蘇] nephew he repaid the kindness of Mr So's [蘇] hospitality by agreeing to train the teenager. Our tradition states that So [蘇] was taken to the Siu Lum / Shaolin temple [少林寺] where he trained under Siu Dak / Zhaode [兆德] / Sam Dak / San De [三德]. He trained for six years until he was 24 years old when he then returned to his home village in the late 1830s. We assume that the stated Siu Lum / Shaolin Temple [少林寺] would more than likely be the Kwangtung Siu Lum / Shaolin Temple [廣東少林寺]. Although it is known that Sam Dak / San De [三德] returned to the Putian Siu Lum / Shaolin Temple [莆田少林寺] several times as part of his duties so it is possible that on one or more of these occasions, So [蘇] would have accompanied him. At this temple, Sam Dak / San De [三德] taught Siu Lum / Shaolin philosophy [少林禪學] and Siu Lum / Shaolin martial arts [少林武術], to So Hak Fu / Su Heihu [蘇黑虎] and other students here. For this reason So Hak Fu / Su Heihu [蘇黑虎] and others called it the Siu Lum / Shaolin Temple [少林寺], as this temple was part of the Siu Lum / Shaolin order and may possibly have been the Kwangtung Siu Lum / Shaolin Temple [廣東少林寺].

Sometime around the early 1840s the Ch'ing / Qing [清朝] authorities found out about these treasonous activities at the West Zen Temple / Sai Sim Ji / Xi Chan Si [西禪寺]. They therefore decided to put an end to this insurrection and hundreds of soldiers were sent to this temple with orders to arrest the abbot [方丈], the Venerable Sam Dak / San De [三德]. It is stated in the book, "The Qianlong Emperor Inspects Southern China / Kin Loong har Kwong Nam / Qianlong Xia Jiangnan [乾隆下江南]", [50b] that the government soldiers were led by Ma Hung [馬雄] and Pui Lung [鮑龍] who were also aided by Ko Chun-chung [高進忠], a disciple [武術弟子] of one of the Shaolin Five Elders / Sui Lum Ng Cho [少林五祖] called White Eyebrow / Bak Mei [白眉]. One night they surrounded the temple, but the noise of the soldiers alerted Sam Dak / San De [三德] to the danger. The commanders of the army, Ma Hung [馬雄] and Pui Lung [鮑龍] ordered Sam Dak / San De [三德] and everyone else in the temple to surrender.

In an attempt to save his students Sam Dak / San De [三德] fought the soldiers as a distraction, while they made their escape. He knew that if he was captured he would be beheaded for treason, which made him fight even more furiously. It is stated that during the fierce battle he beat over fifty men while many of his students fled, making their escape. Unfortunately, he was finally overwhelmed and killed. [81] [81a]

"The Qianlong Emperor Inspects Southern China / Kin Loong har Kwong Nam / Qianlong Xia Jiangnan [乾隆下江南]", [50b] states that Sam Dak / San De [三德] was surrounded by Ma Hung [馬雄], Pui Lung [鮑龍] and many soldiers. He was struggling to deal with so many opponents at one time when he was distracted by the severed head of Wu Wei Kin [胡惠乾] which had been thrown towards him by Ko Chun-chung [高進忠]. Wu Wei Kin [胡惠乾] had been killed by Ko Chun-chung [高進忠] after he had been wounded by arrows from the archers of the Ch'ing / Qing [清朝] army. During this distraction, Ko Chun-chung [高進忠] attacked Sam Dak / San De [三德] with his broadsword. The strike caught Sam Dak / San De [三德] on the right arm causing him to drop his weapon. This strike was followed by another attack from a different opponent who cut into his left shoulder. As Sam Dak / San De [三德] fell to the floor in agony, all the soldiers stepped forward surrounding him and killed him by hacking him to pieces.

Futher details of Sam Dak's / San De [三德] life can be found in the novel entitled, "Monk San De's Three Visits to the Xichan Monastery", written by Woshi Shanren. [82] It is understood that Hong Kong director, Lau Kar Leung utilized this novel in part for the classic, "The 36th Chamber of Shaolin" series in which legendary actor Gordon Liu plays San De / Sam Dak [三德]. Variations on the character can also be found in other films such as Chan Sing's portrayal in 'The Iron Fisted Monk' (1977). [81] [81a] [81b] [81c]

It is understood that after the death of Sam Dak / San De [三德], the Ch'ing / Qing [清朝] authorities replaced all the monks [僧] at the West Zen Temple / Sai Sim Ji / Xi Chan Si [西禪寺] with ones who had no connection or loyalty to Siu Lum / Shaolin [少林].

The Venerable Gwok Yan [覺因]
(sometimes spelt Kwok Yan / Jue Yin [覺因])

The Venerable Gwok Yan [覺因] was a monk from the Siu Lum / Shaolin Temple [少林寺] in Fukien / Fujian Province [福建省] located near Putian [莆田]. Besides studying under the abbot [方丈] Gee Seen [至善禪師] it is stated that he was also tutored by the Venerable Sam Dak / San De [三德] (Tuck). The Buddhist [佛教徒] meaning of the venerable Gwok Yan [覺因] name means "Perceiving Karma". [77] [83]

I believe that Gwok Yan [覺因] may have been in his later years when he either became a monk at the Fukien / Fujian Siu Lum / Shaolin Temple [福建少林寺] or started training in Kung Fu [少林功夫]. I have made this assumption from the information stated by Wong Kiew Kit who asserts that Gwok Yan [覺因] was tutored by the younger Sam Dak / Tuck / San De [三德]. Another reason for coming to this conclusion is that it is recorded that Gwok Yan [覺因] died at the grand age of 110 years when his student, Leung Kwan / Liang Kun [梁坤], more commonly known as Tit Kiu Saam / Tie Qiao San [鐵橋三] was about 21 years old which would have been around the mid 1830s.

It is not known if Gwok Yan [覺因] was at the temple at the time it was attacked and destroyed by the Ch'ing / Qing [清朝] authorities but after the temple's destruction, it is believed that he settled at a temple in Canton [廣州]. The exact temple is not stated, but I have assumed it to have been the Honam Temple [河南寺]. This conclusion comes from the information and short biography of, "Tid Kiu Sam" in the Iron Thread book, which notes at the bottom of page16, [84] that Tid Kiu Sam's Siu Lum / Shaolin teacher [功夫老師] was the Venerable Gwok Yan [覺因]. I have concluded from this, that the following statement possibly refers to his Sifu [師父].

After the famous monastery of Southern Shaolin was burnt to ashes, monks who escaped spread in China "like stars in the sky". Few of them found refuge at the Haichuang (Honam) Monastery where they started to teach monks and later on laymen, the martial arts. This monastery is the cradle of the most famous Kung Fu styles of Southern China – Hung Gar Kuen, Fu Kuen, Li Gar and some others. [85]

It is understood that Gwok Yan [覺因] was skilled in the Tiger style known as Hung Kuen [洪拳], Iron Shirt conditioning / Tee Po Sam / Tie bu shan [鐵布衫] and also of the internal force method known as the Great Majestic Kuen / Tai Hung Kuen [大雄拳] (Triple Stretch Set). He taught this method to his famous student, Leung Kwan / Liang Kun [梁坤] who is better known by his nickname of "Tit Kiu Saam / Tie Qiao San [鐵橋三]", who then used this method to develop the Iron Thread routine [套路]. In Lam Sai Wing's book entitled, "Iron Thread", he states that Gwok Yan [覺因] was one of the greatest masters of the Southern Siu Lum / Shaolin Hung Gar Kuen School [南少

林洪家拳], and that he was known along the whole length of the Yangtse River [揚子江(長江). [84] From the Tiger style (Hung Kuen [洪拳]) it is believed that Gwok Yan [覺因] excelled in both the, Gung Gee Fook Fu Kuen / Taming the Tiger in an I pattern [工字伏虎拳] and Fu Hok Seung Ying Kuen / Tiger & Crane double shape fist [虎鶴雙形], which he then taught to Leung Kwan / Liang Kun [梁坤], (Tit Kiu Saam / Tie Qiao San [鐵橋三]). [66]

(To contradict this, Wong Kiew Kit states that it was the Venerable Cheng Choe, who taught the Great Majestic Kuen / Tai Hung Kuen [大雄拳] (Triple Stretch Set) at the West Zen Temple / Sai Sim Tzi in Canton to Leung Kwan / Liang Kun [梁坤]. This could either be a different monk altogether, or it is possibile is that it was an alias used by Gwok Yan [覺因]. I could not find any sources that mentioned a monk by the name of Cheng Choe for this period.) [83a]

Many sources state that Gwok Yan [覺因] lived till the age of 110 years. It is stated that he accepted the young Leung Kwan / Liang Kun [梁坤] as a disciple [俗家弟子] when he was fourteen years old. He was then taught for seven years by Gwok Yan [覺因]. [66] [152] [156] I believe he must have passed away in the mid 1830s between 1834 to 1836.Unfortunately, for such a famous master [功夫大師] I have been unable to find any more information about him.

The Venerable Chan Fook [陳福]

It is believed that Chan Fook / Chén Fu [陳福] was from the Putian temple [莆田寺]. Wong Kiew Kit believes that Chan Fook [陳福] may have studied under the Venerable Harng Yein who was himself a student of the Venerable Gee Seen [至善禪師]. He was educated in various Siu Lum / Shaolin arts which including the Great Majestic Kuen / Tai Hung Kuen [大雄拳], the Cross-Roads at Four Gates [十字四門拳] and the Dragron Strength Set [龍力運氣拳]. [78a] [85a] [85b]

Wong Kiew Kit states :- *The Cross-Roads at Four Gates / Cantonese; Sap Tze Seai Moon Khoon / Mandarin; Shi Zi Si Men Quan was a fundamental set at the Southern Shaolin Temples at both Quanzhou and Putian. Initial benefits include the consolidation of both footwork and stances. This is followed by the development of many martial skills such as breath control, energy flow, mental focus, internal force management, and speed development. Advanced practitioners can then appreciate the profundity in the philosophy and combat application of this set.* [85c]

The Dragon Strength set is structured to develop internal force from the beginning, followed by combat application. The entire routine [套路] utilises force training to develop two prominent skills of Dragon force and lightning speed. The Dragon force is flowing and internal. The combat applications of this routine [套路] do not rely on defending or blocking attacks but attacks are dealt with by direct counter striking. [85d]

At the time of the Putian temple's [莆田寺] destruction, Chan Fook [陳福] was at his home village in Guangdong [廣東]. One story tells that his village had been harassed by a local villain and his gang of thugs. Chan Fook [陳福] had at first tried to reason with this villain, with no effect, so he resorted to a demonstration of his skills and abilities of Kung Fu [少林功夫]. The conclusion of this demonstration was Chan Fook [陳福] dropping into a deep low Horse stance [馬步] [131a] [131b] in front of a tree and wrapped his arms around it. He then heaved with all of his might and uprooted this tree in front of the shocked villain and his gang members. After witnessing Chan's [陳福] Kung Fu [少林功夫] skills and his strength in uprooting the tree, the villain and his gang fled realising they were no match for the Siu Lum / Shaolin monk [少林僧]. Chan Fook [陳福] later returned to lay life. [85] [85e]

It is rumoured that Venerable Chan Fook [陳福] taught a young So Chan / Su Can [蘇燦] (better known by his nickname of Beggar So / So Hut Yee / Su Qi'er [蘇乞兒]) the Siu Lum / Shaolin Tiger (Hung Kuen [洪拳]) style of Kung Fu [少林功夫] including the use of the staff / Gwun [棍]. [109a] [147] Chan Fook [陳福] is not a Buddhist [佛教徒] name but means Lucky Chan. Chan being the family name, while "Fook" is often used by many Chinese to express their hope that their children will be lucky throughout their lives.

(Unfortunately the only sources I could find regarding information on the Venerable Chan Fook were from Wong Kiew Kit.

Hung Hei-Kwun [洪熙官]

(Hong Xiguan [洪熙官], Original name was Jyu / Zhu [朱])
(can also be spelt as Hung Hei-Goon / -Gun / -Gung etc)
Approximately 1732/45-1825

There are many myths and legends about Hung Hei-Kwun's [洪熙官] life and death. Many of these tend to contradict each other. Several sources state different locations where Hung Hei-Kwun [洪熙官] was born, when he went to the Southern Siu Lum / Shaolin Temple [南少林寺] and other details during his life. Due to this I have therefore shown the following accounts and tried to state possible scenarios to allow for these.

History states that Hung Hei-Kwun [洪熙官] was originally named Jyu [朱], born sometime between 1732 to 1745 (although Wikipedia states 1745). It is stated that he was a distant relation to the old Royal Ming [明] ruling dynasty (a descendant of Prince Leung, a son of the last Ming [明] Emperor Chung Chen / Chongzhen [崇禎] who reigned between 1627 to 1644), that had been overthrown by the current Ch'ing / Qing [清朝] rulers. After some altercation with the Manchurian [滿洲] authorities, he fled to the Siu Lum / Shaolin Temple [少林寺] at Quanzhou [泉州少林寺], with a price on his head. Some stories state that Jyu [朱] got into a fight with a Manchurian soldier [滿洲兵], during which he hit him so hard in the chest that the soldier was fatally injured. He sought refuge at the Southern Siu Lum / Shaolin Temple [南少林寺] and when Gee Seen [至善禪師] saw that Jyu [朱] was a strong, hard working, man with a talent for martial arts [武術], he accepted him as his disciple [武術弟子]. [70] [97]

Wing Lam states that Jyu [朱] (Hung Hei-Kwun [洪熙官]) was born in 1732 in Cheun Jao City / Quanzhou [泉州], Fukien / Fujian Province [福建省], and that he was abandoned by his parents soon after he was born, but was adopted by a local old man. Unfortunately his adopted father passed away when Jyu [朱] was only eight, and he then spent the next two years homeless. This is when he was found by Gee Seen [至善禪師], who was travelling around under the pretence of collecting alms (donations) for the Southern Siu Lum / Shaolin Temple [南少林寺]. Gee Seen [至善禪師] decided to look after the boy and took him with him when he returned to the Southern Siu Lum / Shaolin Temple [南少林寺]. Jyu [朱] lived at the Quanzhou Siu Lum / Shaolin Temple [泉州少林寺] and studied martial arts [武術] under Gee Seen [至善禪師] until he was twenty two years old. He then became a tea merchant [茶商] travelling around the different provinces. This occupation was more likely a cover for his anti-Ch'ing / anti-Qing [反清清朝] activities. [64] It could also possibly be sometime after this that he had a dispute with several Ch'ing / Qing [清朝] officials and had to go into hiding with a price on his head at the Southern Siu Lum / Shaolin Temple [南少林寺].

The Tai Ping Institute state that Jyu [朱] was born around 1743 in Chang-chou / Zhangzhou [漳州], Fukien / Fujian Province [福建省]. His father was a tea merchant [茶商] and a committed Ming [明] supporter who had joined the Heaven and Earth Society / Tiandi hui [天地會]. As Jyu [朱] grew up, he helped his father with the family business, but due to the authorities' strict control, they found it hard to survive in this trade. His father sent him to the temple to train, and also keep him out of the way of the troubles that were taking place in his home town at that time between the Heaven and Earth Society / Tiandi hui [天地會] and the Ch'ing / Qing [清朝] authorities. [14]

Some sources, including Wikipedia, state that he was a tea merchant [茶商], but that he was born in the Huadu district [花都區] north of Guangzhou [廣州]. [97] (Before 1993, Huadu District [花都區] was known as Hua County / Huaxian [花縣]) The distance between Cheun Jao City / Quanzhou [泉州] and Chang-chou / Zhangzhou [漳州] is about 110 kms. If he was born in Quanzhou [泉州] or Zhangzhou [漳州], both in Fukien / Fujian Province [福建省], then the Huadu connection could possibly be from when he settled there around 1782. [14] The Huadu district [花都區] (Hua County / Huaxian [花縣]) is where he lived with his first wife and where they had a son.

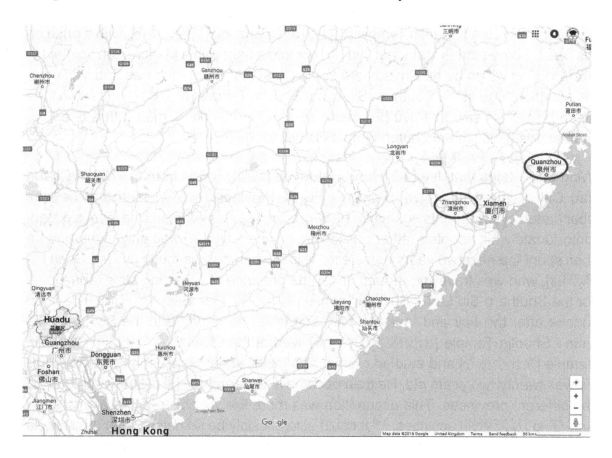

After years of hard training in the Southern Siu Lum / Shaolin Tiger / Fu [虎] and Lohan / Luohan [羅漢拳] styles, he became Gee Seen's [至善禪師] number one disciple [武

術弟子]. A particular routine [套路] which Jyu [朱] was taught was the Shaolin Fook Fu Kuen [少林伏虎拳]. It is stated that he then further expanded this routine [套路] creating the Gung Gee Fook Fu Kuen [工字伏虎拳]. [66] [97a] [97c] [100] [103] [106] [108] [108a] [112]

Luohan quan [羅漢拳], which means "holy Buddhist fist", is a common name for any style of Chinese martial arts that are named after the Arhats. Luohan Style is the oldest style of Shaolin Kung Fu and can sometimes be used to represent the whole system of Shaolin Temple martial arts as there are various Luohan styles. The original roots of this style date back to the early eras of Shaolin temple. It is understood that the Shaolin Luohan 18 hands and Luohan quan are regarded as the root styles on which most of the other Shaolin Kung Fu styles and many other non-Shaolin styles, have been created in other areas of China.

Enlightenment (Nirvana) is the first notion of Buddhism. The Chinese word of Luohan represents the Sanskrit (Indian) word Arhat and refers to those who have attained enlightenment. Therefore, the ultimate goal of the Shaolin monks has always been to achieve the point of becoming Luohans. Therefore, the Luohan(s) have always been holy icon(s) in the daily life of Shaolin temple monks and their martial arts. [97b]

According to the Taiping Institute, when the Quanzhou Siu Lum / Shaolin Temple [泉州少林寺] was destroyed, Jyu [朱] escaped and fled back to his home town of Zhangzhou [漳州]. He became an active member of the Heaven and Earth Society / Tiandi hui [天地會] and taught Kung Fu [功夫] locally to the members. This style of Hung Kuen [洪拳] is now also called Double Branches Fist / Saen Chi Kuen / Shuang Zhi Quan [雙枝拳] in the Zhangzhou [漳州] area. Jyu [朱] was later sent south to Guangdong [廣東], to expand the society in that province. He travelled south with the Red Opera Boat Troupes [紅船粵劇團] and it is believed that it was during this period Jyu [朱] changed his name to Hung Hei-Kwun [洪熙官] to avoid being detected by the Ch'ing / Qing [清朝] authorities. [14] Another version of how he acquired the name, is that while he was teaching Lei Jou Fun [李祖寬] (the founder of the Hung Fut [洪佛] style) and staying at his home, Lei Jou Fan's servants would call him Hung Hei "Kwun [官]" meaning official, and this nickname stuck with him from then on. [97] It is also stated that he chose the name as tribute to the first Ming [明] Emperor Hung Wu [洪武帝]. During these turbulent years travelling on the Red Opera Boats [紅船粵劇團], Hung Hei-Kwun [洪熙官] earned a fierce reputation and became known as the "Southern Fist [南方拳]". [64]

While travelling around, Hung Hei-Kwun [洪熙官] met a lady called Liu Yingchun [廖永春]. They married and settled down to live in the village of Chong She Yuen Tsuen / Cang Shu Yuan Cun [藏書院村] (translates to mean Book storage hall village), near the town of Tan Bu / Tan bou zen / Tanbu Zhen [炭步镇] in Huadu District [花都區]. During this period, this area was called Hua County [花縣]. The village of Chong She

Yuen Tsuen / Cang Shu Yuan Cun [藏書院村] lies approximately 20 kms south west of the town of Huadu [花都] and approximately 30 kms north west of Canton [廣州].

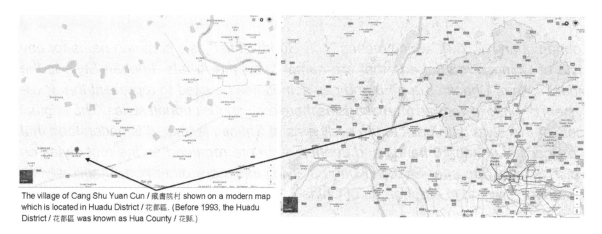

The village of Cang Shu Yuan Cun / 藏書院村 shown on a modern map which is located in Huadu District / 花都區. (Before 1993, the Huadu District / 花都區 was known as Hua County / 花縣.)

At this village, they had a son called called Hung Man Ting / Hong Wending [洪文定], but unfortunately, Hung's [洪熙官] wife, Liu Yingchun [廖永春] died sometime around this period.

It is believed that during these years, Hung Hei-Kwun [洪熙官] was an active member of the Hung secret society (Heaven and Earth Society / Tiandi hui [天地會], members known as Hong Men [洪門]) establishing a group here. He would teach his style of Hung Kuen [洪拳] martial arts during the 1780s in the Huadu [花都區] area. [14] [106]

This period produced many good students, including a man called Tam Min / Tan Min [譚敏]. Tam Min / Tan Min [譚敏] had previously studied his family's style of martial arts [武術] before training under Hung Hei-Kwun [洪熙官]. The Taiping Institute state that during this time, Tam Min's / Tan Min's [譚敏] training included the 3 Extensions Fist / San Zhan Quan [三展拳], 5 Animal (Shapes) Boxing / Wu Xing Quan [五形拳] and a Staff / Gwun [棍] routine [套路]. For this reason a derivative of the Huadu [花都] style became known as Tan Family 3 Extensions 5 Shapes [譚家三展五形拳]. [14] [66]

The NYFK Sports Association [172a] states that Tam Min's / Tan Min's [譚敏] grandfather, who was called Tam Yi Jun / Tan Yijun [譚義均], had trained at the Southern Siu Lum / Shaolin Temple [南少林寺] under Gee Seen [至善禪師]. He had then returned to his home village and taught the Siu Lum / Shaolin [少林] style he had learnt. As a child, Tam Min / Tan Min [譚敏] had not been taught Kung Fu [功夫] by his family because of his aggressive and unruly nature. His grandfather, Tam Yi Jun / Tan Yijun [譚義均] had believed that this, combined with Kung Fu [功夫] skills, would get the young Tam Min / Tan Min [譚敏] into trouble. He had therefore commanded that no one was allowed to teach him. Tam Min / Tan Min [譚敏] had greatly desired to learn Kung Fu [功夫] and so he watched people practicing from the roof tops. He would then go into the forest and from memory, perform the movements and techniques he had witnessed. Tam

Min / Tan Min [譚敏] continued this lone practicing for several years, without anyone finding out.

When Tam Min / Tan Min [譚敏] was seventeen years old he had gone to a festival where he observed another martial artist [武術家] performing. This martial artist [武術家] was called Leung Kwan [梁坤], who was shortly to became famous and more commonly known by his nickname of Iron Bridge Three / Tit kiu Saam / Tie Qiao San [鐵橋三]. During this martial arts performance [武術表演], Tam Min / Tan Min [譚敏] noticed a weakness in the routine [套路] performed by Leung Kwan [梁坤]. Leung Kwan [梁坤] was surprised that this young man had questioned his performance and so challenged Tam Min / Tan Min [譚敏] to prove the issue. News of this challenge match reached Tam Yi Jun / Tan Yijun [譚義均], who hurried to the scene, as he was concerned for his grandson's safety. When Master Tam Yi Jun / Tan Yijun [譚義均] arrived, the match was over and he was approached by Leung Kwan [梁坤] (Iron Bridge Three / Tit kiu Saam / Tie Qiao San [鐵橋三]). Leung Kwan [梁坤] stated that he was impressed with the young Tam Min / Tan Min [譚敏] and that he would like to stay and teach him some conditioning techniques.

Master Tam Yi Jun / Tan Yijun [譚義均] was not only surprised, but also amazed by his grandson's talent. He therefore agreed, and so Leung Kwan [梁坤] stayed several days educating Tam Min / Tan Min [譚敏] in various skills and techniques to condition his arms (bridges). [172a] I believe the facts of this story have been mixed up as the dates do not tie in. Leung Kwan [梁坤] was not born until either 1813 or 1815 and Hung Hei-Kwun [洪熙官] is believed to have died around 1825. Therefore if this did take place I can only assume that either Tam Min / Tan Min [譚敏] had already studied under Hung Hei-Kwun [洪熙官] or that the martial arts performance [武術表演] was by another martial artist [武術家] and not Leung Kwan [梁坤] (Iron Bridge Three / Tit kiu Saam / Tie Qiao San [鐵橋三]). Another Siu Lum / Shaolin [少林] Master [功夫大師] who was known by the name of "Iron arms" (Tien Bay /Tie Bi [鐵臂]) was Sam Dak / San De [三德]. Therefore is it possible that these two have been confused.

It is possible that Hung Hei-Kwun [洪熙官] heard that his teacher [功夫老師] Gee Seen [至善禪師] had re-established himself at the Putian Temple [莆田寺], and travelled back to Fukien / Fujian Province [福建省] to train under him again. While at the Putian Siu Lum / Shaolin Temple [莆田少林寺], Hung also studied the Short Fist / Duan Kuen / Duan Quan [短拳] style under the Venerable Sam Dak / San De [三德]. Sometime after, Gee Seen [至善禪師] sent Hung Hei-Kwun [洪熙官] back to Canton 廣州] to spread their Siu Lum / Shaolin [少林] teachings there. While on these journeys, possibly travelling with the Red Opera Boats [紅船粵劇團] once again, Hung Hei-Kwun [洪熙官] met Fong Wing Chun / Fang Yongchun [方詠春] who was reputed to also be a martial artist [武術家] in the Crane [鶴] style. It is stated that she was either the daughter or niece of Fong Sai-Yuk [方世玉] who was also one of the Siu Lum / Shaolin Ten Best [

少林十傑] under Gee Seen [至善禪師]. As they had both trained under the same Sifu (teacher [功夫老師]), this made Hung Hei-Kwun [洪熙官] and Fong Sai-Yuk [方世玉] Kung Fu brothers [師兄弟].

Several accounts state that Hung Hei-Kwun [洪熙官] was impressed with the Crane [鶴] style and blended it with some of his own movements. The merger of these two styles also led to creation of the Tiger Crane [虎鶴雙形] routine [套路]. While training together, Hung Hei-Kwun [洪熙官] and Fong Wing Chun [方詠春] fell in love and later married. These accounts state that Fong Wing Chun's [方詠春] father had been killed by Bak Mei [白眉] accompanied with some of his students (Wu-tang / Wudang [武當拳] disciples [武術弟子]). Fong Wing Chun [方詠春] wanted revenge for her father's murder and Hung [洪熙官] agreed to help his wife in this task. [14] [66] [100a]

Another possible scenario is that Hung Hei-Kwun [洪熙官] did not train at the Quanzhou Temple [泉州少林寺] but was a tea merchant as a young man. He was also an active member of the Heaven and Earth Society / Tiandi hui [天地會], whose members were known as Hong Men [洪門], and after the altercation with the Manchurian soldier [滿洲兵] he went into hiding at the Putian Siu Lum / Shaolin Temple [莆田少林寺]. He then completed his training as previously stated, but he was now mature and not a young man. The story remains the same but set years later.

When Hung arrived in Canton [廣州], he stayed at the Big Buddha Temple (Dafo Temple [大佛寺]) and due to the political climate, taught in secret. Several sources state that Hung Hei-Kwun [洪熙官] taught covertly at this temple for up to ten years before the authorities eased their restrictions on martial arts [武術] training. In 1785 he opened a martial arts school [武術學校] and began to teach openly. [66] [99] [100]

Wing Lam states that this school [武術學校] was called the "Lok-Sin-San Fong School" [樂善山房學校], which translates to Happy Kind Mountain Training Hall or a modest training hall that brings happiness and kindness. This school [武術學校] was located just inside the West Gate / Sai Kwan / Xiguan [西關] area of Guang Jao (Canton [廣州]). If this is correct then perhaps this was his first school before he had to teach in secret at the Big Buddha Temple / Dafo Temple [大佛寺]. According to Wing Lam, Gee Seen's [至善禪師] Siu Lum / Shaolin Ten Best [少林十傑] were all present at this school's [武術學校] opening along with several other notable masters [功夫大師] including Sam Dak / San De [三德]. Wing Lam also states that during the 1800s, the school had several notable characters three of whom would be one day known as members of the Ten Tigers of Canton / Kwong Tung Sap Fu [廣東十虎] (Guangdong). These martial artists [武術家] are stated as Wong Kei-Ying [黃麒英], Lai Yan-Chiu [黎仁超] and So Hak Fu [蘇黑虎] all of whom were affiliated to this school [武術學校]. It is not known exactly when this was, but we can assume that it was probably sometime between 1830s and 1850s. [64]

Other issues besides the date of this story include the people Wing Lam states were present for the opening. The story tells of a Lion Dance [舞獅] a few days later which included Wong Kei-Ying [黃麒英] and Luk Ah-Choi / Lu A Cai [陸阿采]. This Lion Dance [舞獅] resulted in a fight between the rival lion dance troupe [舞獅團] and followers from another school [武術學校]. The story states that Tit Kiu Saam / Tie Qiao San [鐵橋三] was also involved in the fighting on the side of the Lok-Sin-San Fong School [樂善山房學校]. This again brings the date into question, because it is known that both Wong Kei-Ying [黃麒英] and Tit Kiu Saam / Tie Qiao San [鐵橋三] were not even born until around 1813 to 1815. Therefore, if the events of this story are true we have to assume one of two possibilities. The date could possibly be incorrect, as it must have been either a much later date or these famous masters' [功夫大師] names have been added to embellish this story. *(Please see Wong Kei-Ying's [黃麒英] history for this story.)*

Wong Kiew Kit claims that the school [武術學校] was called the "Siew Lam Hoong Goon" / Siu Lum Hung Kuen [少林洪拳] which translates to the Hoong School of Siu Lum / Shaolin Kung Fu which was actually in Fat Shan / Foshan [佛山] and this was after the destruction of the Siu Lum / Shaolin Temple [少林寺] by the Ch'ing / Qing [清朝] authorities. [65] Unfortunately he does not state if this was the Quanzhou [泉州少林寺] or Putian Siu Lum / Shaolin Temple [莆田少林寺], and I can only assume that during this period of hostility towards Siu Lum / Shaolin [少林] and the destruction of their temple it seems unlikely a martial arts school [武術學校] would use Siu Lum / Shaolin [少林] in its title. Using the name Siu Lum / Shaolin [少林] would only result in unwanted attention from the Ch'ing / Qing [清朝] authorities. If this information is correct, then perhaps it was named several years after the destruction of the Quanzhou temple [泉州少林寺] when hostility towards Siu Lum / Shaolin [少林] from the authorities had relaxed.

We have two different names of schools [武術學校]. My assumption is that perhaps there were two schools [武術學校] but at different times of Hung Hei-Kwun's [洪熙官] life. This would sound more probable than getting the name so completely different if there was only one school [武術學校].

It is stated that after secretly teaching at the Big Buddha Temple / Dafo Temple [大佛寺], Hung Hei-Kwun [洪熙官] later opened a public school [武術學校] in Fa City which is now called Fat Shan / Foshan [佛山]. The city of Fat Shan / Foshan [佛山] is located approximately 18 kms from Canton [廣州]. Another source states that this school [武術學校] opened in 1813 and was called Hung Gar Boxing [洪家拳]. [66] It was around this time that the style became known as Hung Kuen [洪拳] and that the school [武術學校] would be known as the Hung School [洪武術學校]. This name was used to disguise its connection to its Siu Lum / Shaolin origins [少林起源] and so avoid unwanted attention from the Ch'ing / Qing [清朝] authorities. This name was also chosen because it reflects the name of Hung Hei-Kwun [洪熙官] (the founder) and also as a tribute to the first Ming [明] Emperor. [98] [101]

During the early 1800s, Gee Seen [至善禪師] sent his student, Luk Ah-Choi / Lu A Cai [陸阿采] to Hung Hei-Kwun's [洪熙官] school to continue his education in martial arts [武術]. Hung Hei-Kwun [洪熙官] is believed to have lived to be about 93, passing away in 1825. This would make the 1732 date of birth more correct as stated by Wing Lam. [64] Even if he was born in 1745, then he would still be nearly 70 years old when he opened this school [武術學校] in Fat Shan / Foshan [佛山]. Therefore, Gee Seen [至善禪師] would have been older than this and so possibly too old to teach or improve certain techniques that he believed Luk Ah-Choi [陸阿采] needed. Luk Ah-Choi [陸阿采] studied under Hung Hei-Kwun [洪熙官] for several years learning all he could. It is understood that after this, Hung Hei-Kwun [洪熙官] sent Luk Ah-choi [陸阿采] to Canton [廣州] to open a school [武術學校] there. [66]

Unfortunately, like the events in his life, his death follows along the same lines with two different stories. One version is that after he heard that Bak Mei [白眉] had killed his teacher [功夫老師], Gee Seen [至善禪師], he set out to punish him. This was not only to avenge his teacher [功夫老師] but also to take revenge for his wife's family that had been killed by Bak Mei [白眉]. This story has two endings, one with Hung Hei-Kwun [洪熙官] being killed by Bak Mei [白眉], and another with him defeating Bak Mei [白眉]. Wong Kiew Kit states that Bak Mei [白眉] was killed by Hung Hei-Kwun's [洪熙官] son, Hung Man Ting [洪文定] and Wu Ah Piew [胡亞彪], in revenge for not only killing Gee Seen [至善禪師], but destroying the Southern Siu Lum / Shaolin Temple [南少林寺] at Putian [莆田]. (Wu Ah Piew was the son of Wu Wai Thien (Wu Wai Kin [胡惠乾]) who Hung Hei-Kwun [洪熙官] had adopted when his father was killed.) [85]

Another version of his death is that he died after been struck by a young girl he and his wife (Fong Wing Chun / Fang Yongchun [方詠春]) had took into their home. This girl had lied about her circumstances, to avenge her father who Hung Hei-Kwun [洪熙官] had defeated in a duel [決鬥]. Wong Kiew Kit also gives this version of the story stating that Hung Hei-Kwun [洪熙官] was in his eighties when a young girl fainted outside his home. He and his wife took the girl in, who repaid them by working hard, serving them as a devoted daughter they never had. While serving a cup of tea to Hung Hei-Kwun [洪熙官]many months later, she struck him in the ribs with a phoenix-eye fist / Fung Ann Kuen [鳳眼拳] as he raised his cup to drink. The girl then fled, leaving a message that she had done this to avenge her father who Hung had killed in a duel [決鬥] several years before. This strike proved fatal to Hung Hei-Kwun [洪熙官] who while dying, told his family to not seek revenge, as vengeance and the settling of scores would never end. [85] [100a] [107]

According to one source, Hung Hei-Kwun [洪熙官] died in Fa City / Fat Shan / Foshan [佛山] at the age of about 90 years, where his tomb is still located today. [101]

Hung Hei-Kwun's [洪熙官] important contribution like Luk Ah-Choi's [陸阿采], was keeping the style alive during a very dangerous and perilous period when a person was beheaded if found practicing or teaching Kung Fu [功夫] (martial arts [武術]). [108a]

Hung Hei-Kwun's [洪熙官] son, Hung Man Ting [洪文定] remained close friends with Luk Ah-Choi [陆阿采] and trained under him at his martial arts school [武術學校] in Canton after his father's death. [106]

Luk Ah-Choi [陸阿采]
(Sometimes spelt Luk Ah Choy / Lu A Cai [陸阿采])

Approximately 1780s-1850s

It is believed that Luk Ah-Choi [陸阿采] was born sometime around the late 1770s to early 1780s in Guangdong Province [廣東省] where all sources state his father, a Manchurian [滿洲], (Ch'ing / Qing [清朝]), was stationed. Therefore it is assumed that this was in some sort of military position. According to some sources, and the stories that the movie (The story of Luk Ah-Choi, 1960,) is based on, Luk Ah Choi's [陸阿采] original name was Wong Hei Choi [黃喜才] and he was living in Qingjiang town [清江镇人], Qingyuan county [清遠連縣], in Guangdong Province [廣東省].

Unfortunately Luk's [陸阿采] parents both died when he was young and he was raised by an uncle. The uncle treated him as a servant and after several years of frequently being mistreated, Luk [陸阿采] ran away at the age of twelve years. During his wanderings he met a monk by the name of Lei Baak Fu / Li Baihu [李白虎] who was a master [功夫大師] of the Southern Fa Kuen known as the Flower style [花拳]. The monk took pity on the young Luk [陸阿采] and accepted him as his disciple [武術弟子] teaching him at a small temple on a mountain. The monk taught Luk Ah-Choi [陸阿采] his style of Fa Kuen Kung Fu (Flower style / Hua Quan [花拳]) for seven years, after which, the old monk advised Luk Ah-Choi [陸阿采] to continue his studies under the renowned Siu Lum / Shaolin master [少林功夫大師], Gee Seen Sim See [至善禪師]. [64] [70] [101] [102] [103] [107] [108] [112]

All sources agree that Luk Ah-Choi [陸阿采] trained under Gee Seen Sim See [至善禪師] but there are two versions of where this actually took place. Some state that this was at the Hoi Tong Temple [海幢寺] (also known as the Honam Temple [河南寺]) on Honam Island [河南島] located across the Pearl River [珠江] from Canton [廣州], while others state that it was at the Putian Siu Lum / Shaolin Temple [莆田少林寺].

According to Wing Lam's Hung Gar history [64], during his search for Gee Seen [至善禪師], he came across Tong Chin Goon [童千斤] (of the Siu Lum / Shaolin Ten Best [少林十傑]) taught by Gee Seen [至善禪師], who then introduced him to Lei Choi-Ping [李翠屏] (another one of the Siu Lum / Shaolin Ten Best [少林十傑] in Wing Lam's list). Lei Choi-Ping [李翠屏] then wrote a letter of introduction for Luk Ah-Choi [陸阿采], and when Gee Seen [至善禪師] accepted her request, she showed Luk Ah-Choi [陸阿采] where to find him. Lei Choi-Ping [李翠屏] introduced Luk [陸阿采], and although Gee Seen [至善禪師] was in his later years, he accepted Luk Ah-Choi [陸阿采] as his disciple [武術弟子] and taught him the Tiger [虎] style now known as Hung Kuen [洪拳].

The other version states that Gee Seen [至善禪師] was on a trip to Canton [廣州] and in hiding at the Buddhist monastery [佛寺] in Guangzhou [廣州] called the Hoi Tong Temple [海幢寺] (Honam Temple [河南寺]). It was here that Luk Ah-Choi [陸阿采] studied under him learning his style which included routines [套路] such as the Taming the Tiger Fist [工字伏虎拳] [105] and the Five Animals Set / Ng Ying Kuen [五形拳]. Many sources then state that Gee Seen [至善禪師] advised Luk Ah-Choi [陸阿采] to go to Hung Hei-Kwun's [洪熙官] school [武術學校] to continue his education and help him expand the school and its teachings. [64] (A possible reason for this could have been due to Gee Seen's [至善禪師] advanced age and realising that his younger student Hung Hei-Kwun [洪熙官] could push him more, and so progress Luk Ah-Choi [陸阿采] further.)

Other sources, including Yee Chi Wai (Frank Yee), state that Gee Seen [至善禪師] was at the Putian Siu Lum / Shaolin Temple [莆田少林寺] and that Luk Ah-Choi [陸阿采] travelled there to train under him. [101] [102] [107] [108] All sources state that Luk [陸阿采] studied under Gee Seen [至善禪師] for several years. Sources that state Luk [陸阿采] trained at Siu Lum / Shaolin then differ on how he returned to Canton [廣州]. Some claim that he escaped the destruction of the Putian temple [莆田寺] and fled south to Canton [廣州], while others state that he was advised by Gee Seen [至善禪師] to continue his education under Hung Hei-Kwun [洪熙官] at his school [武術學校] in Fa City (Fat Shan / Foshan [佛山]). *(If he trained at Siu Lum / Shaolin I believe it is more likely that he travelled south to train under Hung Hei-Kwun [洪熙官] before the attack on the Putian Siu Lum / Shaolin Temple [莆田少林寺].)*

Possibly around 1813, Luk Ah-Choi [陸阿采] went to train under Hung Hei-Kwun [洪熙官] at his school [武術學校] in Fa City (now called Fat Shan / Foshan [佛山]). It is not recorded whether the two men had met before this or not. What is known is that Hung Hei-Kwun [洪熙官] agreed to teach Luk Ah-Choi [陸阿采] as his Sifu [師父], Gee Seen [至善禪師], had requested. (Wing Lam states Hung Hei-Kwun's [洪熙官] school was called the Lok-Sin-San Fong School [樂善山房學校] [64], while some other sources state it was known as the Hung School). Luk Ah-Choi [陸阿采] combined the teachings of both Gee Seen [至善禪師] and Hung Hei-Kwun [洪熙官] so as to refine his own skills. While studying under Hung Hei-Kwun [洪熙官], Luk Ah-Choi [陸阿采] would also teach other students at the school [武術學校].

It is known that Wong Tai [黃泰] studied under both of these masters [功夫大師], so it is reasonable to assume that this was possibly at the school [武術學校] in Fat Shan / Foshan [佛山]. Sometime later, Luk Ah-Choi [陸阿采] decided to expand the style of Hung Kuen [洪拳], by moving to Canton [廣州] to set up his own school [武術學校]. It is stated that Hung Hei-Kwun [洪熙官] asked Luk Ah Choi [陸阿采] to return to Canton [廣州] to spread the Hung Kuen [洪拳] style in the provincial capital city [省會城市]. One source states that this was after six years of studying under Hung Hei-Kwun [洪熙官]. [103] [104]

Wong Tai [黃泰] was born around 1782 [102a] [102b] [105] and in turn would later teach his son, Wong Kei-Ying [黃麒英], martial arts [武術]. They would work together demonstrating feats of Kung Fu [功夫] and acrobatics / Jop Kai [雜技], during street performances [武術表演], trying to earn a living. Many years later, in the early 1820s, Luk Ah-Choi [陸阿采] spotted the Wongs [黃] performing [武術表演] in the street outside the residence of the general of Guangdong [廣東將軍府]. Luk Ah-Choi [陸阿采] noticed the potential of the young Wong Kei-Ying [黃麒英] and convinced his father to let him train the young man as his disciple [武術弟子]. Luk Ah-Choi [陸阿采] taught the young Wong [黃麒英] for ten years, sometime into the 1830s. It is stated that Luk [陸阿采] taught Wong Kei-Ying [黃麒英] all the aspects of Kung Fu [少林功夫] he had learnt including the Lion Dance [舞獅]. It is recorded that Luk Ah-Choi [陸阿采] studied traditional Chinese medicine [中醫]. It is not stated if he taught this to Wong Kei-Ying [黃麒英] or if Wong had already learnt this from his father, Wong Tai [黃泰]. Another possibility is that they both had a passion for medicine [中醫] and shared their experience and knowledge. [105] [125]

During the 1820s, two of Luk Ah Choi's [陸阿采] other more notable students included Leung Kwan / Liang Kun [梁坤] (known by his nickname of Tit Kiu Saam / Tie Qiao San [鐵橋三]) and Wong Ching-Ho / Huang Chengke [黃澄可]. [106] These three students would later be chosen as members of the Ten Tigers of Canton / Kwong Tung Sap Fu [廣東十虎]. It is not stated if this was before he taught Wong Kei Ying [黃麒英] or if it was at the same time. I can only assume that because these three all trained under Luk Ah Choi [陸阿采] in the same school [武術學校], (even if not at the same time), they would all know each other. Having the same teacher / Sifu [功夫老師] would bring a mutual respect and etiquette which possibly would have given them the opportunity to exchange ideas and practices from time to time. Another notable student at this school [武術學校] was Hung Hei-Kwun's [洪熙官] son, Hung Man Ting / Hong Wending [洪文定].

After completing Wong Kei-Ying's [黃麒英] training at this school [武術學校], Luk [陸阿采] decided to live a peaceful life concentrating more on the study of Chinese medicine [中醫]. He did not teach publicly for several years, and lived a quiet life at his home known as Leshan Lodge / Lok Seen Siu Oak [樂山小屋]. During these later years, Wong Kei-Ying [黃麒英] sought out Luk [陸阿采] who was also renowned as a very skilled practitioner of pole / Gwun [棍] techniques. Wong [黃麒英] had been challenged to a duel [決鬥] using the pole / Gwun [棍] by a rival master [功夫大師] and he requested Luk [陸阿采] to assist him in improving his pole / Gwun [棍] skills. It is stated that because Luk Ah-Choi [陸阿采] was old and ill, he was confined to a bed. He was therefore unable to use a real pole / Gwun [棍], but instead used a pair of chopsticks [筷子] to demonstrate the pole / Gwun [棍] techniques, that Wong Kei-Ying [黃麒英] should learn to counter this rival master [功夫大師]. Propped up by several pillows, Luk [陸阿采] held a chopstick [筷子] in each hand and demonstrated various techniques as he explained the applications. Wong would then imitate these techniques and movements with a pole / Gwun [棍], ensuring he perfected them just as his Sifu [師父] Luk [陸阿采] had shown them. [64] [104] [106b]

Several sources state that Luk Ah-Choi [陸阿采] also taught Wong Kei-Ying's [黃麒英] son, Wong Fei-Hung [黃飛鴻]. It is understood that Luk Ah-Choi [陸阿采] and Wong Fei-Hung's [黃飛鴻] grandfather, Wong Tai [黃泰], were of a similar age, and so he was possibly too old and ill in the 1850s to have taught him for long, if this actually took place. [124]

Luk Ah-Choi [陸阿采] continued to study and practice Chinese medicine [中醫] until he passed away at the age of 68 years around the late 1840s to 1850 at his home of Leshan Lodge / Lok Seen Siu Oak [樂山小屋]. [107] [108] It is stated that Wong Tai [黃泰] and Luk Ah-Choi [陸阿采] were of a similar age but that Luk [陸阿采] was the senior. It is also stated that Wong Tai [黃泰] was born around 1782 [102a] [102b] and so from this I have made the assumption that Luk Ah-Choi [陸阿采] was born sometime around the late 1770s to early 1780s, and therefore must have passed away around the late 1840s to 1850. In the book entitled, "The Ten Tigers of Kwangtung-Trouble at the Sai Shaan Monastery [十虎大鬧西山寺]", it states that Luk Ah-Choi [陸阿采] had a son who was called Kwok Leung [陸國樑]. This book tells the story of the Ten Tigers of Guangdong / Kwong Tung Sap Fu [廣東十虎] accompanying him for his father's funeral. [122] [122a] [122b]

Luk Ah-Choi [陸阿采] is regarded as an important figure in the heritage of Hung Kuen [洪拳], and through his teachings we have the lineage of Wong Tai [黃泰], his son Wong Kei-Ying [黃麒英] and then his son, Wong Fei-Hung [黃飛鴻]. His important contribution, like Hung Hei-Kwun [洪熙官], was keeping the style alive during a very dangerous and perilous period, where a person was beheaded if found practicing or teaching Shaolin Kung Fu [功夫] (martial arts [武術]). [108a]

Tibetan Monk Sing Lung [聖龍]
(Venerable Monk Sing Lung, meaning Sage Dragon [聖龍], (or sometimes Star Dragon [星龍]) was also known as "Golden Hook" Leih Wu-Ji / Jin gou Li huzi [金鈎李胡子])

Approximately late 1700s to mid 1800s

The Manchurians' [滿族] religion was that of Tibetan Buddhism [藏傳佛教] and so after taking over China in 1644, they brought Tibetan monks [藏傳僧] to China to settle. Many of these monks were sent by the Ch'ing / Qing [清朝] authorities to various Buddhist / Chan / Zen / monasteries [禪寺] around the country. Tibetan monks [藏傳僧] were known as Lamas [喇嘛] and were renowned not only for their fighting abilities and being good teachers [功夫老師], but also for their medical knowledge. The Manchurians [滿族] therefore encouraged the spread and settlement of these Lamas [喇嘛] across China in a hope that they would spread their influence around the country.

Sometime around the late 1700s to early 1800s, a Tibetan monk [藏傳僧] called Sing Lung [聖龍] travelled into China from Tibet. It is stated that he first spent some time at O-Mei Shan / Emei [峨眉山] (translates to Great White Mountain) in Szechuan Province (now called Sichuan Province [四川省]) where he wanted to spread his Lion's Roar [獅子吼] Kung Fu and also to expand his own knowledge of martial arts [武術]. It is also rumoured that the Ch'ing / Qing [清朝] government had a political purpose in using Tibetan monks [藏傳僧], but Sing Lung [聖龍] was more interested in spreading his style of Lion's Roar [獅子吼] and Buddhism [佛教], than the hidden political agenda the Manchurians [滿族] had desired. (Sing Lung [聖龍] is reputed to have been the eleventh generation inheritor of the Lion's Roar [獅子吼] system. He was also known by other names, including Rising Virtue / Hing Duk [興德] and by the Chinese name Gam Ngau "Golden Hook" Leih Wu-Ji (Li Hu Ji) [金鈎李胡子]. [86] [87] [89]

112

After a period of time he then travelled further east until he reached the Pearl River / Zhu Jiang [珠江]. A folktale states that at the river he was challenged by the pirate, Cheung Po-Jai (more commonly spelt as, Cheung Po Tsai / Zhang Baozai [張保仔]) who had made his living robbing Ch'ing / Qing [清朝] officials. Sing Lung [聖龍] accepted the challenge and after beating the pirate, accepted him as a student. It was during this period tutoring Cheung Po-Jai [張保仔], that Sing Lung [聖龍] also developed an anti-Ch'ing / anti-Qing [反清清朝] attitude. In 1810, Cheung Po-Jai [張保仔] surrendered to the Ch'ing / Qing [清朝] authorities. It is stated that he struck a deal in order to keep the money he had stolen, by helping the Ch'ing / Qing [清朝] authorities to rid the region of the other pirates [海盜]. He was awarded the rank of captain in the Ch'ing / Qing [清朝] Imperial navy and spent the following years defeating other pirates [海盜]. This betrayal by his student upset Sing Lung [聖龍] who decided to retire to the "Blessed Cloud Monastery" / Hing Wen Chi / Qing yun Si [慶雲寺] on "Ding Wu" Mountain [鼎湖山]. [90] [93] [93a] [93b]

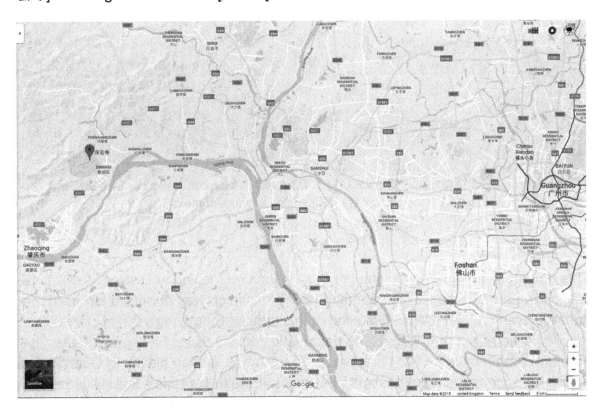

Therefore sometime after 1810, Sing Lung [聖龍] went to the "Blessed Cloud Monastery" [慶雲寺], also known as the ChingYun Jih (*called Qingyun Temple in Mandarin [鼎湖山慶雲寺]*) near the "Ding Wu" Mountain [鼎湖山]. This temple was built in 1633 and was originally called the Lotus Temple [蓮花寺] before later being extended and renamed.
[89a] [89b] [90]

(Many sources state that the Tibetan monk called Sing Lung [聖龍] settled at this temple in 1865. I believe that this date is too late and that it was possibly anytime from 1815 to

the late 1830s. This would then make more sense for him to have taught Wong Yan-Lam [王隱林], and tie in with other known events and dates, such as the incident with the pirate Cheung Po-Jai / Cheung Po Tsai / Zhang Baozai [張保仔] in 1810. Sources also state that the Ten Tigers of Guangdong [廣東十虎] were chosen sometime around the mid to late 1850s and therefore this also contradicts the 1865 date.)

Blessed Cloud Monastery [慶雲寺] on Dinghu Mountain [鼎湖山].

This mountain (now called Dinghu [鼎湖山]) is located in Dinghu District [鼎湖區], 18 km to the east of Shiu Hing / Zhaoqing [肇慶] [94], which was about 80 km from the centre of Canton [廣州]. While teaching at this temple, Sing Lung's [聖龍] Lion's Roar [獅子吼] style of Kung Fu [功夫] also became known as Lama Pai [喇嘛派], after the Tibetan Lama monks [藏傳僧] that practiced this style. During his life in Guangdong [廣東], he accepted several students but most of these kept their teachings behind closed doors. His two students that are renowned for spreading his style are Wong Yan-Lam [王隱林] and Wong Lam-Hoi [黃林開]. It is understood that he taught both of them during the last ten years of his life. My assumption is that Sing Lung [聖龍] taught Wong Yan-Lam [王隱林] and Wong Lam-Hoi [黃林開] sometime possibly from the mid to late 1830s. This would mean that he passed away sometime around the mid to late 1840s.

Before he accepted Wong Yan-Lam [王隱林] and Wong Lam-Hoi, Sing Lung [聖龍] also taught another one of the famed Ten Tigers [廣東十虎]. This was Leung Kwan /

Liang Kun [梁坤], who is better known today by his nickname of, Iron Bridge Three / Tit kiu Saam / Tie Qiao San [鐵橋三]. [86] [89] Several sources state that Leung Kwan / Liang Kun [梁坤] studied under a master [功夫大師] called Lee Hu Si / Li Huzi [李鬍子] which translates to mean Bearded Li and who was also known by the nickname of Golden Hook / / Kam Au Lee Wu Che / Jin Gou Li Huzi [金鈎李鬍子]. These are other aliases that Sing Lung [聖龍] was also known by. [150] [154] [154a] One source asserts that this was when Leung Kwan / Liang Kun [梁坤] was a young boy and that his tuition lasted for a "long time". After this training, Leung Kwan / Liang Kun [梁坤] went in search of more knowledge and skills eventually finding the Siu Lum / Shaolin monk [少林僧] called Gwok Yan / Jue yin [覺因]. [66] If this account is correct, then my understanding would put this training sometime around the the early 1820s.

Southern Shaolin Legends, Fact or Fiction

Much of what we know about the Southern Siu Lum / Shaolin Temple [南少林寺] comes from Southern Chinese folk stories, which may have been embellished as they have been passed down through the generations. I personally believe that these stories are based on true events, which have possibly been exaggerated and mixed up over the years, to make them more appealing and interesting. Many official documents were either altered or destroyed, as previously stated in the Preface of this book. I have therefore included these legends so that the reader can make their own assumptions as to what may be fact or fiction.

Fong Tak [方德] was originally from Pi-ching-fu [平清府] in Kao-yao prefecture, Kwangtung Province / Guangdong Province [廣東省]. He had established the Wan-ch'ang Silk House [宏昌絲綢店], and over the years, the business had flourished. One day, a heavy thunderstorm came across the city, and so Fong Tak [方德] decided to finish early. As he was closing up his silk shop, he saw an old man carrying two large baskets of salt up the street. Fong Tak [方德] felt sorry for the old man, who was wet through due to the heavy rain, so he invited him into his shop to take shelter. This old man was called Miu Hin [苗顯], who had once been known as the unshaved lay disciple [俗家弟子] [111] [111a], one of the legendary Shaolin Five Elders / Sui Lum Ng Cho [少林五祖]. After the death of his wife, he had fallen on hard times and had been forced to become a salt peddler to get by. These hard times had affected Miu Hin's [苗顯] health, which was worsened after being caught out in the thunderstorm. Fong Tak [方德] noticed Miu Hin's [苗顯] poor condition and after some persuasion convinced him to spend the night so that he could recover.

The two men quickly became friends and as repayment, Miu Hin [苗顯] offered to teach Fong Tak's [方德] two sons, Fong How Yuk [方孝玉] and Fong Mei Yuk [方美玉] martial arts [武術]. Fong Tak [方德] agreed to this, realising that his sons would benefit by becoming fitter and stronger, as well as gaining the ability to be able to defend themselves. Miu Hin [苗顯] had a daughter who was called Miu Tsui Fa [苗翠花], whom he had educated in the various skills and methods of Kung Fu [功夫]. Now that she was of age, Miu Hin [苗顯] suggested that she would make Fong Tak [方德] a good wife. Fong Tak [方德] agreed to this proposal and shortly after, they were married. Unfortunately, less than two years later, Miu Hin [苗顯] became very ill and died. Several months after the funeral, Miu Tsui Fa [苗翠花] and Fong Tak [方德] had a son whom they called Fong Sai Yuk [方世玉].

From a very young age, Miu Tsui Fa [苗翠花] would regularly bathe Fong Sai Yuk [方世玉] in a herbal medicine and as he grew older, applied various methods to condition his body. As Fong Sai Yuk [方世玉] became stronger and older, his mother continued to teach him the various skills and techniques of martial arts [武術]. Although the young Fong Sai Yuk [方世玉] was now an accomplished martial artist [武術家], he had a strong respect for justice and integrity, for which he was always fighting and getting into trouble for. When Fong Sai Yuk [方世玉] was only fourteen years old he got into a challenge match on the Lei tai [擂臺].

Lei Hung [雷洪] was more commonly known by his nickname of Lei the Tiger [雷老虎]. He was a big, powerful martial artist [武術家] from northern China. His wife was called Lee Siu Wan [李小環]. Her father, called Lee Pa Shan [李巴山], was regarded as being one of the best martial artists [武術家] in northern China. He had taught his daughter, Lee Siu Wan [李小環] and also her husband, Lei Hung [雷洪] (Lei the Tiger [雷老虎]). Lee Pa Shan's [李巴山] family had been renowned martial artists [武術家] for several generations.

Lei the Tiger [雷老虎] had come to this area due to an invitation from a local Ch'ing / Qing [清朝] official, to set up a martial arts school [武術學校] at his yamen [衙門]. As he had travelled south, he had defeated many challengers already. He had erected a Lei tai [擂臺] after he had been given permission by the local magistrate. On the Lei tai [擂臺] was a large banner that read, "A single punch to knock down all the people of Kwantung Province. One kick to crush the people of Soochow [蘇州] and Hangchow [杭州]." These words had infuriated many local martial artists [武術家] who had taken up this challenge. Unfortunately, they had all been defeated, being either seriously injured or killed. All the names of these defeated were listed on a plaque near the Lei tai [擂臺]. Due to Lei the Tiger's [雷老虎] success, he had become very arrogant believing that the local martial artists [武術家] were inferior to himself.

There was a general feeling of resentment and hatred towards Lei [雷老虎] from the local population because of his arrogant attitude and his boastful comments about how weak and useless the people were in this region. Added to this, was the ruthless way he had dealt with the local challengers and the derogatory signs displayed from the Lei tai [擂臺]. Due to this banner, many people believed that he was in league with the local Ch'ing / Qing [清朝] authorities to incite and flush out rebels or any persons that had any anti-Ch'ing / anti-Qing [反清清朝] sympathies.

When Fong Sai Yuk [方世玉] heard about Lei the Tiger [雷老虎] and his banner, he was so angered that he went to the Lei tai [擂臺] to challenge him. Lei [雷老虎], seeing a young, small boy, at first laughed and mocked the fourteen year old, but Fong Sai Yuk [方世玉] was determined and stood his ground. As Lei the Tiger [雷老虎] tried to push the young lad away, there was a quick exchange of techniques. Lei [雷老虎] then realised that Fong Sai Yuk [方世玉] was no ordinary boy but had some martial arts skills. He therefore decided to quickly defeat this young boy, to avoid being embarrassed in front of the large crowd of spectators. Lei [雷老虎] attacked again, but after several more exchanges, was shocked that Fong Sai Yuk [方世玉] was able to skilfully counter his techniques. Lei the Tiger [雷老虎] became enraged and ferociously attacked, again and again, in an effort to overwhelm his opponent. While continually attacking, Lei [雷老虎] had neglected his own defence, which Fong Sai Yuk [方世玉] took advantage of and countered with his own attacks. The fatal technique came from a kick which caught Lei the Tiger [雷老虎] in the chest. Blood poured from his body as Lei [雷老虎] staggered backwards before falling down and dying on the Lei tai [擂臺] platform.

During the fight, Fong Sai Yuk [方世玉] had also been struck in the chest which made him cough up some blood. This blow should have killed the young Fong Sai Yuk [方世玉] but before the duel [決鬥], he had taken certain precautions. Under his top, he had concealed a metal plate which protected him against Lei's [雷老虎] strikes, and he had also worn shoes which had soles of iron. These had cut and caused the fatal injuries to Lei the Tiger [雷老虎]. With Fong Sai Yuk's [方世玉] victory, the crowd cheered and called him the "Young Hero [少年英雄]". While many of the locals were celebrating the Young Hero's triumph, Lei the Tiger's [雷老虎] students carried their Sifu's body back to his wife, Lee Siu Wan [李小環]. On seeing her husband's blood soaked body, Lee Siu Wan [李小環] realised straight away that these injuries had not been caused by normal unarmed fighting. When she washed and examined the body closer, she noticed the cuts and boot marks. As a skilled martial artist [武術家] herself, she soon realised how these fatal injuries had been caused.

Lee Siu Wan [李小環] wanted revenge for the death of her husband and so challenged Fong Sai Yuk [方世玉]. Although she was a very skilled fighter, she had placed poisoned spikes in her shoes, and during the match managed to kick Fong Sai Yuk [方世玉] who collapsed from this poison. Luckily, Miu Tsui Fa [苗翠花] came to her son's aid and was able to treat him with herbal medicines. Once her son started to recover, Miu Tsui Fa [苗翠花] wrote a letter to Lee Siu Wan [李小環] demanding a duel [決鬥]. Lee Siu Wan [李小環] accepted and the two women met on the Lei tai [擂臺]. Lee Siu Wan [李小環] told Miu Tsui Fa [苗翠花] that Fong Sai Yuk [方世玉] had got what he deserved because he had broken the rules regarding the non use of weapons, which had been agreed by all beforehand. The two women then fought the duel [決鬥]. In one account Miu Tsui Fa [苗翠花] eventually wins [112a] and in the other, the contest continues over three days without a winner. [61d]

This feud then continues as Lee Siu Wan's [李小環] father, Lee Pa Shan [李巴山], gets involved. Due to his great renown as being one of the best Kung Fu [功夫] fighters in northern China, Miu Tsui Fa [苗翠花] seeks the help of the old Buddhist nun [尼姑], Wu Mei Da Shi / Ng Mui Daai Si [五梅大師], the eldest of the legendary Shaolin Five Elders / Sui Lum Ng Cho [少林五祖]. The old Wu Mei [五梅] intervenes in a bid to stop any more feuding, but unfortunately, no words of wisdom, apologies or compensation, would dissuade Lee Pa Shan [李巴山] from seeking his revenge. Lee Pa Shan [李巴山] became angry with the old nun [尼姑] for interfering, and so challenged her. Although he knew Wu Mei [五梅] was once a great master, he now only saw an old, feeble woman in front of him. Wu Mei [五梅] realised that there was no other way and so reluctantly agreed. Initially this duel [決鬥] started on the Lei tai [擂臺], but Lee Pa Shan [李巴山] was surprised that the old nun [尼姑] was still as fast and skilful as her reputation implied, as she easily blocked and countered his attacks.

Lee Pa Shan [李巴山] realised that he had underestimated the old nun [尼姑] and so came up with an idea of how to gain victory. In China there is a well known saying among Kung Fu [功夫] practitioners, that states, "Southern fists and Northern kicks [南拳北腿]". He requested that they stop this contest, but continue on the Plum Flower Posts / Mui Fa Jong [梅花樁]. Wu Mei [五梅] understood Lee's [李巴山] reasoning, but just smiled and agreed to this new contest. *(For duelling [決鬥] purposes, wooden spikes are placed between the posts so that if a person falls they will be impaled seriously, injuring or killing them.)* While the Plum Flower Posts / Mui Fa Jong [梅花樁] were being constructed, the old nun [尼姑] passed the time by instructing Fong Sai Yuk [方世玉] in various highly skilled methods and techniques of Kung Fu [功夫].

Three days later, the Plum Flower Posts / Mui Fa Jong [梅花樁] arena was ready. Once again, Wu Mei [五梅] tried to talk with Lee Pa Shan [李巴山], in a bid to dissuade him from continuing with this deadly contest and his desire for revenge. Unfortunately, Lee [李巴山] believed that the old nun [尼姑] was worried about duelling [決鬥] on the Plum Flower Posts / Mui Fa Jong [梅花樁] and so he mocked her. As Lee Pa Shan [李巴山] was about to climb onto the posts, he whispered into his daughter's ear that if he looked in trouble, she was to throw him a pair of iron rods [鐵棒]. Luckily, Wu Mei [五梅] noticed Lee [李巴山] whisper something to his daughter, so she informed Miu Tsui Fa [苗翠花] and Fong Sai Yuk [方世玉] to watch out for any foul play.

Lee Pa Shan [李巴山] and Wu Mei [五梅] started to duel [決鬥], with both displaying exceptional levels of skill. After many exchanges, Wu Mei [五梅] felt that she had given Lee Pa Shan [李巴山] several chances to stop this contest and so she decided that she should not hold back any longer. She therefore started to attack with all her strength. Lee Pa Shan [李巴山] began to weaken under Wu Mei's [五梅] more powerful attacks and so beckoned to his daughter, Lee Siu Wan [李小環] to pass him the iron rods [鐵棒]. When Fong Sai Yuk [方世玉] saw Lee Siu Wan [李小環] lift the iron rods [鐵棒], he intervened with his own pair of iron rulers [鐵尺], and so she was unable to pass them to her father. Lee Pa Shan [李巴山] became anxious. This affected his concentration, and as he retreated, his stances became unbalanced. Wu Mei [五梅] took advantage of the situation, and delivered a strong kick which sent Lee Pa Shan [李巴山] tumbling from the posts [梅花椿], plunging onto the stakes below. Lee Pa Shan [李巴山] let out a blood curdling scream as he died. Lee Siu Wan [李小環] now wanted to fight the old nun [尼姑] to avenge her father. Wu Mei [五梅] had no weapon, and so Miu Tsui Fa [苗翠花] had to hold her off with a staff while Wu Mei [五梅] grabbed her Buddhist staff [佛家棍].

Wu Mei [五梅] then implored Lee Siu Wan [李小環] to stop all the bloodshed, as enough people had already died, but she would not be reasoned with and attacked the old nun [尼姑]. Wu Mei [五梅] parried each attack as she continually appealed to Lee Siu Wan [李小環] to stop. Unfortunately, Lee Siu Wan [李小環] would not stop attacking, no matter what Wu Mei [五梅] said, so in the end the old nun [尼姑] had no choice and was forced to strike her. The staff caught Lee Siu Wan [李小環] on the head, which turned out to be a fatal blow, and she dropped down dead. When all of Lei the Tiger's [雷老虎] students saw their Sifu's wife die, they feared for they own lives and started to run away. Wu Mei [五梅] called out to them that they had no need to run, as had they not witnessed her on numerous occasions trying to stop all this violence. She then requested that the students take away their teachers' [功夫老師] bodies and bury them in a manner befitting them.

After this incident, the old Buddhist nun [尼姑], Wu Mei Da Shi / Ng Mui Daai Si [五梅大師], returned to her peaceful life back at her temple, and Fong Tak [方德] and his family returned to their ancestral village of Pi-ching-fu [平清府]. Sometime later, Miu Tsui Fa [苗翠花] received word that the Siu Lum / Shaolin abbot [少林方丈], Gee Seen Sim See [至善禪師], was in Canton [廣州]. She therefore suggested to her husband, Fong Tak [方德] that their three sons should study martial arts [武術] under Gee Seen [至善禪師]. Fong Tak [方德] agreed to his wife's proposal and so Fong How Yuk [方孝玉], Fong Mei Yuk [方美玉] and Fong Sai Yuk [方世玉] made ready for the journey to the provincial capital city [省會城市] of Canton [廣州] while Miu Tsui Fa [苗翠花] wrote a letter of introduction for her sons to give to Gee Seen [至善禪師].

Fong How Yuk [方孝玉], Fong Mei Yuk [方美玉] and Fong Sai Yuk [方世玉] went to the Kwong Hau Temple / Guangxiao Si [光孝寺], where their mother, Miu Tsui Fa [苗翠花], had been told Gee Seen [至善禪師] was staying. The abbot of the Kwong Hau Temple / Guangxiao Si [光孝寺] informed them that Gee Seen [至善禪師] was now at the West Zen Temple / Sai Sim Ji / Xi Chan Si [西禪寺] which was located in the West Gate / Sai Kwan / Xiguan [西關] part of the city. They made their way to this area, but as they were passing through the Ti-liu-p'u [大樓排], they saw a young man in his early twenties being attacked by a gang of men. This young man was just trying to protect his head while he was being beaten, and so it was obvious that he had no idea of how to fight. The three brothers intervened and fought off the gang of attackers. Fong Sai Yuk [方世玉] was shocked that there were so many people watching and none had tried to intervene. He shouted this at all the spectators, stating that they should be ashamed of themselves. He was told that the gang belonged to the Chin-lun t'ang Weavers Guild [錦綸堂織工會] who had been trained in martial arts [武術]. If they had interfered, they would have been beaten as well. The brothers picked up this young man and carried him to the West Zen Temple / Sai Sim Ji / Xi Chan Si [西禪寺].

At the temple, they were greeted by one of the monks who took them to see Gee Seen [至善禪師]. They showed their respect by bowing to Gee Seen [至善禪師] before handing him the letter of introduction. As the Siu Lum / Shaolin abbot [少林方丈] read the letter, he smiled and asked about their parents. Fong Sai Yuk [方世玉] helped the young man into a chair as his brothers told Gee Seen [至善禪師] about their parents, and then about Fong Sai Yuk's [方世玉] match with Lei the Tiger [雷老虎], which amused the abbot. After this, Gee Seen [至善禪師] then enquired who the young man was, that they had brought with them. They told him that they did not know his name and about the incident in which they found him being beaten by the gang of men from the Weavers Guild [錦綸堂織工會]. They had brought him to the temple so that he could be cared for. Gee Seen [至善禪師] praised the three brothers for their act of kindness as he instructed some monks nearby to attend to the injured man. He then turned to the brothers and informed them that he would be proud to accept them as his students. In turn, Fong How Yuk [方孝玉], Fong Mei Yuk [方美玉] and Fong Sai Yuk [方世玉] served a cup of tea to Gee Seen [至善禪師] and then took an oath, before the Siu Lum / Shaolin abbot [少林方丈] formally accepted them as his students.

After this ceremony, Gee Seen [至善禪師] went with the three brothers to see the young man they had brought with them. He inquired who he was and why he had been attacked by this gang. The young man told Gee Seen [至善禪師] that his name was Wu Wei Kin [胡惠乾], and that the Chin-lun t'ang Weavers Guild [錦綸堂織工會] had been causing trouble for many years. His father once had a grocery shop and the members of the Guild [錦綸堂織工會] had intimidated his and other businesses in the area extorting money. To avoid any violence, his father had sent him away to work. Wu Wei Kin [胡惠乾] had only returned home two months previously, to be informed by his mother that his father had died two years earlier. He had been so badly beaten by members of the Weavers Guild [錦綸堂織工會] that he died of his injuries. His mother had kept this from him, afraid that Wu Wei Kin [胡惠乾] would get involved and be injured too. Since the death of his father, his mother had been unable to run the shop on her own, and had sold it. Wu Wei Kin [胡惠乾] then informed Gee Seen [至善禪師] that he had only found out about all this a few days ago, but no one would tell him why his father had been beaten. Today he had gone to the Chin-lun t'ang Weavers Guild [錦綸堂織工會] to find out why they had killed his father, but they just pushed Wu Wei Kin [胡惠乾] out into the street and started to beat him. This was when the three men came to his assistance.

Fong Sai Yuk [方世玉] asked Wu Wei Kin [胡惠乾] why he had not gone to the local magistrate and informed him of this affair. He replied that the local magistrates were usually corrupt and accepted bribe money from the Chin-lun t'ang Weavers Guild [錦綸堂織工會]. Any matters brought to them about the Guild [錦綸堂織工會] they would excuse and turn away from. Fong Sai Yuk [方世玉] stated he should become strong so that he could fight this gang to avenge his father. Wu Wei Kin [胡惠乾] thanked everyone for their help and concern, before personally thanking Gee Seen [至善禪師] for attending to his injuries. He stated that unfortunately he was poor and had no money to pay for his treatment. Gee Seen [至善禪師] replied that as he was a man of the Lord Buddha [佛祖], it was his duty to help all people and not to seek worldly riches. Fong Sai Yuk [方世玉] then suggested to his teacher [功夫老師] that he also take on Wu Wei Kin [胡惠乾] as his student.

Gee Seen [至善禪師] stated that he would only teach a person if they wished to improve themselves by following the path of virtue, but, if their only desire was to learn Kung Fu [功夫] for revenge, then he could not consent to this. Wu Wei Kin [胡惠乾] asked if the abbot objected to him seeking revenge, to which Gee Seen [至善禪師] replied that his duty to his father could not be questioned, but it should not be his only purpose in life, for once he had become an accomplished student and achieved justice for his father; he must then devote himself to helping others seek justice. After this, Wu Wei Kin [胡惠乾] performed the ceremony taking the oath to Gee Seen [至善禪師] and he was then also formally accepted as his student.

At the West Zen Temple / Sai Sim Ji / Xi Chan Si [西禪寺], Gee Seen [至善禪師] had set up a gym which included a variety of tools and equipment to enhance his students martial arts [武術家] training. These included various types of wooden dummies, wooden horse, sand bags, throwing disk and the Siu Lum / Shaolin eighteen weapons. [卻言至善在西禪寺開設武場，擺列著埋樁木馬、沙袋飛陀及十八般兵器，件件齊備。] After accepting Fong How Yuk [方孝玉], Fong Mei Yuk [方美玉], Fong Sai Yuk [方世玉] and Wu Wei Kin [胡惠乾], Gee Seen [至善禪師] now had a total of nine students at the West Zen Temple / Sai Sim Ji / Xi Chan Si [西禪寺]. His other five students who had already begun their training, were Lee Kam Lun [李錦倫], Tse Ah Fok [謝亞福], Lee Ah Chun [李亞松], Hung Hei Kwun [洪熙官], and Tong Chin Kan [童千斤]. After six months of teaching, Gee Seen [至善禪師] gathered all his students together and told them that he needed to return to the Southern Siu Lum / Shaolin Temple [南少林寺] because he had been gone for over a year. As he was the abbot there, it was his duty to return to ensure all was well. He then asked them all if they would agree to return with him to this temple which was located in Fukien / Fujian province [福建省].

All the students were excited about going to this temple and willingly accepted Gee Seen's [至善禪師] request. Once this was agreed, they quickly packed their belongings and made the arrangements for this long journey. On the day they arrived at the Southern Siu Lum / Shaolin Temple [南少林寺] there was a great deal of ceremony. The following day, Gee Seen [至善禪師] resumed his students' training in their new home. This began with the rules of the temple and then their daily schedule which was constant every day of every week to ensure that students achieved proficiency in the quickest possible time.

Several years later, Wu Wei Kin [胡惠乾] approached Gee Seen [至善禪師] and asked his permission to return to Canton [廣州]. He stated that he would like to visit his father's grave and see his family. Once he had done this he wanted to obtain justice for his father by seeking revenge on the Weavers Guild [錦綸堂織工會]. Gee Seen [至善禪師] listened to his request and replied that Wu Wei Kin [胡惠乾] was a faithful son who was devoted to his family. Therefore his wish to return to his family was only appropriate and respectable. Nevertheless, when he had first come to the temple he had agreed to abide by the rules and regulations. Wu Wei Kin [胡惠乾] was saddened by his teacher's [功夫老師] words and replied that he had followed the abbot's teachings for several years, but this matter was a great burden on him that constantly played on his mind. Gee Seen [至善禪師] stated that although he sympathised with him, he had not completed his training and therefore could not be given permission to leave. As he had already dedicated a number of years to training here, one more year to complete this would make little difference.

Gee Seen [至善禪師] then stated that if he was to let Wu Wei Kin [胡惠乾] go now without him completing his training, he could possibly fail to avenge his father's death. He should also understand that because he was his student, he was also a representative of the school of Siu Lum / Shaolin [少林武術學校]. Therefore if he failed to accomplish his revenge, he would also shame Siu Lum's / Shaolin's [少林] reputation. Gee Seen [至善禪師] continued by telling Wu Wei Kin [胡惠乾] that he was not trying to discourage from his mission but just to postpone it a year so he could complete his full training. Many of the students at the temple had trained for at least ten years, but because he was a diligent, dedicated, and hard working student, he had progressed a lot faster than most. Wu Wei Kin [胡惠乾] was too eager to seek his revenge, which made him impetuous, and he continued to plead with the abbot. Gee Seen [至善禪師] had made his decision and he was adamant in his refusal to grant permission.

That night while Wu Wei Kin [胡惠乾] lay in bed, many thoughts ran through his head. His desire to seek revenge was so great that he was unable to think rationally and he started to plan his escape from the temple. The walls were strong and thick, the doors were locked and the windows were all barred. He started to feel like an inmate in a prison. Then he remembered the large sewerage pipe that poured out into the sewers below the temple walls. This pipe was made secure by a large iron grill which spanned its entrance and he realised that if he could force the grill away far enough, he would be able to slide underneath it. Wu Wei Kin [胡惠乾] decided that this was the action he should take the following night after he had made some preparations. At midnight the next evening he crept quietly through the courtyard and followed the drain pipes which ran into the large sewerage pipe. Using an iron staff [鐵棍], he forced it through the iron grill and eventually was able to prise an end loose enough for him to crawl though. Wu Wei Kin [胡惠乾] crawled through the pipe until it opened up outside the temple walls, and then continued down the mountain and made his way to the coast. He followed the coastline until he found a harbour where he was able to get a boat back to Canton [廣州]. [112a]

(At midnight, when all persons were in deep sleep, Wu Wei Kin took all his belongings and quietly escape through a drain pipe. He damaged the fencing and jumped across the temple boundary wall. He then made his way to the city of Quanzhou, where he took a boat back to Canton. [50b])

The morning after Wu Wei Kin [胡惠乾] had escaped, it was soon noticed that he was absent from his first lesson. Gee Seen [至善禪師] was informed straight away and he requested that the temple grounds be searched. During the search one of the monks noticed that the iron grill over the sewerage pipe had been tampered with. The monk informed the abbot and Gee Seen [至善禪師] realised that Wu Wei Kin [胡惠乾] had escaped to seek his revenge.

When Wu Wei Kin [胡惠乾] reached Canton [廣州] he went to the West Zen Temple / Sai Sim Ji / Xi Chan Si [西禪寺]. At this temple he was greeted by three of his Kung Fu [功夫] older brothers / Sihing's [師兄] from the Southern Siu Lum / Shaolin Temple [南少林寺]. These were the Siu Lum / Shaolin Monks [少林僧], Sam Dak / San De [三德], Hung Hei Kwun [洪熙官], and Tong Chin Kan [童千斤], who had all completed their training and graduated. They were all pleased to see Wu Wei Kin [胡惠乾] and believed that he too had completed his training and graduated. Wu Wei Kin [胡惠乾] went along with their assumption, and they all celebrated by eating and drinking into the night. During the festivities, they talked about their training at the Southern Siu Lum

/ Shaolin Temple [南少林寺], discussing the various different methods, principles and techniques. During these conversations, Wu Wei Kin [胡惠乾] told his brothers that he had also come to seek his revenge on the members of the Chin-lun t'ang Weavers Guild [錦綸堂織工會] who were responsible for killing his father.

The following day, Wu Wei Kin [胡惠乾] discussed his plans for revenge with his brothers at the West Zen Temple / Sai Sim Ji / Xi Chan Si [西禪寺]. He wanted it publicly proclaimed that he was challenging the Chin-lun t'ang Weavers Guild [錦綸堂織工會]. To emphasise this declaration, he ordered two large red lanterns to be made that had bold wording (Chinese calligraphy [書法]) painted on them, stating, "Wu Wei Kin [胡惠乾] of the West Zen Temple / Sai Sim Ji / Xi Chan Si [西禪寺] will challenge the Chin-lun t'ang Weavers Guild [錦綸堂織工會]." All the local lantern makers were too afraid to do this work as they feared retribution from the Chin-lun t'ang Weavers Guild [錦綸堂織工會], so Wu Wei Kin [胡惠乾] was forced to get the lanterns made outside the city. Once they were ready, he hung them up above the entrance to the West Zen Temple / Sai Sim Ji / Xi Chan Si [西禪寺] for all to see. The local people soon noticed these large lanterns and word of them quickly spread through the whole city.

News of this reached the Chin-lun t'ang Weavers Guild [錦綸堂織工會] and some of their members had also seen the lanterns for themselves. A meeting was quickly organised to decide how they should deal with this matter. They declared it an insult which could not be tolerated. Therefore they proposed to march to the West Zen Temple / Sai Sim Ji / Xi Chan Si [西禪寺] where they would first tear the lanterns down and burn them. They would then enter the temple to give Wu Wei Kin [胡惠乾] a good beating and also punish the monks for allowing this to occur at their temple. Wu Wei Kin [胡惠乾] had anticipated this type of reaction and with a long staff, was guarding the entrance to the West Zen Temple / Sai Sim Ji / Xi Chan Si [西禪寺], with several other students. As a large gang from the Weavers Guild [錦綸堂織工會] approached the temple, they noticed Wu Wei Kin [胡惠乾] standing at the entrance, and so stopped just short. They began shouting, jeering and waving their fists at him, but he just smiled back. After much cursing, they suddenly charged forward, waving their weapons as they ran.

Swiftly and gracefully, Wu Wei Kin [胡惠乾] defended himself with the long staff. As he retaliated with fierce counter strikes the blood of his attackers was sprayed everywhere. A ferocious battle ensued as Wu Wei Kin [胡惠乾] used his staff to cut through the horde of assailants. Some of them had styled themselves as Kung Fu masters [功夫大師], but Wu Wei Kin [胡惠乾] easily outfought them with his own abilities. As the fight continued, many of the Weavers members were left soaked in blood, maimed, and writhing on the floor in agony. The Weavers began to realize that they were defeated, as so many of their men had fallen. They stopped fighting and hastily collected their fallen members, as Wu Wei Kin [胡惠乾] laughed at them while they retreated. Once the Weavers had carried away their fallen members, they soon realised that thirteen were dead, with numerous others badly injured.

The following day the Chin-lun t'ang Weavers Guild [錦綸堂織工會] decided to deal with this incident in another way and so filed a petition of complaint to the magistrates of Nam Hoi / Nanhai [南海] county, which stated,

"The Chin-lun t'ang [錦綸堂織工會], comprising the guilds of both the east and west are represented by their administrator, Ch'en Te-shu [陳帶水], who on behalf of the membership, hereby files a petition reporting an act of violence and injustice. The incident involved the killing of thirteen of our members and the maiming and injuring of more than twenty others.

We are a peaceful group engaged in the weaving of silk. We wish only to abide by the lawful ways of society and want only tranquillity to reign in our community and in our land. We hate violence and are utterly opposed to rough or injurious physical action or might, which we consider brutal. We have never violated any ordinance or acted contrary to the legal code of government.

With your knowledge and authority, we beg you for the proper action so that we may again have peace restored to this area and men like us can return to our peaceable ways. We all bow to your authority."

The magistrate that dealt with this petition, was called, Chou Hung-pin [周洪炳], and he was astounded that one man had performed so many atrocities, on so many people, in such a controlled society. He therefore ordered the arrest of Wu Wei Kin [胡惠乾] straight away. After examining the bodies of the thirteen dead weavers, the magistrate noted that all the injuries were caused by a blunt instrument and there were no sharp cuts. As soon Wu Wei Kin [胡惠乾] had been arrested, he was brought before the magistrate, Chou Hung-pin [周洪炳], in the courtroom to be judged immediately. Wu Wei Kin [胡惠乾] was told to give his name and residence before being informed of the charges made against him. He was then asked to state his version of the incident that led to his arrest, which he willingly did. Chou Hung-pin [周洪炳] had heard many rumours of the troubles caused by the Weavers Guild [錦綸堂織工會] in the West Gate / Sai Kwan / Xiguan [西關] area of the city but there had never been any formal complaint or charges brought against them. He looked again at Wu Wei Kin [胡惠乾] and marvelled at how such a slim young man could possibly inflict so many injuries.

Once Wu Wei Kin [胡惠乾] had finished speaking, the magistrate stated that a crime had been committed, and after hearing his version of events, he was duty bound to investigate this matter further. He then asked Wu Wei Kin [胡惠乾] if he knew any persons who could testify on his behalf, to which Wu Wei Kin [胡惠乾] replied that the magistrate should talk to the storekeepers in the area of his father's old grocery shop. Chou Hung-pin [周洪炳] then stated that Wu Wei Kin [胡惠乾] would be held prisoner until he had completed his investigations.

A few days later, Chou Hung-pin [周洪炳] travelled to the area of Wu Wei Kin's [胡惠乾] father's old grocery shop disguised as a merchant. There, he talked to different storekeepers, and listened to the gossip of the local people. Because they thought he was a merchant from out of the area, they all talked to him freely and openly about how the Weavers Guild [錦綸堂織工會] had intimidated the local residents for many years, including being responsible for Wu Wei Kin's [胡惠乾] father's murder. Then they told him about the fight with Wu Wei Kin [胡惠乾] who was only armed with a staff, while the members of the Weavers Guild [錦綸堂織工會] had swords, knifes and various other weapons. Everyone that talked to him told him the same story, so he was satisfied that he had the true facts. On the magistrate's return, he ordered the guards to release Wu Wei Kin [胡惠乾] and posted a notice in the public square which stated,

"This special notice is posted by the magistrate of the prefecture of Nan-hai [南海].

As an administrator appointed to execute the governmental decrees and to administer justice, all cases before me have been accorded a strict and impartial judgement in order to abide with the will of Heaven and to keep a peaceful community. I have investigated the charges thoroughly and have found that this incident was retribution of a son seeking revenge for the death of his father. This I consider an act of filial piety and the accused person a dutiful son. I have found that there are many who harbour ill feelings against the Chin-lun t'ang [錦綸堂織工會] and accuse them of utmost cruelty and terrorism.

In view of the evidence gathered, I have released the person Wu Wei Kin [胡惠乾] and exonerated him of all charges. I hereby order that the members of the Chin-lun t'ang [錦綸堂織工會] also abide by peaceful ways from this time on and that they amend their ways and ever abide by the will of Heaven. They must walk the path of righteousness and are to forget the past and to correct what they have done. If there should be any further disturbances reported to me of the cruelty of the members of the Chin-lun t'ang [錦綸堂織工會], I will use all my power to punish them and to accord justice and peace in this community. No mercy will be accorded to offenders."

When the Chin-lun t'ang Weavers Guild [錦綸堂織工會] saw this official decree, they realised that there was nothing more they could do about the matter. They had lost face and had to content themselves with resuming their normal business matters. Many of the storekeepers and local citizens were happy with this outcome and celebrated. Unfortunately, Wu Wei Kin [胡惠乾] was not totally satisfied and still harboured yet more thoughts of revenge on the members of the Chin-lun t'ang Weavers Guild [錦綸堂織工會]. To this end, he concealed a pair of iron rulers [鐵尺] under his clothes, and whenever he met any members of the Weavers Guild [錦綸堂織工會] in the streets, he would start a fight. Soon many of these members had been injured and so the administrator, Ch'en Te-shu [陳帶水] of the Chin-lun t'ang Weavers Guild [錦綸堂織工會] called a meeting to discuss how to resolve this situation with Wu Wei Kin [胡惠乾]. All night the members discussed this matter but could not come up with a solution. They therefore agreed to meet the next evening. The following evening when many of the members had thought about this issue, several suggestions were put forward. One person proposed that they should hire another Kung Fu master [功夫大師] to challenge Wu Wei Kin [胡惠乾] to a duel [決鬥]. They then discussed who could possibly be good enough to kill Wu Wei Kin [胡惠乾] during this duel [決鬥].

One of the Guild [錦綸堂織工會] members called Pai An'fu [彭亞福] told them that he had heard of a Wudang style [武當拳] martial artist [武術家], called Niu Hua-chiao [牛化蛟], and he had recently opened up a Kung Fu school [武術學校] in the area of His-pao-t'ai [西炮臺]. (His-pao-t'ai [西炮臺] was located in the area of Shamian / Shameen Island [沙面島].) He then stated that he was nicknamed the Ox because he was so strong, and that he was a student of Fung Do-Duk / Feng Daode [馮道德] (one of the Shaolin Five Elders / Sui Lum Ng Cho [少林五祖]). It was stated that Fung Do-Duk / Feng Daode [馮道德] ranked all his students and Niu Hua-chiao [牛化蛟] the Ox was his third best. When the Guild [錦綸堂織工會] members had heard what Pai An'fu [彭亞福] said, they all agreed to invite Niu Hua-chiao [牛化蛟] the Ox to come to their assistance.

Several of Wu Wei Kin's [胡惠乾] friends at the West Zen Temple / Sai Sim Ji / Xi Chan Si [西禪寺] had heard the news of his recent fights and discussed the matter with him. He was asked to stop fighting and to follow the path of peace. Wu Wei Kin [胡惠乾] told his friends that although he had killed and hurt many of the Weavers Guild [錦綸堂織工會] members, he was still not entirely satisfied as they had not apologised for their actions. He stated that he would not be happy until they had publicly bowed before him, apologised and begged for mercy. His friends understood because he had harboured these feelings for many years, it was now difficult to let them go, but they stated that the Weavers Guild [錦綸堂織工會] had been publicly shamed by the official decree and he had had his revenge; this matter should now be closed, and that fighting in the street was the way of a ruffian and not a Siu Lum / Shaolin disciple [少林俗家弟子]. Wu Wei Kin [胡惠乾] listened to his friends and promised to change his ways.

Ch'en Te-shu [陳帶水], the administrator of the Chin-lun t'ang Weavers Guild [錦綸堂織工會], and Pai An'fu [彭亞福] travelled to His-pao-t'ai [西炮臺] to meet Niu Hua-chiao [牛化蛟] the Ox. Initially, the Ox was not interested in taking another man's life in a duel [決鬥], but he was eventually lured into accepting the deal with the vast offer of 3000 Taels [兩] [12cc] of silver. Ch'en Te-shu [陳帶水] and Pai An'fu [彭亞福] were pleased that they had secured the Ox's services and arranged for a sedan chair [花轎] to take him back to their meeting hall. The Ox arrived with all of his students bar two that he had commanded to stay behind to guard the Kung Fu school [武術學校]. A banquet was hosted by the Chin-lun t'ang Weavers Guild [錦綸堂織工會] to honour the Ox, during which he asked how the dispute had occurred with Wu Wei Kin [胡惠乾]. The Guild [錦綸堂織工會] members gave him a detailed account of all the events, and at the end, the Ox was was satisfied that he had a valid reason for the duel [決鬥]. He stated that he understood why Wu Wei Kin [胡惠乾] would seek revenge but after the matter had been resolved by the official decree, he should have been satisfied; to continue as he had done was not the act of a virtuous or honorable man.

The Ox stated that although he was willing to do their bidding, the duel [決鬥] must be conducted in an honourable manner so there could be no criticism afterwards. To this end the Weavers Guild [錦綸堂織工會] had a notice of this challenge posted in front of the West Zen Temple / Sai Sim Ji / Xi Chan Si [西禪寺], which stated,

"Be it known that the organisation of the Weavers' Guild, the Chin-lun t'ang [錦綸堂 織工會], and the person Wu Wei Kin [胡惠乾] are at odds and harbour ill feelings toward one another. We are of the opinion that our ill feelings have not been spurred without reason because the person in question has not only injured many of our members but also killed some of them. We are helpless against his terror; therefore, we have requested the presence of Master Niu Hua-chiao [牛化蛟] and we are honoured to him aiding us as our champion.

We decree that in three days time, at the I-lin temple [醫靈廟] grounds where there is an outdoor stage called the Shui-yueh t'ai [水月臺], we openly challenge our enemy in the full view of the public. Here will be held a duel [決鬥] which will not be hindered with any rules as to injuries or even death. It will be a fight to the death. We will allow Heaven to decide whether our cause is just and to decide who will win. This duel [決 鬥] will separate the strong from the weak. If he calls himself a man then he should come, else he should be laughed at as a woman. We, the members of Chin-lun t'ang, stand firmly on this resolution."

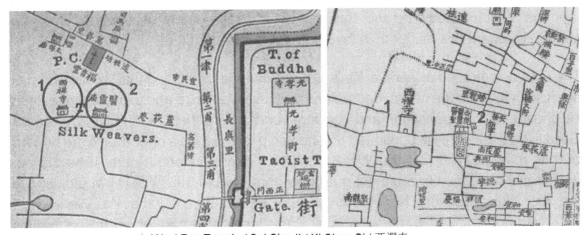

1. West Zen Temple / Sai Sim Ji / Xi Chan Si / 西禪寺

2. Medical Ling Temple / Yi Ling Miao / I lin Temple / 醫靈廟

These maps show how close these two temples were to each other.

When Wu Wei Kin [胡惠乾] saw this notice the following morning, he was so infuriated that after ripping it down, he barged into one of the weavers shops and smashed it up. The weavers raced to their meeting hall to get the Ox, who returned with them to

129

their shop, accompanied by his students. By the time they had arrived, Wu Wei Kin [胡惠乾] had gone back to the West Zen Temple / Sai Sim Ji / Xi Chan Si [西禪寺]. After this incident Wu Wei Kin's [胡惠乾] friends kept him at the temple to avoid any further trouble until the day of the challenge match. During this period, the Ox's students cleaned and decorated the Lei tai [擂臺] in preparation for the match.

On the day of the challenge match, Niu Hua-chiao [牛化蛟] the Ox arrived early at the I-lin temple / Medical Ling Temple / Yi Ling Miao [醫靈廟] and jumped up onto the Lei tai [擂臺] to warm-up. He was a very large, muscular man who was over six feet tall and as he exercised, his speed and skill were obvious to the huge crowd of spectators. He wore a light, padded jacket with a breastplate, and his boots were tipped with an iron spike. Once he had concluded his exercises, he stood before the crowd and bellowed whether the man known as Wu Wei Kin [胡惠乾], dared to show his face. The crowd fell silent as a younger, slender man mounted the Lei tai [擂臺]. In comparison, Wu Wei Kin [胡惠乾] wore a light gown with a black jacket and sandals on his feet. The crowd thought from Wu Wei Kin's [胡惠乾] attire, that he had come to apologise and beg for his life, while the Ox was astounded and asked who had come before him. The young man replied that he was Wu Wei Kin [胡惠乾]. He then informed the Ox of why his grievance was with the Weavers Guild [錦綸堂織工會] and not with a fellow brother of the martial arts [武術]. He continued by stating that he knew the Ox was a student of Fung Do-Duk / Feng Daode [馮道德], and that his teacher [功夫老師] was Gee Seen [至善禪師], so there should be no quarrel between them. Wu Wei Kin [胡惠乾] continued by stating that, as martial artists [武術家], they should follow the path of honour and not be lured by money, but if he scorned this, wishing to fight, then the outcome would be sad; this was not a disagreement between them, so he should disregard this matter as a favour to their masters [師父].

The Ox was outraged at Wu Wei Kin's [胡惠乾] comments, stating that he should have been satisfied with the official decree and that if he wanted to end this challenge, then he should pay compensation and beg forgiveness from the Chin-lun t'ang Weavers Guild [錦綸堂織工會]. He continued that he had only made this offer due to the honour of their masters [師父] as Wu Wei Kin [胡惠乾] had mentioned them. If he did not accept this offer, the Ox could not guarantee that Wu Wei Kin [胡惠乾] would survive the duel [決鬥]. Because Niu Hua-chiao [牛化蛟] the Ox knew that Wu Wei Kin [胡惠乾] had not studied the martial arts [武術] as long as he had, he surmised that his opponent's skill and expertise would be lower than his own. He therefore started to mock Wu Wei Kin [胡惠乾] until he had no option but to fight. The Ox lunged forward to attack and a fierce contest ensued as Wu Wei Kin [胡惠乾] retaliated. Arms and legs were flying everywhere as these two expert fighters exchanged various punches and kicking techniques. While this contest raged on the Lei tai [擂臺], the air was filled with cheering and shouting from the huge crowd of spectators.

Although Wu Wei Kin [胡惠乾] was holding his own against his much bigger and stronger opponent, he felt that it would only be a matter of time before the Ox's size and strength would overcome him. In this moment of doubt, he remembered the method of the "Flowery Fists [花拳]" that his teacher [功夫老師], the Siu Lum / Shaolin abbot [少林方丈], Gee Seen Sim See [至善禪師], had taught him. He leapt into the air, sweeping and circling his body at speed, so that the Ox was unable to hit him. The Ox had not seen this method before and so was confused by it. Wu Wei Kin [胡惠乾] used this moment of confusion and hesitation by his opponent, to suddenly jump to his side, delivering a double handed palm strike called the "butterfly palms [散尾葵]", to the Ox's kidneys. This technique had not only caught the Ox off guard, but also off balance, which knocked him to the floor. As he stood up, Wu Wei Kin [胡惠乾] performed a sweeping kick that completely took the Ox's legs away and he went over the side of the Lei tai [擂臺], crashing to the floor below. Unfortunately, as he hit the floor, his head crashed against the stone pathway which knocked him unconscious.

His students and some of the weavers carried the Ox back to the Chin-lun t'ang's meeting hall and urgently sent for a doctor who came immediately. All efforts were made to save the Ox but his injury was fatal. With blood coming from his mouth, his final words to his students were to seek out his teacher [功夫老師], Fung Do-Duk / Feng Daode [馮道德], at the Wu-tang mountains / Wudang shan [武當山] and request that he send his second best student, called Lu Ying-pu [呂英布], to avenge his death. There was much grieving by the Ox's students at his death and they buried him next to an old temple near the peak of the Twin Mountains [孖岡山].

The members of the Weavers Guild [錦綸堂織工會] asked the students of the Ox who this Lu Ying-pu [呂英布] was, that he had mentioned. The students remarked that he was a highly skilled man, more so than their own teacher [功夫老師], and that he would easily beat Wu Wei Kin [胡惠乾]. This news greatly pleased the weavers who decided to send for his assistance immediately. The four best students of the Ox were sent to the Wu-tang mountains / Wudang shan [武當山] with a sum of 3000 Taels [兩] of silver to pay Lu Ying-pu [呂英布] for his services.

As the victor, Wu Wei Kin [胡惠乾] had the honor of being carried back to the West Zen Temple / Sai Sim Ji / Xi Chan Si [西禪寺] in a sedan chair [花轎]. His friends accompanied him through the crowds who were cheering and celebrating by letting off firecrackers. By the time they arrived at the West Zen Temple / Sai Sim Ji / Xi Chan Si [西禪寺], he was exhausted, so they helped him to his bed. The abbot of this temple was the Siu Lum / Shaolin Monk [少林僧], Sam Dak / San De [三德]. He told Wu Wei Kin [胡惠乾] that he believed that the Ox would die from his injuries, and once his teacher [功夫老師], Fung Do-Duk / Feng Daode [馮道德], heard of this, he would want revenge. Wu Wei Kin [胡惠乾] stated that he had tried to persuade the Ox not to fight, and that he did not even dress for a duel [決鬥]; when the match commenced, the Ox was too skillful and powerful so he had no choice but to kill him, or be killed. If Fung Do-Duk / Feng Daode [馮道德] did seek revenge, he alone would fight him and if he died, he would be satisfied that he had avenged his father's death.

This troubled Sam Dak / San De [三德], who had no plan of how to resolve this matter, so he wrote a letter to his teacher [功夫老師], Gee Seen [至善禪師], asking for his advice. This letter was taken by a messenger to the Southern Siu Lum / Shaolin Temple [南少林寺] in Fukien / Fujian province [福建省]. When the messenger arrived at the temple, Gee Seen [至善禪師] read the letter straight away. He was deeply disturbed by its contents and paced the room as he thought about what to do. After some moments, he called all of his students for a meeting and told them of the events that had occurred in Canton [廣州] which could affect the reputation of the Siu Lum / Shaolin Temple [少林寺]. Because Wu Wei Kin [胡惠乾] was a member of the Siu Lum / Shaolin school [少林武術學校], they had a responsibility to help him and so he would send some students to Canton [廣州]. The abbot [少林方丈] continued by stating that if this matter was not dealt with tactfully, then it could affect the harmonious relationship that existed between the schools of Siu Lum / Shaolin [少林武術學校] and Wu-tang / Wudang [武當武術學校].

Gee Seen [至善禪師] then picked his twelve best students to take the tests that ensured that they had acquired all the skills, and that their training was complete. These various tests and assessments were conducted over three days, and covered their mental and spiritual attitudes, as well as their fighting abilities. The Siu Lum / Shaolin abbot [少林方丈] congratulated the students on completing their training at the Siu Lum / Shaolin Temple [少林寺], but told them to continue their studies of the martial arts [武術]. He then requested that they abide by the way of Heaven and walk the path of righteousness, to help others and never do harm to those that are weaker, and to not be tempted by the spoils of riches. If they continued to follow and live by these codes, they would never disgrace themselves or the good name of Siu Lum / Shaolin [少林]. Gee Seen [至善禪師] then bid them farewell as they departed for Canton [廣州].

In Canton [廣州], Lu Ying-pu [呂英布] had travelled from the Wu-tang Mountains / Wudang shan [武當山] to avenge the death of his fellow student, Niu Hua-chiao [牛化蛟] the Ox. The challenge match had also been held at the I-lin temple / Medical Ling Temple / Yi Ling Miao [醫靈廟], and was a bloody affair, with Wu Wei Kin [胡惠乾] once again achieving victory by killing his opponent, Lu Ying-pu [呂英布]. When news of his death reached Fung Do-Duk / Feng Daode [馮道德] back at the Wu-tang Mountains / Wudang shan [武當山], he was deeply disturbed and saddened by this loss. He called his best and most loved student, Lei Ta-p'eng [雷大鵬], to him. Fung Do-Duk / Feng Daode [馮道德] stated that for the deaths of Lu Ying-pu [呂英布] and Niu Hua-chiao [牛化蛟] the Ox, he was going to challenge Wu Wei Kin [胡惠乾] to a duel [決鬥] to the death. Lei Ta-p'eng [雷大鵬] begged his teacher [功夫老師] to let him fight Wu Wei Kin [胡惠乾] and after much beseeching, Fung Do-Duk / Feng Daode [馮道德] finally agreed.

Fung Do-Duk / Feng Daode [馮道德] accompanied his student, Lei Ta-p'eng [雷大鵬], to Canton [廣州] so that he could witness this match. They rode on horseback to the very gates of the West Zen Temple / Sai Sim Ji / Xi Chan Si [西禪寺] and threw down the challenge to Wu Wei Kin [胡惠乾], who had to be held back by all of his friends from fighting Lei Ta-p'eng [雷大鵬] there and then. News spread throughout the provincial capital city [省會城市] of this incident and the impending challenge match. The population of Canton [廣州] were split as to who they supported, and could do nothing else but discuss this forthcoming duel [決鬥]. This news soon reached the Southern Siu Lum / Shaolin Temple [南少林寺] and Gee Seen [至善禪師] despaired at the situation that was arising between the schools of Siu Lum / Shaolin [少林武術學校] and Wu-tang / Wudang [武當武術學校]. He had heard that the old Buddhist nun [尼姑], Wu Mei Da Shi / Ng Mui Daai Si [五梅大師], (one of the legendary Shaolin Five Elders / Sui Lum Ng Cho [少林五祖]) was in Canton [廣州], so he wrote her a letter, appealing to her to try to resolve the situation if at all possible.

On the day of the challenge match between Wu Wei Kin [胡惠乾] and Lei Ta-p'eng [雷大鵬], many people arrived early at the I-ling Temple / Medical Ling Temple / Yi Ling Miao [醫靈廟], and soon the whole temple grounds were completely full. People started to climb onto the temple walls and nearby trees, in the hope that they could get a view of the Lei tai [擂臺] and the duel [決鬥]. After having breakfast, Lei Ta-p'eng [雷大鵬] and his teacher [功夫老師], Fung Do-Duk / Feng Daode [馮道德], prepared for the fight, running through various tactics and techniques. At the appointed time, they both rode to the I-ling Temple / Medical Ling Temple / Yi Ling Miao [醫靈廟] on a pair of white horses, with Lei Ta-p'eng [雷大鵬] carrying an iron staff [鐵棍]. During this procession, they were accompanied by many of their students and members of the Chin-lun t'ang Weavers Guild [錦綸堂織工會]. When they arrived at the I-ling Temple / Medical Ling Temple / Yi Ling Miao [醫靈廟], the crowd of spectators clapped and cheered as Lei Ta-p'eng [雷大鵬] climbed onto the Lei tai [擂臺]. He was over six feet tall and wore a black cap, black boats, with matching light armour and breastplate. Holding the iron staff [鐵棍] above his head, and with malice, Lei Ta-p'eng [雷大鵬] shouted out his name and why he had challenged Wu Wei Kin [胡惠乾]. He then roared whether anyone was willing to come onto the Lei tai [擂臺] to fight him.

Many of the Siu Lum / Shaolin disciples [少林俗家弟子] were stood near the Lei tai [擂臺] as Lei Ta-p'eng [雷大鵬] made his angry rant. One of these disciples [少林俗家弟子] was called Li Chi-lun [李志倫]. He was usually a peaceful man, but Lei Ta-p'eng's [雷大鵬] outburst infuriated him. He leapt onto the Lei tai [擂臺] to take up this challenge, with a sword in each hand. Lei Ta-p'eng [雷大鵬] rushed forward, swinging his iron staff [鐵棍] and the air was suddenly filled with clinking and clanking sounds from the clash of the iron staff [鐵棍] and the swords. This fierce exchange went on for several minutes, until Li Chi-lun [李志倫] was forced to retreat, and had to jump down from the Lei tai [擂臺] to save himself. Lei Ta-p'eng [雷大鵬] began laughing at Li Chi-lun's [李志倫] humiliating withdrawal, so another one of the Siu Lum / Shaolin disciples [少林俗家弟子], called Hung Hsi-kuan [洪熙官], jumped onto the Lei tai [擂臺] and charged at him in a bid to silence his laughter. Hung Hsi-kuan [洪熙官] fought with a pair of iron rulers [鐵尺], and after a brief but furious encounter, he too was forced to jump from the Lei tai [擂臺] before he was fatally injured.

Lei Ta-p'eng [雷大鵬] paraded confidently on the Lei tai [擂臺] mocking the disciples of Siu Lum / Shaolin [少林俗家弟子]. He enquired if there were any men who could give him a good fight instead of the children he had so far encountered. The men of Siu Lum / Shaolin [少林俗家弟子] were severely provoked by Lei Ta-p'eng's [雷大鵬] comments, and one after another, they climbed onto the Lei tai [擂臺] to fight him, only to be knocked off or forced to jump off to save their own lives. The crowds had been cheering and applauding Lei Ta-p'eng's [雷大鵬] skilful and dominant performances, until a young, slightly built man jumped onto the Lei tai [擂臺]. During this sudden silence, the young man called over to Lei Ta-p'eng [雷大鵬] and asked if wished to have a true match, or if he was content to build a reputation on fighting only novices. Lei Ta-p'eng [雷大鵬] looked at the young man, who wore some light armour with a polished breastplate, and held double ended spears in each hand. He then shouted back, enquiring who dared to come onto his Lei tai [擂臺] and bark insults. Wu Wei Kin [胡惠乾] laughed as he stated that he was surprised Lei Ta-p'eng [雷大鵬] did not know who he was. He then continued by stating that he was an agent for the god of Hades [冥界之神] who had already delivered the souls of Niu Hua-chiao [牛化蛟] and Lu Ying-pu [呂英布], and today he was to deliver Lei Ta-p'eng's [雷大鵬]. The crowd laughed at Wu Wei Kin's [胡惠乾] remarks, but Lei Ta-p'eng [雷大鵬] was so enraged, he could not reply, and just charged forward, swinging his iron staff [鐵棍] towards his opponent's head.

There followed a brief exchange between the two men, with Wu Wei Kin [胡惠乾] demonstrating his speed and agility in avoiding Lei Ta-p'eng's [雷大鵬] power. Both opponents then circled the Lei tai [擂臺] cautiously, as they both realised the skill and expertise of each other. This new found respect ensured that both men were now more cautious, realising their opponent's ability to easily take advantage of any mistake. They continued to duel [決鬥] and after several hours of fighting, both men were covered in sweat, with their clothes ripped and dirty. Lei Ta-p'eng [雷大鵬] had a long cut on his left cheek from a slash with Wu Wei Kin's [胡惠乾] sharp spear. Wu Wei Kin [胡惠乾] had a large nasty bruise over one of his eyes which had swelled so much that he could no longer see out of that eye.

As neither man had gained any real advantage, Wu Wei Kin [胡惠乾] decided to change his tactics in a bid to confuse Lei Ta-p'eng [雷大鵬]. He therefore tried a method called the flowery spear movements [鎗花], where he jumped around in circles looking for an opening. Lei Ta-p'eng [雷大鵬] was not daunted by this, and having a keen eye, was able to counterattack, but every time he counterattacked, Wu Wei Kin [胡惠乾] spun out of the way. Lei Ta-p'eng [雷大鵬] decided to let Wu Wei Kin [胡惠乾] continue this energetic movement so he would exhaust himself, while he stayed on the defensive to conserve his energy. A while later, when he thought Wu Wei Kin [胡惠乾] had tired, he attacked. The attack was blocked by Wu Wei Kin's [胡惠乾] spears, but Lei Ta-p'eng [雷大鵬] was then able to sweep both spears from Wu Wei Kin's [胡惠乾] hands, which sent them flying out into the mass of spectators. Wu Wei Kin [胡惠乾] remained calm, and followed the movement of the iron staff [鐵棍] to enable him to take hold of it. Holding it tightly, he thrust the end of the staff into the floor as he continued to spin while dropping onto one knee. This motion sent both Lei Ta-p'eng [雷大鵬] and his staff spinning. Lei Ta-p'eng [雷大鵬] was forced to let go of his staff. The staff was sent hurtling into the crowd while he rolled forward, then up onto his feet. Now both men were unarmed.

Wu Wei Kin [胡惠乾] was still breathing heavily from all the excursion of performing the flowery spear movements, so Lei Ta-p'eng [雷大鵬] took advantage by attacking again. His attacks were so fierce and unrelenting, that Wu Wei Kin [胡惠乾] was forced to give ground and defend. During this attack, Lei Ta-p'eng [雷大鵬] delivered a mighty kick to Wu Wei Kin's [胡惠乾] chest which sent him flying across the Lei tai [擂臺] platform. Wu Wei Kin [胡惠乾] struggled to his knees as Lei Ta-p'eng [雷大鵬] ran forward to finish him off. Just as Lei Ta-p'eng [雷大鵬] stepped in to deliver a fatal blow, he was suddenly blinded for an instant, as Wu Wei Kin's [胡惠乾] breastplate caught the glow of the setting sun which reflected into his eyes, causing Lei Ta-p'eng [雷大鵬] to miss with his strike. Wu Wei Kin [胡惠乾] was still on his knees, and this gave him the opportunity to counter with a punch to Lei Ta-p'eng's [雷大鵬] vital organs. As he doubled up in agony, Wu Wei Kin [胡惠乾] stood up, and with all his strength, used a technique called, "The two dragons searching for the pearl [二龍爭珠]," which was a twin handed strike simultaneously to both temples. Lei Ta-p'eng [雷大鵬] let out a blood curdling cry as he dropped down dead, blood oozing from his nose and mouth.

The massive crowd erupted, some cheering, and others booing at this outcome, while the Siu Lum / Shaolin disciples [少林俗家弟子] started to make their way up the steps of the Lei tai [擂臺]. At that moment, as all this mayhem started, there was a deafening grief stricken cry as Fung Do-Duk / Feng Daode [馮道德] raced onto the Lei tai [擂臺]. Just as he was about to attack Wu Wei Kin [胡惠乾], the old Buddhist nun [尼姑], Wu Mei Da Shi / Ng Mui Daai Si [五梅大師], intervened. She had been sat in front of the Lei tai [擂臺] in a ringside seat. In that instant, Fung Do-Duk / Feng Daode [馮道德] was seized by several of the men that had reached the Lei tai [擂臺] platform.

Once he had calmed down, Fung Do-Duk / Feng Daode [馮道德] asked Wu Mei Da Shi / Ng Mui Daai Si [五梅大師] why she had stopped him, after Wu Wei Kin [胡惠乾] had killed his three best and favourite students. The old nun [尼姑] replied that there had been enough killing over this issue, and as they were both followers of the will of Heaven, they should walk the path of righteousness; they had both retreated into the mountains to cleanse and search their souls, so why was he letting other people induce him to do violence after his life time of training.

On realising the truth in her words, Fung Do-Duk / Feng Daode [馮道德] dropped his head with embarrassment. He replied that although this was true, a wrong had been done. As she was wise, he would let her judge the matter and so abide by her decision. Wu Mei Da Shi / Ng Mui Daai Si [五梅大師] was already well aware of all the events that had led up to this duel [決鬥], and recited them back to Fung Do-Duk / Feng Daode [馮道德]. She therefore decreed that her verdict was that, Wu Wei Kin [胡惠乾] was to immediately drop onto his knees and beg forgiveness from Fung Do-Duk / Feng Daode [馮道德] in front of the population of Canton [廣州]; then he and his fellow Siu Lum / Shaolin disciples [少林俗家弟子] were to pay 10,000 Taels [兩] of silver as compensation for the deaths of Fung Do-Duk's / Feng Daode's [馮道德] three students for distribution to their families.

Although Wu Wei Kin [胡惠乾] and Fung Do-Duk / Feng Daode [馮道德] agreed to Wu Mei Da Shi's / Ng Mui Daai Si's [五梅大師] judgement, this was the start of conflict and hostility between the schools of Siu Lum / Shaolin [少林武術學校] and Wu-tang / Wudang [武當武術學校]. [50b] [61] [61a] [61b] [61c] [61d] [61e] [61f] [112a]

I have found several versions of these legends which tell the same story but with some variations. (ie In one account written by William C. C. Hu & Fred Bleicher in the Black Belt magazine, the story of Fong Sai Yuk [方世玉] is set in Nanking / Nanjing [南京] and Hangchow / Hangzhou [杭州] while in another [112a] source, this story is set in Canton [廣州].) A main source for this story comes from the novel entitled, "The Qianlong Emperor Inspects Southern China / Kin Loong har Kwong Nam / Qianlong Xia Jiangnan [乾隆下江南]" It is stated that this story was released under a variety of other names which include, "The sacred dynasty's tripods flourish, verdant for ten thousand years / Shengchao ding sheng wannian qing," and "The new tale of the marvellous hero of the everlasting Qing / Wannian qing qicai xinzhuan," (also Qian Long xun xing Jiang nan ji [乾隆巡幸江南記] & Qian Long you Jiang nan [乾隆遊江南]) These novels were first released around 1893. [50c] During the twentieth century, after the fall of the Ch'ing Dynasty / Qing Dynasty [清朝] (1644–1912), the story has been rewritten many times. These rewritten accounts contain various alterations to the original story, to reflect changes in the political climate. [50c]

Siu Lum / Shaolin Tiger to Hung Kuen

Hung Kuen [洪拳] initially developed from the Siu Lum / Shaolin Tiger [少林虎] style blended with the Siu Lum / Shaolin Lohan style [罗汉拳] taught by Gee Seen [至善禪師] at the Southern Siu Lum / Shaolin Temples [南少林寺]. During the late 1700s this combination of styles was further refined into what became known from the early 1800s as Hung Kuen [洪拳]. There are three differing versions of how the name of Hung was derived :-

1. Some believe the name was a tribute to Hung Hei-Kwun [洪熙官] by using his name.
2. Some believe the name was chosen from the Hung / Hong men [洪門] of the secret society that many of the founding practitioners were members of.
3. Some believe the name was derived from the Hung Soan / Red Opera Boats [紅船粵劇團] that founding members used in the early days while in hiding.

Hung Ga (洪家), *Hung Kuen* (洪拳), or *Hung Ga Kuen* (洪家拳), *is a southern style of Chinese martial arts. Due to the character "hung" (洪) being used in the reign name of the emperor who overthrew the Mongol Yuan Dynasty to establish the Han Chinese Ming Dynasty, opponents of the Manchu Qing Dynasty made common use of the character to signify them overthrowing the Qing. It is believed that Hung Hei-Kwun is an assumed name intended to honour that first Ming Emperor and ironically, Luk Ah-Choi was the son of a Manchu. Anti-Qing rebels named their secret society the "Hung Mun" (洪門) which they claimed to be founded by survivors of the destruction of the Shaolin Temple. The martial arts style its members practiced came to be called "Hung Kuen" and "Hung Ga".*

Branches of Hung Kuen :- The syllabus, weapons and routines differ enormously between the various branches of Hung Ga. This is even evident within the different Wong Fei Hung lineages. Various lineages will practice the Five Animal Five Element Fist, while branches that do not descend from Wong Fei Hung, which are sometimes called "old" or "village" Hung Kuen, do not practice the routines he developed. Very few branches practice Iron Wire routine unless they are descended from Tit Kiu Saam. Some branches have grown their syllabus through either the creation or acquisition of additional routines.

The curriculum taught to Hung Hei-Kwun by Jee Sin is stated to have comprised Luohan style, Tiger style, and Taming the Tiger routine. Exchanging techniques and methods with other martial artists allowed Hung to develop and or attain the Tiger Crane Paired Form routine, a combination animal routine, Southern Flower Fist, and several weapons. It is stated that the martial arts Jee Sin originally taught Hung

Hei-Kwun was short range and that the more active footwork, wider stances, and long range techniques commonly associated with Hung Kuen / Ga were added later.

The spreading of Hung Kuen :- *The spreading of Hung Kuen in Southern China, and specifically the provinces of Guangdong and Fujian, was due to the concentration of anti-Qing Hung Mun in that part of the country. It is understood that Hung Mun originated in the 1760s as the Heaven and Earth Society in the area of Zhangzhou in Fujian Province, on its border with Guangdong and Huizhou. The provinces of Guangdong and Fujian remained a stronghold for the Hung Mun, even as it spread around other regions in the decades that followed. Members of the Hung Clan practiced a variety of martial arts styles, but due to the make-up of its membership the characteristics of Fujianese and Cantonese martial arts eventually came to be associated with the names "Hung Kuen" and "Hung Ga". In spite of their differences, the Hung Kuen lineages of Wong Fei Hung, Yuen Yik Kai, Leung Wah Chew, and Jeung Kei Ji (張克治) all trace their origins to this area and this time period, are all Five Animal styles, and all claim Shaolin origins.* [112]

Who Were the Ten Tigers of Gaungdong

Most sources state that the Ten Tigers [廣東十虎] were:-
This list has their real name in Cantonese, with various spellings, followed by the Mandarin (pinyin) way of spelling the name and then their nicknames. [109] [109a] [109b] [109c] [109d] [109e] [122] [122a]

1. Wong Yan-Lam
(traditional Chinese: 王隱林; simplified Chinese: 王隐林; pinyin: *Wang Yinlin*)
Wong Yan-Lam [王隱林] (sometimes spelt Wong Yein-Lam) was a student of the Tibetan monk [藏傳僧] Sing Lung [聖龍], who was a master [功夫大師] of "Lion's Roar [獅子吼]" Kung-Fu [功夫]. Wong Yan-Lam [王隱林] further developed this style which later splintered into Lama Pai / Tibetan Lama Buddhist style [喇嘛派], Hap (Hop) Gar Kuen / Hap family style or Chivalrous boxing [俠家] and Bak (Pak) Hok Pai / White Crane style [白鶴派].

2. Wong Ching-Hoh
(traditional Chinese: 黃澄可; simplified Chinese: 黄澄可; pinyin: *Huang Chengke*)
Wong Ching-Hoh [黃澄可] (sometimes spelt Wong Cheng-Ho) was a student of Luk Ah Choi / Lu A Cai [陸阿采]. He became a master [功夫大師] of the Nine Dragon Fist style [九龍拳] of Kung Fu [功夫] which he had created from the various styles he had previously studied.

3. So Hak Fu
(traditional Chinese: 蘇黑虎; simplified Chinese: 苏黑虎; pinyin: *Su Heihu*)
So [蘇] was more commonly known by his nickname of So Hak Fu [蘇黑虎] (sometimes spelt Sou Hak Fu & So Hark Fu). He was a student of the Siu Lum / Shaolin monk [少林僧] Sam Dak / San De [三德] (who was also known by various aliases including Siu Dak / Zhao De [兆德] & Iron Arms / Tien Bay / Tie bi [鐵臂]). So Hak Fu [蘇黑虎] studied at the Kwangtung Siu Lum / Shaolin temple [廣東少林寺] and the Putian Siu Lum / Shaolin Temple [莆田少林寺]. He later created his own style called Hak Fu Mun [黑虎門] (Gate of the Black Tiger style).

4. Wong Kei-Ying
(traditional Chinese: 黃麒英; simplified Chinese: 黄麒英; pinyin: *Huang Qiying*)
Wong Kei-Ying [黃麒英] (sometimes spelt Wong Khei-Yin) first studied under his father, Wong Tai [黃泰] before becoming a student of Luk Ah-Choi / Lu A Cai [陸阿采] who trained him in the Hung Kuen [洪拳] style. Wong Kei-Ying [黃麒英] was also a highly skilled practitioner in the Siu Lum / Shaolin pole [少林棍] and was also trained in traditional Chinese Medicine [中醫]. He had his own clinic called Po Chi Lam / Bao Zhi Lin [宝芝林].

5. Lai Yan-Chiu

(traditional Chinese: 黎仁超; simplified Chinese: 黎仁超: pinyin: *Li Renchao*)

Lai Yan-Chiu [黎仁超] was a practitioner of the Hakka Kuen [客家拳] style also known as Southern Praying Mantis [南派螳螂]. He was not a full-time Kung Fu master [功夫大師] like many of the other Tigers, but had his own business running a Pawn Shop called Shun Hang Pawnshop [信亨押店]. He was renowned for his skill in performing the Seven Star Fist / Chuk Sing Kuen / Qi Xing Quan [七星拳] routine [套路].

6. So Chan / So Huk Yee

(traditional Chinese: 蘇燦; simplified Chinese: 苏灿; pinyin: *Su Can*)

So Chan [蘇燦] was more commonly known by his nickname of So Huk Yee [蘇乞兒] (sometimes spelt So Hut Yee) which means Beggar So. He was originally trained in a Hung Kuen [洪拳] style by the Siu Lum / Shaolin Monk [少林僧] known as the Venerable Chan Fook [陳福]. He was famous for his "Drunken" style of Kung Fu / Jade Kuen / Zui quan / 醉拳 and was an expert of the Siu Lum / Shaolin pole [少林棍].

7. Leung Kwan / Tit kiu Saam

(traditional Chinese: 梁坤; simplified Chinese: 梁坤; pinyin: *Liang Kun*)

Leung Kwan's [梁坤] nickname was Tit kiu Saam / Tie Qiao San [鐵橋三] (sometimes spelt Tit Kew Sam) which literally means "Iron Bridge Three" and he was a Hung Kuen [洪拳] practitioner. He had several teachers as a boy, but the Siu Lum / Shaolin monk [少林僧] known as the Venerable Gwok Yan [覺因] is credited as being the most significant and influential during his youth. Although he would take on students, he spent most of his life continuing to learn and study martial arts [武術] from other Masters [功夫大師].

8. Chan Cheung-Tai / Tit Chee Chan

(traditional Chinese: 陳長泰; simplified Chinese: 陈长泰; pinyin: *Chen Changtai*)

Chan Cheung-Tai [陳長泰] was more commonly known by his nickname of Tit Chee Chan [鐵指陳] (sometimes spelt Tit Ji or Chi Chan / Chen Zhi Tie) which means Iron Finger Chan. He was an expert at the Siu Lum / Shaolin method of Diamond Finger / Yak Chee Sim Kung Fu / Yi Zhi Jin Gang Fa [一指禪功夫] (Siu Lum Kam Kung Chee [少林金剛指]). Chan Cheung-Tai [陳長泰] was trained in both the Hung Kuen [洪拳] style and the Siu Lum / Shaolin [少林] style of Eagle Claw / Jing Jar [鷹爪] Kung Fu [功夫]. It is not known who his teacher was, but it is believed to have been a Siu Lum / Shaolin Monk [少林僧].

9. Tam Chai-Kwan

(traditional Chinese: 譚濟筠; simplified Chinese: 谭济筠; pinyin: *Tan Jijun*)

Tam Chai-Kwan [譚濟筠] (sometimes spelt Tam Chai Hok or Tam Chai Wen) was also known by the nickname of Sam Kuk Tam / Tanji He [三脚譚], which means Three Leg Tam due to three types of kicks he would use when fighting. Tam Chai-Kwan [譚濟筠]

was trained in the Huadu style of Hung Kuen [花都洪拳] by Tam Min / Tan Min [譚敏] who was a former disciple [武術弟子] of Hung Hei-Kwun [洪熙官].

10. Chau Tai

(traditional Chinese: 鄒泰; simplified Chinese: 邹泰; pinyin: Zou Tai)

Chau Tai [鄒泰] (sometimes spelt Jau Taai or Chow Thye) was a student of a monk called Law Mui Hing / Luo Mao Xing [羅茂興], who was a disciple from the lineage of Yeung Ng Long / Yang Wulang [楊五郎]. Chau Tai [鄒泰] was skilled in the Yang Family martial arts and an expert in the Yang Family Spear / Yeung Ka Cheong / Yang Jia Qiang [楊家枪] from which he formulated his own style of Zhou Family Bagua Staff / Chau Gar Ba Gua Gwun [周家八卦棍].

The majority of sources agree with these ten names. It is stated that Wong Fei-hung / Huang Feihong [黃飛鴻] who was the son of Wong Kei-ying / Huang Qiying [黃麒英] has often been referred to as the Tiger after the Ten Tigers. [109] [109b] [109c] [109d] [109e]

How the Ten Tigers were chosen

Many refer to the 1800s as the Golden Age of Kung Fu [功夫], and during the mid 1800s ten heroes arose in southern China, who would become legends and patriots for their anti-Ch'ing / anti-Qing [反清清朝] (anti-Manchurian) beliefs. These ten Kung Fu masters [功夫大師] lived in Guangdong Province [廣東省] and assumed the title of the "Ten Tigers of Canton", or the "Ten Tigers of Kwangtung [廣東十虎]", depending on the different dialects. In more recent years they have also been known as the "Ten Tigers of Guangdong" / Guangdong shi hu [廣東十虎], which is the modern name for this region.

One source confirms that the Ten Tigers of Kwangtung [廣東十虎] "were all real people who were well-known not only because of their Kung Fu skills, but also because they were always ready to help the poor, the deprived and the needy". [122] [122a] Some sources state that during the mid to late 1850s, many prominent citizens and martial artists [武術家] from the city of Canton [廣州] (Guangzhou [廣州]), gathered to debate who the best Kung Fu masters [功夫大師] were at this time. During this period, several Kung Fu masters [功夫大師] had earned themselves such eminent reputations for being exceptionally skilled, that it is reputed they were known throughout China. During this debate, they discussed the fighting abilities / Chin Duo Lung Lake [戰鬥能力] and prowess of the various masters [功夫大師], as well as their martial arts [武術] skills. Besides this, other attributes were taken into consideration such as their reputations, their characters of virtue and honour (known as Mao Dak / Wude [武德]) as well as their promotion of the martial arts [武術].

For the Shaolin monks, and other traditional Chinese martial arts schools, the study of martial arts was not just for self-defense or mental training, but also included a system of ethics. This can be described as Wude (武 德) which can be translated as "martial morality" (wu (武), means martial, and de (德), means morality). Wude is split into; "morality of deed" and "morality of mind". The morality of deed relates to social relations while morality of mind relates to cultivating the inner harmony between the emotional mind (心; Xin) and the wisdom mind (慧; Hui). The ultimate goal is to reach "no extremity" (無 極; Wuji) where both wisdom and emotions are in harmony with each other. [2] [2a]

	DEED				**MIND**		
CONCEPT	**CANTONESE**	**MANDARIN**		**CONCEPT**	**CANTONESE**	**MANDARIN**	
HUMILITY	*HIM*	*QIAN*	謙	*COURAGE*	*YUNG*	*YONG*	勇
VIRTUE	*SING*	*CHENG*	誠	*PATIENCE*	*YAN*	*REN*	忍
RESPECT	*LAI*	*LI*	禮	*ENDURANCE*	*HANG*	*HENG*	恒
MORALITY	*YI*	*YI*	義	*PERSEVERANCE*	*NGAI*	*YI*	毅
TRUST	*SEUN*	*XIN*	信	*WILL*	*JI*	*ZHI*	志

After all the talking and deliberating was completed, they voted to elect the ten best, who from that time on, would be known as the Ten Tigers of Canton / Kwong Tung Sap Fu [廣東十虎] (Guangdong). It is understood that these debates and the results, were reported in the local newspapers of the day. [50] [50a] [51] [51a] [108b] [109]

In Wong Lam's book entitled, "Southern Shaolin Kung Fu Ling Nam Hung Gar," he states that Canton [廣州] had a growing martial arts community [武術界] with over a hundred schools [武術學校] of different styles. The community [武術界] assembled together to elect the ten best martial artists [武術家] in the city. The criteria for judging each martial artist [武術家] was based on each master's [功夫大師] skill, reputation and of their promotion of martial arts [武術]. The ten who were elected by the community [武術界] then became known as the Ten Tigers of Guang Jao [廣東十虎]. [64]

A writer named Woshi Shanren [我是山人] (pseudonym of Chen Jin) in the 1940s to 1960s wrote many books referring to this period, and of the Ten Tigers of Guangdong / Kwong Tung Sap Fu [廣東十虎]. In the preface of one of his books titled, "Two Tigers of the Martial Arts World" (Mo Lum Yee Fu / Wulin Er Hu [武林二虎]), he summarised the events and situation that led to the rise of these ten martial artists [十武術家].

"Numerous masters appeared as the techniques were passed on from generation to generation. In the middle years of the Qing Dynasty, ten eminent martial artists appeared in Guangzhou, known variously as the Mad Tigers' or as the Ten Tigers of Guangdong'. They were: Wang Yinlin, Huang Chengle, Su Heihu, Huang Qiying (Huang Fei-Hong's father), Li Renchao, Su Qier (Beggar Su), Huang Fei-Hong, Tieqiao San (Iron Stance') Tiezhi Chen ('Iron Finger') and Tan Jijun. Each had a distinct area of expertise, and each founded his own school." [81] [82]

Woshi Shanren has listed nine of the accepted Tigers and has included Wong Fei-Hung / Huang Fei-Hong [黃飛鴻], instead of Chau Tai / Zou Tai [鄒泰] in his list. However, Wong Fei-Hung [黃飛鴻] is generally accepted as being called the "Tiger after the Ten Tigers" and was not one of the original Ten Tigers [廣東十虎]. [109]

Another source states that the Ten Tigers [廣東十虎] were chosen by word of mouth, by the general population. There was no official voting or competition, and this is the reason that there are slight variations in the group. Generally, Chinese people have a high ethical standard when it comes to martial arts [武術]. Using force to resolve or settle matters is regarded as intimidating and oppressing, and considered bad. Only when martial arts [武術] are combined with virtuous and chivalric intentions is it respected by the general Chinese population. [142] [151]

It is stated that the ten chosen Kung Fu masters [功夫大師] had unprecedented martial arts [武術] skills. This, combined with their character for integrity and honour, and anti-Ch'ing / anti-Qing [反清清朝] sympathies, made them revered by all during this period. Any stories concerning the ten martial artists [武術家] regarding their actions or deeds become captivating and astonishing, and would make them living legends thereafter.

The **Ten Tigers of Canton** or **Ten Tigers of Guangdong** *(Guangdong Sap Fu) refers to a group of ten Chinese martial artists who lived in or around Canton (Guangdong), in China, during the late Qing Dynasty (1644–1912). They were reputed to be the best fighters in southern China at that time. Much of their lives has been embellished by folk legends and stories passed down through the generations. The martial arts lineage of the Ten Tigers originated from the Southern Shaolin Monastery in the Jiulian Mountains in Fujian province.* [109]

It is claimed that although they lived in Guangdong Province [廣東省] in the 1800s, they did not all appear as one organised group as portrayed in the 1979 Hong Kong film, the "Ten Tigers of Kwangtung" [廣東十虎]. This film depicts them as one group of avengers working together, but this is a fictitious story. To contradict this theory, the book entitled," <u>The Ten Tigers of Kwangtung-Trouble at the Sai Shaan Monastery</u> [十虎大鬧西山寺]," [122] [122a] [122b] depicts the Ten Tigers [廣東十虎] as friends meeting together for the funeral of Luk Ah-Choi [陸阿采]. From my research, I believe that several of the Ten Tigers [廣東十虎] did know each other and were friends who exchanged ideas and techniques. It is fair to assume that the Ten Tigers [廣東十虎] were friends, possibly before, but definitely after their honorary title of the Ten Tigers of Guangdong / Kwong Tung Sap Fu [廣東十虎]. The sharing and exchange of knowledge and ideas between masters [功夫大師] has occurred throughout history. It was a common practice at the Siu Lum / Shaolin Temple [少林寺]. It is therefore only reasonable to assume that this exchange also took place within this group, but possibly it may not have been advertised, either to save face or to let the general public believe that certain techniques were their own creation.

In fact, other styles and influences besides Siu Lum / Shaolin [少林], also played a part in forging some of these ten great martial artists [十武術家]. It is known that most of the Ten Tigers [廣東十虎] were initially trained in the Tiger [虎] style, that at the time was in the process of being refined and developed into the style known as Hung Kuen [洪拳]. The Hung Kuen [洪拳] trained practitioners were taught by different masters [功夫大師] in the various branches of Hung Kuen [洪拳]. Although many of the Ten Tigers [廣東十虎] were originally taught the Hung Kuen [洪拳] style, they all had their own individual skills and specialties which made them unique. Some of them went on to add their own ideas and methods, and so continued to develop their own different techniques, eventually formulating either their own styles or variations of Hung Kuen [洪拳].

The three of the Ten Tigers [廣東十虎] who were not Hung Kuen [洪拳] trained were Lai Yan-Chiu / Li Renchao [黎仁超], Chan Cheung-Tai / Chen Zhangtai [陳長泰], who was also know by his nickname of Iron Finger Chen / Tit Chee Chan / Tie Zhi Chen [鐵指陳] and Chau Tai / Zhou Tai [鄒泰]. Lai Yan-Chiu / Li Renchao [黎仁超] was a skilled practitioner of the local San Tau / Shantou [汕頭] boxing style of Hakka Kuen [客家拳], also known as Southern Praying Mantis Kung Fu [南派螳螂]. Chan Cheung-Tai / Chen Zhangtai [陳長泰] (Iron Finger Chen / Tit Chee Chan / Tie Zhi Chen [鐵指陳]) was a skilled practitioner of the style of Eagle Claw / Jing Jar [鷹爪] and Chau Tai / Zhou Tai [鄒泰] was a skilled practitioner of the Yang Family [楊家拳] style. Many sources state that because Wang Yin-Lam / Wang Yinlin [王隱林] was a practitioner of the Lama Pai [喇嘛派] style, he was not Hung Kuen [洪拳] trained. As a young boy, however, before he had studied Lion's Roar [獅子吼] Kung-Fu [功夫] under theTibetan monk [藏傳僧] Sing Lung [聖龍], he had been initially trained in the Siu Lum / Shaolin Hung Kuen [洪拳] style. This was taught to him by his father, Wong Ping [王平], who was also known by his nickname of the Bronze foot / Ching Tung Kerr / Qingtong Jiao [青銅腳].

Some of the Ten Tigers [廣東十虎] were classed as lay-disciples [俗家弟子], meaning that although they were not monks, they were directly connected to, or trained within the temple. Most had been taught by either Siu Lum / Shaolin monks [少林僧] who had escaped the Siu Lum / Shaolin Temples at Putian [莆田少林寺] or Quanzhou [泉州少林寺], or by their unshaved lay disciples [俗家弟子][111] [111a] giving them the Siu Lum / Shaolin connection and allegiance [與少林的連繫及忠誠].

(A Buddhist lay disciple has taken two steps:
1. *By going for Refuge to the Three Jewels they make the solemn commitment to accept the Three Jewels which are the Buddha, the Dharma, and the Sangha, as the guiding ideals in their life.*
2. *Undertaking the Five Precepts they express a determination to bring their conduct into accord with these ideals.*

Both steps are usually undertaken in a ceremony conducted by monks and nuns in a Buddhist temple. Although the ceremony might seem short and simple, it marks a dramatic turning point in their life, opening the way to all future progress in the practice of the Dharma. [110]

This means that a lay disciple is a respectful follower of Buddhism attached to or living at a temple.

The lay prātimokṣa (a list of rules governing the behaviour of Buddhist monks) consists of five vows that are also known as the Five Śīlas:
1. *To refrain from killing.*
2. *To refrain from stealing.*

145

3. *To refrain from false speech.*
4. *To refrain from sexual misconduct.*
5. *To refrain from using intoxicants.*

They are not obliged to take all five vows. The list below describes the seven types of lay followers:
1. *Promising to keep just one vow.*
2. *Promising to keep certain vows.*
3. *Promising to keep most of them.*
4. *Promising to keep all five.*
5. *Keeping all five and also promising to keep the pure conduct of avoiding sexual contact.*
6. *Keeping all five, pure conduct, and wearing robes with the promise to behave like a monk or a nun.*
7. *Lay follower of mere refuge. This person is unable to keep the vows but he promises to go for refuge to the triple gem until death.*

Although they were tutored by Monks, they did not have to observe all the monastic vows while studying and living at the temple. [111])

Wang Yin-Lam [王隱林] was a unshaved lay disciple [俗家弟子] and trained under the Tibetan Lama Monk [藏傳僧], Sing Lung [聖龍], at the Blessed Cloud Monastery / Hing Wen Chi / Qing yun Si [慶雲寺] for ten years.

So [蘇] (more commonly known by his nickname of So Hak Fu [蘇黑虎]) was a unshaved lay disciple [俗家弟子] of the Siu Lum / Shaolin monk [少林僧] Sam Dak / San De [三德], who he studied under at the Kwangtung Siu Lum / Shaolin temple [廣東少林寺] and the Putian Siu Lum / Shaolin Temple [莆田少林寺].

Leung Kwan [梁坤] (more commonly known by his nickname of Iron Bridge Three / Tit kiu Saam / Tie Qiao San [鐵橋三]) spent much of his life living at the various monasteries in and around Canton [廣州]. It is believed that Leung Kwan [梁坤] was an "ordained novice", which is a layman / Or Hong Yan [外行人] attached to the temple, who followed Buddhist [佛教徒] teachings, but did not follow the monastic vows that monks did. Although he had a great love of Buddhism [佛教] and many of its practices, Leung Kwan [梁坤] would continue to eat meat and drink alcohol from time to time.

So Chan [蘇燦] (more commonly known by his nickname of Beggar So / So Huk Yee [蘇乞兒]) was trained in a Hung Kuen [洪拳] style by the Siu Lum / Shaolin monk [少林僧] known as the Venerable Chan Fook [陳福].

Chau Tai [鄒泰] was trained in the Yang Family [楊家拳] style by the monk Law Mui Hing / Luo Mao Xing [羅茂興] at his martial arts school [武術學校] in Nanhai County / Nam Hoi Yuen [南海縣].

Wong Ching-Hoh [黃澄可] and Wong Kei-Ying [黃麒英] were trained by Luk Ah Choi / Lu A Cai [陸阿采] who was a lay-disciple [俗家弟子] of the Siu Lum / Shaolin Abbot [少林方丈] Gee Seen [至善禪師].

Jianghu Lifestyle [江湖]

Many of the "Ten Tigers" [廣東十虎] spent parts of their lives living the Jianghu [江湖] lifestyle. I have therefore added this detailed account to enable the reader to have a better understanding of what this lifestyle was, what it entailed and the code they lived by.

The "jianghu" (江湖; literally means "rivers and lakes") refers to the social world of martial artists and other ruffian types. "Wulin" (武林; meaning "martial forest") is a word more commonly used with regards to this community. The jianghu is made up of a number of martial artists who are sometimes congregated in sects, families, disciplines and various schools of martial arts. This group is also inhabited by others such as youxia ("wandering martial artists"), nobles, thieves, beggars, priests, healers, merchants and craftsmen.

A common aspect of the jianghu is that all disputes and differences (within their community) are resolved by members of the community, instead of the normal courts of law. This can be either through, mediation, negotiation or force, requiring the need for the code of xia and acts of chivalry. Law and order within the jianghu community are upheld by the various traditional and honourable sects and champions.

A leader is elected from among the jianghu community to govern them and ensure law and order. This position is called the "wulin mengzhu" (武林盟主; meaning "master of the wulin alliance"). The leader is generally someone with a high level of mastery in martial arts and has a great reputation for righteousness. A role of the leader is to preside and judge over all injustices and disputes.

Relationship with the official authorities
Members of the jianghu are required to keep their distance from any government offices or officials, without necessarily being hostile, although it is acceptable for Jianghu members who are reputable members of society (usually owning properties or big businesses) to maintain respectful but formal relationship with the officials, such as paying due taxes and attending certain local community events. These members are expected to protect a fugitive from the law or at the least not to turn them over to the officials unless the crimes also violated some of the moral rules of jianghu; then jianghu members may assist the government officials.

Jianghu code
1. *Unless there is a deep personal grievance, one must not resort to dirty tricks such as eye-gouging during personal combats.*
2. *Personal feud does not extend to family members.*

3. *Respect for seniority by status or age.*
4. *Complete obedience to one's shifu (martial arts instructor).*
5. *No learning martial arts from another without prior permission from one's shifu.*
6. *No using martial arts against those unskilled.*
7. *No violating of womenfolk.*
8. *No sexual relationship with the wives of friends.*
9. *One's word is one's bond.*

[95]

The Code of xia

Eight common characteristics of the xia are benevolence, justice, individualism, loyalty, courage, truthfulness, disregard for wealth and desire for glory. The code of xia also emphasises the importance of repaying benefactors who have given acts of en (恩; "grace", "favour"), as well as seeking chou (仇; "vengeance", "revenge") bringing certain villains to justice. However, the significance of vengeance is controversial, as a number of wuxia works emphasise Buddhist principles, of forgiveness, compassion and no killing.

Jianghu martial artists are expected to be loyal to their master (Sifu). This can sometimes give rise to the formation of several complex trees of master-apprentice relations as well as the various sects such as Shaolin and Wudang. Disputes between martial artists are expected to settle their differences choosing the honourable way of fighting a duel. [95]

For further detailed meanings of Jianghu and Wuxia the following website is recommended:-
http://wenku.baidu.com/view/4bb3af8984868762caaed5c9 [95a]

Wong Yan-Lam [王隱林]

(Traditional Chinese: 王隱林; simplified Chinese: 王隐林; pinyin: *Wang Yinlin*)

Approximately 1830-1930

In the province of Guangdong [廣東], approximately 70 km west from the city of Guangzhou [廣州] (Canton [廣州]), close to the Dinghu Mountain (Dinghu Shan / Ting Hu) [鼎湖山] in the village of Shiu Hing / Zhaoqing [肇慶], there lived a Siu Lum / Shaolin master [少林功夫大師]. This Kung Fu master [功夫大師] was called Wong Ping [王平], who was also known by the nickname of the "Bronze foot / Ching Tung Kerr / Qingtong Jiao [青銅腳]". He was renowned for performing his Kung Fu [功夫] in public for all to see. On the nearby mountain, there was a temple called the Blessed Cloud Monastery / Hing Wen Chi / Qing yun Si [慶雲寺] (also known as the Ching Yun Jih and called Qingyun Temple in Mandarin [鼎湖山慶雲寺]) where a Tibetan Monk [藏傳僧], by the name of Sing Lung [聖龍], had settled. It is stated that Sing Lung [聖龍] was also known by several other nicknames, such as, Lee Hu Si / Li Huzi [李鬍子], which translates to mean Bearded Li and Golden Hook / Kam Au Lee Wu Che / Jin Gou Li Huzi [金鈎李鬍子]. [150] [154] [154a] While at the temple, Sing Lung [聖龍] had heard many stories of Wong Ping's [王平] exploits, so one day decided to visit the village of Shiu Hing / Zhaoqing [肇慶] and observe this local Kung Fu master [功夫大師] for himself.

After watching him perform at a demonstration [武術表演], Sing Lung [聖龍] was impressed by his skill and techniques. Unfortunately, when he tried to introduce himself, there was a misunderstanding which resulted in Wong Ping [王平] thinking he was being challenged. Sing Lung's [聖龍] Chinese was not very good and Wong Ping [王平] attacked him. As Wong Ping [王平] performed a leg sweep on Sing Lung [聖龍], the Tibetan monk [藏傳僧] countered this sweep by performing a technique called the "Gam Gong Hung Lung / Jingang Xiang Long [金剛降龍]", (this translates to mean the indestructible body of Buddha to surround dragon), by which he jumped into the air and then landed on the sweeping leg, breaking Wong's [王平] knee. After this unfortunate injury, Sing Lung [聖龍] had time to explain his intentions, and so correcting the misunderstanding that Wong [王平] initially had. Now the air was cleared between the two men, Sing Lung [聖龍] offered to heal the broken knee using his knowledge of Tibetan medical techniques / Joon Chuen Yee Suit [藏傳醫術]. Wong Ping [王平] was impressed with Sing Lung's [聖龍] skills and this resulted in both men becoming good friends, with Wong [王平] asking the monk [藏傳僧] if he would teach his son. Wong Ping's [王平] son, Wong Yan-Lam [王隱林], was accepted by the old Tibetan Monk [藏傳僧] and so became his layman disciple [俗家弟子]. The young Wong Yan-Lam [王隱林] then returned with the monk [藏傳僧] to the Blessed Cloud Monastery [慶雲寺] on Dinghu Mountain [鼎湖山]. [87] [90]

Blessed Cloud Monastery / Qingyun Temple / 慶雲寺 on Dinghu Mountain / 鼎湖山

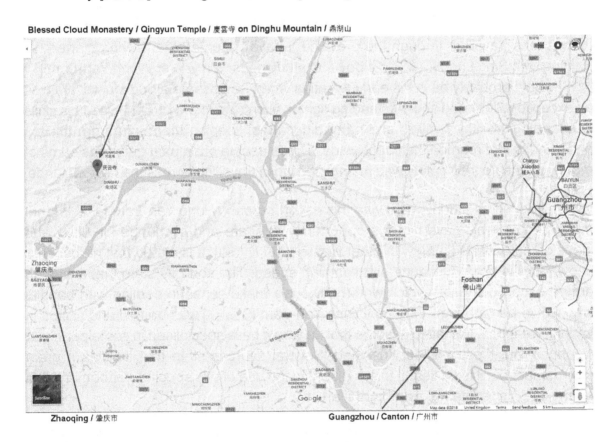

Zhaoqing / 肇庆市   **Guangzhou / Canton / 广州市**

It is understood that Wong Ping [王平] taught his son, Wong Yan-Lam [王隱林], Siu Lum / Shaolin martial arts [少林武術] prior to him studying under Sing Lung [聖龍]. It is stated that this was in the Hung Kuen style [洪拳]. [96] At the Blessed Cloud Monastery [慶雲寺] on Ding Wu Mountain [鼎湖山], Wong Yan-Lam [王隱林] studied the Lion's Roar / Si ji Hau / Shizi Hou [獅子吼] style of martial arts [武術] for ten years. During this period he was also educated in Tibetan medical techniques / Joon Chuen Yee Suit [藏傳醫術] and the internal methods of both Lo Han Myuhn / Luohan men [羅漢門] / Boddhisattva division (Gate / Door) and the Gam Gong Myuhn / Jingang men [金剛

門] / Diamond division (Gate / Door). Sing Lung [聖龍] had several students during this period, but his two best and most important, were Wong Yan-Lam [王隱林] and Wong Lam-Hoi [黃林開]. Unfortunately, in the tenth year of Wong Yan-Lam's [王隱林] martial arts [武術] training, the old Tibetan Monk [藏傳僧], Sing Lung [聖龍] passed away. [96]

(The style of Lions Roar [獅子吼] changed names in Guangdong [廣東] after Sing Lung [聖龍] passed it onto Wong Yan-Lam [王隱林] and Wong Lam-Hoi [黃林開]. From this period onwards the successors of Wong Yan-Lam [王隱林] and Wong Lam-Hoi [黃林開] would call their styles by several other names. These styles and branches are Lama Pai [喇嘛派], Hap / Hop Gar [俠家] and White Crane [白鶴派].)

Lama Pai [喇嘛派] history states that Wong Yan-Lam [王隱林] then travelled north as far as Shan Xi Province / Shanxi Sheng [山西省] where he found employment as a bodyguard. This was for an escort company that provided armed protection to caravans travelling through the province. I have assumed that having started his training with Sing Lung [聖龍] as a boy and studying for ten years, Wong Yan-Lam [王隱林] would probably be in his early twenties when he became a bodyguard. He was an exceptionally skilled and outstanding fighter. Wong Yan-Lam [王隱林] used his skills in escorting wealthy families and other dignitaries, keeping them safe from thieves and bandits that roamed the countryside. These people often paid generous sums of money to ensure their safety was maintained while travelling across the lawless lands.

Whilst working as a bodyguard with this escort bureau, Wong Yan-Lam [王隱林] met many people. This gave him the opportunity to share and exchange his skills and ideas of martial arts [武術] with other masters [功夫大師]. It is stated that he became known for his powerful hands and lightning speed. The sources state that it was an armed escort company, which would obviously make sense in dealing with bandits who would be carrying weapons. Wong Yan-Lam [王隱林] was trained and skilled in various weapons. It is fair to assume that he would have specialised in some particular weapons, but these are not specified. Several sources state that he was a great swordsman, but it is unclear if this is meant in the use of this specific weapon or if this referred to his reputation as a martial artist.

Some accounts say it was during this period, that Wong Yan-Lam [王隱林] gained his nickname. Because of the many good deeds he performed, he was given the nickname of Hap, meaning Knight or Hero, (Hap / Hop meaning "chivalrous knight" / Haap Ga / Xia Jia [俠家]) and Gar, representing "family", which was a common practice with Southern Chinese styles. During these years of travelling, Wong Yan-Lam [王隱林] adopted the dangerous life of a Wuxia (Jianghu [江湖]), and observed first hand, the tyranny and oppression of the Manchurian (Ch'ing / Qing [清朝]) government. After witnessing the cruelty of the government, he developed an anti-Ch'ing / anti-Qing [反清清朝] attitude and became a revolutionary. [87] [90] [96] [96a]

Wuxia, *translates to "martial hero". Wuxia is split into two elements, wu (meaning "martial", "military", or "armed") and xia (meaning "honourable", "chivalrous", or "hero"). Martial artists who follow the code of xia are often referred to as a xiake (translates: "follower of xia") or youxia (translates: "wandering xia"). In some works of wuxia, the martial artist is sometimes called a "swordsman" or "swordswoman" even though he or she may not necessarily use a sword.* [95]

Several years later, around the early to mid 1850s, Wong Yan Lam [王隱林] decided to return home to Guangdong [廣東] and open his own school [武術學校] teaching Lama Pai [喇嘛派] Kung Fu. He thought the best way to do this, would be to go to Canton [廣州], (Guangzhou [廣州]) and build a reputation by proving his fighting skills and abilities. He therefore decided to have a large wooden stage built, known as a Lei-tai [擂臺], in front of the Honam Temple [河南寺] (Hoi Tong Monastery [海幢寺], on what is now the island district of Haizhu [海珠區]), and publicly proclaimed he would fight any challengers. It is stated that Wong Yan-Lam [王隱林] declared that, "None could beat his Lama Pai Kung Fu", and this proud boast brought forward many martial artists [武術家] to confront him to dispute his boast.

During this period, Guangdong [廣東] and in particular, Canton [廣州] was regarded as Southern China's foremost city for Kung Fu masters [功夫大師], and fighters of the toughest and highest quality. Fighters wore no protective equipment, and matches continued until one side conceded defeat, was forced off the Lei-tai [擂臺], or through injury was unable to continue. These challenge matches on the Lei-tai [擂臺] were taken very seriously, and had nearly no rules or restrictions, which could frequently result in either permanent injury, or sometimes, death. The matches were presided over by a referee who would witness both competitors signing a written document called a "Death Waiver / Sang Say Jong [生死狀]", which was a declaration of their commitment and courage, and a legal agreement to accept the outcome of the fight regardless. These death waivers / Sang Say Jong [生死狀] would then be displayed at the winner's school [武術學校], proving the combat effectiveness of that style and teacher [功夫老師], to attract new students and enhance their reputation.

(The film "Fearless", starring Jet Li, shows different versions of the Lei-tai [擂臺], and also gives an account of the "Death Waiver / Sang Say Jong [生死狀]" showing its significance.)

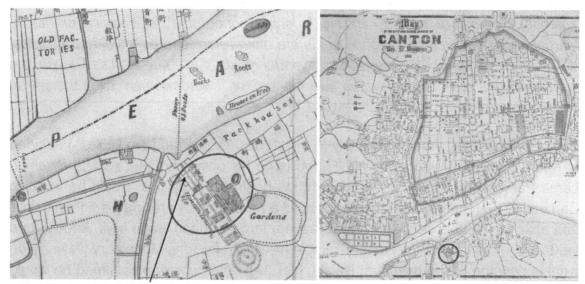

Wong Yan Lam had a Lei-tai erected in front of Honam Temple / Hoi Tong Monastery

(*This temple was commonly known as the Honam Temple during this period, which in Cantonese means south of the river. It is also known and spelt as: Haitong, Hoy Tung, Haizhuang, Haichung or Sea Monastery [海幢寺].*)

It is reputed that there were so many challengers, that the fights on the Lei-tai [擂臺] lasted for eighteen days. Wong Lam-Yan [王隱林] fought over one hundred and fifty contenders, winning all matches. He is reputed to have exercised the principles of his style during these challenge matches, but ensuring that one in particular, called "Chan [殘]", was used, which means to destroy. Some regard this principle as cruelty, as it is to severely injure or maim the opponent, ensuring that they are unable to return to the fight and cause any further harm. David Ross, of Lama Pai [喇嘛派], states that some were knocked unconscious and three were choked into submission. On completion of all the challenge matches, Wong [王隱林] had fought all the best fighters in the area that were willing to challenge him, and he had displayed an unprecedented fighting capability. He had remained victorious and his reputation spread enormously, enabling him to open his new Lama Pai School [喇嘛派武術學校] without delay. Due to his performance, it is reputed that Wong Yan-Lam [王隱林] was considered probably the best fighter in southern China. [15] [87] [90] [96] [96a]

Wong Yan-Lam [王隱林] then looked for a good location for his new school [武術學校]. He chose a site across the Pearl River / Zhu Jiang [珠江] from the Hoi Tong Monastery [海幢寺], near Wong Sa Road (Huangsha Avenue [黃沙大道]), in the West Gate / Sai Kwan / Xiguan [西關] (now called the Liwan district [荔灣區]) area of Canton [廣州]. The building was located in Kim Sin Street / Jianshan Jie [兼善街], just off Wong Sa

Road [黃沙大道] (present day location is just off Huangsha Avenue [黃沙大道] and near Penglai Road [蓬萊路].) This was a thriving and prosperous area, with several other schools [武術學校] located in the same vicinity. The news of Wong's [王隱林] epic challenge matches had an instant effect in attracting students to his new school [武術學校].

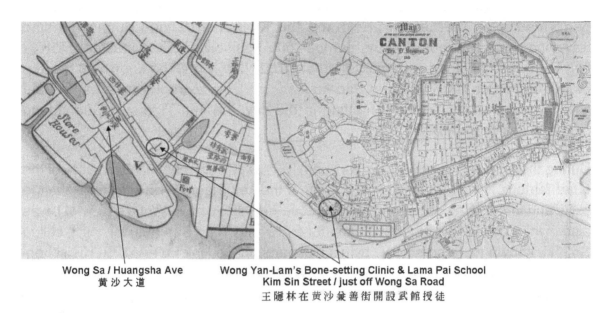

Wong Sa / Huangsha Ave
黃沙大道

Wong Yan-Lam's Bone-setting Clinic & Lama Pai School
Kim Sin Street / just off Wong Sa Road
王隱林在黃沙兼善街開設武館授徒

After such an impressive public performance on the Lei-tai [擂臺], people flocked to Wong's [王隱林] school [武術學校], wishing to be taught his fighting style and the secrets of Lama Pai [喇嘛派] Kung Fu. It is said that during challenge matches, Wong Yan-Lam [王隱林] would not allow a challenger to leave his school [武術學校] without being either maimed or killed, ensuring he had demonstrated the principles and theories of Lama Pai / Lama Pai (dick chin duo yuen lay) [喇嘛派的戰鬥原理]. These principles are listed below:

Chan [殘] (ruthlessness): *Chan [殘] represents the mental state that must be achieved. When attacked, there is no room for ambivalence or hesitation. The student must commit themselves to being totally ruthless. All strikes must be executed full force, and all blocking motions must destroy the opponent's limbs.*

Sim [閃] (dodge, evade, avoid): *Sim [閃] represents the preferred defensive method. It is considered superior to evade all attacks whilst simultaneously striking exposed vital points. This is achieved through footwork, body positioning, and jumping.*

Chyuhn [穿] (to pierce, penetrate): *Chyuhn [穿] represents the primary offensive goal, for all strikes to pierce and destroy vital points. It also refers to vital point striking.*

Jit [截] (to stop, intercept): *Jit [截] represents the second line of defence. Attacks that cannot be evaded must be intercepted and the attacking limb destroyed.* [87]

Shortly after the challenge matches on the Lei-Tai [擂臺], many prominent members of the community and Kung Fu masters [功夫大師] gathered to elect the current ten best martial artists [武術家]. Due to Wong Yan-Lam's [王隱林] recent impressive performance on the Lei-Tai [擂臺] and the reputation gained during his time travelling, he was elected to the number one position of these masters [功夫大師]. From then on, these top martial artists [功夫大師] would be known as the Ten Tigers of Canton / Kwong Tung Sap Fu [廣東十虎]. An extract from a Lama Pai [喇嘛派] poem states, "A lot of fighting in the city, the Ten Tigers of Guangdong made the earth tremble." [90]

During the following years, Wong Yan-Lam [王隱林] would meet up with some of the other famous Kung Fu masters [功夫大師] of the Ten Tigers [廣東十虎] to exchange skills and ideas. A neighbouring school [武術學校] close by to Wong's [王隱林], was also owned by a fellow Tiger of Guangdong / Kwong Tung Sap Fu [廣東十虎], called So [蘇], known more commonly by his nickname of So Hak Fu [蘇黑虎]. His school [武術學校] was located only several hundred metres away, in Wong Sa Road / Huangsha Avenue [黃沙大道]. Hak Fu Mun's [黑虎門] oral history states that besides teaching Lama Pai [喇嘛派] Kung Fu [功夫], Wong Yan-Lam [王隱林] was also running a bone setting clinic / Tip Da Yee Kwun [跌打醫館] and practicing Tibetan medicine [藏傳醫術] from his building at Kim Sin Street / Jianshan Jie [兼善街]. Wong Yan-Lam [王隱林] and So Hak Fu [蘇黑虎] were friends, and they exchanged ideas and techniques. From this exchange, So Hak Fu [蘇黑虎] incorporated some of the upper body movements, with certain powerful long arm attacking techniques, into his style of Hak Fu Mun [黑虎門]. Both styles also have their own versions of Kam Kong Kuen [金剛拳] routine [套路] (spelt Dai Gum Gong Kyuhn [大金剛拳] in the Lama Pai [喇嘛派] style). From this exchange, it is believed that Wong Yan-Lam [王隱林] incorporated certain Hak Fu [黑虎] techniques into his Lama Pai [喇嘛派] style, such as the Tiger Claw [虎爪]. This technique can be used to strike vunerable areas such as the face and throat, as well as seizing to either choke or control joints.

Nearby was another one of the Ten Tigers [廣東十虎], by the name of Lai Yan-Chiu [黎仁超] of the Hakka Kuen [客家拳] style, also known as Southern Praying Mantis [南派螳螂]. Hak Fu Mun [黑虎門] oral tradition states that he was a money lender and owner of the Shun Hang pawn shop [信亨押店] which was located on Wong Sa Road / Huangsha Avenue [黃沙大道]. The three masters [功夫大師] became close friends, exchanging their knowledge, and become known as the "Three Heroes of Wong Sa [黃沙三傑]". [50] [50a] [51]

The Three Heroes of
Wong Sa Road / Haungsha Avenue
黃沙三傑

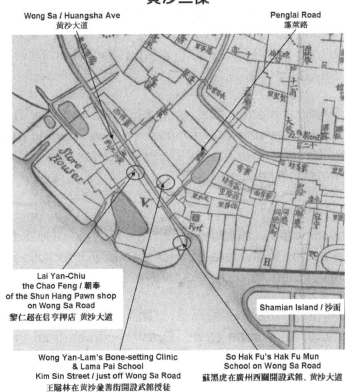

Wong Sa / Huangsha Ave
黃沙大道

Penglai Road
蓬萊路

Lai Yan-Chiu
the Chao Feng / 朝奉
of the Shun Hang Pawn shop
on Wong Sa Road
黎仁超在信亨押店 黃沙大道

Shamian Island / 沙面

Wong Yan-Lam's Bone-setting Clinic
& Lama Pai School
Kim Sin Street / just off Wong Sa Road
王隱林在黃沙鑫善街開設武館授徒

So Hak Fu's Hak Fu Mun
School on Wong Sa Road
蘇黑虎在廣州西關開設武館, 黃沙大道

It is also known that Wong Kei-Ying [黃麒英] and his son Wong Fei-Hung [黃飛鴻] both exchanged ideas with Wong Yan-Lam [王隱林]. It is stated that the long arm techniques in the Tiger and Crane / Fu Hok Seung Ying Kuen [虎鶴雙形] and the Five Element Fist / Ng Haang Kuen [五行拳] (now found in the Five Animal Five Element Fist / Ng Ying Ng Haang Kuen [五形五行拳] routine [套路]) are an outcome of this exchange in the Wong's [黃麒英] & [黃飛鴻] Hung Gar [洪家] lineage. It is understood that Wong Yan-Lam [王隱林] learnt the Hung Kuen [洪拳] Five Animal Fist / Ng Ying Kuen [五形拳] from Wong Kei-Ying [黃麒英] and his son Wong Fei-Hung [黃飛鴻]. From these techniques Wong Yan-Lam [王隱

林] created the Small Five Animal Fist / Siu Ng Ying Kuen (also spelt Siu Nhg Yihng Kyuhn) [小五形拳], which he later incorporated into his Lama Pai [喇嘛派] style. [87]

It is understood that at this time, Wong Yan-Lam's [王隱林] training syllabus included the following [88a] :-

Twelve bridges / Sub Yee Chee Kiu [十二支橋]
Small Lo Han Kuen / Siu Lo Hon Kuen [小羅漢拳]
Tiger & Crane Fighting / Fu Hog Zhui Du [虎鶴相鬥]
Great Lo Han Kuen / Ta Lo Hon Kuen [大羅漢拳]
Knight Style Knife / Hop Kai Duo [俠家刀]
Nine Point Twelve Spurs Loud Staff / Kow Dip Sub Yee Cheong Hong Gwun [九點十二鎗響棍].

I would like to thank Sifu David Rogers of the Rising Crane Centre located in Bedford, UK, for providing the following descriptions of these methods and routines [套路]. David stated that unfortunately, the different lineages (of Hap Gar [俠家], Lama Pai [喇嘛派], Bak Hok Pai [白鶴派]) have Wong Yan-Lam [王隱林] teaching different sets (routines [套路]). However, he stated that these were certainly the sets (routines [套

路]) that are preserved in his line, with the exception of the last one, the Nine Point Twelve Spurs Loud Staff / Kow Dip Sub Yee Cheong Hong Gwun [九點十二鎗響棍]. David was not familiar with this particular routine [套路] but stated that in his lineage, their staff form (routine [套路]) is called the "Yellow Dragon Staff / Wong Lung Gwun [黃龍棍]", and that Yellow Dragon / Wong Lung [黃龍] was Wong Yan-Lam's [王隱林] nickname. David learnt all these routines [套路] in Canton [廣州] (Guangzhou [廣州]) from his Sifu [師父], Master Deng Jan Gong [鄧鎮江].

(Sifu David Rogers has trained in Chinese martial arts since 1984. He is an indoor disciple of Master Deng Jan Gong. He is the only non-Chinese to have learned the entire Deng family Hap Kune system directly from Master Deng in Canton. For more information please visit :- http://www.risingcrane.co.uk/) [88b]

Twelve bridges / Sub Yee Chee Kiu [十二支橋] :- This is a training set for developing the strength of the grip as well as building powerful forearms. This method also aids the development of connecting the power to the practitioner's core. It is practised slowly with abdominal pressure, similar to the 'Iron Thread' form of Hung Kuen [洪拳].

Small Lo Han Kuen / Siu Lo Hon Kyuhn (Kuen) [小羅漢拳] : This is a fundamental fighting set which uses the 'long bridge' and large steps. Evasion comes from the footwork and power is generated in large arcs. This set encompasses most of the main hands techniques of the style.

Tiger & Crane Fighting / Fu Hog Zhui Du [虎鶴相鬥] : This is an intermediate level routine [套路]. The general method is more for utilising counter attacks and mixing both 'Hard' and 'Soft' techniques.

Great Lo Han Kuen / Ta Lo Hon Kyuhn (Kuen) [大羅漢拳] : This is an advanced level routine [套路] that requires a high degree of skill and hand conditioning. Evasion is by movement with the head or body. Attacks are aimed at the vital points on the opponent predominately using hand techniques such as the 'phoenix eye' or 'Needle finger'. It also includes Wave Punch and other distinctive long arm strikes of the system.

Knight Style Knife / Hop Kai Duo /[俠家劍刀] : The sword used for this routine [套路] resembles that of a Japanese Katana. It has a long, thin blade which is sharpened on one side. This routine [套路] has many techniques typical of the Broadsword [刀], and also Straight Sword [劍], combined. Although it contains mostly single handed techniques, there are some two handed methods as well. It involves fast turns and powerful cutting movements, with stabbing attacks in all directions.

Yellow Dragon Staff / Wong Lung Gwun [黃龍棍] : Although this weapon is shorter than the long pole of Southern Siu Lum / Shaolin, for the majority of the routine [套路]

(approximately 80%), it is still used in the 'single head' method. This weapon routine [套路] also contains the flowers method and also has double ended techniques within.

David Rogers also stated that his Sifu [師父], Master Deng Jan Gong [鄧鎮江], told him that at the time of the Ten Tigers [廣東十虎], all of the masters [功夫大師] would meet up for Yum Cha [飲茶] at the tea houses. Here, they would freely exchange techniques. Styles were not so insular then, and cross training was the norm. He was not familiar with exactly who taught whom, which techniques, as it was more of what the Cantonese call, "Mo Shut Gau Lau [無師自通]". This means that this cross training occured without the Sifu [師父], student-disciple / todai [徒弟] formality and was therefore more like a friendly exchange.

Yum Cha [飲茶] is a southern Chinese style of morning or afternoon tea, which involves drinking Chinese tea and eating dim sum (點心).

Yum cha translates to mean drink tea and dim sum (點心) refers to the wide range of small dishes, but in Cantonese yum cha, or "drinking tea", refers to the entire meal.

The Cantonese term of yam cha or yum cha mostly refers to the tradition of morning tea in Cantonese cuisine represented by the traditional tea houses of Guangzhou (Canton). [88c]

During the late 1800s, Wong Yan-Lam [王隱林] continued to focus on expanding his school and teaching his students. During this period, he built up a group of proficient disciples to help him with this task, as he was growing older. In the early 1900s, Wong Yan-Lam [王隱林] gave his number one disciple [武術弟子], Wong Hon-Wing [黃漢榮], more responsibility for looking after his school [武術學校]. This worked out well, and sometime later, Wong Yan-Lam [王隱林] decided to retire. Once in retirement, Wong Yan-Lam [王隱林] returned to his home village of Shiu Hing / Zhaoqing [肇慶] at the foot of Dinghu Shan [鼎湖山], and while there, he allowed Wong Hon-Wing [黃漢榮] to run his school [武術學校] entirely.

In the early 1900s, there was a growing tide of nationalism, and therefore resentment of foreign influences and systems. The name Lama Pai [喇嘛派] was associated with the Tibetan Monks [藏傳僧] who had introduced this style under the Manchurians [滿族]. It is understood that due to this, Wong Hon-Wing [黃漢榮] was advised by Dr. Sun Yat-Sen [孫逸仙], to alter the name. Wong Hon-Wing [黃漢榮] therefore chose the old nickname of his teacher, and renamed the style, Hap (Hop) Gar [俠家]. It is believed that the students of Wong Lam-Hoi [黃林開] (a fellow student of Wong Yan-Lam [王隱林] under the Tibetan monk [藏傳僧], Sing Lung [聖龍]), were offended by naming the style after their elder uncle, which would deny any credit to their own teacher [功夫老

師]. Nhg Siu-Chung [吳肇鐘] therefore chose the alternative name of White Crane / Bak (Pak) Hok Pai [白鶴派], to represent their style under the lineage of Wong Lam-Hoi [黃林開].

There are several accounts of Wong Yan-Lam's [王隱林] later years from the different lineages of his style. These sources state how he passed on the style during the final years of his life.

During Wong Yan-Lam's [王隱林] retirement, his disciple [武術弟子], Wong Hon-Wing [黃漢榮], opened several more schools [武術學校] to expand the style further. Unfortunately, several disputes occurred, with rumours that Wong Hon-Wing [黃漢榮] was either not passing on certain teachings, or not paying royalties to his teacher [功夫老師] Wong Yan-Lam [王隱林], or that Wong Yan-Lam [王隱林] was bored and so unable to stay in retirement. The rumours resulted in Wong Hon-Wing [黃漢榮] losing his position, and Wong Yan-Lam [王隱林] coming out of retirement to teach again, taking on new disciples [武術弟子]. One of these later students, was a young man by the name of Jyu Jik-Chyuhn [朱亦傳], who had previous experience in several styles of Kung Fu [功夫] including Hung Kuen [洪拳], Choy Lay Fut / (also spelt Choy Li Fut) [蔡李佛] and Southern Eagle Claw / Jing Jar [鷹爪]. It is reputed that he had also just spent the previous seven years studying under Wong Lam-Hoi [黃林開], learning all his open-hand and weapons routines [套路]. Near the end of his training under Wong Lam-Hoi [黃林開], he introduced himself to Wong Yan-Lam [王隱林]. At this introduction, Jyu Jik-Chyuhn [朱亦傳] requested that he be taken on as Wong Yan-Lam's [王隱林] student so he could learn his style of Lama Pai [喇嘛派]. Wong Yan-Lam [王隱林] accepted his request and taught him the different forms [套路] (routines) and techniques in his style over the next several years.

At nearly ninety years old, one of Wong Yan-Lam's [王隱林] last students was a young man by the name of Choi Yit-Gung. Choi Yit-Gung was from a wealthy family and had been introduced to the old Wong Yan-Lam [王隱林] when he was eleven years old. Unfortunately Wong Yan-Lam [王隱林] had by now lost his eyesight, and so Choi Yit-Gung arranged for him to live at his home and be taken care of by his servants. Wong Yan-Lam [王隱林] was very grateful, and in return, he agreed to teach the young man. Choi Yit-Gung then spent the next eight years dedicating his time to studying under Wong Yan-Lam [王隱林], mastering his Lama Pai style [喇嘛派] of Kung Fu [功夫].

By doing the maths and working backwards, I have made the following assumption: *It is known that Wong Hon-Wing [黃漢榮] was for a period, Wong Yan-Lam's [王隱林] successor, until his loss of position due to various issues. Wong Hon-Wing [黃漢榮] had adopted the style name of Hap / Hop Gar [俠家] (Wong Yan-Lam's [王隱林] old nickname) at the recommendation of Dr Sun Yat-Sen [孫逸仙] during the period shortly after the founding of the Chinese Republic in 1912. Wong Yan-Lam [王隱林] came out of retirement and started to accept disciples at an advanced age. One of these was Wong Hon-Wing's [黃漢榮] senior disciple called Lei Ying-Chuen [黎應全], and the other was a young boy of eleven called Choi Yit-Gung. It is stated that Choi Yit-Gung started his training when Wong Yan-Lam [王隱林] was 90 years old and lasted 8 years. Jyu Jik-Chyuhn [朱亦傳] was born in 1892, and had trained in various other styles before first studying under Wong Lam-Hoi [黃林開] for 7 years, and then he continued his education in Lama Pai [喇嘛派] under Wong Yan-Lam [王隱林]. It is stated that Ng Yim-Ming [吳冉明] trained under the now blind Wong Yan-Lam [王隱林] for 8 years, until 1928. [91] I therefore believe that Wong Yan-Lam [王隱林] died sometime around 1930, which means he was probably born sometime between the late 1820s and 1830. A branch of the Netherlands Hop Gar [俠家] state that Wong Yan-Lam [王隱林] was born in 1830, [88] although the Taiping Institute differs, and states that Wong Yan-Lam / Wang Yinlin [王隐林] was born in 1801 and passed away in 1882. [96]*

Another branch of Hop Gar [俠家] states that Ng Yim-Ming [吳冉明] studied under Wong Yan-Lam [王隱林] from 1920 to 1928. Ng Yim-Ming [吳冉明] (later known as Harry Ng) trained in a local opera troupe / Kat Tuen [劇團] from the age of four. When he was twenty he started training in one of Wong Yan-Lam's [王隱林] schools [武術學校], which was at this time, being run by Wong Hon-Wing [黃漢榮]. Because Ng Yim-Ming [吳冉明] had little money to pay for many lessons, he was unable to advance at the same rate as his fellow students. It is stated that Wong Hon-Wing [黃漢榮] would only teach what his students could afford. But due to Ng Yim-Ming's [吳冉明] hard work and dedication, his teacher [功夫老師], Wong Hon-Wing [黃漢榮] sent him on errands to Wong Yan-Lam [王隱林].

Wong Yan-Lam [王隱林] was lonely and spent much time talking to Ng Yim-Ming [吳冉明]. This time together helped develop a good relationship, and one day, the elderly Wong [王隱林] asked Ng Yim-Ming [吳冉明] to show him what he had learnt. Because Wong Yan-Lam [王隱林] was now blind, Ng Yim-Ming [吳冉明] asked that as he could not see, how would he be able to judge his abilities. The elderly Wong [王隱林] replied that he would listen to his movements, and so judge the power and correctness due to the sound. After a small demonstration, the elderly Wong stopped Ng Yim-Ming [吳冉明] and informed him that he would instruct him. Ng Yim-Ming [吳冉明] was told to continue going to the school [武術學校] during the day, and then to come on an evening, so he could train under Wong Yan-Lam [王隱林] personally, on a one to one basis. This continued until 1928 when Ng Yim-Ming [吳冉明] was forced to move out of the area with the opera troupe / Kat Tuen [劇團]. [91] [92]

The Chinese Wikipedia [96b] states that Wong Yan-Lam's [王隱林] more notable students included :-   Cho / Zhu [朱]

Wong Hon Wing / Wang Hanrong [王漢榮]
Wong Lun / Wang Lun [王倫]
Wong Lum / Wang Lin [王林]
Poon Kame / Pan Jian [潘鑒]
Ng Yee Kon / Wu Yi Gong [吳懿恭]
Siu Chung / Zhao Zhong [肇鍾]

The Taiping Institute [96] confirms these, and states that Wong Hon Wing / Wang Hanrong [王漢榮] called the style Hop Gar [俠家], that Ng Yee Kon / Wu Yi Gong [吳懿恭] called the style Lama Pai [喇嘛派] and that Nhg Siu-Chung [吳肇钟] called it White Crane / Bak (Pak) Hok Pai / Baihe Pai [白鶴派].

It is believed that sometime around 1930, Wong Yan-Lam [王隱林] passed away due to natural causes.

Wong Ching-Hoh [黃澄可]

(sometimes spelt Wong Cheng Ho. Traditional Chinese: 黃澄可; simplified Chinese: 黃澄可; pinyin: *Huang Chengke*.)

According to the Taiping Institute, Wong Ching-Hoh [黃澄可] was born in the district of Sam Shing / Sanshui [三水]. [14] Other sources state he was from the small village Mar Tong / Ma Dong [麻東村]. [115] [115a] Unfortunately, there are several small villages dotted around Guangdong Province [廣東省] named Mar Tong / Ma dong [馬洞], but only one spelt the same as the source [麻東村]. One option, is a village named Madong [马洞] located near Sam Shing / Sanshui [三水] (formerly Sam Shing City / Sanshui [三水]) city. This location would tie in with the Taiping Institute source, and also make sense with

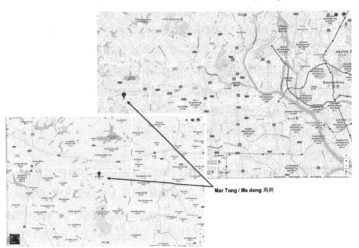

Mar Tong / Ma dong 馬洞

the connection of Luk Ah-Choi / Lu A Cai [陸阿采] wandering around this area. Madong [馬洞] is located approximately 16 kms in a south easterly direction from Sam Shing / Sanshui [三水]. This village lies approximately 22 kms west of Guangzhou [廣州] (Canton) and only about 12 kms north west of Fat Shan / Foshan [佛山].

Another possible option is that Wong Ching-Hoh [黃澄可] was actually from the village called Mar Tong / Ma dong [麻東村], but this is located much further away in the Chung Shan / Zhongshan [中山] district. (During the 1800s, this area was called Heungshan / Xiangshan [香山], but was renamed to Chung Shan / Zhongshan [中

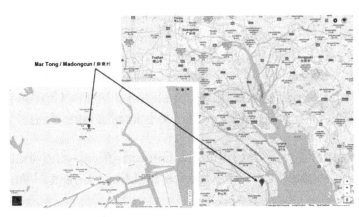

Mar Tong / Madongcun 麻東村

山] in 1925, in honour of Sun Yat-Sen [孫逸仙] who is known in Mandarin as Sun Zhongshan. Sun Yat-Sen [孫逸仙] (1866-1925) was born in Cuiheng village [翠亨村] in Nanlang Township [南蓢鎮], of what was then Xiangshan County. [115b]) The village of Mar Tong / Ma dong Cun [麻東村] is located approximately 72 kms in a south easterly direction of Guangzhou [廣州] (Canton [廣州]).

It is believed that Wong Ching-Hoh [黃澄可] was born sometime just before 1820, during the reign of the Emperor Kar Hing Dai / Jiaqing [嘉慶帝] (9th February 1796 – 2nd September 1820).

During the late 1820s, Luk Ah-Choi / Lu A Cai [陸阿采] was being hunted by the Ch'ing / Qing [清朝] army. While evading the pursuing Ch'ing / Qing [清朝] soldiers, he wandered into a village called Mar Tong / Ma dong [麻東村]. As he cautiously made his way through the village, he was noticed by a young man called Wong Ching-Hoh [黃澄可], who realised that soldiers in the area were pursuing him. Like many Han Chinese [漢族], Wong [黃澄可] did not like the Manchurians [滿族] (Ch'ing / Qing [清朝]), who were generally cruel and arrogant towards the Hans [漢族]. He did not wish the wanderer to be caught and possibly executed, and so decided to help him. The young Wong [黃澄可] offered to assist Luk [陸阿采] by providing food and shelter, hiding him from the soldiers. Luk Ah-Choi [陸阿采] accepted Wong's [黃澄可] help, and in return for the kindness, offered to teach the young man martial arts [武術]. Wong Ching-Hoh [黃澄可] stated that he was not interested in martial arts [武術], so Luk [陸阿采] taught him some basic skills described as key techniques of Hung Kuen [洪拳], instead. While Luk [陸阿采] taught him, he observed that Wong [黃澄可] was an honest, hard working, young man with a talent for Kung Fu [功夫].

Wong Ching-Hoh [黃澄可] was an intelligent person, but unfortunately from a poor family. He had no prospects and was looking for something to focus on, which would give him some direction in his life. When Luk Ah-Choi [陸阿采] was leaving, he invited the young Wong [黃澄可] to come to Canton [廣州] with him. Luk [陸阿采] informed him that he was going to the provincial capital [省會城市] to establish a school [武術學校] there, and so spread the style of Hung Kuen [洪拳]. Luk [陸阿采] saw that Wong Ching-Hoh [黃澄可] was a kind-hearted, generous person who was happy to help others. For these reasons, Luk [陸阿采] invited him to take up Kung Fu [少林功夫] and train with him at his school [武術學校]. Wong [黃澄可] accepted this invitation, believing it would give him new challenges and experiences. It is not stated if Wong [黃澄可] travelled with Luk Ah-Choi [陸阿采] to Canton [廣州], or followed on at a later date.

It is recorded that Wong Ching-Hoh [黃澄可] did move to Canton [廣州], and that sometime later, he lived in a building located on Benevolence and Love Street / Wai Oi Street [惠愛街].

(The current location of Benevolence and Love Street / Wai Oi Street [惠愛街] is now the Zhongshan Sixth Road [中山六路].) This street was situated in the old walled city of Canton [廣州], and was part of the main avenue that ran from the West Gate / Sai Kwan / Xiguan [西關] to the East Gate / Dung Kwan / Dongguan [東關]. Also located on this street, were many Ch'ing / Qing [清朝] government buildings. [106] [113] [115] ("惠愛街", 沿街分布有廣州主要的官署衙門， 如清代的布政司、巡撫部院、廣東都司等." [115c])

Wong Ching-Hoh's house located within this area.

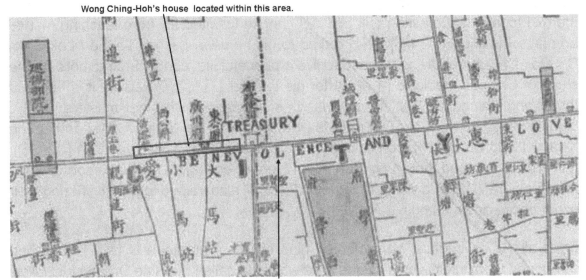

惠愛街 / Benevolence and Love Street / Wai Oi Street

Wong Ching-Hoh [黃澄可] was a clever and talented young man, who trained very hard under Luk Ah-Choi [陸阿采] for many years at his school [武術學校]. During this time, he also met and befriended two other students of Luk Ah-Choi [陸阿采] who would later become renowned masters [功夫大師] themsleves. These two fellow students were Wong Kei-Ying [黃麒英] and Leung Kwan / Liang Kun [梁坤], who is now known better by his nickname of Tit kiu Saam / Tie Qiao San [鐵橋三] which literally means "Iron Bridge Three". Wong Ching-Hoh [黃澄可] trained with both of these during this period, gaining more knowledge, skills and experience. Techniques that he thought proved effective and practical, he added to his own repertoire.

According to Wong Kiew Kit, [85] and several other sources including Wikipedia [109b] [114a], Wong Ching-Hoh [黃澄可] was also famous for his Iron Head skill. Iron Head / Tee Tau Kun / Tie tou gong [鐵頭功] is one of the famed 72 arts of Siu Lum / Shaolin, and perfecting this skill takes several years of dedicated practice. It is stated that to achieve this skill, the practitioner initially wraps several dozen layers of soft, usually silk fabric around his head. Within these layers of silk are up to two layers of thin metal plate. They will then strike a wall with their head, a few times each day, with only a little force to start with. As time goes by, the amount of force is gradually increased, as are the amount of times striking the wall. After a year of this continual training, a few layers are removed, to lessen the cushioning. One hundred days later, more layers of fabric are removed, and this process continues until after two years, all the layers of fabric are taken off. This is the final stage of training, and the practitioner will continue to strike the wall with his head. At first this is unpleasant, but this feeling gradually lessens. When the head becomes as hard as stone, the objective of Iron Head [鐵頭功] conditioning has been achieved. [114]

It is believed that Wong Ching-Hoh [黃澄可] trained under Luk Ah-Choi [陸阿采] until the mid to late 1830s, when Luk [陸阿采] choose to withdraw from teaching martial arts [武術] publically. Luk [陸阿采] retired to his home of Leshan Lodge / Lok Seen Siu Oak [樂山小屋], having decided to live a peaceful life, concentrating more on the study of Chinese medicine [中醫]. After his teacher [功夫老師] retired, it is believed that Wong Ching-Hoh [黃澄可] continued his education with other masters [功夫大師] including his two Kung Fu brothers [師兄弟], Wong Kei-Ying [黃麒英] and Leung Kwan / Liang Kun [梁坤] (Iron Bridge Three / Tit kiu Saam / Tie Qiao San [鐵橋三]). It is also understood that Hung Man Ting / Hong Wending [洪文定] (the son of Hung Hei-Kwun [洪熙官]) and Wong Ching-Hoh [黃澄可] also trained together, sharing their experiences and methods.

From all his experience, he perfected nine styles of martial arts [武術], and then developed them into his own unique style which he called the Nine Dragon Fist / Kow Loong Kuen [九龍拳]. This style contained a wide range of diverse techniques, utilising both soft and hard forms. Wong Ching-Hoh [黃澄可] was a master of this style. [109] [109e] [113] [164]

The nine methods of his style were called :-

The Gliding Dragon movement / Yau Loong Sai [遊龍勢]
The Turning Dragon movement / Suen Loong Sai [旋龍勢]
Capture the Dragon movement / Kame Loong Sai [擒龍勢]
The Swinging Dragon movement / Buy Loong Sai [擺龍勢]
The Sinking Dragon movement / Champ Loong Sai [沉龍勢]
The Circling Dragon movement / Poon Loong Sai [盤龍勢]
Dividing the Dragon movement / Fun Loong Sai [分龍勢]
The Coiling Dragon movement / Chen Loong Sai [纏龍勢]
The Flying Dragon movement / Fai Loong Sai [飛龍勢]

It is stated that when combining all these nine methods into one Nine Dragon Fist / Kow Loong Kuen [九龍拳] movement, this whole movement would be like Nine Dragons Soaring into the Sky with infinite possibilities ["九龍沖天", 幻變無窮]. [113]

It is recorded that Wong Ching-Hoh [黃澄可], trained under Luk Ah-Choi [陸阿采], Wong Kei-Ying [黃麒英] and Leung Kwan / Liang Kun [梁坤] (Iron Bridge Three / Tit kiu Saam / Tie Qiao San [鐵橋三]), who were all predominately Hung Kuen [洪拳] masters [功夫大師]. He must have therefore also trained under other Kung Fu masters [功夫大師] of different styles, to eventually formulate his own unique Nine Dragon Fist / Kow Loong Kuen [九龍拳]. This assumption is made from the description of the Nine Dragon Fist / Kow Loong Kuen [九龍拳] style which states that it combined both hard and soft forms [終自創出一套剛柔並重, 變化無窮的"九龍拳"].

During this period in China, times were very hard and there was much corruption. Wong Ching-Hoh [黃澄可] would promote a spirit of Chivalry by combating these problems, and in so doing, became a local hero to many ordinary people. The following is one such story about the deeds of Wong Ching-Hoh [黃澄可] that helped to elevate him in the eyes of his peers and the general public.

A story of Wong Ching-Hoh saving a beautiful lady from the Ch'ing / Qing [清朝]

Wong Ching-Hoh [黃澄可] was living in Benevolence and Love Street / Wai Oi Street [惠愛街] in the old city of Canton [廣州] (Guangzhou [廣州]). One day, at Kat Har Street [旗下街] which was close by Wong Ching-Hoh's [黃澄可] home, a Ch'ing / Qing [清朝] military officer called Tung Tin-Ba [佟天霸] was walking along the crowded street escorted by several soldiers. Tung Tin-Ba [佟天霸] was a military attache [武官] who had been posted to Canton [廣州] on a short term secondment. As they marched along Kat Har Street [旗下街], Tung Tin-Ba [佟天霸] noticed a very beautiful lady who was being carried in a sedan chair [花轎]. This lady was of Han Chinese [漢族] origin and her name was Siu Ying [秀英].

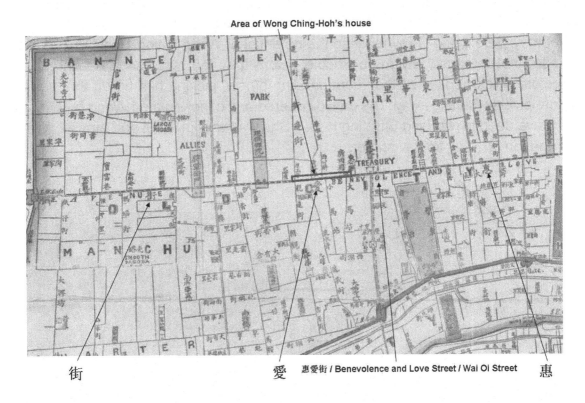

Area of Wong Ching-Hoh's house

街　　　　　　　　愛　惠愛街 / Benevolence and Love Street / Wai Oi Street　　惠

Tung Tin-Ba [佟天霸] greatly desired her and because he realised she was Han Chinese [漢族] decided to kidnap her as he knew his superiors would not be concerned. He therefore commanded his soldiers to stop the sedan chair [花轎] and so help him capture her. As the soldiers began to seize Siu Ying [秀英], she screamed for help and all this commotion started to attract a large crowd of people. Wong [黃澄可] happened

167

to be passing by at the same time, and could not bear to stand by, watching as the Ch'ing / Qing [清朝] soldiers were trying to abduct this beautiful lady. Wong Ching-Hoh [黃澄可] stepped forward to intervene and told the soldiers to leave the young woman alone. Tung [佟天霸] didn't pay any attention to Wong [黃澄可], and carried on with his men in the kidnapping of the beautiful Siu Ying [秀英]. She continued screaming at the solidiers and shouting out at people in the crowd pleading with them to save her.

Wong Ching-Hoh [黃澄可] was outraged at the disgraceful behaviour of these Ch'ing / Qing [清朝] troops and quickly leapt forward to help the young woman. Tung Tin-Ba [佟天霸] was carrying double broadswords [雙刀] and as he saw Wong [黃澄可] coming forward to interfere, he slashed at him with these. Wong [黃澄可] easily evaded the clumsy attack and countered with a kick, knocking the swords [雙刀] from Tung's [佟天霸] hands. Tung Tin-Ba [佟天霸] was furious that a common Han [漢族] peasant was meddling with his plans so he again attacked Wong Ching-Hoh [黃澄可], throwing many punches at him. Wong [黃澄可] easily blocked these, and retaliated with several punching and kicking techniques which swiftly defeated Tung Tin-Ba [佟天霸].These counter strikes sent Tung Tin-Ba [佟天霸] crashing to the floor where he lay squirming around, moaning in pain with broken ribs. When the Ch'ing / Qing [清朝] soldiers saw that their commanding officer had been so easily defeated, they all suddenly stopped what they were doing. They realised the potential of Wong Ching-Hoh [黃澄可], and decided not to cause any more trouble before they too received a beating. They therefore quickly collected their commanding officer, picking him up off the ground, before quickly running away. The crowd cheered and congratulated Wong [黃澄可] for his brave deed in rescuing Siu Ying [秀英]. She was very grateful and thanked Wong Ching-Hoh [黃澄可] for saving her.

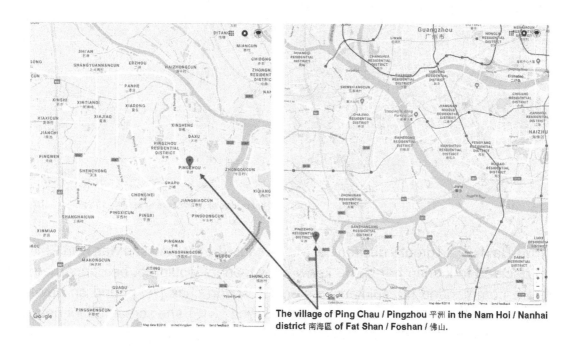

The village of Ping Chau / Pingzhou 平洲 **in the Nam Hoi / Nanhai district** 南海區 **of Fat Shan / Foshan /** 佛山.

Wong Ching-Hoh [黃澄可] gained a lot of respect from the people for this incident, but unfortunately, he was now classed as a criminal due to the assault on the Ch'ing / Qing [清朝] military attache [武官], Tung Tin-Ba [佟天霸]. As a wanted man, Wong [黃澄可] had no other choice but to quickly flee Canton [廣州] and go into hiding. It is stated that he moved with his family to the village of Ping Chau [平洲], in the Nam Hoi Yuen [南海縣] (now Nanhai district [南海區]) of Fat Shan / Foshan [佛山].

Fortunately, shortly after this incident, Tung Tin-Ba [佟天霸] was transferred to a different region away from Canton [廣州]. When Wong Ching-Hoh [黃澄可] was told the news that Tung Tin-Ba [佟天霸] had been transferred from Canton [廣州], he was able to come out of hiding. It is believed that the physical description that the Ch'ing / Qing [清朝] authorities had of him was quite poor, and the only person who could positively identify him was Tung Tin-Ba [佟天霸]. Now that the coast was clear, Wong [黃澄可] and his family were able to return to Canton [廣州]. It is not certain if this was to their original home at Benevolence and Love Street / Wai Oi Street [惠愛街] or elsewhere in the city. [115]

Incidents like this helped to promote Wong Ching-Hoh [黃澄可] and he started to be regarded as a hero by the general public. It is stated that Wong Ching-Hoh [黃澄可] put his knowledge and skills to the test in many life or death fights. Unfortunately, it is not recorded if these fights were just challenge matches, or for other possible reasons. What is recorded, is that when he did fight, he was very fearless, not being concerned if his head was hit or his blood was split. It is understood that his preferred technique when fighting or duelling [決鬥] was to use his renowned skills of Iron Head / Tee Tau Kun / Tie tou gong [鐵頭功]. This would be to strike at his opponents, head or abdomen, in order to defeat them. [109c] He was respected as an honest, kind-hearted and generous person, who was always happy to help others. These traits, plus his fearless attitude during numerous life or death fights, earned him a highly esteemed reputation amongst his fellow martial artists [武術家]. During the mid to late 1850s, many prominent members of the community and Kung Fu masters [功夫大師] gathered to elect the ten best martial artists [武術家] at that time. Wong Ching-Hoh [黃澄可] was chosen, and from that time on was known as one of the Ten Tigers of Canton / Kwong Tung Sap Fu [廣東十虎].

One source states that Wong Ching-Hoh / Huang Cheng Ke [黃澄可] had many disciples [武術弟子] in Guangdong Province [廣東省]. [106] Therefore he must have either established a school [武術學校], or accepted disciples privately, and taught them his unqiue style of the Nine Dragon Fist / Kow Loong Kuen [九龍拳]. However, this same source only mentions the Hung Kuen [洪拳] style which was known to be taught by one of his disciples [武術弟子].

Unfortunately, I have been unable to find any information about Wong Ching-Hoh's [黃澄可] later life after these events. The only information I could find was from Tony (José Antonio) Rey García's web site [106a], stating that one of Wong Ching-Hoh's [黃澄可] later disciples [武術弟子] was a man called Wong Ying Oi / Huang Ying E [黃英娥]. He was born in 1864, so I can only assume that he studied under Wong Ching-Hoh [黃澄可] sometime from the late 1870s onwards. It is stated that Wong Ying Oi / Huang Ying E [黃英娥] had studied under both Wong Ching-Hoh / Huang Cheng Ke [黃澄可] and Hung Man Ting / Hong Wending [洪文定] (the son of Hung Hei-Kwun [洪熙官]). Wong Ying Oi / Huang Ying E [黃英娥] became a Buddhist [佛教徒] and later in life, moved to a village near Toishan / Taishan [台山] (Southwest of Kongmoon / Jiangmen [江門]) where he established his own martial arts school [武術學校] called the Shan Tong Wu Tong / Shang Tang Hui Tang Academy [山塘會堂].

So Hak Fu [蘇黑虎]

(So / 蘇 was more commonly known by his nickname of So Hak Fu (or So Hark Fu) traditional Chinese: 蘇黑虎; simplified Chinese: 苏黑虎; pinyin: *Su Heihu*)

Unfortunately, only So's [蘇] family name has been passed down in time and his full name has been lost. This is because he was commonly known by his nickname of So the Black Tiger / So Hak Fu [蘇黑虎] and this is the only name that has been recorded over the years. So [蘇] was born just before the reign of the Tao Kuang Ti Emperor / Daoguang [道光帝] who came to power on the 3rd October 1820. He lived in a village close to Pek Ho Town (what is now Beijiaozhen [北滘镇], translates to North Kau town) in the district of Shunde [順德區], which is approximately 23 km south of the city of Canton [廣州]. Shunde [順德區] is now an outer district of the city of Fat Shan / Foshan [佛山]. He was from a reasonably wealthy family, as his uncle, Mr So [蘇] was the local Han gentry squire [漢族鄉紳] and a large land holder in the area. As a village leader, he had the responsibility for ensuring law and order within the local community, and made his living by renting out this land to many of the local farmers. Due to Mr So's [蘇] position, he was regarded as a man of standing with a very respectable reputation.

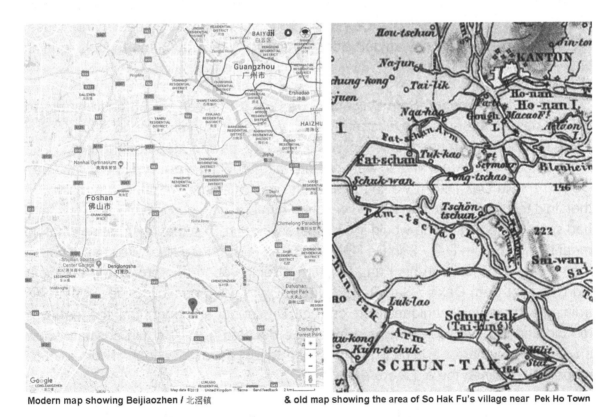

Modern map showing Beijiaozhen / 北滘镇   & old map showing the area of So Hak Fu's village near Pek Ho Town

During the 1830s, a Siu Lum / Shaolin monk [少林僧] called Siu Dak / Zhaode [兆德] (which translates to mean Fortune Virtue and an alias name of the Siu Lum / Shaolin monk [少林僧] better known as Sam Dak / San De [三德], meaning Three Virtues, who was the abbot [方丈] of West Zen Temple / Sai Sim Ji / Xi Chan Si [西禪寺] in the West Gate / Sai Kwan / Xiguan [西關] (now Liwan district [荔灣區]) area of Canton [廣州]) was travelling around Guangdong, [廣東省] begging for alms and also visiting associates. The collection of alms was a cover for meeting other anti-Ch'ing / anti-Qing [反清清朝] sympathisers and recruiting new students. Heading south on the outskirts of the city of Canton [廣州] (Guangzhou [廣州]), he arrived at a village near North Kau town [北滘镇 / 北崗鄉] in the district of Shunde [順德區]), where he met a local gentleman named Mr So [蘇].

Mr So [蘇] was a charitable man, and offered to accommodate the monk for a few days while he was in this region. When the monk, Sam Dak / San De [三德] (Siu Dak [兆德]), was staying at Mr So's [蘇] home, he would awake early each morning as was his normal practice. His window looked onto the rear garden where he noticed a teenager practicing martial arts [武術]. Through the practice of martial arts [武術], this young man had developed strength and a good physique, but the monk noticed that although the teenager's striking power was strong, his technique was poor, lacking refinement and true skill. Even though the young man's training was obviously improving his health and making him stronger, it was of little use for practical fighting or self-defence. As Sam Dak / San De [三德] (Siu Dak [兆德]) was a guest in the house, he thought it best not to say anything or offer to rectify the young man's technique, in case it offended his hosts.

Several days later, when Sam Dak / San De [三德] (Siu Dak [兆德]) had completed his business in the area and was ready to leave, he went to say goodbye to Mr. So [蘇]. As he walked around looking for Mr So [蘇], he saw the teenager training once again in the rear garden, and so went out into the garden to meet him. Sam Dak / San De [三德] (Siu Dak [兆德]) walked over to the teenager and introduced himself. He then told the young man that he had watched him practicing on a few occasions, and had some observations he would like to share with him. The teenager asked what he meant, and so Sam Dak / San De [三德] (Siu Dak [兆德]) tried to explain to the young man the shortcomings in his Kung Fu [功夫]. Being young and proud, the teenager didn't accept Sam Dak's / San De [三德] (Siu Dak [兆德]) opinion, believing that his training and martial techniques were correct. The teenager thought that the man was too old and that because he was a monk, he doubted that he could possibly know anything about martial arts [武術]. The young So [蘇] gave him a look of contempt as he politely declined the old monk's advice.

Sam Dak / San De [三德] (Siu Dak [兆德]) realised that the young man didn't understand what he meant and so asked him if he would be willing to take a test to prove his point. Again still believing that his training was correct, the young man was happy to accept and immediately punched at Sam Dak's / San De [三德] (Siu Dak [兆德]) stomach.

Sam Dak / San De [三德] (Siu Dak [兆德]) demonstrated his skill evading these strikes with perfect timing and almost effortless movement, maintaining correct balance and posture. Sam Dak / San De [三德] (Siu Dak [兆德]) waited for the moment during this relentless attack, until he noticed a look of frustration on the young man's face. He then countered by blocking the young man's punch with his left hand and slightly pushed his shoulder with right hand palm. This resulted in the teenager losing his balance and he fell to the ground.

Sam Dak / San De [三德] (Siu Dak [兆德]) immediately picked him up and asked his name. The young man replied that his name was So [蘇], and that he was a nephew of Mr. So [蘇] who the monk had been staying with. The young So [蘇] didn't complain, realising that the monk was obviously a skilled Kung Fu master [功夫大師], immediately beseeching Sam Dak / San De [三德] (Siu Dak [兆德]) to teach him. The monk initially refused because he had completed his work in this region and needed to return to his temple. The young So [蘇], was persistent, and stated that if was unable to stay here and teach him, he was willing to follow Sam Dak / San De [三德] (Siu Dak [兆德]) to Siu Lum / Shaolin and learn there. During this conversation, Sam Dak / San De [三德] (Siu Dak [兆德]) felt the young man's passion for learning, and knew that he had great potential for Kung Fu [功夫], so he told him that he would discuss the matter with his uncle, Mr So [蘇].

Sam Dak / San De [三德] (Siu Dak [兆德]) then returned into the house in search of Mr So [蘇]. When he found Mr So [蘇], Sam Dak / San De [三德] (Siu Dak [兆德]) inquired more about the young So [蘇] and what he was like. Mr So [蘇] told him that he was his nephew and that he was looking after him. He then explained that his family were successful in business with a distinguished reputation, but his nephew was a problem because he was always getting into trouble, mainly because of fighting. Sam Dak / San De [三德] (Siu Dak [兆德]) believed the teenager lacked guidance and discipline, and so asked Mr So [蘇] if he could take him to the temple to teach him. The monk stated that this would be a way to repay Mr So [蘇] for his kindness and generosity, but also because he believed that the young man had a raw talent, that under the correct tutelage, could go far. In appreciation for this, Mr So [蘇] provided the monk with food and financial assistance for his return trip.

After discussing matters with Mr So [蘇] and finalising the arrangements, Sam Dak / San De [三德] (Siu Dak [兆德]) then took the young So [蘇] with him to the Siu Lum / Shaolin temple (Kwangtung Siu Lum / Shaolin Temple [廣東少林寺]) and started educating him in the arts of the renowned masters [功夫大師].

The young So [蘇] soon settled into the hard, disciplined regime of temple life and began his studies in earnest. The first part of his training was Siu Lum / Shaolin conditioning [少林內息調理功] using various tools to help toughen his hands and arms.

One of these tools was called the stone spring wheel / Chu Shek Lun [轉石輪], which was a large circular stone attached to a long wooden shaft. The shaft was held in one hand, and spun so the other end of the shaft would then roll down the arm. Due to the weight of the stone, the wooden shaft bears down on the bone and nerves, and this then conditions the forearms. Another tool that So [蘇] would use, was the throwing stone lock / Pow Shek Shaw [拋石鎖] which had a handle at one end with a large stone attached to it. As So [蘇] held the handle, he would swing his arm up, and then suddenly punch out, snapping his hand forward, raising the forearm for the stone to bounce off as it swung over the rotating handle. Initially this was practiced one arm at a time, and when he had skilfully mastered this, he progressed to doing both arms together. This was done by holding a throwing stone lock in each hand and simultaneously performing this technique.

The conditioning tools with the stone weights also helped to improve So's [蘇] stance besides toughening his arms. If his stance was weak, then the weight of the stone would unbalance him while he was practicing. To coincide with using these conditioning tools, So [蘇] also trained in other Shaolin techniques / Siu Lum Moo Hook [少林武學]. One of these Siu Lum / Shaolin arts is known as the, "Skill of the Iron Arm" (Tein Bak Kuen / Tie Bi Gong [鐵臂功]). This method is performed using the inner and outer forearms striking initially against a pole. Each day, the amount of strikes and the power, would steadily increase to strengthen the arms. As the arms toughened up, this method was then used on trees with a rough bark surface. Another method he practised, was the Shaolin striking pole / Siu Lum Mood Chee Kwun [少林木柱功]. This was a thick wooden or bamboo shaft of between ten to twelve inches (25-30cm) in diameter wrapped tightly with thick hemp cord. So [蘇] would stand in front of this pole delivering various striking, pushing and cutting techniques, using his fists, palms, forearms, elbows, shoulders, legs and feet. After a period of prolonged training, pain felt by the practitioner is reduced as the skin and muscles become thicker and stronger. After three years of diligent practice, it is stated that the striking parts of the body start to feel as if they are made of iron. This art is called, "The Pole of the Falling Star," (Lau Sing Kwan / Liu Xing Zhuang [流星棍]). [114]

Paul Burkinshaw arm conditioning using the Stone Spring Wheel at GM Wong Cheung's Bute St gym, Mongkok, Hong Kong, 2006.

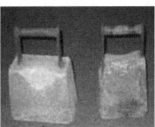

Arm conditioning using
the Throwing Stone Lock

Alan Low / Low Shiu Lun
Head Coach, Hong Kong

Paul Burkinshaw
Head Coach, UK

So [蘇] was also instructed in the use of the Shaolin Striking Dummy / Siu Lum Mood Chong Kwun [少林木樁功]. This method involved using his arms, elbows, hips, legs, knees and feet, for various blocking and striking techniques, and is called striking at the wooden dummy (Da Mood Chong / Da Mu Chun [打木樁]). The dummy stands between five to six feet tall, (152 -183cm) with a short pole fixed horizontally around shoulder height, to represent outstretched arms. The body and head are wrapped with cotton-wool, and then leather on the outside, to provide a little cushioning. Besides strikes, pressing, pushing and grasping techniques are also performed at the various parts of the dummy, on a daily basis. Using this dummy also ensured that his hand and arm positions were correct when hitting and blocking.

Fred Woo performing the Hak Fu Mun Dan Chong (Black Tiger Single Dummy) at a demonstration in Hong Kong, approx 1973

So [蘇] was renowned for his Iron Palm / Tin Sa Cheung [鐵砂掌] technique. [109d] [109e] During these years, he included the traditional Siu Lum / Shaolin training method of conditioning his hands in the skill of Shaolin iron gravel palm / Siu Lum Tee Sha Chen [少林鐵沙掌]. There are two main methods to achieve this conditioning skill. One method is the striking of a canvas bag filled with iron grains, cooked into a mixture with a secret medicine. This art is called, "Palm of Iron Sand" (Tee Shek Chen / Tie Sha Zhang [鐵石掌]). The other method is to thrust the hands

175

into a box, filled initially with beans. As the hands harden, this substance is changed to rice, then sand, and finally to iron filings. All these conditioning, training methods cause the hands and arms to swell and bruise. Therefore after each session, the hands and arms were bathed and treated with conditioning medicines such as Dit Da Jow [跌打酒].

Dit Da Jow is a Chinese liniment used to heal external injuries such as bruises or sore muscles. Various recipes which are considered "secret formula" for Dit Da Jow, have been passed down through oral and written history of Traditional Chinese medicine, martial artists, and modern Western science.

Dit Da Jow is an painkilling liniment traditionally used by Chinese style martial artists. Usually a martial arts master / sifu combines their mixture of various aromatic herbs such as myrrh and ginseng, which are mixed to stimulate circulation, reduce pain and swelling, and improve healing of certain injuries and wounds. [116]

It is understood that the days at the temple were very long, starting as early as 5.00am and continuing until 11.00pm at night. Besides the demanding training regime, students also had to perform menial duties, such as cleaning, cooking, fetching, chopping wood, working the land etc, which were all part of the general maintenance of daily temple life. After the first three years of So's [蘇] training at the Kwangtung Siu Lum / Shaolin Temple [廣東少林寺], he had covered the basic skills to improve his stamina, flexibility and balance as well as his power skills. He had conditioned both his arms (bridges [橋手]) to be as strong as iron and his stances now had correct posture with very good balance. This period prepared him for the next part of his training which was to cover the combat skills [實戰技巧]. Siu Lum / Shaolin combat methods, applications and strategies were taught to So [蘇] via the open-hand routines [套路] of the Ten Animals form / Sap Yin Kuen [十形拳] and Drunken Eight Immortals / Chue Ba Sin [醉八仙] as well as the weapon routines [套路] of Black Tiger Broadsword / Hak Fu Dao [黑虎刀], and Kam Kong Pole / Kam Kong Kwun [金剛棍].

During this next phase of So's [蘇] Siu Lum / Shaolin combat training, his favourite open-hand form [套路] (routine) which he was taught, was the Ten Animals form / Sap Yin Kuen [十形拳]. The ten animals within this routine [套路] were the Dragon / Lung [龍], Snake / Se [蛇], Tiger / Fu [虎], Leopard / Paau [豹], Crane / Hok [鶴], Elephant / Cheung [象], Lion / See [獅], Horse / Ma [馬], Monkey / Hau [猴], and Marten [貂]. [116a] [116b] Every animal in the form [套路] (routine) has approximately thirty movements, and the form / routine [套路] was divided into three parts. The three parts are the Front dummy / Chin Chong [前椿], Middle dummy / Chung Chong [中椿], and Rear dummy / Hau Chong [後椿], which include both hard and soft movements. During these years of training at the temple, So [蘇] had been given the nickname of So Hak Fu / Su Heihu [蘇黑虎] by his brothers (fellow students). This was because So [蘇] had a dark complexion and favoured the Tiger [虎] moves and applications in his training, hence he was called "So the Black Tiger" [蘇黑虎].

Description of Ten Animals Hak Fu Mun [黑虎十形拳]

Dragon Style [龍形]

[龍形拳]是根據古代流傳至今文獻中有關"龍"的傳說, 如相貌、形態、身體特徵等, 所衍生創造而成的拳法。自古以來, 中國視"龍"為代表皇帝象徵, 相傳龍能呼風喚雨, 上天下海, 神通廣大, 來無蹤, 去無跡! 神龍見首不見尾, 所以練習 [龍形拳] 的特點是首先需要氣聚丹田, 重意不重力, 一舉手, 一投足需瀟灑利落。

The Dragon style fist was created based on the "dragon" of legends written in ancient literature for its physical characteristics such as appearance and shape. In China, the dragon is also the representative symbol of the emperor. According to legend, the Dragon has the power of calling the wind and the rain, with the ability to move around the sky and into the sea, to come and go as it wants without leaving any trace. One can see the head of the dragon but not the tail. That is why the characteristics of practicing the Dragon style should focus on the accumulation of air at the Dan Tian. This is achieved by concentrating on the mood rather than power, with every movement of hands or feet being clear and precise.

"龍"外形據傳是擁有兩角、四腿, 身長如蟒並長有鱗片, 故此能左顧右盼, 首尾兼顧, 當活動時有如龍在九天, 有浮沉吞吐, 排山倒海之勢; 至於馬步浮中帶實, 每當一動一靜, 就有如龍在雲中浮沉: 浮者轉動輕盈; 沉者穩如泰山。

The Dragon of legend has two horns with four legs and a long python type body covered with scales. It moves as if almost floating with lightness when turning up, but steady like a mountain when dropping down. Due to its movement of weaving from side to side the Dragon has the ability to see all around. The movements of the practitioner should therefore simulate that of the dragon moving up and down in the clouds. Hence the step should be solid with a certain degree of floating lightness.

[龍形拳] 的心法是以柔為主, 外柔內剛, 剛柔並濟, 步法靈活, 手法多變, 動作舒緩, 協調連貫, 一氣呵成。

The concept of the Dragon style fist is mainly of the soft style. Soft outside while hard inside with the two forces working together in harmony. The characteristics of this are flexible footwork and changeable hand movements with continuous coordinated targeting.

功法多以纏鬥、裹勁為主, 身形步法乃要龍形蛇腰, 虎座橫步, 貓行獅蹲, 體態軟綿成曲蜷之勢, 前手為龍, 後手為虎, 並成鹿伏之狀, 手、腳及身體配合而作出旋轉之法~左旋相生, 右旋相克, 左右旋轉產生「生」與「克」的奧妙變化。

The fighting style is mainly to pursue an opponent utilising internal strength. The body structure should be the stepping movement of the dragon, with snake waist, a tiger type lateral step, cat walk, lion squat, expressed coiling body, dragon for front hand and tiger for back hand looking like a coiling deer. Hands and feet work together for turning the body, to generate power when turning left and suppression of an opponent's power when turning right. The rotation change of the body is key to the creation and suppression of power.

至於內在氣勁和呼吸的控制，動作如流水般靈活、活動的步法以帶出有力的掃腿、拳及前手攻擊，內勁的使用增強攻擊時的爆發力，使用快速及連貫的攻擊動作使對手無法還擊。

In regard to the internal strength and the control of breathing, the movement should be flexible like flowing water to produce powerful kicks, punching and forearm attacks. The internal strength enhances the explosion of power during attack. Utilising speed and continuous attacks limits an opponent's ability to fight back.

［龍爪手］手法特別，尤其以兩爪合抱之勢，出名招式有：「烏龍吐珠」，「毒龍搶珠」，其他手法是用以擒拿對方的前臂、耳朵或其他伸出的部份以便使用掃腿、推倒或拋開對手。

The Dragon claw is a special type of hand technique. The black dragon throws the pearl up and poisoned dragon capturing the pearl are two particular types of dragon claws which are of an encirclement style. The other Dragon claw methods are used for grabbing an opponent's forearms, ears or parts of the body in order to use pushing, throwing or sweeping leg techniques on them.

腿法則模仿龍尾動作擺動掃向敵人，如「蟠龍腿」、「烏龍擺尾」等。

The leg simulates the movement of a dragon's tail sweeping the opponent e.g. coiling dragon leg and black dragon swinging tail.

Snake Style [蛇形]

［蛇拳］的特點是以模仿蛇的盤纏、咬擊動作和搏鬥的各種動態形式所創造的拳法。特性是使用輕巧靈活、飄忽而流暢的動作身法，以盤纏、鎖扣緊纏的手法，用曲線（模仿蛇以S形活動方式）、飄忽，難以捉摸的的活動來糾纏對手，繼而產生突然爆發性速度出擊，以刁鑽的角度，準確地攻擊對手致命的部位，要一擊即中目標。這些掩藏而又騙人的技術，需要很高的準確度、力度集中出擊，同時亦可以用不同手法擋格順勢出擊對方，借力打力，過橋上樹，一氣呵成。運用掌形或不同手指的佩合，攻擊敵人各要害及脆弱部位，例如眼睛、耳、喉嚨、腋下及所有穴位，表現時要運用特別的呼吸方法以引發內氣的力量。一般握法: 分「蛇公」及「蛇乸」，「蛇公」用一或二隻手指，「蛇乸」用平掌。

The snake style is created by simulating the shape of a coiling snake, its biting action and the shapes it takes when fighting against different animals. The key characteristic of this style is the light, flexible and smooth body movement. The snake style uses different methods to block, such as diverting the power from an opponent's strike to attack back in one motion. It also uses the techniques of coiling, locking and catching to attack an opponent in an unpredictable curved path. Different combinations of palm and finger techniques are utilised to formulate powerful, precise attacks which are targeted at the vital and vulnerable parts of an opponent with explosive speed. These target areas can include the eyes, ears, throat, armpits and all the acupuncture points.

Tiger Style / 虎形

[虎形拳] 的特點是模仿老虎獵食、跳躍及奔馳的各種形態，威猛又剛勇。

The Tiger style simulates the fierce and valiant shape of the tiger when fighting and hunting its prey.

老虎以巨大身軀、驚人力量的「虎爪」、雄渾的「虎嘯」、正所謂「靜如虎踞、動若靈貓」。

Tiger style is expressed by the immense size and power of the tiger's body, its considerable claw strength and the powerful tiger howl. This is known as, "quiet with the stealth of a tiger squatting, but moves like a dynamic cat".

[虎形拳]特性是 ⌒ 含胸拔背、沉肩墜爪 ，以強而有力的進攻方式壓倒對手， 直接向對方的目標使用殺着，在最短時間內擊倒對手，主要目標是面部、 喉嚨及身體脆弱部分。攻擊時多數使用「虎爪」。

The characteristic of tiger style fist is to contract the chest and extend the back, while keeping the shoulders down. The hand position adopts the shape of the Tiger Claw. In order to overwhelm opponents and defeat them in the shortest time, there is a large emphasis on the use of power and strength while attacking. The Tiger Claw is mainly used when attacking the main target areas such as the face, throat and other weak points of the body.

「虎爪」的正確手法是五指分開，而每指成勾曲狀，側面看以英文字母 "C" 字，使用時必須氣沉丹田，力貫指尖，才能硬如鋼鐵，抓向敵人，一擊殺著!

The correct technique of tiger claw is to separate the fingers with each finger bent in the shape of a curved hook (like letter C in the alphabet). When using the Tiger Claw, the practitioner must accumulate air in the Dan Tian and concentrate strength in the finger tips making them as hard as steel. The Tiger Claw strike is delivered with such intent as to kill in one action.

虎爪手法亦可作 "擒拿" 制服敵人。還可以利用手背攻擊下巴、面額及頭頂。其他可以配合拳和掌交替使用。

The Tiger claw can also be used to catch an opponent, while the back of the hand can be used to attack the chin, forehead, or top of the head to dominate an opponent. The Tiger Claw attacks are also used interchangeably with fist and palm strikes.

「虎尾腳」亦是常用招式。注意在使出虎爪時要發出「虎嘯」聲，以震懾敵人，令敵人聞風喪膽，因此失去戰意!

The Tiger Tail Kick is also another technique that is commonly used. While fighting, the Tiger growl is often used to shock or frighten an opponent in order to reduce their determination to fight.

Leopard style [豹形]

[豹形拳] 是模仿 "豹" 的身形、動作特性而成拳。"豹 " 的身形比虎細小，氣力不及虎、獅這類猛獸，而且同屬於「貓科」，不過，但只有 "豹" 能上樹，故縱跳翻騰，以豹為冠! [豹形拳] 雖然不及[虎形拳] 剛猛威武，但[豹形拳]特別敏捷、靈活、陰險! 而且[豹形拳] 絕大

動作均以半蹲半跪的馬步作出攻擊, 故此, 在基本功上要多下苦功, 因為這姿勢較「龍、虎、蛇」三形難練。

The Leopard style simulates the movement and characteristics of a leopard. The body structure of the leopard is comparatively small and less powerful than the tiger or lion. Leopards are excellent at jumping and have the capability of climbing trees. Although the leopard fist is less powerful than the tiger fist, it is very sinister due to its flexibility and speed. As most of the leopard fist strikes are delivered from low stances, basic training is particularly hard in comparison to other styles such as dragon, tiger and snake.

[豹形拳] 拳法的特點是剛中帶柔, 發力迅速而猛烈, 拳勢暴烈, 以練勁力、靈敏性及速度為主。利用[豹手] 快速攻擊敵人的軟弱部位, 如眼、耳、太陽穴、頸、下陰及關節。因為用[豹形拳] 的人多以低馬姿態出現, 故此往往乘敵人下路空虛而出奇制勝。這些準確的攻擊志在盡快帶給對手傷痛。其他攻擊包括使用睜、膝、低腳等短而有爆發力, 能快速地擊倒對手。

The characteristic of the leopard style fist is hard combined with soft style utilising explosive speed with fierce powerful attacks using impulsive strength. Speed and flexibility are the key points using the leopard fist to quickly attack the soft vulnerable parts of an opponent's body such as their eyes, ears, temples, neck, groin and the bone joints. The leopard fist strike is generally delivered from lower stances targeting susceptible areas to hurt an opponent quickly and also making it harder for them to block. Other forms of attacks in the Leopard style include the use of elbows, knees, and lower kicks, utilising short explosive power to overwhelm an opponent.

「豹手」又稱「豹爪」 是[豹形拳]中的特式, 他與「虎爪」不同, 「豹手」更窄小, 先將五指屈曲, 四指的頭兩節向內屈曲成中空, 大拇指則壓向食指而構成菱形的尖銳角, 攻擊時掌心向下, 連環扣擊, 殺傷力量很強。

The leopard fist can also be known as the panther claw/fist. The Leopard fist is narrow with the fingers bent almost flat and the thumb pressing into the index finger forming a diamond shape. The claw should face downwards when attacking and create continuous attacks with strong destructive power.

Crane style [鶴形]

[鶴拳]的特色是模仿 "鶴" 的形態、特性、性格•••等, "鶴" 是非常瀟灑及高傲的生物, 警覺性強, 不會謬然攻擊對方,
是以靜制動, 敵不動, 我不動, 敵人一出手, 它就立刻作出針對性攻擊, 因為當敵人出手先, 會露出破綻, 此時就一擊即中了。

The Crane style simulates the shape, movement and manner of the crane which is an elegant and proud bird with a high alertness. Its tactics are to stay calm in a bid to try and control the movements of an opponent, only moving when its opponent moves, preferring to counter attack. When an opponent attacks they can expose a weak *or vulnerable area which provides the opportunity for a counter attack, allowing the Crane to strike back immediately at the targeted area.*

[鶴拳] 是用圓線的閃避移動亂對方直至雙方約一臂之距就進行攻擊。

The style of the Crane fist is to use a circular type movement to avoid an attack from an opponent and then strike back at a distance of arm's length.

「鶴咀」是常用的手法，以快速、閃電式攻擊，會使用於不需要接近的情況下擊敗對方，攻擊目標是較遠弱的部位如眼、耳、太陽穴、喉嚨、心臟、肋骨，因此對速度、準確度的要求比力量高，主要原理是借用對方進攻時的衝力及力量反擊而打敗對手。還有「鶴頂拳」，以近身重擊為主，再配合「鶴扣手」或稱「鶴鈎手」，更是天衣無縫的一攻一守的鶴拳特色，最佳配搭手。至於馬步，一般採用高樁馬，如吊馬、單蹄馬•••等，因為戰鬥時，要配合手法、換馬、轉身、起腳踢腿、易於靈活變動身形。

Crane beak is a common fast technique of this style which can be used at arm's length and so avoiding the need to get too close to an opponent. The target areas are the weaker or vulnerable parts of the body such as the eyes, ears, temples, throat, heart, and ribs. The main concept of this style is making use of the opponents' attacking momentum to strike back and defeat them. Hence the necessity on speed and accuracy, more than the use of power, are important. Another striking technique is the crane head (top of) fist which is mainly used for close range powerful attacks. This can be incorporated with crane hook hand to form a perfect attacking and defensive combination. The footwork is normally higher adopted stances such as the hanging step and single hoof step, etc. The stances are more flexible and so easy to incorporate the changing steps, body turning and kicking.

Lion style [獅形]

[獅形拳]乃取自獅子「萬獸之王」的特色。獅王雄霸一方，威風凜凜！所以拳法出手，以中上路為主，硬打硬入，進攻時無懼敵人強弱、多寡，務必全力以赴！那怕你我一拳，互相駁搥，誓要把敵人殲滅，打倒對方，如「獅子撲兔」的打法。特色是使用全身的力量產生強而有力、兇猛駭人的攻擊，低身法及大幅度的步法，堅定、強硬、低身法是對付對手的必要元素，同時佩合強力的中低腿，主要攻擊會使用獅爪快速及不斷的攻擊。

The Lion is regarded as the king of all animals; therefore this style follows the characteristics of this impressive and prestigious beast. All attacks are delivered with full all-out effort and are mainly focused on the middle and upper part of the body. Regardless of how strong an opponent may be, no fear is shown as they are struck with numerous powerful strikes until they are defeated, "Like a lion bashing a rabbit". This expresses the meaning of a very powerful move to bash a tiny thing. The main characteristic is the use of strength which is generated by utilising the whole body to create the biggest and most powerful strikes. These are delivered in a continuous, ferocious and determined manner from low, wide stances. The Lion style utilises fast, continuous, Lion paw strikes combined with low to middle kicks.

Elephant style [象形]

［象形拳］是模仿＂大笨象＂強壯健碩的體型，沉重穩健步伐，並以長驅直進、勇往直前的進攻方式，來個正面直接擊倒敵人，而創造的拳法。練者要講求先天條件，體格魁梧，高大威猛者比較適合！特點主要是＂大笨象＂象鼻的先天優點，它富彈性而擁有捲物能力及強力擺動動作，似一隻既長而又能捲物的手臂，配以大身形，攻向敵人的中心位置，以自己身形和體重，施加壓力在敵人身上，令對方背負你的重量，從而破其腰馬，兼且控制住對方的身形和位置，輕者把敵人推倒於地上；重者則打斷敵人的關節，及重擊頭部致命，例如「天罡搥」。注意攻擊時下盤的馬步要穩健，上肢輪臂有如象鼻般霸道氣勢迫人，用拳頭的全部面積作出攻擊，而並非只用手指的關節部分，亦可用一隻手像象鼻捲著對手然後用另一隻手攻擊，扎實的馬步是必須的否則難以發揮重擊的效果。

The Elephant style simulates the big, strong muscular body of the elephant, offensively driving straight forward in a courageous and heavy way at a steady pace. The main weapon of attack is the elephant's trunk which it uses in large swinging motions as well as having the flexibility to enable it to be used for coiling. This style suits practitioners with a big, strong physique. Long, bending or double arm techniques are used to strike an opponent's centre. The mass and weight of the practitioner is utilised to bear down on and pressurise an opponent. These attacks are generally simple and direct. The goal is to buckle an opponent pounding them into the floor. This method can be either to crush their stance, break their bones or joints, and also even delivering fatal strikes to the head such as 'Tien Kong fist'. (One forearm protects the forehead horizontally while the other arm performs a hammer-fist strike to the opponent's head.) A key feature is the low, stable stances to enable the upper body to generate the strong, powerful, swinging arm movements to represent the elephant's trunk. The whole fist is used instead of just the knuckle area. One arm can be used to hold an opponent (like the trunk coiling around) while the other arm can then be used to strike.

Horse style [馬形]

［馬形拳］的特點是拳勢激烈，快而有力的手法佩合敏捷而靈活的身法，如戰馬般衝鋒陷陣，進攻敵人時氣勢恍如渴馬奔泉，手不停，邊打邊走，絕不回頭。

Characteristics of the horse style are the intensive, fast, powerful hands combined with brisk, flexible, agile foot work. This is to simulate the momentum of a thousand war horses making an assault on the battle field to attack the enemy. The attacks are non-stop, which are generated by continuous movement.

手法包括不同的掌法和拳法夾雜著有力的腳法，很多都是大範圍的攻擊對於同時要對付幾名對手時特別有用，一般會使用飛身或跳躍以轉變攻擊的方式。

The attacking methods of the Horse style incorporate palm and fist strikes as well as powerful kicks. This style is particularly useful for dealing with several opponents at the same time due to a large area covered during attacking. It is normal while attacking an opponent to jump or rotate to alter the manner or form of the assault on them.

Monkey style [猴形]

［猴形拳］乃取自猴子本能特長，模仿＂猴子＂的身形，要求縮脖、聳肩、含胸、圓背、束身、屈肘、垂腕、屈膝演練成拳。練［猴形拳］主要是取其心敏意捷，以靈敏而制笨拙，取其刁抓意發神速，乘機取巧的優點，只是象形而取意，而不是象形而取形，以智慧而勝勇猛，以多謀而勝魯莽，因此在搏鬥中需要心神安靜，形式純正，身體輕便靈敏，因此而命名為［猴形拳］。＂猴子＂的特點是敏捷和雜技式的出乎意料的動作，另外這些動作亦可以攪亂和困惑對手從而制做機會出擊，攻擊目標：上路有頭頂、面部、眼睛及喉嚨；中路有左右腋下、肋骨、腹溝；下路有下陰、膝蓋等，都以脆弱部分為主。由於佩合各種虛招及難以估計的進攻方法，使對手難以招架，攻擊時一般使用猴手（猴拳獨有）佩合多種踢腳和步法，從低處或蹲下的位置打出，會隨著閃避動作之後作出突然而連續的反擊。還需要配合跌、撲、翻、滾的動作同時使用。「身法」有：剛、柔、輕、靈、綿、巧、躲、閃等。「手法」有：刁、採、抓、拿、扣、甩、切等。「腳法」有：頂、膝撞、蹬腿、彈腿、釘腿等。「步法」有：躍、竄、吊馬、蹲撐步、跪步、半馬步、腳尖步、小跳步、交叉步等。「手型」有：拳（四指捲屈，大拇指扣貼於食指第二指節，拳心虛空）、掌（五指伸直并攏，掌心微凹成谷手狀）、勾（屈曲手腕，五指捲屈，大拇指和食指扣貼成環形，手心空，指尖扣貼手腕）。另外有些動作如猿猴出洞、入洞、窺望、摘果、嬉戲、驚竄、蹲坐、捉虱、抓耳撓腮、掠痕、翻跟斗及各種猴子的小動作，並無多大意義！只是粉飾套路的可歡性及娛樂性，對實戰並無甚作用。招式有：猴子偷桃」、「靈猴上樹」、「雄猴看果」等。

The Monkey style imitates the nature and movements of the monkey. This is characterised by simulating the body shape of a monkey, such as to contract the neck while lifting up the shoulders and curving the back. The body adopts lower squatting or crouching positions, with bent and sagging arms moving around on all fours (hands and feet). The key requirements of practicing the monkey style fist are speed and agility with a sharp mind. The movements may appear uncontrolled and clumsy but these are used to trick an opponent. Sensitivity, coupled with speed of motion are used to take advantage of the opponent.

Wisdom and strategy are used to defeat fierce, reckless attacks. As such, during fighting, it is imperative to stay calm while maintaining the monkey style features keeping the body light and flexible. The Monkey style characteristics of agile, with acrobatic unpredictable movements confuse the opponent, creating opportunities to attack. The target areas on the upper body include the face, eyes, throat, arm pits and, ribs, while on the lower body they include the groin and knees.

Marten Style [貂形]

[貂形拳]乃模仿＂貂鼠＂與其他動物搏鬥的情況而創出拳法。＂貂鼠＂體型細長如水獺, 鼻子及面部尖出、大耳朵、頭部成三角形, 四肢短, 五趾長有彎曲而銳利的尖爪, 粗尾巴。牠移動迅速十分敏捷, 身體柔軟度極高, 因為＂貂鼠＂脊椎長, 所以爆發力就越強! 覓食的手法快速, 乾淨利落, 動作靈巧輕取, 簡直就是長了手腳的蛇。

The Marten style simulates the movements of the marten when it fights with other animals. It has a long slim body with a thick long tail. Its head is triangular shaped with an extended face and nose with pronounced ears. It has four short legs that have five fingers with sharp curved claws on them. Due to the marten's long backbone it is highly flexible and can use this to generate strong explosive power which can make its movements very fast. Its hunting tactics are to overwhelm a prey with fast, clean, nimble actions like a snake with four limbs.

＂貂鼠＂其實在發力的技巧上比蛇更高明。

But in fact, a marten is more skillful than a snake in its technique of exerting force.

＂蛇＂發力是從S形變直的, 牠最多只能用到脊椎肌肉一半發力, 左半或者右半。為了最大發力, 蛇把身體卷曲打圈, 這樣的機械傳動效率不高, 因為脊椎骨要平直才能最大承力, 所謂立木承千斤。

In order to create the greatest power, a snake coils its body to attack straight. This power is created from its spinal muscular movement of either half left or half right and so is only able to use half of this force. This transmission of energy is not very efficient as the backbone has to be balanced when it is under such high pressing pressure. (It is also known as, "wood could sustain tone of force". This means that when the body is standing up straight and steady, a person can sustain a very heavy vertical loading. The loading can transfer from the arm or shoulder to floor through the legs.)

＂貂鼠＂聰明在於能善用自己身材的特點~身體長, 把脊椎的肌肉全部運用, 就是控制肌肉「旋轉」身體, 撲向敵人, 因為脊椎骨角度小, 立木承千斤了。

Martens are smart animals in that they can make use of the whole length of their bodies utilising their spinal muscles to control the twisting force. They are able to make use of their small angular backbone to sustain the greatest force.

因為「旋轉」所發出的力量是最強的, 就是這點, [貂形拳]以快速動作, 靈巧的身形, 加埋敏捷的步法, 刁鑽的角度, 向敵人打出致命一擊, 令對方無法招架。

Due to the fact that twisting can create the most powerful force, the marten style practitioner is able to have fast, flexible body movement with agile footwork. This allows them to deliver lethal attacks from cunning and awkward angles on an opponent which they are unable to parry.

[貂形拳]攻擊的目標, 多數是脆弱的要害: 如眼睛、耳朵、喉嚨、腋窩、雞心、肋骨等。

Target areas include the vulnerable and weak points such as the eyes, ears, throat, arm pits, heart and ribs.

Written by Franco Lok / Lok Wai Fai [駱華輝] and also in photos demonstrating the characteristics. (Martial Arts Executive of Hak Fu Mun [少林黑虎門益群堂黃祥體育會])

Drunken Eight Immortals

Drunken Fist [醉拳] is a style of Chinese martial arts that replicates the movement of a drunken person. In southern China it has been preserved intact by the styles of Hak Fu Mun [黑虎門] and Hung Fat [洪佛派]. The Northern styles of Mantis [螳螂門] and Da Sheng Pi Gua [大聖劈掛門] also have drunken routines which have been passed down.

There is authentic and fictitious information regarding the origins of Drunken Fist [醉拳] that has been circulated over the last hundred years. The 1978 Jackie Chan movie, "Drunken Master", tells of one of these stories. Numerous present day routines and concepts were created for the Jackie Chan movie of Drunken Master and since this movie has been broadcast many magazines and books have published articles about Drunken Fist [醉拳]. Unfortunately various drunken routines have been created from these which have no authentic practical value.

Hak Fu Mun [黑虎門] and Hung Fat [洪佛派] styles in Hong Kong, still preserve several Drunken Fist style routines. In Hak Fu Mun [黑虎門] there are three "Drunken Fist [醉拳]" routines which are called, The Great Drunk, Drunken Snake and Drunken Eight Immortals [醉八仙]. Hung Fat [洪佛派] Style also has the Drunken Eight Immortals [醉八仙] and a routine called the Four Great Lame [四大跛拳] which was modified from Drunken Eight Immortals [醉八仙]. So Chan [蘇燦] of the legendary "Ten Tigers of Guangdong", performed this routine, but unfortunately, it is difficult to research historical materials regarding So Chan [蘇燦].

Regarding the origin of Drunken Fist [醉拳], there is the Song of the Drunken Eight Immortals [醉八仙] which has been passed down through the centuries. This song has existed since the time of the Qing Dynasty and possibly as early as even the Ming Dynasty. However, even though it has the name of the Eight Immortals it is difficult to prove that the song is directly related to Drunken Fist [醉拳], but it does explain the eight parts of the body and elements of fighting techniques. It is because it describes Chinese boxing theories that it has been accepted by the martial arts community.

Song of Drunken Eight Immortals

It is generally understood that there are several songs regarding the Drunken style which are "Tai Pak Drunk [太白醉酒]", "Woo Chun Drunken Fall [武松醉跌]", "Drunken Lo Chi Sum Break the Temple Gate [魯智深醉打山門]", and "Drunken Eight Immortals [醉八仙]". In relation to the song of the Drunken Eight Immortals [醉八仙], there are lyrics within it explaining the use of eight parts of the human body. However, this alone does not guarantee that it is directly related to the style of Drunken Fist.

醉八仙歌訣 **Verses from the song of the Eight Drunken Immortals**

A person who is drunk is immoral. His head is so strong that he believes he can touch the top of the North polar star. His shoulders are unbeatable, hips as hard as iron, elbow like thunder, fist like a pole and hands like the wind in smoke. He uses the knee to lift people and his feet to injure them. Strikes are started from the head and shoulders to deliver cuts, claws and palms as the body moves in a mad and wild manner. Stepping here and there makes it difficult to recall or remember their movements. The Eight Immortal style is regarded as a gorgeous sight to see.

First Section:

Han Chung Lai (Zhongli Quan [漢鐘離 / 汉钟离]) is a drunken immortal who puts a fenugreek (can be used as a container to hold wine) on his shoulders. He allows the fenugreek to decide where he wants to be carried. Although he is a fallen mountain due to his decadence, he is also kind hiding behind the immortal's shadow. Knees pushing up both sides which is skillful but should be avoided as being too causal. He should step forward to give the momentum and carry by movement of the shoulders.

Second Section:

Lui Tung Pun (Lu Dongbin [呂洞賓]) is a drunken immortal who carries double straight swords on his back. He can choose to cut the hand or cut the leg, it is all up to him. Although his two hands are like arrows, he can also punch with fists like lead. Retreats by stepping to the back and while leaning his body to the side which guards his scrotum. Then drives forward like the pressure of a rock mass rolling down a mountain.

Third Section:

Han Sen Chi (Han Xiangzi [韓湘子]) is a drunken immortal who holds a flute in his hand. It is his will to choose to hit heavy or slight tap. Although he can strike using the flute to any position, he also incorporates the hidden fist and kicks. With a forceful fist he hits to the head like the beating of a drum and occasionally he unexpectedly can kick to the scrotum. Knows when to fight by sweeping in to overcast, then moves out hiding in the shadows.

Fourth Section:

Cho Kwok Kau (Cao Guojiu [曹國舅]) is a drunken immortal who holds a whisk in his hand. As he steps forward the movement is in harmony with his body to be strong. With a strong arm, elbows up to break the defense of his enemy, then hits by elbowing down. The upper body and hip move together turning around. As the body rotates, the right elbow goes to the hip and the left arm swings out.

Fifth Section:

Nun Ho (He Xiangu [何仙姑]) is a drunken immortal with a hidden iron claw finger. It is her will to choose to claw up or down. Although by dropping forward and leaning her body she is able to rotate. Her iron claw finger is better than a iron whip as when touched by it, it leaves a trail of blood. It can be extended or shortened like the arm of an ape.

Sixth Section:
Lam Cho Wo (Lan Caihe / 藍采和) is a drunken immortal who holds a splendid flower basket. At will he is able to pull down or lift up with a punch and can then move away like a dragonfly skimming across the water. Moves quickly approaching an enemy with the eyes looking down to watch for any foot movement, while blocking punches and kicks, then attacks with fists.

Seventh Section:
Cheung Gor Low (Zhang Guolao [張果老]) is a drunken immortal holding an iron chain that slices, which he can use to strike at will. This weapon can also be wrapped around his own body and so therefore used to protect him. With a twist of his body he is able to avoid heavy strikes and then he can counter attack using fist or palm.

Eighth Section:
Iron Disabled Lee (Li Tieguai [李鐵拐 / 李铁拐]) is a drunken immortal wearing an inverted golden head ring. He can throw to the left or hit to the right as he chooses. Although the golden head ring protects his head, he also needs to use good foot and body movement to guard against attacks. He can strike with a leg hook kick from the back on his enemy then step forward and rotate to knock them down.

These Eight Drunken Immortal Song tactics are taken from "Summary of Fist Theory and Techniques" and "Fist Scripture"

The song of Eight Drunken Immortals is intended to use the name of the eight immortals to insert the key elements into the song. It explains how to use the eight portions of the body: head, shoulder, arm, elbow, fist, palm, knee, and leg. These methods are also applicable for other styles of martial arts, and so are not exclusive to the drunken style.

Traditional Drunken Fist in Taiwan
In the early 20ᵗʰ Century during the Republican era of China, there were many famous masters of Drunken Fist routines. They are very different, depending on the style of the masters. This is what we classified as [Traditional Drunken Fist in Taiwan].
1. Tai Yi Drunken Fist [太乙醉拳]: this is one of the many routines of Tai Yi Mun. This routine has excellent drunken movements. Tai Yi Mun is also famous in Monkey Fist and Tai Kung Fist.

2. Lu Zhishen Drunken Fist [魯智深 醉拳]: this routine has in total 20 steps and therefore is relatively short. It is based on the lean, stumble and strike method. (Lu

Zhishen, nicknamed "Flowery Monk", is a fictional character in the Water Margin, one of the Four Great Classical Novels of Chinese literature)

3. *Eight Drunken Immortal Fist* [醉八仙拳]: the most famous master is Cheung Sik Yam and the routine has 32 steps. The movement and the name of the steps are similar to Lu Zhishen Drunken Fist.

Traditional Drunken Fist in Hong Kong
The following lists the types of drunken fists in Hong Kong.

1. *Eight Drunken Immortal Fist of Hung Fat Style* [洪佛派醉八仙拳]: This is one of the famous routines of the Hung Fat [洪佛派] Style. It mainly simulates the drunken movements of the eight immortals. Some sources state that the Drunken Fist of Jackie Chan has made reference to this routine.

2. *Drunken Lohan* [醉羅漢]: It was spread by the famous master Law Kwong-yuk of the Mantis Style [螳螂拳名拳師羅光玉先生]. Mainly expresses the movement of falling, rotating, summersault, etc, having the capability of nearly drop down but still be stable.

3. *Eight Drunken Immortal Fist of Hak Fu Mun* [黑虎門醉八仙拳]: One of the Drunken Fists of Hak Fu Mun [黑虎門] spread by the Grand Master, Wong Cheung [黃祥宗師] of Hak Fu Mun [黑虎門]. This routine simulates the drunken movements of the eight immortals. The movement methods are typical of the martial arts styles of Canton.

4. *Great Drunk* [大醉]: One of the Drunken Fists of Hak Fu Mun [黑虎門] spread by the Grand Master, Wong Cheung [黃祥宗師], of Hak Fu Mun [黑虎門]. This routine adopts long arm and leg movements. The larger scale movements of this routine are very different to the style of the traditional Eight Drunken Immortal Fist. This style is more akin to the Crane Fist of Lama Style.

5. *Drunken Snake* [醉蛇]: One of the Drunken Fists of Hak Fu Mun [黑虎門], spread by the Grand Master, Wong Cheung [黃祥宗師], of Hak Fu Mun [黑虎門]. This routine is a combination of the Eight Drunken Immortal Fist and Snake Fist, the style of which is different to the normal drunken fist.

6. *Drunken Monkey Fist* [醉猴拳]: This is one of the five Monkey Fists of Tai Sing Pup Kai Mun, which was spread by the Grand Master, Ken Tai-hoi. His followers, Chan Shu-chung and Hui Hoi-chi have spread this style to the general public. [117]

Description of the Black Tiger Broadsword routine [黑虎刀]
黑虎刀》乃少林黑虎門「武術套路」系列內之《黑虎系列》中的一套刀法, 屬初級套路。 《黑虎刀》同樣是由少林黑虎門宗師˜蘇黑虎學自少林寺的。 一般授予初學者。雖然如此! 但亦要求練習者必須步履矯健、身形靈活, 隨着步法的起落擺動, 身法的左旋右轉, 變化出劈、撩、抹、帶、攤、截、刺、纏頭、過腦、走步刀花、內外劏刀⋯⋯等刀法! 綿綿不斷, 滔滔不絕, 所謂「刀若猛虎、劍似游龍」, 變化萬千, 可見於此。

《黑虎刀》採用厚度較薄的柳葉刀, 所以自然不會以硬架猛砍為動作的基礎, 而是利用靈動 的身形步法, 順身使力、藉腰帶刀的基本功法, 將刀的刁鑽精悍展露在套路之中。　刀是戰 場上的常規兵器, 常常使用于戰場拼殺格鬥, 所以《黑虎刀》的演練風格更貼近實戰, 格架 掃進, 神出鬼沒, 劈擋撩刺、威猛非常。

《黑虎刀》不但要有逼人的氣勢和簡明的節奏, 更強調的是刀法的實用性, 所以非常強調刀 和手的互相配合, 刀和身的互相配合, 從而要達到刀身合一的境界, 所以有說：「　單刀睇 手,　雙刀睇走」。

The Black Tiger Sword of Siu Lum Hak Fu Mun [少林黑虎門] is a primary level broadsword routine within the 'Series of Black Tiger martial arts'. This routine originated from Siu Lum / Shaolin Temple [少林寺]. So Hak Fu [蘇黑虎], the founder of Hak Fu Mun [少林黑虎門], learnt this routine while he was at the Kwangtung Siu Lum / Shaolin Temple [廣東少林寺].

Although it is a relatively easy routine, it requires the practitioners to have various physical strengths combined with several skillful attributes. These include strong flexible body movements that are synchronised with the foot movements. The trunk of the body needs to rotate left and right so as to generate power for the variation of movements such as cut, push, guide, lead, spread, block, point, passing head, crossing head, moving while performing flowers with the sword, inside and outside slide sword, etc. These movements are continuous and smooth. It is said "Broadsword like fierce tiger, straight sword like grinding dragon" This motto expresses the vast variability of broadsword.

The Black Tiger Sword is a relatively thinner kind of bamboo leaf sword than the normal standard broadsword. Obviously, due to this it is not suitable for some methods such as hard chopping. Instead, it is more beneficial to incorporate the flexible, fast body movements with agile foot work, so as to utilise the skill of power generated from waist rotation movement. Although it is a basic routine, it demonstrates some cunning methods and characteristics of the broadsword.

In fact, the broadsword was a conventional weapon of the common soldier used for close fighting on the battlefield. As such, the style of the Black Tiger sword follows that of actual realistic and practical combat applications. The combinations of blocking, holding, sweeping and forward moves, make the attacks very unpredictable, while the chopping, holding, lead and point movements, also make the attacks aggressive. The pressing momentum, combined with the clear rhythm movements, enhances the practicality of the Black Tiger sword. There is a great emphasis on hand and sword co-ordination, combined with body and sword co-ordination, in order to unify all the movements together. There is a saying that, "The single sword watch the hand, while double sword watch the foot movement".

Description of Kam Kong Kun / Kam Kong Pole (Guardian God Staff) [金剛棍]

《金剛棍》乃少林黑虎門「武術套路」系列內，《金剛系列》中之一套棍法，屬初級套路，一般授予初學者。

《金剛棍》源自少林寺，由少林黑虎門宗師~蘇黑虎學自少林寺，據說是僧侶們常常練習的，其功能有二 ： 一則強身健體運動，二則又能保護寺院的功能。

《金剛棍》是一套 "雙夾單" 的棍法，演練套路一開始，就開式比禮，以合掌抱棍勢，如武僧護法般，守護寺院。其招式簡單而直接，一招一式，硬朗剛勁，絕不花巧，《金剛棍》內容並沒有如《李家棍》的細緻動作，如圈、點……之類; 也沒有《衝團棍》的密集招式，流水行雲、動如猛虎、靜若靈貓; 當然也沒有《猴子棍》的樸地翻滾、穿胯飛腳吧……!

但《金剛棍》雖然是初級套路，以學武格言所謂 :「拳為種，棍為師，雙刀為父母。」此套路確是基礎的典範。

The Guardian God Staff [金剛棍] of Siu Lum Hak Fu Mun [少林黑虎門] is one of the staff routines belonging to the "Guardian God Series". This staff routine is a primary level routine normally taught to beginners.

The Guardian God Staff [金剛棍] routine originated from Siu Lum / Shaolin Temple [少林寺]. So Hak Fu [蘇黑虎], the founder of Hak Fu Mun [少林黑虎門], learnt this routine while he was at the Kwangtung Siu Lum / Shaolin Temple [廣東少林寺]. It was said that Siu Lum / Shaolin monks [少林僧] practiced this staff routine very often for two reasons. One was to strengthen their physical capability and the second was to protect the temple should the need arise.

The Guardian God Staff [金剛棍] routine combines both methods of single head staff and double head staff techniques. The routine starts with a salute movement, by holding the staff horizontally on closed Buddhist palms [以合掌抱棍勢]. This method represents a martial monk protecting Buddhism and the temple (ie, a Guardian of the temple). The contents of this routine are relatively clear and straight forward. All movements and techniques are hard and bold, without any fancy or elaborate actions. The Guardian God Staff [金剛棍] does not have the details such as the circling and pointing movements that are common in the Lee Ga Staff [李家棍] routine, and it certainly does not have the rolling floor movements and jumping kicks of the Monkey Staff [猴子棍] routine. Neither does it have the concentrated moves of "Rush Out Staff [衝團棍]", such as presenting the staff like water and clouds flowing, or moving like fierce tiger and quiet like agile cat.

Although Guardian God Staff [金剛棍] is a primary level staff routine, one martial motto says, "fist is the base, staff is the teacher, and double sword is the parent". This routine is a typical example of that motto.

Description of Black Tiger Sword of Siu Lum Hak Fu Mun [少林黑虎門] & Guardian God Staff [金剛棍] routines by Franco Lok / Lok Wai Fai [駱華輝]. (Martial Arts Executive of Hak Fu Mun [少林黑虎門益群堂黃祥體育會])

After six years of training, So [蘇] had learned all the secret martial arts [武術] from the monk, Sam Dak / San De [三德] (Siu Dak [兆德]). During these years, when Sam Dak / San De [三德] (Siu Dak [兆德]) would return to the Putian Siu Lum / Shaolin Temple [莆田少林寺] as part of his duties, So [蘇] would accompany him and study there as well. He then went on to develop and formulate his own style, from the various aspects of Siu Lum / Shaolin Kung Fu [少林功夫] taught to him. [164] This style was named after So [蘇], and called Hak Fu Mun [黑虎門], (Gate of the Black Tiger style) which was then taught at the temple by him to other monks. So Hak Fu's [蘇黑虎] style of fighting could be described as cunning, treacherous and unpredictable, striking at the vulnerable target areas located around the body. Initial instruction consisted of speed training to develop fast movement, and a very high degree of conditioning [少林內息調理功] to harden the body. Due to a considerable amount of body conditioning [少林內息調理功] during training, this results in both delivering strong powerful strikes, as well as being able to withstand a large amount of punishment in return. Techniques and applications were rooted in real combat, with swift movement for breaking and entering, grabbing and striking to perceived weak points by the shortest and most direct route.

After many years at the temple, So [蘇] was feeling homesick and wished to return to his home village. At the age of 24, after gaining the approval of his teacher [功夫老師], Sam Dak / San De [三德] (Siu Dak [兆德]), So Hak Fu [蘇黑虎] left the Kwangtung Siu Lum / Shaolin Temple [廣東少林寺] and returned to his home village near Pek Ho Town (what is now Beijiaozhen [北滘镇], translates to North Kau town) in the district of Shunde [順德區], to visit his parents. Once back in the village, his clan were soon very impressed by his standard of Kung Fu [少林功夫] and he was invited to teach martial arts [武術] there. So [蘇] was given an area at the local fruit wholesalers company, to set up his gym and teach his martial arts [武術] to his clan there. This school [武術學校] proved popular with many locals, but due to the village's rural location, was limited in size. After three successful years, it was suggested by his clan brothers, that he expand by travelling to Canton [廣州] (Guangzhou [廣州]) and open a gym there. So Hak Fu [蘇黑虎] had already realised that his options were restricted if he stayed in his village, and if he moved into to the provincial capital city [省會城市] of Canton [廣州], he would have greater prospects. There, he would have the opportunity to enhance his reputation and be able to attract more students. This would not only spread his style of Kung Fu [少林功夫], but also he could become more prosperous, enabling him to have a better life.

At the age of 27, So [蘇] handed over his school [武術學校] to one of his students. With several of his clan brothers, he left his home village and travelled to the city of Canton [廣州]. Once in the city, he looked for a good location to start his new school [武術學校]. So [蘇] eventually found a site in the West Gate / Sai Kwan / Xiguan [西關] (now called the Liwan district) in the flourishing west part of Canton [廣州] (Guangzhou [廣州]), which was on the northeast bank of the Pearl River [珠江]. This was an area located at a busy fruit market close to Wong Sa Road / Huangsha Avenue [黃沙大道].

He was familiar with this area of Canton [廣州], as he had studied not too far away at the West Zen Temple / Sai Sim Ji / Xi Chan Si [西禪寺]. So Hak Fu [蘇黑虎] referred to this temple as the Kwangtung Siu Lum / Shaolin Temple [廣東少林寺] because he had trained in Siu Lum / Shaolin philosophy [少林禪學] and martial arts [少林武術] there. This temple was also part of the Siu Lum / Shaolin order. So Hak Fu [蘇黑虎] started teaching his Black Tiger style [黑虎門] at this location, and attracted more students, expanding until his teaching had become a steady business.

In the early 1850s, after three years teaching at this fruit market, he decided to look for a property to enable him to set up his own school [武術學校]. So [蘇] wanted a permanent building because of the increasing number of people that wanted to study under him. Because he was known in this area, he looked close by until he found an appropriate building for his school [武術學校]. So Hak Fu [蘇黑虎] soon found suitable premises for his school [武術學校] in Wong Sa Road / Huangsha Avenue [黃沙大道] near to the Wong Sa / Huangsha Ferry Pier [黃沙碼頭] and Shamian Island [沙面島]. Present day location would be near to the Zhujiang Pearl River Tunnel exit [珠江隧道出口], straight across from the White Swan Hotel on Shamian Island [沙面島]. Shamian only became an island when digging out the waterway, which began in 1859, and was completed in 1862. It was then separated from the north bank of the Pearl River [珠江], and a stone bridge was built in the east to connect it to the north bank. Therefore when So Hak Fu [蘇黑虎] established his school [武術學校] around the 1850s, Shameen as it was called then, was a large, crowded sand bank area with thousands of people living on boats.

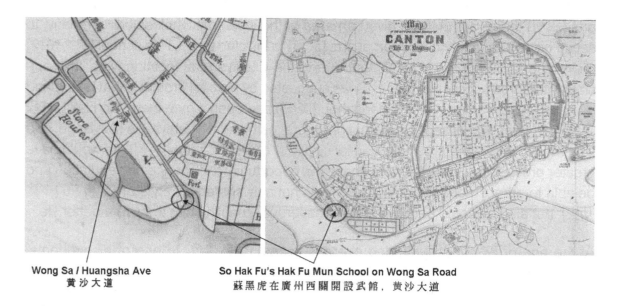

Wong Sa / Huangsha Ave
黃沙大道

So Hak Fu's Hak Fu Mun School on Wong Sa Road
蘇黑虎在廣州西關開設武館，黃沙大道

The Waterfront area of Liwan district to Yuexiu district is the historical part of the city of Canton (starting from Yan Jiang Zhong Road, by the foot of Jiangwan Bridge to Yan Jiang Xi Road at Renmin Bridge). This area is the oldest and once the most energetic part of the old city of Canton. This district was always filled with people, various markets and many ramshackle and dilapidated buildings. There are some colonial buildings grouped near the old Customs House when you walk towards west end of the road, which is typical of how Canton (Guangzhuo) looked like in the old colonial period.

At the back of White Swan Hotel is Shamian Island. Dating back to centuries ago, westerners were restricted to Shamian Island where they operated their factories. This 2 sq. km small island was leased to the French and British after the Opium War. Ironically the Chinese were not allowed to enter the island during that period of occupation. The pace inside the island is very different from outside. All the Victorian-style houses, grand villas, churches and other facilities remain unchanged except they are no longer occupied by foreigners. [119]

With the aid of some of his students, So [蘇] got the building ready and started to promote his new gym [武術學校], with several demonstrations of his skills. He quickly built up a good reputation as a skilled martial artist [武術家] and soon more students joined his new gym [武術學校]. In Canton [廣州] he became more commonly known by his nickname of So Hak Fu [蘇黑虎].

Over the next few years, So Hak Fu [蘇黑虎] gained a reputation as an outstanding Kung Fu master [功夫大師], with many people wanting to study at his school [武術學校]. Unfortunately, due to his success, some other local Sifus [師父] became jealous. One of these was a Wu-tang / Wudang style [武當拳] Sifu [師父] called Liu Wing [呂榮]. Liu Wing [呂榮] decided that he would teach this new upstart a lesson, and so one day, went to So Hak Fu's [蘇黑虎] gym [武術學校] with, it is claimed, as many as thirty of his own students. When Liu Wing [呂榮] arrived at So's [蘇] gym [武術學校], he challenged So Hak Fu [蘇黑虎] to a fight. While this was going on, Liu Wing's [呂榮] students began to smash up So's [蘇] school. So Hak Fu [蘇黑虎] had no alternative but to accept this challenge and fight with Liu Wing [呂榮] and his students.

A very fierce battle then commenced, with So Hak Fu [蘇黑虎] having to fight for his life against not only Liu Wing [呂榮], but also his students. Due to his many years of training and conditioning [少林內息調理功], So Hak Fu [蘇黑虎] was able to withstand many strikes that caught him while he blocked, and struck thunderous blows to his opponents. With speed and power, he dodged in and out, first hitting to one person's eyes, then another's groin, followed by a strike to someone's throat, as well as hitting the joints, breaking arms and legs, to overwhelm his foes. He swiftly moved through the horde of assailants, leaving a moaning multitude of injured or maimed opponents, withering on the floor in agony. Liu Wing [呂榮] was the last person standing, but So [蘇] quickly sent him crashing to the floor under a barrage of furious strikes. Finally at the end of the battle, So Hak Fu [蘇黑虎] was victorious and had defeated Liu Wing [呂榮] and his students.

News of this battle soon spread through Canton [廣州] (Guangzhou [廣州]), and So Hak Fu [蘇黑虎] became famous. His enhanced reputation as a skilled and fierce fighter increased his popularity, with more students wishing to join his gym. Shortly after the famous battle with the Wu-tang / Wudang [武當拳] Sifu [師父], Liu Wing [呂榮] and his students, many prominent members of the community and Kung Fu masters [功夫大師] gathered to elect the ten best martial artists [武術家] at that time. So Hak Fu / Su Heihu [蘇黑虎] was honoured by being selected as one of the Ten Tigers of Guangdong / Kwong Tung Sap Fu [廣東十虎]. This honour was bestowed upon him not only because of his phenomenal prowess as a fighter, but also because of his principled character traits such as decency and integrity. His decency extended to the local populace, with many acts of charitable deeds, and he was also popular because of his anti-Ch'ing / anti-Qing [反清清朝] (anti-Manchurian) attitude.

So Hak Fu [蘇黑虎] had made friends with several other local Kung Fu masters [功夫大師], two had businesses nearby, who were Lai Yan-Chiu / Li Renchao [黎仁超], the Chao Feng [朝奉] (chief in charge) and owner of the Shun Hang Pawnshop [信亨押店], which was also located a little further up on Wong Sa Road / Huangsha Avenue [黃沙大道]; the other was Wong Yan-Lam / Wang Yinlin [王隱林] of Lama Pai [喇嘛派], who had a bone setting clinic on Kim Shin Street [兼善街], which was located just off Wong Sa Road. From this building, he was also running a Kung Fu school [武術學校], teaching his style of Lama Pai [喇嘛派]. These three masters [功夫大師] became known as the "Three Heroes of Wong Sa [黃沙三傑]".

**The Three Heroes of
Wong Sa Road / Haungsha Avenue
黃沙三傑**

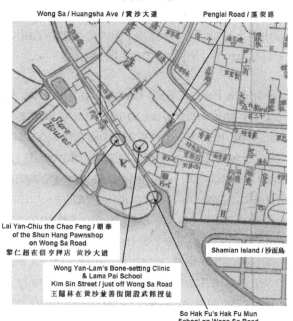

Wong Sa / Huangsha Ave / 黃沙大道   Penglai Road / 蓬萊路

Lai Yan-Chiu the Chao Feng / 朝奉
of the Shun Hang Pawnshop
on Wong Sa Road
黎仁超在信亨押店 黃沙大道

Wong Yan-Lam's Bone-setting Clinic
& Lama Pai School
Kim Sin Street / just off Wong Sa Road
王隱林在黃沙兼善街開設武館授徒

Shamian Island / 沙面島

So Hak Fu's Hak Fu Mun
School on Wong Sa Road
蘇黑虎在廣州西關開設武館. 黃沙大道

So Hak Fu [蘇黑虎] continued to develop his style over the next several years, adding methods and techniques that he thought would create or enhance skills that were practical and useful. He achieved this by training with other great masters [功夫大師], such as his friend Wong Yan-Lam [王隱林]. So [蘇] and Wong Yan-Lam [王隱林] would exchange ideas and methods. The style of Hak Fu Mun [黑虎門] has certain aspects of the Lama Pai [喇嘛派] style within it, which corroborates this exchange. A good example of this can be found in the Hak Fu Mun [黑虎門] routine [套路] called the Great Drunk [大醉]. It is understood that So [蘇] utilised upper body movements with certain powerful long arm attacking techniques, from this exchange with

Wong Yan-Lam [王隱林]. Both styles also have versions of a Kam Kong Kuen [金剛拳] (spelt Dai Gum Gong Kyuhn [大金剛拳] in the Lama Pai [喇嘛派] style) routine [套路]. As well as using these techniques in practical fighting applications, these methods were also incorporated into several Hak Fu Mun routines [黑虎門套路] to ensure that they could be practiced and passed on. It is believed that one of the techniques that So Hak Fu [蘇黑虎] helped Wong Yan-Lam [王隱林] develop from this exchange, was the Tiger Claw [虎爪]. This technique can be used to strike vunerable areas such as the face and throat, as well as seizing to either choke or control joints.

Grandmaster Wong performing the Chopstick and bowl form.

Another Kung Fu master [功夫大師] that So Hak Fu / Su Heihu [蘇黑虎] collaborated with, was So Chan [蘇燦], who was more commonly known by his nickname of So Hat-Yee [蘇乞兒] which means Beggar So. So Chan [蘇燦] was also honoured as one of the Ten Tigers of Guangdong / Kwong Tung Sap Fu [廣東十虎] and from him, So Hak Fu / Su Heihu [蘇黑虎] learnt the Iron Chopstick and Golden Bowl [金碗鐵筷] routine. It is known that So [蘇] had acquired several enemies during his life in the city, and because he led an open lifestyle in the public domain, he was always expecting a trap or surprise attack. His belief was that this Chopstick and Bowl routine would be a very practical method, so that even when he was eating, he would still be prepared in case an opponent tried to ambush him. This routine contains many practical applications which were useful not only to defend himself with, but could be devastatingly utilised for attacking as well.

(This routine [套路] has been passed down through the generations with the last Grandmaster of Hak Fu Mun [黑虎門], Wong Cheung [黃祥宗師] teaching it to several of his students. One of these students was a Hong Kong actor called Philip Kwok [郭追] (also known as Kuo Chui, Kwok Chui, Kwok Chun-Fung). In the film entitled Shaolin Rescuers aka "Avenging Warriors of Shaolin" (a Shaw Brothers film from 1979), both Philip Kwok and Grandmaster Wong Cheung [黃祥宗師] starred and demonstrated some comical techniques using a chopstick and bowl during a meal scene. In the final grand fight scene of the film, Philip Kwok (in white) demonstrates several other Hak Fu Mun [黑虎門] weapons including the Wooden Bench [板櫈], Double Tiger Hooks [虎頭雙鈎] and Chopstick and Golden Bowl [金碗鐵筷]. When he picks up the Chopstick and Bowl, his opponent asks what style that is and Philip Kwok replies that it is Black Tiger Kung Fu / Hak Fu Mun [黑虎門].)

Coincidently, also in 1979, Philip Kwok [郭追] played the part of Beggar Su Chan [蘇乞 兒] in the Ten Tigers from Kwantung [廣東十虎與後五虎], another film made by Shaw Brothers. It is understood that his Sifu, Grandmaster Wong Cheung [黃祥宗師] taught Philip Kwok [郭追] the drunken methods of Hak Fu Mun [黑虎門], which So Hak Fu [蘇黑虎] had learnt and passed on.

It is also known that So Hak Fu [蘇黑虎] and So Chan [蘇燦] (Beggar So / So Hat-Yee [蘇乞兒]) were very good friends who exchanged various ideas and methods for their respective drunken styles. It is even stated in Hak Fu Mun [黑虎門] oral history that they were cousins. This fact was confirmed by the last Grandmaster, Wong Cheung [黃祥], but I have been unable to prove or even disprove this thought with any other evidence. It is understood that So Hak Fu [蘇黑虎] and So Chan [蘇燦] shared their knowledge of the Drunken Eight Immortals / Chue Ba Sin [醉八仙] which they had both learnt. The Great Drunk [大醉] routine [套路] was developed during this period by So Hak Fu [蘇 黑虎] from his exchange with several of the other Ten Tigers of Guangdong / Kwong Tung Sap Fu [廣東十虎]. It has already been mentioned that this routine contains certain characteristics of the Lama Pai [喇嘛派] style from So Hak Fu's [蘇黑虎] exchange with Wong Yan-Lam [王隱林], but the main influence was due to his collaboration with So Chan [蘇燦]. So Chan [蘇燦], was well known for his high level of drunken style, that was both unique and practical in its fighting technique, to handle different situations. As a sign of respect for his friend, So Hak Fu [蘇黑虎] named this routine [套路] the Great Drunk [大醉] in honour of his good friend, (cousin) So Chan [蘇燦]. [50a]

So Hak Fu [蘇黑虎] was also good friends with Wong Kei-Ying [黃麒英], and later, when he became of age, his son Wong Fei-Hung [黃飛鴻]. From this friendship, various methods and ideas of their Kung Fu [功夫] styles were exchanged. It is understood that So Hak Fu [蘇黑虎] taught the Hak Fu Mun [黑虎門] Tiger methods to Wong Kei-Ying [黃麒英], from which he then formulated a routine [套路] which he simply called the Black Tiger Fist / Hak Fu Kuen [黑虎拳]. This routine was taught to Wong Fei-Hung [黃飛鴻] by his father and has become part of the curriculum which has been passed down through this lineage. In return, Wong Kei-Ying [黃麒英] taught So Hak Fu [蘇黑虎] various methods of the umbrella for which he was famous for. So Hak Fu [蘇黑虎] formulated these ideas into a routine [套路] which he intergrated into his style. [50a] [66] [112]

During So Hak Fu's [蘇黑虎] life time, he trained with numerous Kung Fu masters [功夫大師] in various other styles. Several of these were friends, and the remainder acquaintances who, over time, would also become his friends. While training with these Kung Fu masters [功夫大師], certain methods and techniques that he thought were useful and practical, he incorporated into his own style of Hak Fu Mun [黑虎門]. By the time he had completed Hak Fu Mun [黑虎門], it is understood that it was formulated from the merging of the various skills and methods of a dozen or so different styles.

Legend states that So Hak Fu / Su Heihu [蘇黑虎] was challenged many times over the years and was never defeated. Unfortunately, due to the sometimes brutal and extreme conditioning [少林內息調理功] required at the initial stages of training in Hak Fu Mun [黑虎門], it never became a mainstream style. So [蘇黑虎], now in his later years, had decided to leave the worldly life behind and had retired to a more peaceful existence at the Honam Temple [河南寺]. During So's [蘇] early lifetime, he had been an unshaved lay disciple [俗家弟子] of the Siu Lum / Shaolin monk [少林僧] Sam Dak / San De [三德] and had spent years at the Siu Lum / Shaolin Temple [少林寺], so had been familiar with Buddhist practices and temple life.

Shortly after the young Fung Ping Wai [馮平慧] had settled at the Honam Temple [河南寺], he had started to study martial arts [武術] under "So the Black Tiger" [蘇黑虎]. After an initial period of training, Fung Ping Wai [馮平慧] become a disciple of So Hak Fu [蘇黑虎] and his true education of Hak Fu Mun / Black Tiger style [黑虎門] began. Initially, Fung Ping Wai's [馮平慧] training included a large part of conditioning [少林內息調理功] as well as studying various martial techniques with Hak Fu Mun / Black Tiger style [黑虎門] open hand and weapon routines. He was also told about his teachers' / Sifu's history and linage of the Shaolin temple and the master's that had come before. His martial arts training [武術] was in harmony with his education in Buddhism and some years later when he became of age, he was ordained as a monk.

It is understood that in the middle to late 1880s, "So the Black Tiger" [蘇黑虎] passed away from natural causes and his body was cremated with his ashes placed in the burial ground at the temple. Fung Ping Wai [馮平慧] continued his practicing of Hak Fu Mun / Black Tiger style [黑虎門] while he resided at the Honam Temple [河南寺]. During the early 1900s, Fung Ping Wai [馮平慧] had decided to leave the temple. After discussing this matter with the abbot, he disrobed and left the Buddhist temple life behind him, returning to a worldly existence. A few years later, around 1910, he travelled to Hong Kong [香港], where he found employment with the British family at Bowen Road [寶雲道], which was located on the mid-levels of Victoria Peak [太平山].

He had been with the family for a number of years and had become a trusted and highly valued member of the staff. During breaks from his work schedule, Fung Ping Wai [馮平慧] would continue his training in Hak Fu Mun / Black Tiger style [黑虎門]. Then, in 1920, a young man called Wong Cheung [黃祥] started working for the British family as a gardener, and early in the morning and during his breaks he would practice his martial arts [武術]. His would include performing Three wraps of iron thread boxing / Saam Jin Tit Sin Kuen [三輾鐵線拳], staff work (Chai Mei Kun), and Dragon Ba Gua Palm / Lung Yin Ba Gua Cheong [龍八卦掌].

Not long after the young Wong Cheung [黃祥] had started this new job, Fung Ping Wai [馮平慧] saw him training and was impressed by his relentless practice and commitment to his Kung Fu [功夫]. Wong Cheung [黃祥] was training with his staff when one day this co-worker who had been watching him asked if he could borrow it to demonstrate his technique. Wong Cheung [黃祥] obliged and the co-worker started imitating Wong's technique, but he wielded the staff with grace and such power that it broke into two pieces. His co-worker apologised for breaking the staff and then started to go back to work. Wong [黃祥] realised that his co-worker must be a master of Kung Fu and so therefore asked him his name and where he had learned such powerful Kung Fu.

The co-worker introduced himself as Fung Ping Wai [馮平慧] and briefly told him his story. The young Wong Cheung [黃祥] was understandably impressed at the level of skill of such a master and asked if he could be accepted as Fung's [馮平慧] student. Fung Ping Wai [馮平慧] had been observing Wong Cheung [黃祥] for some time, and after witnessing his commitment, his dedication, his general attitude and conduct had planned that this would happen. He therefore accepted Wong [黃祥] as his student (apprentice) and shortly after arranged the Bai Si [拜師] ceremony in keeping with traditional formalities.

Fung Ping Wai [馮平慧] would educate Wong Cheung [黃祥] every day in the martial arts [武術] of Hak Fu Mun [黑虎門]. During these periods, Fung Ping Wai [馮平慧] would talk about the history and his Sifu (teacher), So the Black Tiger [蘇黑虎], his Si Gung, Siu Lum / Shaolin monk [少林僧] Sam Dak / San De [三德] as well as explaining the various techniques and principles of the style. During the next few years, Fung [馮平慧] and Wong [黃祥] became very good friends. Due to the young Wong Cheung's [黃祥] previous experience and devoted attitude, he was able to learn and progress at a rapid rate. This continued until 1923 when they found out that their employers were moving back to Britain. Fung Ping Wai [馮平慧] had been invited to travel with the family back to Britain and continue his employment there. In the final few months before Fung [馮平慧] left, he imparted what remained of the style for Wong [黃祥] to learn. As Fung Ping Wai [馮平慧] was ready to leave, he requested that Wong Cheung [黃祥] continued to practice Hak Fu Mun [黑虎門] and pass on the style as his disciple's obligation to him. Wong Cheung [黃祥] readily accepted this responsibility to pass on Hak Fu Mun [黑虎門] and continue the lineage, stating that it was an honour for him to do so. [50] [50a] [50d] [51] [120] [121]

Fung Ping Wai [馮平慧] left Hong Kong and made the voyage to Britain on an ocean liner travelling with the British family. Unfortunately, all further information on Fung Ping Wai [馮平慧] is unknown after he left Hong Kong.

Before Wong Cheung [黃祥] trained under Fung Ping Wai [馮平慧] he had also studied under other Kung Fu masters [功夫大師]. One of these was Sifu Fu Man [傅文] who was the brother of the famous Iron Palm Fu Chen-Sung / Fu Zhen Song [傅振嵩] [117a].

Wong Cheung [黃祥] studied aspects of the Fu Style Baguazhang [傅式八卦掌] [117b] with Fu Man [傅文] for four years before he arrived in Hong Kong. During the early to mid 1920s Wong Cheung [黃祥] also studied Hung Kuen [洪拳] with Kwong Gang San / Kuang Gengchen [鄺賡臣], who was a disciple of Wong Fei Hung [黃飛鴻]. Through Kwong Gang San / Kuang Gengchen [鄺賡臣], Wong Cheung [黃祥] met Wong Fei Hung [黃飛鴻] and they became friends in the few years before he passed away in 1924.

In 1928 Wong Cheung [黃祥] opened up his school [武術學校] at Wellington Street [威靈頓街] in the Central district, on Hong Kong Island. Over the next several years, he had built up a large following until this was brought to a dramatic end when the Japanese invaded Hong Kong in December, 1941. Wong [黃祥] decided to leave Hong Kong returning back to his home town of Punyu [番禺], in Canton. Once back in his home town, he soon found work as a doorman at a local bar. Over the next few years he established himself and soon owned his own bar and casino. During the war, Wong [黃祥] would provide food and shelter for other fleeing masters [功夫大師] trying to escape the Japanese. This enabled Wong [黃祥] to train with these other masters [功夫大師] and besides honing his own skills, it was reputed that during this period, he also learnt several high level secret aspects of Kung Fu [功夫] as repayment for providing food and shelter to travelling masters [功夫大師] who had been made refugees during the war.

Once again, Wong's [黃祥] affluent life was brought to a sudden end in 1949 when the Communist party took over China. They outlawed martial arts, and so consequently many Kung Fu masters [功夫大師] who had enjoyed revered positions, now escaped persecution by fleeing China via Hong Kong. Wong Cheung [黃祥] was forced to leave Punyu [番禺] and once again returned to Hong Kong with thousands of other Chinese refugees also fleeing the Communist government. Wong [黃祥] soon found employment working for various restaurant and employees associations located at Pei Ho Street [北河街] and Shanghai Street [上海街] in Mong Kok [旺角], who wished their workers to learn Kung Fu [功夫]. In the 1950s, he was also employed to train the workers on the railways by the Kowloon and Canton Railway Workers Union [九廣鐵路職工會]. This position enabled him to set up his own gymnasium in a siding at Mong Kok railway station. This gym remained in use until the area was redeveloped for the MTR in around 1980.

Grandmaster Wong Cheung at the Mong Kok Railway sidings, 1970s.

With the fame of Bruce Lee and explosion of people interested in learning Kung Fu [功夫], Wong's [黃祥] students encouraged him to formally open the Black Tiger Association and set out a more rigid and standardised syllabus. This culminated in the official opening of the Wong Cheung Black Tiger Gymnasium in 1973, first at 332-334 Portland Street [砵蘭街] and then in 1974, at its final home in Bute Street [弼街], Mong Kok [旺角]. This gymnasium was on the roof level (8th floor) and had a large outdoor training area on the roof top, as well as an indoor area. Wong Cheung [黃祥] maintained this school [武術學校] until his death on the eve of Chinese New Year 1989.

Ceremony to celebrate the official opening of the Wong Cheung Black Tiger Gymnasium, 1973.

Wong Cheung [黃祥] was a small man of about 5 feet tall, who over many years of arduous training, had achieved a very high degree of body conditioning, with extremely well-conditioned hands. His teaching method was therefore to emphasise stealth and deception over raw power, using sneaky techniques and a high degree of body conditioning. The majority of the kicks in the style are low, and the preferred hands strikes are gouging, clawing, and raking to vulnerable areas of the body. During Wong Cheung's [黃祥] life, he exchanged ideas and methods with various other masters [功夫大師] so as to continue to expand his knowledge and skills. In the same manner as So Hak Fu [蘇黑虎] had devised his system, combining his knowledge of many systems, Wong Cheung [黃祥] re-designed the system further, adding skills and concepts he had studied. This was not to change the style of Hak Fu Mun [黑虎門], but to expand it further. Many of the routines [套路] were slightly adapted to give them a common feeling and standardisation within the Hak fu Mun [黑虎門] system.

During his lifetime, Wong Cheung [黃祥] exchanged ideas and methods with various other Kung Fu masters [功夫大師] including the follow :-
Hung Fut [洪佛] from the "White Hair Devil" Hung Jiu Sing [洪照成].
Choi Lei Fut [蔡李佛] from Jeung Loi [張來]
Qigong from Jeung Loi [張來], and Lei Gau [李九]
Staff [棍] from Lei Yi [李義], including Yau Lung Gwun [游龍棍], Baat Gwa Gwun [八卦棍], Chung Wai Gwun [衝圍棍] and Jui Gwun [醉棍].
Various weapons from Pun Fai Shan [潘輝] (南海人), including 點子扇, 點子蕭, 黃金鐧, 八卦梅花鞭, 青龍偃月刀, 夜遊刀, 孫臏拐, 梅花槍, 三節棍, 太師座, 八仙劍等.

A brief account of So Hak Fu's [蘇黑虎] and Wong Cheung's [黃祥] lives can be found in the magazine entitled "Real Kung Fu", 1976 edition, pages 5 to 7. [50d]

Another branch of Hak Fu Mun [黑虎門] is more commonly known today as Fu Jow Pai [虎爪派]. According to Fu-Jow Pai / Tiger Claw [虎爪派] history, Wong Bil Hong [黃標雄] was born in 1841, and originally studied Hung Kuen [洪拳] under Wong Kei-Ying [黃麒英], and then later under his son, Wong Fei-Hung [黃飛鴻]. In 1876, Wong Bil Hong [黃標雄] was engaged in a duel [決鬥] with another Kung Fu master [功夫大師] at the Honam temple [河南寺] (Hoi Tung Temple [海幢寺]), when suddenly a monk from the temple intervened. This monk subdued both men, then acted as a mediator, eventually accepting them as disciples [武術弟子]. Unfortunately, this monk's name is not recorded, only that he was of the Siu Lum / Shaolin [少林] order who taught the style of Hak Fu Mun [黑虎門].

Late Grand Master Wong Moon Toy

Wong Bil Hong [黃標雄] later passed on this style to his nephew, Wong Moon Toy [黃文采] and a servant in 1927. Just before he passed away in 1934, it is stated that Wong Bil Hong [黃標雄] renamed the style Fu Jow Pai of the Hoy Hong Temple [海幢寺虎爪派]. Fu Jow Pai / Tiger Claw [虎爪派] history states that shortly after, the servant also passed away, and that Wong Moon Toy [黃文采] then became the second generation of this Fu Jow Pai / Tiger Claw [虎爪派] style. During the same year, Wong Moon Toy [黃文采] left Guangdong [廣東] and settled in New York City in the USA, where he began to teach the style of Fu Jow Pai / Tiger Claw [虎爪派]. Wong Moon Toy [黃文采] passed away on 14th March, 1960 and the third generation successor is Ng Wai Hong [伍偉康]. [118] [118a] [118b] [118c]

Wong Kei-Ying [黃麒英]

(traditional Chinese: 黃麒英; simplified Chinese: 黃麒英; pinyin: *Huang Qiying*)

Approximately 1815-1886

Wong Kei-Ying [黃麒英] was born about 1815, in the village of Luk Chow / Louzhou [祿州] [123] [130] (although Wikipedia states Sai Chiu Tsuen / Xiqiaocun [西樵村]), which is about 4 kms east [105] [105a] and is situated at the foot of the Sai Chiu Mountain / Xiqiao [西樵山] in the Nam Hoi county / Nam Hoi Yuen [南海縣] (now district [南海區]) of Fat Shan / Foshan [佛山]. This village is located approximately 21 kms from Fat Shan / Foshan [佛山] and 40 km South West of the old city of Canton [廣州] (now Guangzhou [廣州]). Some sources state that Wong Kei-Ying [黃麒英] was born a little earlier, around 1810. [102b] [105a]

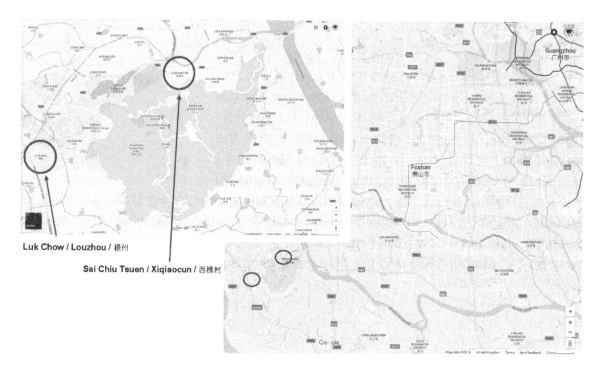

Luk Chow / Louzhou / 祿州

Sai Chiu Tsuen / Xiqiaocun / 西樵村

202

The young Wong Kei-Ying [黃麒英] had been taught Kung Fu [少林功夫] by his father, Wong Tai [黃泰]. Wong Tai [黃泰] had also learnt martial arts [武術] and had studied at Hung Hei-Kwun's [洪熙官] school [武術學校] in Fat Shan / Foshan [佛山], in the Hung Kuen style [洪拳]. While at this school [武術學校], Wong Tai [黃泰] had met Luk Ah-Choi / Lu A Cai [陸阿采] with whom he had become good friends. He later continued his education in Hung Kuen [洪拳] under the tutelage of Luk Ah-Choi [陸阿采]. Wong Tai's [黃泰] main occupation was as a Traditional Chinese doctor, specialising in bone setting and herbal medicine [中醫]. [105]

Traditional Chinese medicine (TCM; simplified Chinese: 中医; traditional Chinese: 中醫; pinyin: zhōng yī; literally: "Chinese medicine") has been practiced in China for over 2,000 years. TCM is a wide variety of medical procedures which comprises various types of herbal medicine, acupuncture, massage (Tui na), exercise (qigong), and dietary therapy. [125]

It is believed that Luk Ah-Choi [陸阿采] left Hung Hei-Kwun's [洪熙官] school [武術學校] in Fat Shan / Foshan [佛山], sometime around 1820 to set up his own school [武術學校] in Canton [廣州]. After Luk Ah-Choi [陸阿采] moved to Canton [廣州], Wong Tai [黃泰] focused more on his medicine business than studying Kung Fu [功夫], and returned to his home village. From a very young age, he taught his son, Wong Kei-Ying [黃麒英], martial arts [武術] and acrobatics / Jop Kai [雜技]. To supplement his income, Wong Tai [黃泰] would also perform public Kung Fu demonstrations [武術表演] with his son, and the young Wong Kei-Ying [黃麒英] would assist his father demonstrating martial arts [武術] and acrobatics / Jop Kai [雜技] in these street performances [武術表演]. The performances [武術表演] would attract a large crowd of spectators, to which Wong Tai [黃泰] could then promote his medical skills and herbal remedies.

During the 1820s, Wong Tai [黃泰] travelled around the various towns and villages of the region with his son, performing these demonstrations. On one of these trips they had gone to the provincial capital city [省會城市] of Canton [廣州] to ply their trade there. One day, they had gone to one of the more prosperous areas to perform, hoping that the richer residents might possibly spare more money for their demonstration and herbal medicines [中醫]. While doing their usual performances [武術表演] outside the residence of the general of Guangdong, the young Wong [黃麒英] was noticed by his father's Hung Kuen [洪拳] master [功夫大師], Luk Ah-Choi / Lu A Cai [陸阿采]. Luk Ah-Choi [陸阿采] could see that the young Wong Kei-Ying [黃麒英] was a skilful acrobat / Jop Kai [雜技] who had a talent for martial arts [武術]. After seeking permission from his old friend and student, Wong Tai [黃泰], he persuaded Wong Kei-Ying [黃麒英] to become his disciple [弟子]. [105a] [115a] [124] [126]

Wong Tai [黃泰] left his son in Canton [廣州] to live with, and be trained by Luk Ah-Choi [陸阿采]. The young Wong Kei-Ying [黃麒英] then spent the next ten years studying under Luk Ah-Choi [陸阿采], learning the style of Hung Kuen [洪拳]. [105a] During his training, he learnt various forms [套路] (routines) and weapons which included "Single Hard Fist", "Double Hard Fist", "Taming the Tiger Fist / Gung Gee Fook Fu Kuen [伏虎拳]", "Mother & Son Butterfly Knives [子母雙刀]", "Angry Tiger Fist", "Fifth Brother Eight Trigram Pole [五郎八卦棍]", "Flying Hook", and the "Black Tiger Fist [黑虎拳]". [105] (Wikipedia states that the "Black Tiger Fist [黑虎拳]" was taught by Luk Ah-Choi [陸阿采], but it is understood that this routine was initially taught to Wong Kei-Ying [黃麒英] by So Hak Fu [蘇黑虎], sometime around the 1850s. I believe that this routine was part of Wong Kei-Ying's [黃麒英] early syllabus and so assume that he had learnt it from Luk Ah-Choi [陸阿采].) Wong Kei-Ying [黃麒英] had a great aptitude for martial arts [武術], and achieved an extraordinary level of mastery in his Kung Fu [少林功夫] over these ten years.

A story relating to a Lion Dance with Luk Ah-Choi [陸阿采] and Wong Kei-Ying
(This story is told in Wing Lam's History of Hung Gar [64])

A local temple would organise an annual parade to celebrate one of the Northern Gods. Various groups and organisations were invited to take part which including dancers, musicians, acrobats / Jop Kai [雜技] and Lion Dancers [舞獅]. Many of the local Kung Fu schools [武術學校] were represented by their Lion Dance troupes [舞獅團] supported by flag and banner holders parading with the lions. Along the route of the parade, various stores and businesses had set up Chings [採青] (a green with a red envelope that has a cash reward inside) for the different lions to attempt to retrieve.

One business had placed their Ching [採青] at a difficult height, and as the lions in the parade approached, they set off firecrackers to draw the attention to their Ching [採青]. Several lions approached, but after seeing the business' sign, passed by without attempting the Ching. Luk Ah-Choi [陸阿采] was the lion head, and Wong Kei-Ying [黃麒英] was leading the lion. Wing Lam states that they were representing Hung Hei-Kwun's [洪熙官], Lok-Sin-San Fong School [樂善山房學校]. They were one of the last troupes [舞獅團] in the parade, and Wong Kei-Ying [黃麒英] was about to pass by, also believing that the Ching [採青] was too difficult to get, when Luk [陸阿采] called him back. Luk [陸阿采] stated he had an idea and was going to take this Ching [採青]. He started to perform a powerful yet skilful dance in front of this Ching [採青], before suddenly running forward towards it and leaping into the air. As he leapt, he held the lion head in one hand while throwing a dart with the other at the rope holding the Ching [採青]. The dart hit the rope, slicing it through and releasing the Ching [採青]. As it fell, Luk [陸阿采] opened the mouth of the lion to swallow the prize.

The watching crowd were amazed by this skilful display and started shouting and cheering in appreciation. This commotion made several of the other lions that had passed by, look back to see what was happening. When one Sifu [師父] in particular realised that the Ching [採青] had been taken, he became angry at the credit that Luk's [陸阿采] lion troupe [舞獅團] were getting. This Sifu [師父] was called Chan [陳], who was a powerful and talented master [功夫大師] himself. He came back towards Luk Ah-Choi [陸阿采] and Wong Kei-Ying [黃麒英], shouting that they had been disrespectful for taking that particular Ching [採青] after the others schools' [武術學校] lions had chosen not to attempt it and passed it by. He stated that it wasn't because the other lions couldn't have acquired it, but the reason they had left it was because that business had dealt with foreigners, and they didn't want that sort of money.

Luk Ah-Choi [陸阿采] replied that the Ching [採青] was part of the parade and so could be taken by any lion, and that several other business and stores had also dealt with foreigners, but their Chings [採青] had been taken by the other lions. Sifu [師父] Chan [陳] was outraged at Luk's [陸阿采] response, and rushed forward attacking him with a punch. Luk Ah-Choi [陸阿采] dodged this strike by moving to the side, but Sifu [師父] Chan [陳] then decided to attack again, to which Luk [陸阿采] continued to evade, hoping to prevent the situation escalating into a deadly fight. Unfortunately, Sifu [師父] Chan [陳] not wishing to lose face in front of so many people, would not stop his relentless attacks. Luk [陸阿采] realised that Sifu [師父] Chan [陳] was not going to stop, and was therefore forced to counter with a palm strike to the chest. This strike caught Chan [陳] perfectly, sending him crashing to the floor. Sifu [師父] Chan [陳] had trained in the Iron Body skill and so was not hurt by the palm strike. He was, however, infuriated that he had been knocked down in front of his students, and therefore jumped up and renewed his attack on Luk Ah-Choi [陸阿采]. Luk [陸阿采] assumed that as his basic counter strikes were having no effect on Sifu [師父] Chan [陳], he must have trained in the Iron body conditioning (also known as Iron Shirt / Tee Po Sam / Tie bu shan [鐵布衫].) He realised that in order to stop Sifu [師父] Chan [陳] he would have to strike at a more vulnerable target area.

Luk Ah-Choi [陸阿采] stepped back as Chan [陳] charged in, throwing a powerful right punch with all of his might. Luk [陸阿采] countered this attack and delivered a kick to Chan's [陳] solar plexus. Sifu [師父] Chan [陳] stumbled backwards before collapsing to the floor. Chan's [陳] students, upset at seeing their Sifu [師父] floored, surrounded Luk [陸阿采] with weapons drawn. Wong [黃麒英] and the supporting members of the Lok-Sin-San Fong School [樂善山房學校] joined the fight to assist Luk Ah-Choi [陸阿采]. Chan's [陳] students outnumbered Luk's [陸阿采] by three to one as they were a long established martial arts school [武術學校] in this area. A mass fight ensued and because many of Luk's [陸阿采] students were novices, a great deal of them were soon injured. Others fled, leaving Luk Ah-Choi [陸阿采] and Wong Kei-Ying [黃麒英] on their own, fighting back to back against an overwhelming crowd. Chan's [陳] students managed to separate Wong Kei-Ying [黃麒英] from Luk Ah-Choi [陸阿采] and in the ensuing battle, the young Wong [黃麒英] was injured.

Fortunately at that moment, several masters [功夫大師] from the Lok-Sin-San Fong School [樂善山房學校], including Hung Hei-Kwun [洪熙官], Leung Kwan / Liang Kun [梁坤] (known as Iron Bridge Three / Tit Kiu Saam / Tie Qiao San [鐵橋三]) and Wu Wei Kin [胡惠乾], got there just in time. They had heard news of the battle from the other students and had rushed to the scene in order to assist their brothers. The battle raged on until all of Sifu [師父] Chan's [陳] students were either injured or had fled. The next morning, the area was awash with blood and thirty dead bodies were counted lying in the street. Members of the Lok-Sin San Fong School [樂善山房學校] had only suffered minor injuries including Wong Kei-Ying [黃麒英]. News of this fight spread through the city, which was to further enhance the names of Luk Ah-Choi [陸阿采], Hung Hei-Kwun [洪熙官] and Wu Wei Kin [胡惠乾] as members of the Siu Lum / Shaolin Ten Best [少林十傑], but it also was the start of reputations for Wong Kei-Ying [黃麒英] and Leung Kwan / Liang Kun [梁坤]. It is also stated that Hung Hei-Kwun [洪熙官] and Luk Ah-Choi [陸阿采] were full of remorse for the unfortunate outcome of this event and had Buddhist monks [和尚] perform a ceremony for the dead. They also offered compensation for the dead and injured of Sifu [師父] Chan's [陳] school [武術學校]. [64]

(This story was taken from Wing Lam's book, but unfortunately, some of the details of this story raise several questions. Either the date could possibly be incorrect, as it must have occurred much later, or these famous masters' [功夫大師] names have since been added to embellish the story. It is very possible that this story is true, but obviously some details have either been mixed up or confused.)

Lion dance (simplified Chinese: 舞獅, traditional Chinese: 舞獅, pinyin: wǔshī) is a traditional part of Chinese society performed during various occasions such as Chinese New Year and other Chinese traditional, cultural and religious festivals. It can also be performed on various other occasions such as business openings, special celebrations or weddings, or to honour special guests.

The Chinese Lion Dance was originally performed by Kung fu (Wushu (武術)) schools and the dancers were martial artists.

During the Chinese New Year, Chinese martial arts schools' Lion Dance would visit shops of the Chinese community to perform the traditional custom of "cai qing" (採青), which means "plucking the greens". This involves the lion plucking the green vegetables (like a lettuce), which are either hung from a pole or placed on a table in front of the property. Usually a "red envelope" containing money is tied to the green vegetables, which is the prize for the lion. The Chinese believe that the lion dance brings good luck and fortune to the business.

Historically, the lettuce was hung far above the ground so that only a highly skilled martial artist could reach the red envelope. These occasions sometimes turned into a public challenge, with large money rewards. Sometimes at these events, when lions from different Kung Fu schools approached the "Green" at the same time, they would try to outdo each other, to gain the crowds judgement as to which school was the most skilled [127]

I have been unable to find the location of Luk Ah-Choi's [陸阿采] school in Canton [廣州], but I have established that Wong Ching-Hoh [黃澄可] was also at this school, and for a time, so was Leung Kwan / Liang Kun [梁坤] (known as Iron Bridge Three / Tit Kiu Saam / Tie Qiao San [鐵橋三]) [106] [113] Around the mid to late 1830s, Luk Ah-Choi [陸阿采] decided to withdraw from teaching martial arts [武術] publically and his only student after this was Wong Kei-Ying [黃麒英]. Besides teaching Wong [黃麒英], Luk [陸阿采] had committed himself to the further study of Chinese medicine [中醫]. It is not stated if Luk [陸阿采] taught Wong Kei-Ying [黃麒英] Traditional Chinese Medicine [中醫] on top of what he had learnt from his father, Wong Tai [黃泰]. This could have also been a passion that they shared, and that they exchanged ideas and practices with each other, or Luk [陸阿采] expanded on Wong Kei-Ying's [黃麒英] knowledge.

Now that Wong [黃麒英] had completed his training under Luk Ah-Choi [陸阿采], he sought employment and became a martial arts instructor [功夫老師], teaching the soldiers in the General of Guangdong's army [粵軍部兵技擊教練] based in Canton [廣州]. [105] [115] [128] [130] Several sources state that this was after he had completed his training with Luk Ah-Choi [陸阿采], but it is unclear if this was straight away or a few years later. It is also unclear how long Wong Kei-Ying [黃麒英] maintained this job, teaching the troops in the General of Guangdong's infantry regiment. Due to the poor wages he received from teaching martial arts [武術] (monthly salary was approximately 3.6 ounces of silver), Wong had to supplement his earnings as a doctor of Chinese medicine [中醫] and by selling herbal medicines as his father, Wong Tai [黃泰], had done.

During the 1840s, Wong met a lady called Pu Lai Ai [朴麗娥] that he wished to marry. Unfortunately, her parents were not happy about this relationship and were strongly opposed to their daughter marrying a martial artist [武術家]. They felt that due to the way Wong Kei-Ying [黃麒英] lived this dangerous lifestyle, many things could be uncertain for their daughter's future. They were therefore concerned about the stability and welfare of their daughter, but because she admired and respected Wong [黃麒英], she ignored their objections and married him. Within a year or two of being married, they had a son whom they named Wong Fei-Hung [黃飛鴻]. He was born on the 9th, July, 1847 in Fat Shan / Foshan [佛山] town. [105a]

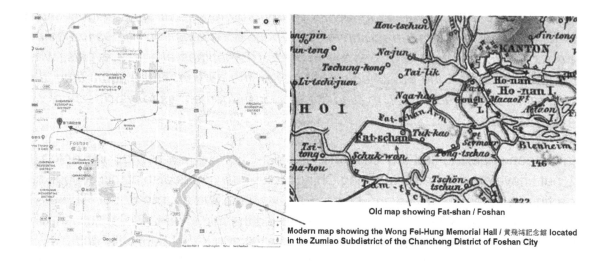

Old map showing Fat-shan / Foshan

Modern map showing the Wong Fei-Hung Memorial Hall / 黃飛鴻記念館 located
in the Zumiao Subdistrict of the Chancheng District of Foshan City

*(Wikipedia and other sources state that Wong Fei-Hung [黃飛鴻] was born in what
is now the Zumiao Subdistrict of the Chancheng District of Foshan City. The Wong
Fei-Hung Memorial Hall [黃飛鴻記念館] was built at this location,* [129] *although several
other sources state that Wong Fei-Hung [黃飛鴻] was born in Luk Huern Yan Village,
Sai Chu County, Lam Hoi.* [132] [133] [134] *My assumption is that this refers to Wong Kei-
Ying's [黃麒英] ancestral home of Luk Chow / Louzhou [祿州], near Sai Chiu / Xiqiao
Mountain, Namhoi.)*

I believe that the reason for these different locations is because Wong Kei-Ying [黃
麒英] was continuously moving around, living the life of Jianghu / 江湖. [95] During the
late 1840s, Wong opened up a school teaching martial arts [武術學校].

A story relating to the opening of Wong Kei-Ying's school
(This story is told in Wing Lam's History of Hung Gar [64] and in a detailed article
written by Anthony at practical hungkyun [106b]. This article was originally from an issue
of "Real Kung Fu" magazine, pages 22 to 23. The Wing Lam source states that the
local teacher was called Sifu Gum [64], while Anthony at practical hungkyun states
Kam. [106b]) [128]

Wong Kei-Ying [黃麒英] started to become well known in Canton [廣州] for his skill
in Kung Fu [少林功夫]. He was also gaining a reputation as an honourable man with
a great respect for others, always willing to help out the poor and needy. With this
enhanced reputation, Wong [黃麒英] decided to open up his own school [武術學校]
and teach martial arts [武術]. Once his new school [武術學校] opened, it attracted a
reasonable amount of students, which then continued to gradually increase as his
reputation as a good teacher [功夫老師] continued to spread.

A local master [功夫大師] by the name of Sifu [師父] Gum / Kam who already had an
existing thriving school [武術學校] in the same neighbourhood, started to lose students.

This local Sifu [師父] had been making a good living for many years teaching Kung Fu [功夫], prior to Wong's [黃麒英] school [武術學校] opening in the same neighbourhood. He soon realised that many of his students were in fact defecting from his school [武術學校] to join Wong Kei-Ying's [黃麒英] new school [武術學校]. The loss of students meant that Sifu [師父] Gum's / Kam's income was reduced, which therefore started to affect his standard of living. In an attempt to reverse his loss of income and increase his students by proving he was a better Kung Fu master [功夫大師], he decided to challenge Wong Kei-Ying [黃麒英]. Sifu [師父] Gum / Kam was not a bad person, and as there was no dispute or feud between them, he decided the most appropriate why to do this was by inviting Wong [黃麒英] to take part in a contest with staffs / Gwun [棍]. He sent a letter to Wong Kei-Ying [黃麒英] regarding the contest to establish who was the more skilled with this weapon. He requested that they meet at a certain location on the outskirts of the town, within an appropriate timescale.

When Wong Kei-Ying [黃麒英] received the letter, he knew he had to accept, as refusing would cause him to lose face, which would bring dishonour on him and his school [武術學校]. He therefore told the messenger who had brought the letter, that he would meet with Sifu [師父] Gum / Kam in two days time at noon. Wong [黃麒英] found out that Sifu [師父] Gum / Kam was a big powerful man who was renowned for being skilled with the staff / Gwun [棍]. He also discovered that two of his preferred techniques were attacks to the groin and the throat. To ensure that he was properly prepared for this contest, Wong Kei-Ying [黃麒英] decided that he should go to see his teacher [功夫老師], Luk Ah-Choi [陸阿采], and seek his advice.

That same evening, Wong [黃麒英] travelled on a boat along the river to Luk's [陸阿采] home at Leshan Lodge / Lok Seen Siu Oak [樂山小屋]. He greeted his teacher [功夫老師], Luk Ah-Choi [陸阿采], who unfortunately was ill and confined to his bed. After informing Luk [陸阿采] of the challenge, and of his opponent's skills, Wong [黃麒英] then sought his teacher's [功夫老師] opinion in countering these staff / Gwun [棍] techniques. Luk Ah-Choi [陸阿采] asked Wong [黃麒英] to sit him up, supported by pillows, and fetch him two chopsticks [筷子] so that he could demonstrate the movements. Luk [陸阿采] then held a chopstick [筷子] in each hand to represent two staffs / Gwun [棍] and while moving them, explained the principle methods and applications to counter the attacks preferred by Wong's [黃麒英] opponent. While he was doing this, Wong Kei-Ying [黃麒英] stood next to the bed and imitated the movements using a real staff / Gwun [棍]. Once he had mastered these movements, he thanked his teacher [功夫老師] and bid him good health till they meet again.

On the day of the challenge match, Wong Kei-Ying [黃麒英] travelled to the location with two students who also carried a staff / Gwun [棍] each, for their Sifu [師父] to use. News had spread around the community of this match between the two masters [功夫大師], and a large crowd had gathered to watch. Wong [黃麒英] and his two students made their way through the mass of onlookers, and when they got to the centre, they found Sifu [師父] Gum / Kam with several of his students already there waiting for them. Introductions were made, and then Sifu [師父] Gum / Kam adopted his guard posture of cat stance, holding his staff / Gwun [棍] like a fishing pole which pointed directly at Wong [黃麒英]. Wong Kei-Ying [黃麒英] responded by dropping into a horse stance [馬步] [131a] [131b] with his staff / Gwun [棍] aimed towards his opponent. The crowd fell silent in anticipation waiting for what was about to happen next, but nothing happened. Both masters [功夫大師] knew that this was a waiting game, as the one that attacked first would be open to their opponent's counter strike. Wong [黃麒英] knew that his opponent was strong and skilled with the staff / Gwun [棍], therefore he could not afford to be reckless.

As the waiting continued, Sifu [師父] Gum / Kam became impatient and invited Wong [黃麒英] to attack. Wong [黃麒英] replied that as Sifu [師父] Gum / Kam had requested this challenge, then it was obvious he should attack first. Sifu [師父] Gum / Kam realised that this was true and so was forced to respond. He slammed his staff / Gwun [棍] down against Wong's [黃麒英], then thrust the staff / Gwun [棍] forward stabbing towards Wong's [黃麒英] armpit. Wong [黃麒英] immediately countered this attack by lifting his staff / Gwun [棍] up. This caught Sifu [師父] Gum's / Kam's staff / Gwun [棍], forcing them to cross. Both masters [功夫大師] vied for control, trying to get their weapon on top, which caused the staffs / Gwun [棍] to circle. After a few rotations, Sifu [師父] Gum / Kam then changed and attacked towards Wong's [黃麒英] lead hand, striking down. He then thrust it forward, stabbing towards Wong's [黃麒英] body, who again, quickly blocked this move. Wong [黃麒英] immediately stepped forward and attacked, thrusting his staff / Gwun [棍] into Sifu [師父] Gum's / Kam's chest. Sifu [師父] Gum / Kam dropped his weapon as he staggered back a few steps. Winded, he dropped to his knees as he struggled to breathe. Several minutes later, Sifu [師父] Gum / Kam was able to get back up on his feet. He realised that the strike could have seriously injured him, but Wong [黃麒英] had showed some restraint. He therefore showed respect to Wong Kei-Ying [黃麒英] by bowing, before leaving in defeat. [64] [106b]

Shortly after this challenge match, Luk Ah-Choi [陸阿采] passed away at his home known as Leshan Lodge / Lok Seen Siu Oak [樂山小屋], at the age of 68 years. One source states that Wong Kei-Ying's [黃麒英] father, Wong Tai [黃泰], also passed away at about the same time as Luk [陸阿采], but several other sources state that Wong Tai [黃泰] passed away around 1867. [102a] [102b]

Wong Kei-Ying [黃麒英] would travel around the province to collect and trade his herbal medicines. On these trips, he would also perform martial arts demonstrations [武術表演] on the streets. This was another method to supplement his income as well as advertise his skills, as not just a Kung Fu master [功夫大師], but as a doctor. During his travels, he would exchange ideas and methods with other skilled martial artists [武術家]. [126] [129]

Due to his strong character and sense of justice, Wong Kei-Ying [黃麒英] was always busy living the life of Jianghu [江湖]. Whilst away living this life, and dealing with various matters, his neglected wife became critically ill. Unfortunately, when Wong [黃麒英] realised his wife was so ill, it was too late to save her. Her last request before she died was that he took care of their son, Wong Fei-Hung [黃飛鴻]. Wong [黃麒英] was full of remorse and guilt at the death of his wife. Because of this, together with accusations and bad feelings from her parents, he decided to leave his ancestral home at the village of Luk Chow / Louzhou [祿州] near Sai Chiu / Xiqiao Mountain [西樵山] in 1852, with his five year old son. It was from this time on, that he started to teach his son Kung Fu [少林功夫] and about Chinese medicine [中醫]. Wong [黃麒英] did not talk to his son about the guilt and regret regarding the life he had had with his wife, but kept this sadness to himself. It is rumoured that this lack of communication did cause some misunderstanding between father and son, but Wong Kei-Ying [黃麒英] cherished his son and was fiercely protective towards him. [130]

It is understood that Wong Kei-Ying [黃麒英] was based in the provincial capital [省會城市], where it is recorded that he expanded his Traditional Chinese Medicine [中醫] business and opened up a medical clinic and herbal dispensary. This was called Po Chi Lam Clinic / Bao Zhi Lin [宝芝林] and was located in Jingyan Street / Chan Yun Street [靖遠街] of Canton [廣州]. It is also believed that at these premises, he also had a school teaching martial arts [武術學校]. [105a] What is not stated, is whether Wong Kei-Ying's [黃麒英] Po Chi Lam Clinic / Bao Zhi Lin [宝芝林] was located on this site before or after the Battle of Canton (October 1856 to January 1858). If it was before this battle, I think it is fair to assume that the building would have been damaged or totally destroyed, due to its close proximity to the Thirteen Factories. [135] If the clinic was established after October 1856, then this area was clear of foreigners as they had relocated across the Pearl River [珠江] on Honam Island [河南島], and so the area was relatively safe during the remainder of the conflict.

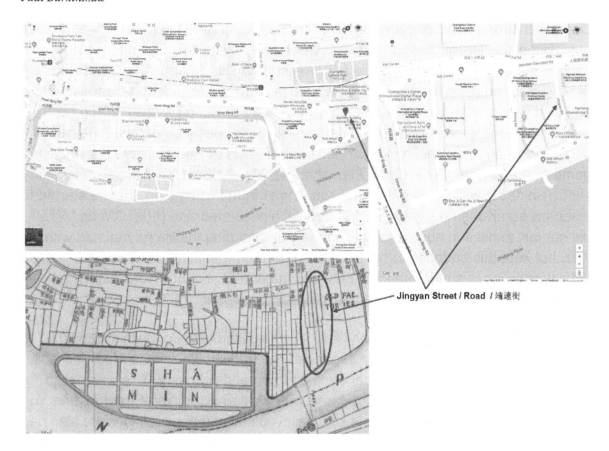

Jingyan Street / Road / 靖遠街

The Thirteen Factories was an area in Canton, China, in the 18th century where the first foreign trade was allowed. (It was also sometimes called the "Thirteen Hongs" or the "Canton Factories". This system came to an end in 1842 with the Treaty of Nanking. The present day location where the factories stood, is now Wenhua Park, and Thirteen Hong Street and the factories backed onto Shisanhang Road.

The Factories were buildings occupied by foreigners and used as trading posts and were located outside the city walls of Canton. The name came from the term "factors", meaning foreign agent, who arranged trading deals with the Chinese. The Chinese citizens would call these places "Barbarian Houses".

The factories were burnt down in 1856, during the Second Opium War. Western traders moved to warehouses across the Pearl River on Honam Island, until Shamian Island was developed in 1859.

The Factories were set back one hundred yards from the river, with the trading warehouses located on the first floors, and living apartments on the second and third floors. The square area in front of these factories was fenced, and for foreigners only. The streets surrounding the factories were named Thirteen Factory Street, Old China Street, and Hog Lane, and were full of local shops selling a wide range of Chinese goods. [135]

Wong Kei-Ying [黃麒英] ensured that his son, Wong Fei-Hung [黃飛鴻], was taught all aspects of traditional Chinese medicine [中醫], as a herbalist, as well as bone setting and acupuncture; the same went for his Hung Kuen [洪拳] style of martial arts, including Lion Dance [舞獅]. It is reputed that in years to come, his son became so good at Lion Dance [舞獅] that he would be known in Canton [廣州] (Guangzhou [廣州]) as "Wong Fei-Hung, King of the Lions [黃飛鴻獅王爭霸]". The young Wong Fei Hung [黃飛鴻] was famed for his "no-shadow kicks", but several sources state that Wong Kei-Ying [黃麒英] was also renowned for this kick before his son mastered it. [115a]

Wong Kei-Ying's [黃麒英] "Small Deception-Kick" / Gwai Ji Geuk [拐子腳], commonly called the "Shadowless Kick", includes the "Yin-Lifting Kick" / Liu Yam Geuk 撩陰腿, "Court-Sweeping Leg" / So Tong Geuk [掃堂腿], "Propping-Rooster Leg" / Chang Gaai Geuk [撐雞腳], and "Single-Standing Golden Rooster Leg" / Gam Gaai Duk Laap Geuk [金雞獨立腳]. Because issuing such a counter is so extremely fast that the opponent is unable to detect a shadow, these skills are therefore called the "Shadowless Kicks" / Mou Ying Geuk [無影腳].

The "Small Deception-Kick" of the Siu Lam Hung Ga system, likewise a "Shadowless Kick", is referred to as a Gwai Ji / "Small Deception". The idea of it is to "Counter with Emptiness" / Heui Jiu [虛招]. When issuing this counter-attack against an opponent, it is first necessary to strike forth by means of emptiness, "signalling the east to attack the west", thus distracting the opponent's ears and eyes. This type of empty counter is referred to as the "Small Deception" / Gwai Ji [拐子], and is also called the "Shadow-Strike" / Ying Da [影打]. Written by: Ngo Si Saan Yan [我是山人], as told by Jyu Yujai [朱愚齋], disciple of Grandmaster Lam Sai-Wing. [131]

One source also states that the umbrella, was in fact one of Wong Kei-Ying's [黃麒英] favourite objects to use as a weapon. [131c] The umberella can be carried during all seasons for keeping the rain, snow and sun off the holder. It has the advantage of appearing totally inoffensive when carried around, but having a point at one end and a hook at the other, allows for numerous attacking and defensive applications. Due to the general weak, springy body of the umbrella, it is mainly used to a parry an attack, with the more effective strikes performed by using the pointed end to pierce an opponent, or striking with the stronger hook handle. The handle can also be used for hooking an opponent's arms, legs or even around their neck. During the next few years, Wong [黃麒英] would be challenged from time to time and was always victorious which earnt him the honour of being named as one of the Ten Tigers of Guangdong / Kwong Tung Sap Fu [廣東十虎]. This honour was not only bestowed upon him because of his fighting skills, but also because of his virtuous and honourable character traits. He would always treat the poor, charging only what little they could afford. Any shortfalls would then be supplemented by charging his wealthier clients according to their means or making up the difference himself.

Wong [黃麒英] would continue to expand his knowledge and improve his skills by exchanging ideas with other renowned Kung Fu masters [功夫大師]. One of these masters [功夫大師] was Wong Yan-Lam [王隱林], who taught Lama Pai [喇嘛派] and was also one of the Ten Tigers [廣東十虎]. It is stated that Wong Kei-Ying [黃麒英] taught the Hung Kuen [洪拳] Five Animal Fist / Ng Ying Kuen [五形拳] to Wong Yan-Lam [王隱林], and that from these techniques, he created the Small Five Animal Fist / Siu Ng Ying Kuen (also spelt Siu Nhg Yihng Kyuhn) [小五形拳] which he later incorporated into his Lama Pai [喇嘛派] style. In return, Wong Yan-Lam [王隱林] taught Wong Kei-Ying [黃麒英] long arm techniques, which he incorporated into the Tiger and Crane Double Fist / Fu Hok Seung Ying Kuen [虎鶴雙形] and the Five Element fist / Ng Haang Kuen [五行拳] techniques (now found in the Five Animal Five Element Fist /Ng Ying Ng Haang Kuen [五形五行拳] routine [套路]). [87] It is also possible that the two exchanged ideas about medical practices as well.

On the same road as Wong Yan-Lam's [王隱林] bone setting clinic and school [武術學校], another renowned master [功夫大師] had his school [武術學校]. This master [功夫大師] was called So, more commonly known as So Hak Fu / Su Heihu [蘇黑虎], (So the Black Tiger) and during this period, Wong Kei-Ying [黃麒英] became good friends with him. So Hak Fu [蘇黑虎] was also one of the Ten Tigers of Guangdong / Kwong Tung Sap Fu [廣東十虎] and it is believed that they would often train together, exchanging ideas and methods of their Kung Fu [功夫]. It is understood that So Hak Fu [蘇黑虎] taught various Hak Fu Mun [黑虎門] Tiger methods to Wong Kei-Ying [黃麒英], which he then formulated into a routine [套路] that he simply called the Black Tiger Fist / Hak Fu Kuen [黑虎拳]. In return, Wong Kei-Ying [黃麒英] taught So Hak Fu [蘇黑虎] various methods of the umbrella, for which he was famous. So Hak Fu [蘇黑虎] formulated these ideas into a routine [套路] which he intergrated into his Hak Fu Mun [黑虎門] style. [50a] 66] [112]

During the late 1850s to early 1860s, Wong Kei-Ying [黃麒英] would again travel around the province, living the life of Jianghu [江湖]. The young Wong Fei-Hung [黃飛鴻] would accompany his father on these trips, and they would spend a lot of time over the next several years travelling around together. Also, like his father had done as a boy, Wong Fei-Hung [黃飛鴻] would assist him in the street performances, demonstrating martial arts [武術表演] and promoting their family business.

It was on one of these trips, travelling around the district of Shunde [順德區] and into the town of Fat Shan / Foshan [佛山] around 1860 that Wong Kei-Ying [黃麒英] was challenged by another local Sifu [師父]. The Wongs [黃麒英 & 黃飛鴻] were performing one of their Kung Fu demonstrations [武術表演] at a town in the region, and at the same time, there was another martial arts demonstration [武術表演] going on. This other demonstration [武術表演] was being conducted by a local Sifu [師父] called Cheng Tai Hung [鄭大雄]. It is stated that Sifu [師父] Cheng Tai Hung [郑大雄] was exhibiting his skills of his famous left handed fishing pole techniques [左手釣鱼棍法]. Cheng Tai Hung [鄭大雄] became very angry because more locals were turning away from his performance [武術表演] and going over to watch the Wongs' [黃麒英 & 黃飛鴻] demonstration [武術表演]. He felt that because he was the local teacher [功夫老師], the Wongs [黃麒英 & 黃飛鴻] were being disrespectful, for first, encroaching on his territory, and secondly, performing at the same time as him. The local teacher [功夫老師] feeling offended and humiliated, approached Wong Kei-Ying [黃麒英] with his staff / Gwun [棍] in hand and challenged him to a duel [決鬥].

Wong Kei-Ying [黃麒英], knowing that the challenger was not equal to him, just smiled as he offered the match to his thirteen year old son, Wong Fei-Hung [黃飛鴻]. The young Wong Fei-Hung [黃飛鴻] accepted his father's invitation and took up his staff / Gwun [棍]. Before the match, Wong Kei-Ying [黃麒英] advised his son to use the techniques of Ng Long's Eight Diagram Long Pole / Ng Long Baat Gwa Gwan [五郎八卦棍]. The young Wong [黃飛鴻] easily outclassed Sifu [師父] Cheng Tai Hung [鄭大雄], defeating him in front of the large crowd. News of this challenge match and the young Wong's [黃飛鴻] victory soon spread around the province. After this incident, Wong Fei-Hung [黃飛鴻] was known as the "Young Hero [少年英雄]". [14] [129b] [132] [133] *(NB, Cheng Tai Hung / Zheng Daxiong [鄭大雄] can be spelt slightly different depending on source, ie Jeng Daai Hung* [132]*, & Gwan Dai Hung* [133]*)*

In the same year of 1860, while on this trip, they came across another Kung Fu teacher [功夫老師] performing a demonstration [武術表演] in one of the towns. This Kung Fu teacher [功夫老師], Lam Fook Sing [林福成], was a student of Leung Kwan / Liang Kun [梁坤], known more by his nickname of Tid Kiu Sam (Iron Bridge Three), who was also one of the Ten Tigers of Guangdong / Kwong Tung Sap Fu [廣東十虎]. Wong Kei-Ying [黃麒英] and his son stopped to watch this martial arts performance [武術表演], and unfortunately during the demonstration, a spectator was accidentally injured by Lam Fook Sing [林福成]. Wong Kei-Ying [黃麒英] and his son, Wong Fei-Hung [黃飛鴻], offered their services as doctors and treated the injured man. Lam Fook Sing [林福成] was very grateful for their help and so he offered to teach them the Tit Sin Kuen / Iron Wire Fist / Tie Xian Quan [鐵線拳] in return. This famous internal form (routine) [套路] had been taught to him directly by his Sifu [師父], Leung Kwan [梁坤], who was also one of the Ten Tigers of Guangdong / Kwong Tung Sap Fu [廣東十虎]. Wong Kei-Ying [黃麒英] and his son accepted the offer and were taught the Tit Sin Kuen [鐵線拳]. [64] [129] [134] *(NB, 林福成 spelt slightly different depending on source, ie Lam Fook Sing* [64]*, Lam Fuk Sing* [129]*, Lam Fok Sing* [134]*)*

It is recorded that in 1863, Wong Fei-Hung [黃飛鴻] was helped by some local workers to open up his own martial arts school [武術學校]. This was at Shui Ker / Shuijiao [水腳], which was located in the West Gate / Sai Kwan / Xiguan [西關] area of Canton [廣州]. This school [武術學校] was located near the 7th ward area, close to the water. *(It is understood that Shui Ker / Shuijiao [水腳] could possibly also translate to mean pier of the canal).* Unfortunately, this didn't work out for some unstated reason, and so in 1865, he was employed by the Sam Lan Hong / San Lan Xing [三欄行] (三欄行 which means the Three Markets Company - Fruit, Vegetable and Fish) traders as a martial arts teacher [功夫老師]. [14] [129] [129a] [129b] At this time, Wong Fei-Hung [黃飛鴻] was still a teenager (16-17 years old), and so I think it is fair to assume he was possibly living with his father. If this is the case, then Wong Kei-Ying [黃麒英] was himself still living in this area of Canton [廣州], until sometime into the mid 1860s.

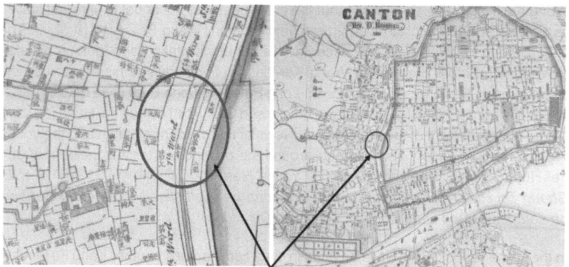

Location of Wong Fei-Hung's / 黃飛鴻 school

Sometime around the mid to late 1860s, Wong Kei-Ying [黃麒英] chose to return to his ancestral home in the village of Luk Chow / Louzhou [祿州], located near Sai Chiu / Xiqiao Mountain [西樵山]. He wanted to pay his respects to his late wife's grave. Although many years had passed since he was last there, the sight of his old home still filled him with much sorrow. His old house had recently been occupied by his aunt Po [寶姨], who had just returned home after spending some time abroad. His aunt [寶姨] was very open minded in her outlook compared to Wong's [黃麒英] beliefs, which caused some disagreements between them. Wong Kei-Ying [黃麒英] suffered her opinions with a patient attitude. His tolerance eventually paid off, and they established some harmony, with subtle feelings towards each other. [130]

Now in his fifties, Wong Kei-Ying [黃麒英] decided to leave the Jianghu [江湖] lifestyle behind, and concentrate on his medical profession. He opened another herbal dispensary and clinic, using the same name of Po Chi Lam / Bao Zhi Lin [寶芝林]. This clinic was located in the Ren'an [仁安], area of Canton [廣州]. 仁安街 translates into Benevolence Street, therefore it is assumed that the Po Chi Lam / Bao Zhi Lin [寶芝林] clinic was located in the area of Benevolence Street. (Some sources state that this area is now part of Xiaobei Road [小北路], in the Yuexiu District [越秀區]. From this information, the current location would be in the area of Zhongshan 4th Road [中山四路] and Cangbian Road [倉邊路], leading into Xiaobei Road [小北路]). [129] [133] [137]

(However, I have found some other sources which state that the Po Chi Lam / Bao Zhi Lin [寶芝林] clinic was in Fat Shan / Foshan [佛山].)

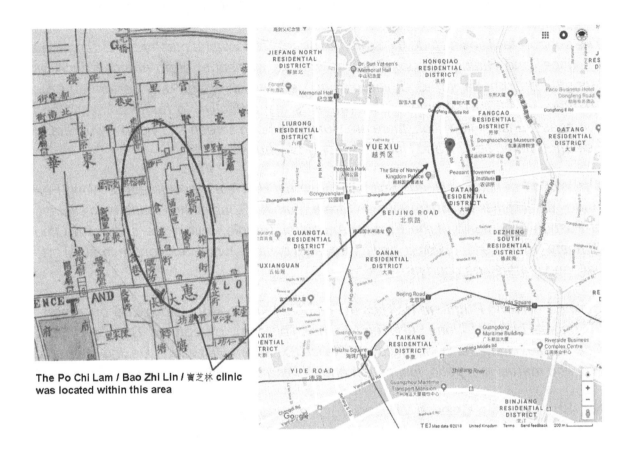

The Po Chi Lam / Bao Zhi Lin / 寶芝林 clinic
was located within this area

Wong Kei-Ying [黃麒英] was very well respected in his clinic, and was known for his generosity and compassion treating any and all patients, regardless of their finances or attitude. His charitable nature of treating patients that couldn't afford to pay, secured him a large amount of admiration from the local community. He would also secretly treat political activists and rebels who fought against the corrupt Ch'ing / Qing [清朝] authorities. Wong Kei-Ying [黃麒英] passed away in 1886, and his son, Wong Fei-Hung [黃飛鴻], inherited his father's Po Chi Lam / Bao Zhi Lin [寶芝林] clinic. [14] Wong Fei-Hung [黃飛鴻] at this time, was working for the army, but shortly after his fathers death, he resigned and took over the running of his late father's clinic [飛鴻辭去軍中技擊教練職務，在廣州仁安街設跌打醫館 "寶芝林"]. Wong Fei-Hung [黃飛鴻] maintained the Po Chi Lam [寶芝林] clinic until late 1924. During October of that year, troops from the then Republic of China's Nationalist government [中華民國國民政府] were battling the Canton Merchant Volunteers Corps [廣州商團]. Unfortunately, during the suppression of this uprising, the Po Chi Lam [寶芝林] clinic was destroyed. [137a]

Wong Fei-Hung (Huang Feihong) Memorial Hall *is located in the north part of the Ancestral Temple. The building is modelled after the wok-handle fire-walled house of the Qing Dynasty. It reproduces the style of folk residence and ancestral temple when Huang Feihong – the great martial arts master was alive. The building is divided into a show room, Huang Feihong Cinema, a hall, and patio for practicing Wush;, all of these represent the charism of the great master to the life.*

The support facilities include the statue booth of "Ten Wushu masters of Guangdong Province" and Huang Feihong Park as well as traditional performances such as Gongfu, "dragon-playing" and "lion-playing", etc, which will be duly performed from 10.00am to 4.00pm. All these performances are attractive to many domestic and overseas tourists. In addition, there are Huang Feihong screen and video town, Huang Feihong Wushu school and Huang Feihong Wushu village. [136]

The Wong Fei-hung or Huang Feihong Memorial Hall is a museum about Wong Fei-Hung [黃飛鴻]. It is located in Xinwen Street, Zumiao Road in the Chancheng District, of Foshan City, north of the Foshan Ancestral Temple. It is in the style of a Qing Dynasty (1644–1911) building, and features an exhibition hall, auditorium, martial arts hall, and martial arts courtyards. [136a]

Huang Fei Hong Pugilism Hall *lies at the foot of Xiqiao Mountain in Luzhou village - the original home of Wong Fei Hong's Father. This complex features: Bao Zhi Lin, Bai Cao House, Hung Fei Hong Historical Relics Exhibition Hall, Guan Dexing Memorial Hall and martial arts patio, instruction and training schools.* [136b]

NB. Strangely, the Chinese Wikipedia [129a] and some other sources [129b] state that Wong Fei-Hung [黃飛鴻] may have been born in 1856. Consequently, the dates of the incidents in his early life are also out following his age instead of when they actually occurred. This continues until around the time of his father's (Wong Kei-Ying [黃麒英]) death in 1886.

Lai Yan-Chiu [黎仁超]

(Traditional Chinese: 黎仁超; simplified Chinese 黎仁超; pinyin: *Lí Renchao*)

Lai Yan-Chiu [黎仁超] was born in the expanding port town of San Tau / Shantou / 汕頭, on the coastline of the South China Sea in Guangdong Province [廣東省] in the early 1800s, possibly sometime between 1825 and 1830. The town's importance during this period would continue to grow, when it was designated as one of the treaty ports to the British after the conclusion of the First Opium War in 1842. San Tau / Shantou [汕頭] is approximately 350 kms east of Guangzhou [廣州] as the crow flies. This area of Guangdong was known as Hakka [客家] land, after the Han Chinese [漢族] had predominately settled in this region east of the Pearl River Delta [珠江三角洲]. The style of martial arts [武術] practised in this region was generally referred to as either Hakka Kuen [客家拳] or Southern Praying Mantis [南派螳螂], and this is the style of martial arts [武術] that Lai Yan-Chiu [黎仁超] was renowned for. [14] [109] [138]

Southern Praying Mantis is a Chinese martial arts style that originated from the Hakka people. This style emphasises close-range fighting with concise power techniques, and has both internal and external methods. The majority of techniques consist of hand and arm, with a minimal amount of low kicks. This close combat style makes it appear, to what many would say looked like "street fighting." The hands are used mainly for attacking and defending the upper part of the body. The practitioner uses brutal and ruthless techniques to cause serious injury to their opponent. Fast footwork is utilised to get in and out of range, so as to protect and defend the practitioner. Attacks with the feet are limited to short, low kicking techniques so as to ensure they are not off-balance and so left vulnerable. [138a]

Legend has it that in the late 1700s and early 1800s, Hakka Kuen [客家拳] was strongly influenced by the Siu Lum / Shaolin monk [少林僧], Gee Seen Sim See [至善禪師]. The Fukien temples / Fujian si [福建寺] were located in Hakka [客家] lands, and so local people who joined these temples would have learnt this Siu Lum / Shaolin style [少林拳]. After leaving the temples, they in turn taught with variations due to differences in their knowledge, ability and preferred techniques. After the destruction of the Southern Siu Lum / Shaolin Temple [南少林寺] at Quanzhou [泉州] in the 1760s, Gee Seen [至善禪師] avoided the Ch'ing / Qing [清朝] troops by travelling south along the coastline and rivers into Guangdong Province [廣東省]. He made his escape hiding out with the Red Boat Opera Troupe [紅船粵劇團] that toured the waterways around this region. During this period, he would continue to teach his Siu Lum / Shaolin style of Kung Fu [少林功夫], and was a supporter of the anti-Ch'ing / anti-Qing [反清清朝] movement. [139]

It is stated that Lai Yan-Chiu [黎仁超] (Lai [黎] is his surname, Yan [仁] means kindness, and Chiu [超] means superior) was from a very wealthy family that had paid for him to be academically educated, as well as giving him a good tuition in martial arts [武術]. He studied the local San Tau / Shantou [汕頭] Hakka Kuen [客家拳] style, known also as Southern Praying Mantis [南派螳螂] Kung Fu. Lai [黎仁超] was from a large family and had at least six sisters. Little is known of his early life, but it is stated that when he was young, he was materialistic and dishonest. But after some bad incident in his teenage years, his attitude totally changed and he became a reformed character. This was possibly about the time that the family moved from San Tau / Shantou [汕頭] to Canton [廣州]. [109] [115] [141] One source states that Lai's [黎仁超] parents got into some kind of situation, and that he was orphaned as a result of this. He continued to study Kung Fu [功夫] so that he could one day avenge their death. [109a] [109c] This incident could also be a reason why he left San Tau / Shantou [汕頭] with the rest of his family and moved to Canton [廣州].

According to Wing Lam's history of Hung Gar [64], Lai Yan Chiu [黎仁超] is recorded as being affiliated to Hung Hei-Kwun's [洪熙官] school [武術學校] in Fat Shan / Foshan [佛山]. This would make him Kung Fu brothers [師兄弟] with several of the other Ten Tigers [廣東十虎], who it is stated, were members. These other members are recorded as being Wong Kei Ying [黃麒英], Leung Kwan [梁坤] (more commonly known as Iron Bridge Three / Tit Kiu Saam [鐵橋三]) and So Hak Fu [蘇黑虎]. Unfortunately, no dates are stated in this book to give a record of when their affiliations were. It is not known when Lai Yan-Chiu [黎仁超] moved into the West Kwan [西關] area (now called the Liwan District [荔灣區]) of Canton [廣州], but he was living at a house in the 10th Ward / Sap Sai Kwan [西第十] during the 1850s. [141]

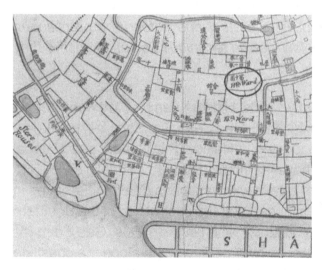

Xiguan or ***Sai Kwan*** *(simplified Chinese: 西关; traditional Chinese: 西關; pinyin: Xīguān; "West Gate") refers to an historical area of Canton / Guangzhou. The area outside the west gate of Guangzhou was collectively called **Xiguan**.*

Lai Yan-Chiu [黎仁超] was not a full-time martial artist [武術家] like several of the other Ten Tigers [廣東十虎], but due to his education and upbringing, he had his own business as a money lender, managing a pawn shop. He was the (Chao Feng [朝奉]) chief in charge of Shun Hang Pawnshop [信亨押店] which was located on Wong Sai Road / Huangsha Avenue [黃沙大道]. It is stated that Lai Yan-Chiu [黎仁超] was a smart, handsome, well dressed man and that first impressions gave no indication of him being an excellent martial artist [武術家]. Although he had a full time job, he continued his education in Kung Fu [功夫]. [141]

Wong Sa / Huangsha Ave   Lai Yan-Chiu the Chao Feng / 朝奉 of the Shun Hang Pawnshop on Wong Sa Road
黄沙大道   黎仁超在信亨押店　黄沙大道

Lai Yan-Chiu [黎仁超] was renowned for his skill in the Seven Stars Fist / Chuk Sing Kuen / Qi Xing Quan [七星拳] routine. [109] [109d] [109e] [115a] [164] This is a common Siu Lum / Shaolin routine [少林套路] which gets its name from the constellation of stars known as the "Big Dipper". This is because the footwork in this form [套路] (routine) follows a similar pattern to this star formation. It is stated this is an old form (routine [套路]) dating back to the 17th century. During the late 17th century, several forms (routines [套路]) were fully developed, of which one of the most notable still practiced today is the Seven Stars Fist / Chuk Sing Kuen / Qi Xing Quan [七星拳] routine. This routine has characteristic leg postures, as well as hand shapes, of the rooster [公雞], also called Feng Shou (wind hands) for the splayed fingers. The Seven Stars Fist / Chuk Sing Kuen / Qi Xing Quan [七星拳] has been preserved over the centuries, largely unmodified and is today part of the core curriculum of the Siu Lum / Shaolin Temple [少林寺] system.

The Seven Stars Fist / Chuk Sing Kuen / Qi Xing Quan [七星拳] is a brief fighting form [套路] (routine) which was designed for close quarter combat, and suits practitioners of a smaller stature fighting against a larger opponent. It is based on practical techniques and its method is therefore to evade direct confrontations of strength or power. It consists of short range defensive and pressing attacking techniques, which focus on speed and accuracy, with power generated from the waist. It is an energetic form (routine [套路]) that contains some well structured attacking and defensive techniques, that have been described as flexible and ingenious in their practical fighting application. The area required to perform this routine [套路] is relatively small, therefore it makes it particularly effective and practical for fighting in a small, compact area. This fierce routine [套路] is also known as the Seven Hurt Fist as its emphasis is to kill or destroy an enemy in one step.

A story about Lai Yan-Chiu and the oil porters union members

One day, Lai Yan-Chiu [黎仁超] was walking along Guanyin Roadway [觀音大巷] to his place of work at the Shun Hang Pawnshop [信亨押店], from his home in the 10th Ward / Sap Sai Kwan [西關]. During this period, some of the streets of Canton [廣州] (Guangzhou [廣州]) were very narrow, particular the Guanyin Roadway [觀音大巷] which was only about four feet wide. This road [觀音大巷] was always very busy and crowded with bustling people. On this particular day, Lai Yan-Chiu [黎仁超] was blocked by two porters (known as "coolies [苦力]") that were walking very slowly in front of him. They were carrying large oil barrels suspended from two bamboo poles [竹竿] that were across their shoulders. These oil barrels were about three feet in diameter, and so due to their size, they nearly blocked off the whole walkway. There were only small gaps on either side of the barrels, but this was less than seven or eight inches wide. It was a hot summer's day and the surfaces of the barrels were covered with grease and dirt. Lai Yan-Chiu [黎仁超] was wearing brand new clothes and a summer gown which was floating in the air as he walked along. Lai [黎仁超] was in a hurry as he had some urgent business to attend to, and so was pressed for time. However, he knew that if he tried to pass by, his new clothes would wipe against the barrels and be stained with the grease. As such, he had to be patient, walking slowly behind them.

However, after only passing a few shops, the two porters then stopped, placing the oil barrels down in the middle of the roadway. They took off the ropes from the bamboo poles [竹竿]. Lai [黎仁超] understood they were going to perform an "oil barge" (*[駁油] oil barge means transfer the oil from the movable oil barrels to the fixed oil containers in the oil shop*) which would block the roadway for several hours. The porters (coolies [苦力]) were members of a large union that covered the upper and lower West Gate / Sai Kwan [西關], (Xiguan, West Suburbs) area of Canton [廣州]. This was a powerful organisation, known as the "virtuous gangs [聚賢館人馬]", that had a bad reputation for not only harassing shop keepers to gain their business, but also rampaging through the streets intimidating the local people. The union's organised criminal activities were protected by corrupt local officials and so the porters (coolies [苦力]) were arrogant and inconsiderate to the local community, knowing there would not be any reprisals or punishment from the authorities.

Lai [黎仁超] told the porters (coolies [苦力]) that blocking the road this way was unreasonable, and therefore urged them to quickly move the drums so that people could continue to pass by. The two porters (coolies [苦力]) replied that they were not going to move the oil barrels, but if Lai [黎仁超] thought they were an obstruction, he could move them himself. Lai [黎仁超] was not impressed with their selfish attitude and so sharply told them that because of their inconsiderate manner, he would like to smash their oil barrels. But he knew this would affect the business of the shops that they were delivering the oil to, so he decided to punish them in another way. Lai [黎仁超] quickly thought of an alternative method which would also demonstrate how formidable he was. Due to the obstruction of the roadway and this disturbance, a large crowd had now gathered around this shop. Lai [黎仁超] removed his overgown and handed it to an on-looker who was next to him. He then rolled up his sleeves and took hold of the oil barrel, shouting, "up".

Lai [黎仁超] then lifted up the oil barrel into the air and placed it onto a four foot high dwarf wall on the right hand side of the oil shop front door. Everyone was surprised and couldn't believe how powerful this polite, well dressed young man was. The onlooking crowd started to cheer as Lai [黎仁超] then continued down the alleyway, lifting several more oil barrels up onto the dwarf walls, at different shops along this road [觀音大巷]. The two porters (coolies [苦力]) were stunned into silence as they realised that Lai's [黎仁超] actions were an astounding feat. Once Lai [黎仁超] had finished, he then cleaned his hands, put his gown back on and walked away. The two porters (coolies [苦力]) had hoped to monopolise the businesses in this road by their actions, but due to Lai's [黎仁超] intervention, they had lost time and money. They were then forced to find two more of their companions to help them lift the oil barrels down from the dwarf walls, at each of the different shops along Guanyin Roadway [觀音大巷].

As the porters (coolies [苦力]) were doing this, they asked the onlookers in the roadway if any of them knew who this young man was. A person in the crowd had recognised Lai Yan-Chiu [黎仁超], and told them that he was the owner of the Shun Hung pawnshop [信亨押店] which was located on Wong Sa Road / Huangsha Avenue [黃沙大道]. This incident had caused them a loss of face as well as money, so the two porters (coolies [苦力]) returned to their factory and told their boss what had happened. They hoped that he would then deal with this embarrassment caused by Lai [黎仁超]. The boss was a prudent man and decided that before retaliating straightaway, he would first look into Lai's [黎仁超] Shun Hung pawnshop [信亨押店] and his background.

A day or two later, Lai [黎仁超] was working at his Shun Hung pawnshop [信亨押店] and during a busy period, when the shop was full of people, a man came in to deliver a parcel. As Lai [黎仁超] went to accept the parcel, the man threw it at him, but Lai [黎仁超] skilfully dodged it. The parcel smashed as it hit the wall and floor of the pawnshop [信亨押店]. Inside the parcel was a "dung pot [屎桶]", which was an earthenware pot full of dung, grass-hoppers and cockroaches. The back area of the shop was now a dirty mess which started to produce a foul stench as the grass-hoppers and coaches scurried around the floor. As soon as this despicable man had thrown the dung pot [屎桶], he had run off and by the time Lai [黎仁超] was able to run after him, the man had disappeared.

Lai [黎仁超] wondered why anyone would want to do such a thing, as he had never incurred such hatred from anyone like this before. After a couple of moments, he remembered the incident with the two porters (coolies [苦力]) in Guanyin Roadway [觀音大巷] a few days previously. He wondered whether they had held a grudge and this was their stupid way of getting back at him. Lai [黎仁超] decided to find out if the porters (coolies [苦力]) were behind this shameful act. He therefore used some money to investigate the man that had thrown the dung pot [屎桶], and found out he was a member of the porters (coolies [苦力]) union. Once Lai [黎仁超] had found this out, he decided to go to their factory and confront these three members. When he arrived at the factory, the people there thought he had come to do some business because of the way he was dressed and his polite manner. He was therefore greeted very graciously and treated with respect. Lai [黎仁超] pretended that he wanted to do business and asked about the three men he was seeking. At the same time he picked up some bamboo [竹竿] and walked into the factory to see if he could see the men. As he did this, he was informed that the three particular porters (coolies [苦力]) were out working at the time.

After hearing that the men he was after were not here, he informed them that he would come back the next day to meet the three porters (coolies [苦力]). As Lai [黎仁超] was about to leave, he asked if he could sample the strongest bamboo poles [竹竿] the factory men had. The members working at the factory thought nothing of this and served him as they would any other normal customer. One coolie returned with a bamboo pole [竹竿] which was the thickness of a rice bowl. Lai [黎仁超] took the pole [竹竿] and placed it across his knee. He then placed his hands either side, and using his skill and strength, bent it over his knee. With a very loud crack, the bamboo pole [竹竿] snapped into two pieces. Everyone was shocked and couldn't believe how this customer could break such a thick bamboo pole [竹竿]. Lai [黎仁超] then suggested that, the piece of bamboo [竹] was too weak as it broke so easily and asked for a bigger pole [竹竿]. All the members looked at each other, not knowing what to say. Lai [黎仁超] then selected another bamboo pole [竹竿] and broke it in the same fashion, which stunned everyone there.

Lai Yan-Chiu [黎仁超] then continued to snap all the bamboo poles [竹竿] that were in sight. Although these bamboo poles [竹竿] were not expensive, they were the tools that the porters (coolies [苦力]) used to make their living. All the porters (coolies [苦力]) present felt helpless, and after witnessing his strength and excellent Kung Fu [功夫] skill, they did not dare to stop or challenge Lai [黎仁超]. Once he had broken all the poles [竹竿], Lai [黎仁超] then informed them where he was from and what had happened a few days previously. He explained that this was the reason that he wanted to find the three porters (coolies [苦力]). He then made it clear to them that he had broken the bamboo poles [竹竿] as a warning. As Lai [黎仁超] left, he told them his name and warned them that if this lesson had not convinced them, then they were welcome to come to the Shun Hung pawnshop [信亨押店] on Wong Sa Road / Huangsha Avenue [黃沙大道] where he would gladly give them another lesson.

Some of the union members from the factory then went searching for their boss. When they returned with him later that day, they showed him all the broken bamboo poles [竹竿] and told him what had happened. The boss realised that Lai Yan-Chiu [黎仁超] was excellent at Kung Fu [功夫] and so too powerful to mess with. He therefore told all his members not to seek revenge as this would only bring about more trouble for them. The boss understood that any more incidents with Lai Yan-Chiu [黎仁超] would cost them dearly and would result in them losing even more face. This story soon started to spread throughout Canton [廣州], and Lai [黎仁超] became noticed among the general public and martial arts community alike [漸漸傳颺出去, 武術界和社會人士對他也注意起來.]

A story about Lai Yan-Chiu and the thief

During the mid 1800s, there were many wealthy people living in the West Gate / Sai Kwan [西關] area. (*West Kwan, West Suburbs of Canton*) Therefore this vicinity attracted many thieves who usually struck during the night. To combat this, the local authorities had employed more officers in this area and also offered a reward in an effort to reduce the thefts. Unfortunately, the authority's attempts to combat these crimes had proved ineffective so far. Lai Yan-Chiu [黎仁超] lived in this area, so he was fully aware of the problem with the thieves.

One evening after work, Lai Yan-Chiu [黎仁超] had returned to his home in the 10th Ward of the West Gate / Sai Kwan / Xiguan [西關] area. While he was resting in his study, he heard a tapping sound on the roof. Lai [黎仁超] realised straightaway, that this was the typical sound of a thief testing the roof before climbing onto it. He assumed that if the thief came over the roof, he would then enter the house by the window. Lai [黎仁超] decided to catch the thief as he was leaving, with any stolen property on him. He therefore quietly left the room, going to the front of the house, and discreetly climbed up onto the roof. Lai [黎仁超] then hid in the shadows, waiting for the thief to climb up. As expected, the thief soon appeared, making his way over to the edge of the roof and using a rope, climbed down to the window. Lai [黎仁超] could tell from the way this person moved, and then climbed down the rope, that they were strong with a reasonable level of skill. When the thief was out of sight, Lai [黎仁超] made his way over to the rope and untied it, before then using a plant pot to hold the rope in the same position.

Lai Yan-Chiu [黎仁超] then jumped down through the open window into the study. The thief heard Lai [黎仁超] land behind him, and immediately reacted by leaping onto a five foot cabinet. As soon as he was on top of this cabinet, he attacked Lai [黎仁超]

with a chain whip *(also known as a nine section whip [九節長鞭])* he had concealed in his coat. The dart end of the whip [九節長鞭] headed straight towards Lai's [黎仁超] face. He was surprised by the speed and accuracy of this attack, and was forced to somersault backwards several feet to avoid being hit by this weapon. He thought the thief might carry a knife [匕首短刀], but was shocked that he had a chain whip [九節長鞭] which was not a common thief's weapon but used more by martial artists [武術家].

In his haste to trap the thief, Lai [黎仁超] had not had any time to prepare himself with a weapon. He quickly looked around the room for something to arm himself with, and so be able to counter the chain whip [九節長鞭]. Near the door was a three foot long wooden locking pole [木門押,長有三尺] which he realised he could use as a small staff / Gwun [棍]. Lai [黎仁超] then rushed to this pole and as he grabbed it, attacked the thief with a vertical strike to the jaw. *(This movement is known as, "Pushing a fire torch upward [舉火燎天]".)* The thief easily evaded the strike, and countered by waving the chain whip [九節長鞭] up and down. Lai [黎仁超] realised that because the thief had the higher ground, he therefore had the advantage, and so he dived forwards into a roll towards the cabinet. As he came out of the roll, he delivered a "Tiger Tail" kick [虎尾掃堂腿] to the leg of the cabinet, which snapped, making the cabinet collapse. As the furniture gave way, the thief jumped down shouting, "no good."

Just before landing on the floor, the intruder attacked, lashing outwards horizontally with the chain whip [九節長鞭]. This attacking movement is called, "wearing a jade belt [玉帶環腰]". Lai [黎仁超] countered this attack with a technique called, "fishing staff [董公垂釣]", to block the whip [九節長鞭]. He raised the staff / Gwun [棍] upward which caused the chain whip [九節長鞭] to be thrown back. The thief cleverly ducked down under the rebounding whip [九節長鞭] which would have struck him in the face. The thief felt tension and power coming from the staff / Gwun [棍], which worried him. He now appreciated Lai's [黎仁超] skill at Kung Fu [功夫] and looked for a way to escape. Unfortunately, he realised that he was trapped and he would have to try and fight his way past Lai [黎仁超] to get out of the house. The thief decided the best way to do this, would be to try and unarm Lai [黎仁超] using his chain whip [九節長鞭]. Lai [黎仁超] anticipated the intruder's intention and decided to go against the usual fighting methods practiced against this flexible weapon. Although Lai's [黎仁超] strategy was contrary to the standard manner, he was confident that he had the skill and strength to counter the intruder's intended technique.

Suddenly, the thief reacted with a fast technique, striking down with the handle. This was a unique movement he had developed, and so was very confident that he would succeed with this strike. *(This movement is known as, "Covering by falling snowflake [雪花蓋頂]").* Lai [黎仁超] blocked this attack with his wooden pole, but purposely left a gap for the thief to use. The thief seeing the opening, believed he had an opportunity he could not miss. He lashed out with the whip [九節長鞭] and as he did this, he flicked his wrist, making the chain ripple like waves on water. As the chain hit Lai's [黎仁超] staff / Gwun [棍], it coiled around it several times. The thief then pulled sharply, trying to disarm Lai [黎仁超]. But as he pulled with all of his strength, he felt a sharp pain in his hand and arm. This pain was caused by Lai [黎仁超] pulling and twisting back with his staff / Gwun [棍], which ripped the chain whip [九節長鞭] from the intruder's grasp. The shocked intruder was astounded by this unconventional move. In a panic, he ran for the window, jumping onto a table which was next to it. As he grabbed the rope and stepped out of the window, it gave way. The thief fell to the ground, and as he tried to stand up, Lai [黎仁超] was at his side using the wooden staff / Gwun [棍] pressing onto his back, forcing him back down. The thief was apprehended and taken back into the house.

Lai Yan-Chiu [黎仁超] started to enquire who this intruder was, and why he was stealing. The thief told him that his name was Ng Tong [吳棠] but he was known by his nickname of Scabbed Head Tong [癩痢棠]. He had lost his father as a child, and because he was not educated, had turned to stealing so he could provide for himself and his mother. The thief became upset, and then started to cry as he was telling Lai [黎仁超] about his miserable life. Lai [黎仁超] was taken aback after witnessing the sincerity of this poor man's story and decided to show him some compassion. He told the thief that if he was to take him to the government offices, he would almost certainly be executed for all his crimes. But if he was to do this, what would then become of his poor old mother. This situation troubled Lai [黎仁超], so he decided to show him some mercy and kindness instead. Lai Yan-Chiu [黎仁超] gave the poor intruder some money, and told him that this was for him to start a new life, setting up some small business venture.

Ng Tong [吳棠] was completely shocked by Lai's [黎仁超] mercy and generosity. He kneeled down in front of Lai [黎仁超] as a sign of respect and thanked him for his humanity. Ng Tong [吳棠] then proclaimed that because Lai [黎仁超] had shown him such kindness he promised never to do a bad deed again and follow Lai's [黎仁超] advice. He declared he would be a changed man and requested that Lai [黎仁超] keep the chain whip [九節長鞭] as he would not need it from now on. Ng Tong [吳棠] suggested that it could be a token of remembrance of the compassion he had shown him. Lai [黎仁超] accepted Ng Tong's [吳棠] words with all sincerity and was pleased that Ng Tong would now follow a new path in his life. As Ng Tong [吳棠] received the money (silver [銀子]) from Lai [黎仁超] he repeatedly thanked him and kowtowed / Kau tau [磕頭] many times due to the respect he now bore him.

Kowtow, comes from Cantonese kau tau and is an action performed to show deep respect. To Kowtow is to kneel down and bowing so low that the practitioner's head touches the floor. [138b]

227

Out of gratitude and respect, Ng Tong [吳棠] told many people of the kindness and mercy shown him by Lai Yan-Chiu [黎仁超] and that Lai [黎仁超] was not only a great and skilful Kung Fu master [功夫大師] but that he was also a kind and benevolent man. This story soon spread throughout Canton [廣州], and Lai Yan-Chiu [黎仁超] became respected among the general public and martial arts community alike.

A story about Lai Yan-Chiu and the Flower gang

During the lawless times of the 1800s, China was plagued by various criminal gangs and organisations. One of these types of gangs was more commonly known as "Flower gangs [花子團]". Flower gangs [花子團] would harass ordinary people's wedding parties, trying to take advantage of the auspicious ceremonies and proceedings. They would blackmail the families, threatening to disrupt or ruin the celebrations unless they were given money, food or wine. If they were not satisfied with what they were given, they would disturb the wedding party by making fun and intimidating the families. These gangs [花子團] were generally made up of beggars, ruffians and rogues [由乞丐、流氓、地痞、無賴等組成] who made their living in this way. One such gang [花子團] in the West Gate / Sai Kwan [西關] area (*West Kwan, West Suburbs of Canton*) would gather at an old abandoned temple to the Chinese deity Kwan Yu / Guan Yu [關帝], and so were known locally as Guan hall men [關帝廳人馬]. This ruined building was the Meizhou hall [湄州會館], Man Cheong Venue which was located on Lower Nine Road [下九路], which in present day Guangzhou [廣州] would be just off from Wenchang South Road [文昌南路].

Guan Yu is generally referred to as "Emperor Guan" (關帝), which comes from his Taoist name "Saintly Emperor Guan" (關聖帝君), and also "Guan Gong" meaning Lord Guan. Around mainland China, Hong Kong, Macau, and Taiwan, many temples and shrines can be found which are dedicated exclusively to Guan Yu[143]

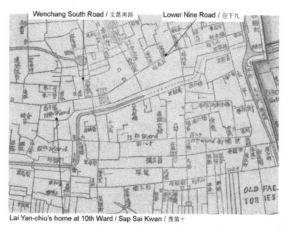

Lai Yan-chiu's home at 10th Ward / Sap Sai Kwan / 西第十

On the wedding day of Lai Yan-Chiu's [黎仁超] sixth youngest sister, the local flower gang [花子團] turned up and requested they were given some of the lucky money, food and wine. They threatened that if their demands were not met, they would take away the bridal sedan chair [大红花轎]. This act would delay the scheduled timings of picking up the bride and groom from their homes, which was felt would bring bad fortune on the couple's future. This bridal sedan chair [大红花轎] had been carefully selected by the couple to bless their future relationship and prosperity.

The bridal chair was very important for a bride to be carried to her wedding ceremony. A shoulder carriage / 肩輿 was normally hired. These chairs were richly ornamented and gilded and lacquered, in an auspicious shade of red with red silk curtains to hide the bride from onlookers. [144] [144a]

This intimidation of the wedding party made everyone angry. They were also concerned that the auspicious timings would be disrupted and so bring bad luck on the bridal couple. Lai Yan-Chiu [黎仁超] was particularly offended, believing that this gang [花子團] had no respect for him whatsoever. Due to this total disregard, Lai [黎仁超] decided to go to the flower gang's [花子團] meeting building at the Meizhou hall [湄州會館]. When he arrived at the ruined temple, he entered the building noticing that it was completely empty with no furniture, just bare walls. As he turned around to leave, there was a sudden loud bang as the temple doors were kicked open. In ran over a dozen men, who quickly scurried around the hall and surrounded Lai [黎仁超]. These men were followed by their leader, who was known by the nickname of "Disaster Chi [大難齊]". Disaster Chi [大難齊] was about thirty years old and was known for doing many evil deeds with his gang [花子團]. He was skilled with the Yanling Dao [雁翎刀], and had a reputation for being a fearless and ferocious fighter.

Disaster Chi [大難齊] moved forward with his Yanling Dao [雁翎刀] in his hand, giving Lai [黎仁超] a dirty, fierce look. He then grinned and told Lai [黎仁超] that if he wanted to leave here alive, he would have to pay a hefty ransom in silver [銀子]. Disaster Chi [大難齊] also threatened to kidnap members of Lai's [黎仁超] family unless he gave his gang [花子團] brothers food and wine as well. This was all done in a very aggressive and nasty manner, to ensure that Lai [黎仁超] knew these were not idle threats but the gang's [花子團] true intentions if their demands were not fulfilled. The threats made Lai [黎仁超] very angry, but he listened in silence, concealing his true feelings for the sake of his sister's wedding and returning with the bridal chair [大红花轿] on time. He calmly assured Disaster Chi [大難齊] that he did not have enough money on him, but if they were to follow him back to his home with the bridal chair [大红花轿], he would give them what they wanted.

Disaster Chi [大難齊] did not believe him and insisted that Lai [黎仁超] pay the full amount of ransom money in silver [銀子] immediately. Lai [黎仁超] was adamant that he did not have enough silver [銀子] on him, and so the two men quarrelled about what was to be done. When Chi [大難齊] realised that Lai [黎仁超] would not give him the silver [銀子] there and then, he ordered his men to attack Lai [黎仁超]. Many of the Flower gang [花子團] were carrying various weapons [武器], and Lai [黎仁超] realised he was at a serious disadvantage being alone and unarmed. To give himself a fighting chance, he quickly removed his long silk overgown and used it as a whip. Lai [黎仁超] had excellent internal power [內功], and he skilfully turned his silk gown into a weapon [武器], whipping the gown out towards his attackers. As the silk gown slashed across their hands and faces, the attackers felt a sharp, hot, burning sensation which left red raw marks. Through the fear and pain, the gang [花子團] members were forced back.

Disaster Chi [大難齊] expertly blocked Lai's [黎仁超] attacks using his thin bladed Yanling Dao [薄刃的雁翎刀] and pushed forward with his strikes, chopping, cutting and thrusting. He was aware of how to counter against the long gown as it whipped out towards him and so he pressed forward, looking for a weakness to exploit. Lai [黎仁超] saw that Chi [大難齊] was an experienced fighter and in response to Chi's [大難齊] attacks, he used light, agile footwork, adopting a technique movement called "rat step, snake slide [鼠步蛇行]". He successfully avoided Chi's [大難齊] strikes but his silk gown was now becoming shredded and cut down in length, as it blocked the blade of the Yanling Dao [雁翎刀]. Soon the gown was too short to be effective, as pieces had been cut away, and Lai [黎仁超] was becoming exhausted from all the excessive jumping and moving around he had done to avoid Chi's [大難齊] Yanling [雁翎刀] cuts. He became concerned that he could be defeated.

At that moment from behind him, Lai [黎仁超] was suddenly surprised to hear his name being shouted out. He glimpsed back to see Ng Tong [吳棠] on top of a broken section of the temple wall. Ng Tong [吳棠] stated that that he had come to help his esteemed friend, Lai Yan-Chiu [黎仁超], as he threw a metal object towards him. Lai [黎仁超] understood straightaway, that this was a chain whip (Nine section whip [九節長鞭]), which was a favoured weapon of the reformed thief Ng Tong [吳棠] who he had not seen for some time. Lai [黎仁超] was not only surprised to see his old friend, but also happy, especially in his moment of need.

Since Ng Tong [吳棠] had been given a second chance by Lai Yan-Chiu [黎仁超], he had turned his life around completely. He had used the money provided by Lai [黎仁超] to become a successful businessman. Since that time, Ng Tong [吳棠] always had thoughts of, and appreciation of, Lai's [黎仁超] benevolence. He had been meaning to visit and thank Lai [黎仁超] for some time, but had been too busy with his new work. It just so happened that on this day, Ng Tong [吳棠] had taken a day off from his business to visit Lai [黎仁超]. He had gone to Lai's [黎仁超] home with a gift of fruit, when family and guests from the wedding party informed him of what had happened. Worried about Lai [黎仁超], Ng Tong [吳棠] had hurried here to ensure his friend's safety and assist him if needed.

As Lai [黎仁超] caught the chain whip [九節長鞭] thrown to him, Ng Tong [吳棠] jumped into the middle of the flower gang [花子團] wielding a bamboo pole [竹竿]. He then fiercely attacked the gang [花子團] members around him with powerful and accurate techniques. With the chain whip [九節長鞭] now in his hand, Lai [黎仁超] rejoined the attack with the ferocity of a tiger. Disaster Chi [大難齊], seeing that the situation was starting to turn against his gang [花子團], moved around and jumped in to attack Lai's [黎仁超] back with a horizontal slash. Fortunately, Lai [黎仁超] saw the attack coming and immediately used the chain whip [九節長鞭] to block this strike, which coiled around the blade. He then wrenched the whip [九節長鞭] back which caused sparks, with a loud clanging sound, as part of the blade of the sword broke. While this was happening, Ng Tong [吳棠] had beaten several gang [花子團] members, who were laid out unconscious or subdued on the ground. Disaster Chi [大難齊] realised that he had no chance of winning and so became frightened. He now looked for a way to escape, but the front temple door was blocked by Ng Tong [吳棠].

Lai Yan-Chiu [黎仁超] wished to resolve this situation as quick as possible so that he could return to the wedding party. He therefore pressed forward pressurising Chi [大難齊] who had lost concentration as he looked for an escape route. Lai [黎仁超] used a step called, "Dragon Light Shoot [龍光射鬥]", and Chi [大難齊] was forced to retreat quickly to avoid this attack. However, this was a decoy movement which Lai [黎仁超] then followed with a technique using the whip [九節長鞭] called, 'Meteor chasing the moon [流星趕月]'. The whip [九節長鞭] curved in and out, in a zigzag movement, towards Chi [大難齊] with lightning fast speed. He raised his arm to block the whip [九節長鞭], which struck him on the wrist. There was a sudden sickening, snapping sound as Chi's [大難齊] wrist broke, and as his arm went limp, the Yanling Dao [雁翎刀] fell to the floor. Lai [黎仁超] moved forward grabbing him by the collar with one hand, and placing his knee into the small of Chi's [大難齊] back to restrain him. Disaster Chi [大難齊] was totally subdued and unable to move, as Lai [黎仁超] demanded that the bridal chair [大红花轿] be returned to his home for the wedding ceremony. Chi [大難齊] had no alternative but to agree with this demand as Lai [黎仁超] told him he should have done so initially, before trying to extort money from him.

Ng Tong [吳棠] then returned with Lai Yan-Chiu [黎仁超] to the wedding party after Disaster Chi [大難齊] had promised to quickly return the bridal chair [大红花轎]. When the bridal chair [大红花轎] arrived at Lai's [黎仁超] home, there was a card with a written apology. With this, Disaster Chi [大難齊] had also sent some food and wine as a sign of his regret to Lai Yan-Chiu [黎仁超] and his family. Lai [黎仁超] then sent his sister off in the bridal chair [大红花轎] to pick up her future husband, while he greeted his relatives and friends. Later, at the dinner, Lai [黎仁超] introduced Ng Tong [吳棠] to everyone and told them how he had come to his rescue that day. He stated that if it had not been for Ng Tong's [吳棠] help, he would not be with them that night. Lai [黎仁超] and all the guests then drank a toast to honour Ng Tong [吳棠]. From that day on, they became as brothers and lifelong friends.

The following day, Lai Yan-Chiu [黎仁超] returned to the Meizhou hall [湄州會館] so that he could speak with Disaster Chi [大難齊]. Chi [大難齊] was very surprised to see Lai [黎仁超] and was worried, wondering why he had come. Lai [黎仁超] cautioned Chi [大難齊] about his future business dealings, stating that intimidation and evil deeds would only bring him problems and trouble, whereas good deeds and hard work would be rewarded with kindness and prosperity. To prove his point, Lai [黎仁超] then thanked Chi [大難齊] for returning with the bridal chair [大红花轎], and as a good gesture, rewarded this with a small amount of silver [銀子]. Disaster Chi [大難齊] accepted this, and acknowledged Lai Yan-Chiu [黎仁超] as a man of prestige and kindness from then on.

Although Lai Yan-Chiu [黎仁超] was an excellent martial artist [武術家], he never boasted about his skills or flaunted his abilities in public. This was in stark contrast to when he was a young man, but he had since matured and totally changed his attitude. He was now a reformed character who was renowned for his good deeds and efforts to help the poor. [141]

Due to his outstanding martial arts' [武術] skills and his now reformed, admirable reputation for helping the poor and needy, he was elected as one of the Ten Tigers of Canton / Kwong Tung Sap Fu [廣東十虎] in the mid to late 1850s. It is also said Lai Yan-Chiu [黎仁超] was the most patient of the Ten Tigers [廣東十虎] and that he was a very serious and sombre sort of a person. In confrontations he used his intelligence and was regarded as a smart and clever sort of a fighter that would use his wisdom to achieve success. [142]

The Three Heroes of Wong Sa Road/ Haungsha Avenue 黃沙三傑

Lai Yan-Chiu the Chao Feng / 朝奉 of the Shun Hang Pawn shop on Wong Sa Road / 黎仁超在信亨押店 黃沙大道

Wong Sa / Huangsha Ave 黃沙大道

Wong Yan-Lam's Bone-setting Clinic & Lama Pai School Kim Sin Street / just off Wong Sa Road 王隱林在黃沙兼善街開設武館授徒

Shamian Island / 沙面島

So Hak Fu's Hak Fu Mun School on Wong Sa Road 蘇黑虎在廣州西關開設武館，黃沙大道

Hak Fu Mun [黑虎門] tradition states that Lai Yan-Chiu [黎仁超] was one of three Tigers on Wong Sai Road. On the same road, were two other tigers known as So Hak Fu [蘇黑虎] and Wong Yan-Lam [王隱林]. These three tigers were friends and exchanged various ideas and methods with each other. Collectively, they were known to the general public as the "Three Heroes of Wong Sa [黃沙三傑]". [51] [52]

Little is known of his later life and it is stated that he passed away towards the end of the 1800s, during the reign of the Kuang-hsu Emperor / Guangxu Emperor [光緒帝] (14th August 1871 – 14th November 1908).

So Chan [蘇燦]

(traditional Chinese: 蘇燦; simplified Chinese: 苏灿; pinyin: Su
Can, known by his nickname of So Hut Yee / Beggar So / Su Qi'er
/ traditional Chinese: 蘇乞兒 / simplified Chinese: 苏乞儿)

It is believed that So Chan [蘇燦] was born in the early 1800s, possibly sometime
between 1815 and 1825. According to the Taiping Institute [14], So Chan [蘇燦] was
born in Nanhai / Nam Hoi [南海]. This may be referring to the actual town of Nanhai /
Nam Hoi [南海镇] which is located close to Fat Shan / Foshan [佛山], or it may just be
referring to Nanhai County / Nam Hoi Yuen [南海縣] (now Nam Hoi / Nanhai district
[南海區]) in the province of Guangdong [廣東省]. The county of Nam Hoi / Nanhai [
南海] was located to the west of the old provincial capital city [省會城市] of Canton [
廣州] (now Guangzhou [廣州]) which covers quite a large area that almost encircles
the city of Fat Shan / Foshan [佛山]. Other sources just state Guangdong Province [
廣東省]. [109b] [109c]

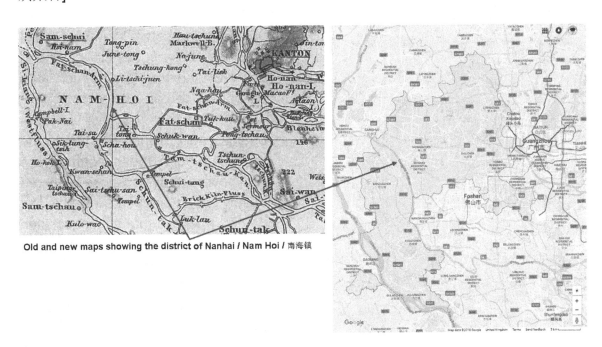

Old and new maps showing the district of Nanhai / Nam Hoi / 南海镇

233

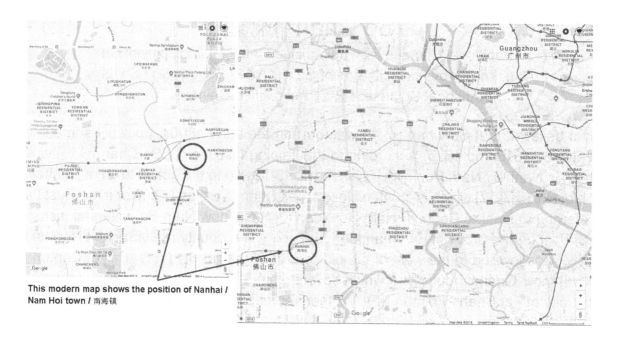

This modern map shows the position of Nanhai / Nam Hoi town / 南海镇

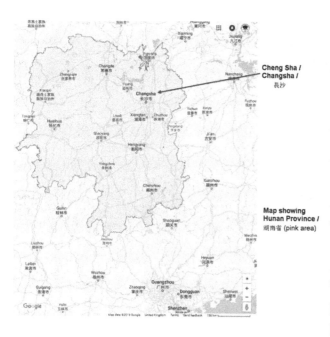

Map showing Hunan Province / 湖南省 (pink area)

Cheng Sha / Changsha / 長沙

Other sources state that So Chan [蘇燦] was born in the city of Cheng Sha / Changsha [長沙], which is in the province of Hunan [湖南省]. Hunan Province [湖南省] borders Guangdong Province [廣東省] to the north. Although these sources are from several movies whose plots are loosely based on events from his life. [145a] [146] I believe that his association with the city of Cheng Sha / Changsha [長沙] came later on in his life, during his wanderings. Even the Chinese Wikipedia is uncertain and so states both Nam Hoi / Nanhai [南海] and Hunan [湖南省]. [145]

It is stated that So Chan [蘇燦] was from a wealthy family, and had a good lifestyle as a child. His father had paid for him to be taught martial arts [武術] as he believed that this would help to focus So Chan [蘇燦] and aid him to become strong and successful. Wong Kiew Kit states that So Chan [蘇燦] was taught by a Siu Lum / Shaolin monk [少林僧] called Chan Fook [陳福], but it is not stated when during his life, that this took place. I think it is fair to assume that it would have been sometime during the early part of his life. Chan Fook [陳福] had been at his home village in Guangdong Province [廣東省], at the time of the destruction of the Fukien Siu Lum / Shaolin Temple [福建

234

少林寺] at Putian [莆田]. So Chan [蘇燦] was initially taught a Hung Kuen [洪拳] style of Kung Fu [少林功夫] from Chan Fook [陳福]. Sources also state that So Chan [蘇燦] was especially skilled in the use of the staff / Gwun [棍]. [78a] [85] [109] [109b] [109c] [145] [147] I assume that he either learnt the use of the staff / Gwun [棍] from Chan Fook [陳福] or that the monk [少林僧] helped So Chan [蘇燦] to refine and improve his skills.

As So Chan [蘇燦] was growing up, he began to have misunderstandings with his father. He could not understand his father's ways, who he believed would always compromise when dealing with matters. Due to this difference of opinion between father and son, So Chan [蘇燦] started to form a rebellious attitude. With this defiant nature, he would generally be lazy, eating and drinking all day. As a young man, he was living an extravagant lifestyle and spending his father's money. It is stated that although So Chan [蘇燦] was kind-hearted, he could also have an aggressive side. He became disruptive and unruly, using, martial arts [武術] in a bad way. During this time, he was happy and because of his family's wealth, he could do what he wanted and live an excessive lifestyle.

During these years, So Chan [蘇燦] was known for his rowdy behaviour and fighting. For these reasons, he became regarded as a local bully. Unfortunately, with his activities, this brought him into conflict with a local axe gang [斧頭幫]. This conflict with the axe gang [斧頭幫] escalated from a dispute over an incident with a man called Smith, who was a westerner and the local comprador [買辦]. It is understood that there was some conspiracy regarding a business deal, and So Chan's [蘇燦] family lost all their money. So Chan [蘇燦] went to see the comprador [買辦] about this matter but unfortunately he was under the protection of the local axe gang [斧頭幫]. [115]

*A **comprador** or **compradore** / 買辦, is the name of a local manager of a European business in East and South East Asia.*

The word comprador is a Portuguese term that means buyer. Originally, this name was used for a local servant in European households in Canton or the neighbouring Portuguese colony at Macao in southern China, who went to market to trade their employer's merchandise. Compradors had important roles in southern China buying and selling tea, silk, cotton and yarn for foreign businesses, as well as working in foreign-owned banks. [148]

The history of So Chan [蘇燦] states that, when he was a young man, both of his parents tragically died and that he was possibly responsible because of his lifestyle. *(My assumption about this is that the local axe gang [斧頭黑幫] which was known to have hatred towards So Chan [蘇燦] murdered his parents in an act of retaliation.)* At the same time as his parents being killed and losing all the family wealth, So Chan's [蘇燦] girlfriend / lover was also killed in the incident with the axe gang [斧頭黑幫]. All these events deeply disturbed him and he turned to drink. Due to his drinking and the loss of his family's money, So Chan [蘇燦] started living the life of a beggar. He then became a recluse, with only wine as his companion. In an attempt to escape these circumstances, he wandered around living the Jianghu lifestyle [江湖]. It is believed that during this period, he was a heavy drinker and that while intoxicated, he would still try to practice his Hung Kuen [洪拳] style of Kung Fu [功夫]. This could explain his style of Drunken Fist [醉拳] for which he is famed. [109] [109c] [109d] [109e] Some sources state that during this period of wandering around, that he was accompanied by his sister. [115] [145]

The Drunken [醉拳] style imitates the irregular, and unpredictable movements of an inebriated person staggering, swaying and falling over. But these moves are intended to confuse an opponent as well as being defensive, dodging and evading movements when being attacked, hiding their true combative nature. From these unorthodox positions, the practitioner will suddenly explode into an attack with the intention of catching their opponent totally by surprise. Practitioners require a high degree of acrobatic / Jop Kai [雜技] skill and balance to successfully master this style.

Zui quan / 醉拳, means Drunken Kung Fu and is a common name for all the styles of Chinese martial arts that mimic the movements of a drunkard person. The Buddhist style is connected to the Shaolin Temple while the Daoist style originates from the Daoist story of the drunken Eight Immortals. These styles of Chinese martial arts incorporate hitting, grappling, locking, dodging, feinting, ground and aerial fighting.

Shaolin Zui Quan is not a complete system, but consists of a small number of hand and weapon forms [套路] (routines). The main weapon used in this style is the staff, but other weapons including the sword are also practiced. Generally the technical contents are almost the same, but the the forms [套路] (routines) differ depending on the lineages.

The technical characteristics of Zui Quan are based on imitating a drunken person. The core body technique is called sloshing, which refers to "Hollow Body, Wine Belly" concept, which is the lower abdomen (丹田; dantian) filled with wine instead of Qi, which curculates around the body giving power to the movements. The weight and momentum of the whole body drives the postures by staggering around, which creates sudden power from awkward positions. The Drunken style seems strange and unstabile, but the acrobatic movements require a great degree of balance and coordination. Trying to perform these techniques while drunk could be possible, but certainly would be dangerous.

The swaying, and falling movements are used to throw off opponents and the drinking from a wine cup is grabbing and striking techniques. The main hand position emulates holding a small wine cup as a fist is rarely used. Back of the hand, fingers, palms, wrists, forearms, and other parts are used to attack and defend, to grab or throw, and to lock or release. The unorthodox movements are intended to trick an opponent into situations of attack and defence. Aerial and floor dodges and falls can be used to either avoid certain attacks or to trap attackers to the floor while vital points are struck. [149]

It is possible that as part of So Chan's [蘇燦] martial arts [武術] training, he was also taught the Siu Lum / Shaolin routine [少林套路], the Drunken Eight Immortals / Chue Ba Sin [醉八仙] by the Siu Lum / Shaolin monk [少林僧] called Chan Fook [陳福]. It is stated that he knew this routine and was famed for it. [117] [145] My assumption would be that he merged the characteristics of this routine with his Hung Kuen [洪拳] style when he was inebriated, to form his own unique style of Drunken Fist [醉拳] which he became famed for. *(A detailed account of the Drunken Eight Immortals / Chue Ba Sin [醉八仙] is contained within So Hak Fu's / Su Heihu's [蘇黑虎] history as this was one of the routines [套路] he was taught while at the Kwangtung Siu Lum / Shaolin Temple [廣東少林寺].)*

Wong Kiew Kit states that So Chan [蘇燦] was not actually a beggar, but his famed nickname was given to him because of his drunken, unkempt appearance, and the manner in which he would casually wander around the region. Because of this, and his unorthodox style of Kung Fu [功夫], he became known as So Hut Yee [蘇乞兒] which translates to So the beggar. He is also reputed to have preferred the life of a wanderer, which could have also contributed towards his nickname. During this period of travelling, he would often earn money by performing martial arts demonstrations [武術表演] in the streets. So Chan's [蘇燦] (Beggar So's / So Hut Yee / Su Qi'er [蘇乞兒]) style of Kung Fu [功夫] was still the Hung Kuen [洪拳] he had originally learnt but performed in his own drunken manner. [147] Some sources also state that during these performances [武術表演], he was assisted by his sister.

Due to the perils and constant danger of being ambushed while living the Jianghu lifestyle [江湖], So Chan [蘇燦] wanted to be always prepared for hostilities. He had created his own method so that even when it was not practical to carry a weapon, he was still armed. This method involved the use of chopsticks [筷子] and a bowl [碗] as weapons that could easily be utilised at any moment if he was ambushed. Over a period of time, he developed various techniques of blocking and attacking using these eating utensils. To be more practical and durable for combat, he used iron chopsticks [鐵筷] and a metal bowl [金屬碗]. The bowl [金屬碗] is utilised more for blocking applications and the chopsticks [鐵筷] mainly for attacking, striking to many of the body's acupuncture points. So Chan [蘇燦] crafted these applications into a routine [套路] which he named the Iron Chopstick and Golden Bowl form [金碗鐵筷]. [145]

He spent the next several years wandering around Guangdong Province [廣東省], and north into the neighbouring Hunan Province [湖南省]. During this period of roaming, he met and became friends with two other people that were also living the Jianghu lifestyle [江湖]. These two fellow martial artists [武術家] were Yue Fung [余楓] and Leung Kwan / Liang Kun [梁坤] who was more commonly known by his nickname of Iron Bridge Three / Tit kiu Saam / Tie Qiao San [鐵橋三]. Once they became aware of So Chan's [蘇燦] misfortune, they decided to try and aid him. While they travelled together, Yue Fung [余楓] and Iron Bridge Three [鐵橋三] constantly tried to help So Chan [蘇燦] get over his troubled past. When they had travelled together for some time, and got as far north as the city of Cheng Sha / Changsha [長沙] in Hunan Province [湖南省], all their encouragement and support finally had an effect on So Chan [蘇燦]. *(Cheng Sha / Changsha [長沙] is located approximately 567 km north of Canton / Guangzhou [廣州].)* Here, he at last regained his spirits, with a better and more positive attitude. As they travelled back towards Canton [廣州], So Chan's [蘇燦] character changed with a much improved sense of morality. The virtues of decency, integrity and honour, encouraged him to improve his martial arts [武術] skills. With his reformed attitude, So Chan [蘇燦] now dedicated himself to fighting for justice on behalf of the poor. [115]

Obviously, if So Chan [蘇燦] was born in Hunan Province [湖南省] and after the tragic events with the axe gang [斧頭黑幫] that led to the deaths of his parents and his girlfriend / lover, he started his wanderings from there. As he travelled south, he would leave Hunan Province [湖南省] and enter Guangdong Province [廣東省]. While travelling, he met Leung Kwan / Liang Kun [梁坤] (Iron Bridge Three) and Yue Fung [余楓]. His travelling companions eventually lifted his spirits, and he arrived in the provincial capital city [省會城市] of Canton [廣州] as a reformed character.

Leung Kwan / Liang Kun [梁坤] (Iron Bridge Three) was also a highly skilled Kung Fu master [功夫大師], and he and So Chan [蘇燦] worked together, exchanging ideas and practices. This enabled them both to improve their knowledge and abilities, which enhanced their skills. Sometime around the late 1840s to early 1850s So Chan [蘇燦] arrived back in the provincial capital city [省會城市] of Canton [廣州]. During the 1850s, So Chan [蘇燦] (Beggar So / So Hut Yee / Su Qi'er [蘇乞兒]) became prominent amongst the people of Canton [廣州] for fighting for the justice of the poor people of the city. During these years, he would continue to improve his martial arts [武術] skills, exchanging ideas and methods with other Kung Fu masters [功夫大師].

So Chan [蘇燦] (Beggar So / So Hut Yee / Su Qi'er [蘇乞兒]) was now a respected Kung Fu master [功夫大師] himself, and people were now seeking him out to study under him. He therefore opened up his own martial arts school [武術學校] in Canton [廣州]. One source states that this school [武術學校] was called the Saam Sing Se / Sansheng She [三聖社] which was located at a building in Canton [廣州]. [115] [145] [145a]

[146] Saam Sing Se / Sansheng She [三聖社] can translate to mean, "Three Saints / Holy / Sacred community or social club", which represents the past, present and future of the Great Buddha. *(After some research, I found that Longjin West Road was originally named Social / Community Three Saints Street. [龍津西路原是「三聖社大街」].* [146a]*)*

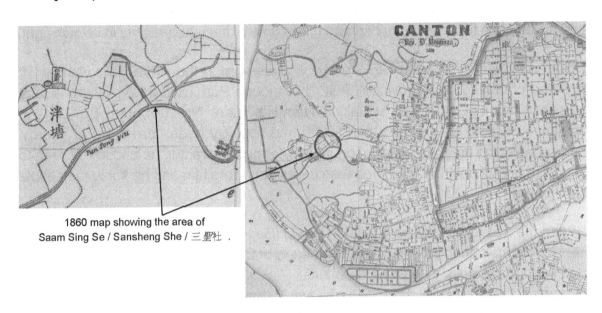

1860 map showing the area of
Saam Sing Se / Sansheng She / 三聖社 .

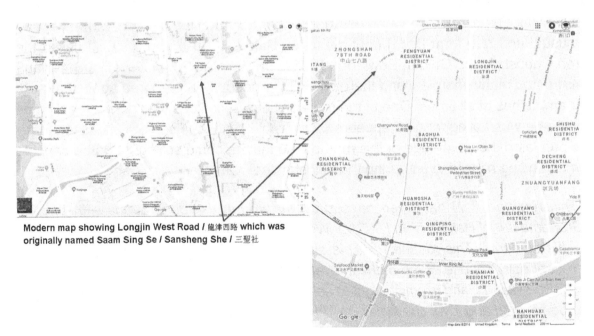

Modern map showing Longjin West Road / 龍津西路 which was
originally named Saam Sing Se / Sansheng She / 三聖社

I have gauged the location of this street to be in the area of the village of Pun Tong [泮塘], and that during the time period of the Ten Tigers of Canton / Kwong Tung Sap Fu [廣東十虎], the suburbs of Canton [廣州] fell just short of this area, *(This is shown in the old 1860 map below.)* From reading old reports, Pun Tong [泮塘] village had many wealthy inhabitants with large mansions, and was located only a mile from the city wall of Canton [廣州]. As well as possibly attracting inhabitants from this village, the suburbs of West Kwan / Sai Kwan / Xiguan [西關] area are very close. It is therefore reasonable to assume that students would travel this short distance from these suburbs, to So Chan's [蘇燦] martial arts school [武術學校]. Unfortunately, due to the nature of this unorthodox style, not many students could master it. It is for this reason that his drunken fist style did not spread or become a mainstream style in its own right.

Some sources [14] state that So Chan [蘇燦] was born in the Nam Hoi / Nanhai [南海] area of Guangdong Province [廣東省]. Although Pun Tong [泮塘] village is very close to Canton [廣州], it was actually in Nam Hoi Yuen / Nanhai county [南海縣]. An assumption could be that So Chan [蘇燦] had possibly been born there or nearby, and so knew the area well. On becoming a reformed character, he chose this area to establish his school [武術學校] because it was familiar to him and he knew the people in this area.

During the mid to late 1850s, So Chan [蘇燦] (Beggar So / So Hut Yee / Su Qi'er [蘇乞兒]) became famed as one of the Ten Tigers of Canton / Kwong Tung Sap Fu [廣東十虎] due to his skills as a Kung Fu master [功夫大師], and his reformed benevolent character. During these years, he is known to have exchanged ideas with another one of the Ten Tigers [廣東十虎] called So [蘇], who is better known by his nickname of So Hak Fu [蘇黑虎]. So Chan [蘇燦], (Beggar So / So Hut Yee [蘇乞兒]) taught an unusual and rare form [套路] (routine) to So Hak Fu / Su Heihu [蘇黑虎] called the Iron Chopstick and Golden Bowl form [金碗鐵筷]. So Hak Fu [蘇黑虎] like So Chan [蘇燦], had many enemies, and therefore felt the need to be prepared against attacks or ambushes at all times. One of the most obvious occasions was during meal times when he was eating, and so appeared vulnerable. So Hak Fu [蘇黑虎] consequently appreciated the advantage of this method, so that he could still fight and be capable of defending himself even during these instances.

(This routine [套路] has been passed down through the generations with the last Grandmaster of Hak Fu Mun [黑虎門], Wong Cheung [黃祥宗師] teaching it to several of his students. This routine [套路] is still preserved in Hak Fu Mun [黑虎門] to the present day. It is one of the highest level routines [套路] within the the Hak Fu Mun [黑虎門] syllabus, and is only taught to selective students that have proved themselves to be of good and loyal character. [50] [50a]

One of Wong Cheung's [黃祥宗師] students was a Hong Kong actor known as Kuo Chui or Philip Kwok [郭追]. In the film entitled Shaolin Rescuers aka "Avenging Warriors of Shaolin" (a Shaw Brothers film from 1979 which was originally entitled, "Jie shi ying xiong"), both Philip Kwok [郭追] and Grandmaster Wong Cheung [黃祥宗師] use the chopstick and bowl, demonstrating some comical techniques during a meal scene. More serious techniques of the Chopstick and bowl are demonstrated in the final grand fight scene. Interestingly, in the film called the Ten Tigers of Kwangtung [廣東十虎與後五虎] (also made 1979), Philip Kwok [郭追] played the role of Beggar So Chan [蘇乞兒].)

So Hak Fu [蘇黑虎] had also learnt the Siu Lum / Shaolin routine [少林套路] of the Drunken Eight Immortals / Chue Ba Sin [醉八仙], when he had studied at the Kwangtung Siu Lum / Shaolin Temple [廣東少林寺] under the renowned Siu Lum / Shaolin Monk [少林僧] called Sam Dak / San De [三德] (also known as Siu Dak / Zhaode [兆德]). As he had this routine in common with So Chan [蘇燦], they would practice it [少林套路] together and exchange ideas and techniques regarding the methods of the Drunken Fist [醉拳] style. It is known that So Hak Fu [蘇黑虎] was greatly inspired by So Chan's [蘇燦] style of drunken fist [醉拳], and they became very good friends. In Hak Fu Mun [黑虎門] oral history, it is rumoured that they may have even been cousins. Although they share the same family name of So [蘇], I have been unable to prove or even disprove this thought. If they were related, then it is also more probable that So Chan [蘇燦] was born locally, within the province of Guangdong [廣東省], south of Canton [廣州] in Nanhai County / Nam Hoi Yuen [南海縣], near Fat Shan / Foshan [佛山].

So Hak Fu [蘇黑虎] was born at Pek Ho Town (within the red circle) which is now North Kau town / Beijiaozhen [北滘镇] in the district of Shunde [順德區]. Therefore it is possible that So Chan [蘇燦] was also born local to Fat Shan / Foshan [佛山].

So Chan [蘇燦] was well known for his high level of unique and practical drunken fighting techniques to handle different situations. So Hak Fu [蘇黑虎] used this collaboration and exchange of ideas and techniques, to formulate a new routine [套路] which he named the Great Drunk [大醉]. It is understood that this name is in honour of So Chan [蘇燦]. This routine [套路], and the Iron Chopstick and Golden Bowl routine [金碗鐵筷], were incorporated into So Hak Fu's [蘇黑虎] Black Tiger / Hak Fu Mun [黑虎門] style with the approval of So Chan [蘇燦]. [50] [50a]

So Chan [蘇燦] is also stated as exchanging ideas with Wong Kei-Ying [黃麒英] (another fellow Ten Tiger of Canton [廣東十虎]), and his son Wong Fei-Hung [黃飛鴻]. It is believed that there was a very strong friendship between these characters and that So Chan [蘇燦] aided the Wongs [黃麒英 & 黃飛鴻] in developing their Drunken Fist [醉拳] style. [122] [122a] [145] Wong Kiew Kit states that although they they had learnt the Drunken Fist [醉拳] style from So Chan [蘇燦] (Beggar So / So Hut Yee [蘇乞兒]), it was not passed down in their lineage of Hung Kuen [洪拳]. Although he does not mention Wong Kei-Ying's [黃麒英] fights or challenges, he does state that Wong Fei-Hung [黃飛鴻] very occasionally used it in them. [147] [147a]

It is stated that So Chan [蘇燦] modified the Drunken Eight Immortals [醉八仙] routine [套路] to create the Four Great Lame [四大跛拳] / Disabled Boxing [殘拳]. This routine [套路] covers the disabilities of blindness, deafness, being dumb and so unable to speak, and being lame, which would affect movement. To be able to counter and therefore combat an opponent, this routine [套路] relies on enhancing the other remaining senses. A blind person would utilise their senses of hearing and touch to a much higher degree, while a deaf person would utilise their sight and sense of touch more. As So Chan [蘇燦] was an expert in the Drunken Fist [醉拳] of irregular and unpredictable movements, it is easy to appreciate how some of these techniques could be developed for a lame person, who would struggle with normal foot work. Hung Fut [洪佛] have a routine by this name, but it is not known if these two routines are the same or totally different. [117] [145]

Many movies have been made about So Chan [蘇燦] (Beggar So / So Hut Yee / Su Qi'er [蘇乞兒]), which show him as a Hung Kuen [洪拳] drunken style master. [164] Some of these cover the relationship between himself and the Wongs [黃麒英 & 黃飛鴻], which assert that he was closer to Wong Fei-Hung [黃飛鴻]. [109] Although these movies contain much fiction, some do have certain facts which are loosely based on events in his life. Unfortunately, I have been unable to find any information about So Chan's [蘇燦] later life or when he passed away, but it is assumed it was during the earlier part of the reign of the Kuang-hsu Emperor / Guangxu Emperor [光緒帝] (14th August 1871 – 14th November 1908).

Leung Kwan [梁坤]

(Chinese: [梁坤]; pinyin: Liang Kun, known as Iron Bridge Three / Tit Kiu Saam / Tie Qiao San / traditional Chinese: 鐵橋三; simplified Chinese: 铁桥三)

1813-1886 or 1815-1888

Leung Kwan / Liang Kun [梁坤] (one source [150a] states that his full name was Leung Ah Kwan) was born in Nam Hoi Yuen / Nanhai county [南海縣] in the province of Guangdong [廣東省], during the reign of the Emperor Kar Hing Dai / Jiaqing [嘉慶帝] (9th February 1796 – 2nd September 1820). *(However, the Taiping Institute states that he was born in the neighbouring Punyu district of Canton / Guangzhou [廣州] [14])* His date of birth is given as either 1813 or 1815, depending on the source. He was the third son of a wealthy family, and his father, wishing him to grow up to be strong and competent, paid for him to study martial arts [武術] from a very young age, under prominent teachers [功夫老師].

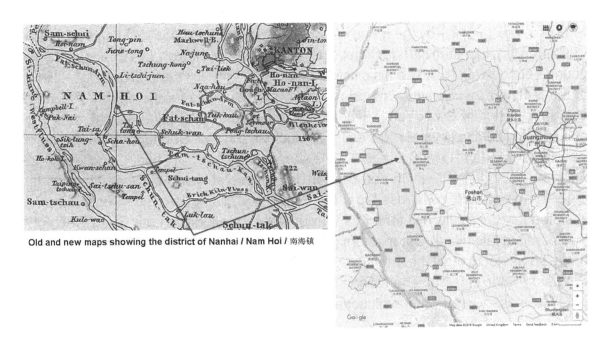

Old and new maps showing the district of Nanhai / Nam Hoi / 南海镇

243

It is stated that as a child, he studied under several teachers [功夫老師]. Records assert that initially, as a youth, he was taught by a master [功夫大師] called Bearded Li, also known as "Golden Hook" / Lei „Wuji / Li Huzi [金鉤李胡子]. These are the other names that the Tibetan monk, Sing Lung [聖龍], was also known by. No times are stated of when or for how long this education lasted under Sing Lung [聖龍], although one source [66] does assert that it was a long time. *(If this is true, it confirms the fact that Sing Lung [聖龍] was in the Canton [廣州] area well before the date of 1865).* [66] [86] [87] [150] [154] [154a] [154b]

During my research, I came across a source [151] which states that Leung Kwan [梁坤] trained with the Siu Lum / Shaolin monk [少林僧], Gwok Yan [覺因], from the age of fourteen, at the NengrenTemple [能仁寺] on Baiyun Shan / White Cloud Mountain, near Canton [廣州]. [入廣州白雲山能仁寺]. [153] The problem with this, is that this temple was not built until the 1850s, and Leung Kwan [梁坤] would have started his training with Gwok Yan [覺因] around 1827 to 1829, depending on which date of birth we go by. Another source states that it was the White Cloud Temple / Baak Waan Temple / Baiyun Si [白雲寺] on White Cloud Mountain / Baak Waan Mountain / Baiyun Shan [白雲山], but here he was a disciple [武術弟子] of the abbot, Wai Cheung [慧長方丈]. This same source also states that he learnt the Iron Wire Fist / Tit Sin Kuen / Tie Xian Quan [鐵線拳] from the abbot Wai Cheung [慧長方丈], instead of developing it later as a young man. After this, he then went to the Haichuang / Haizhaung Temple or Hoi Tung Temple [海幢寺] (Honam Temple [河南寺]) and studied under the Siu Lum / Shaolin monk [少林僧], Gwok Yan [覺因]. [150a]

At the age of fourteen, Leung Kwan [梁坤] started to travel, seeking other knowledgeable masters [功夫大師] to learn from. [154] He wanted to acquire new techniques and ideas as well as to improve his existing skills. During this time, he came across a Siu Lum / Shaolin monk [少林僧] by the name of Gwok Yan [覺因], who was residing at a temple in Canton [廣州]. After introductions, the venerable Gwok Yan [覺因] accepted the young Leung Kwan [梁坤] as his disciple [俗家弟子]. [154a] [154b] Leung Kwan [梁坤] lived at the temple as a layman / Or Hong Yan [外行人], studying for the next seven years under the tuition of Gwok Yan [覺因]. In this time, Leung [梁坤] was taught many arts and skills, including several routines [套路] such as "Fu Hok Seung Ying Kuen", which translates to mean "Tiger & Crane double shape fist [虎鶴雙形]", and "Gung Gee Fook Fu Kuen [工字伏虎拳]" which can be translated several ways, such as "Taming the Tiger in an I pattern" or "Cross Tiger Fist Form" and "Conquering the Tiger Form". It is stated that originally, this form [套路] (routine) was called Siu Lum Gung Gee Fook Fu Kuen, but later Hung Gar masters [功夫大師] dropped the Siu Lum / Shaolin [少林] name so as not to draw the attention of the Ch'ing / Qing [清朝] authorities to them as Siu Lum / Shaolin [少林]. The reason for this, was at certain times Siu Lum / Shaolin [少林] was associated with revolutionary sympathies. [66] [151]

Tiger Crane Paired Form [虎鶴雙形] can been found in almost every Hung style. Although many of these routinese are not as long as the Wong Fei Hung [黃飛鴻] version, they generally contain 108 movements / techniques.

"工" Taming the Tiger Fist [工字伏虎拳] (pinyin: gōng zì fú hǔ quán; Yale Cantonese: gung ji fuk fu kuen.)
This is a long routine, that trains the practitioner in the basic techniques of Hung Ga while building stamina. It is believed to date back to Jee Sin, who is said to have taught a version of Taming the Tiger to both Hung Hei-Kwun [洪熙官] and Luk Ah-Choi [陸阿采]. The "工" Character in the name of this routine is because the footwork traces the path of the character "工". [112][155]

I believe that Leung Kwan [梁坤] first trained on White Cloud Mountain / Baak Waan Mountain / Baiyun Shan [白雲山] under the abbot, Wai Cheung [慧長方丈], before going to either the Haichuang / Haizhaung Temple (also called the Hoi Tung Temple [海幢寺] or the Honam Temple [河南寺]) to study under the Siu Lum / Shaolin monk [少林僧] Gwok Yan [覺因]. I can only assume that the facts have been confused or mixed up by some sources. After reading the Iron Thread book, I assumed that Gwok Yan [覺因] was at the Honam temple [河南寺], located just across the river from the provincial capital city [省會城市] of Canton [廣州]. Some other sources also confirm this, stating that Leung Kwan [梁坤] studied under Gwok Yan [覺因] at the Honam Temple [河南寺]. [150a] [150b] It is stated that after the destruction of the Putian Siu Lum / Shaolin Temple [莆田少林寺], monks that escaped, spread like stars in the sky. Some found refuge at the Honam Temple [河南寺] (Haichuang Temple) where they started to teach monks, and then later on, laymen, the Siu Lum / Shaolin martial arts [少林武術]. [84] *(The Honam Temple [河南寺] is also called the Haichuang, Haizhaung Temple or Hoi Tung Temple [海幢寺] and was located on the island district of Haizhu [海珠區]. But the population of Canton [廣州] often referred to it as Honam [河南], meaning "south of the river").* [156]

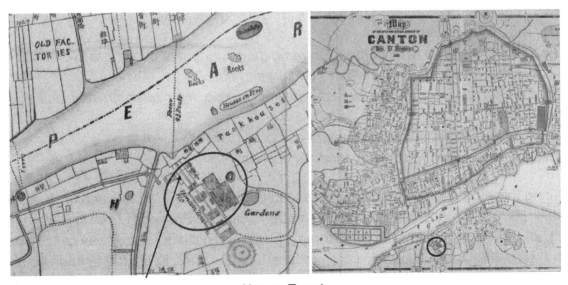

Honam Temple

Leung Kwan [梁坤] learned much from his teacher [功夫老師], Gwok Yan [覺因], including the Great Majestic Kuen / Tai Hung Kuen [大雄拳] (Triple-Stretch Set). Due to Leung Kwan's [梁坤] obsessive dedication and hard work during his training, he developed tremendously strong stable stances combined with solid muscular arms that many described as being like iron. It is also probable that Leung Kwan [梁坤] derived the skills, methods and techniques of the Tit Sin Kuen (Iron Wire Fist / Tie Xian Quan [鐵線拳]) from the Great Majestic Kuen / Tai Hung Kuen [大雄拳] (Triple-Stretch Set) which he would formulate in the years to come. It is reputed that the Venerable Sam Dak / San De [三德] and Hung Hei-Kwun [洪熙官] were both highly skilled in this routine [套路]. When Hung Hei-Kwun [洪熙官] was about 80 years of age he instructed Leung Kwan [梁坤] (Tit Kiew Sam [鐵橋三]) on the finer points of the Great Majestic Kuen. [157]

Leung Kwan [梁坤] trained diligently to develop and improve his bridge hand / Kiu Sau [橋手]. His conscientious, hard training paid off as he became highly skilled and competent in these techniques.

The Twelve Bridge Hand Boxing / Sap Yi Ji Kiu Sau [十二橋手] consists of the following :

Hard (Gong): *Striking hard with "Heavy Hand" to end the confrontation as fast as possible.*

Soft (Yau): *If an opponent is stronger, "Use" their strength against them.*

Press (Bik): *Press the opponent back and so forcing them to retreat and defend.*

Straight (Jik): *If you lose contact, continue like a spring with straight attacks.*

Separate (Fan): *To separate and break contact if necessary.*

Fix (Ding): *To control and fix an opponent so as to use close range attacks with elbows or finger pokes etc,.*

Inch (Chyun): *Controlling an opponent so they can't evade so as to attack the vital points such as throat and eyes.*

Lift (Tai): *Lift an opponent up.*

Keep (Lau): *"Receive what comes", allowing the opponent to come in close with their attacks so as to enable you to capture them.*

Send (Wan): *If an opponent presses forward, using their strength and pull them forward.*

Control (Jai): *To subdue the opponent and control them.*

Adapt (Ding): *Adapting to an opponent's actions.* [84] [171]

During this time, Gwok Yan [覺因] introduced Leung Kwan [梁坤] to a senior Buddhist monk [和尚] who had travelled from the northern Qinghai Province [青海] to Canton [廣州], and was staying at the Honam Temple [河南寺]. This elder monk was called Wan Sing [永星和尚], and Gwok Yan [覺因] requested that Leung Kwan [梁坤] address him as older uncle / Si-Baak [師伯]. He also told him that Wan Sing's [永星和尚] martial arts

[武術] skills were unassailable, and that Leung [梁坤] should praise his skills. Although he agreed to his teacher's requests, his face gave away his objections. When the elder monk Wan Sing [永星和尚] noticed this, he smiled and informed Gwok Yan [覺因] that although his student was still young, to praise his achievement too much would diminish his motivation and enthusiasm, which could make him proud and arrogant. Leung Kwan [梁坤] was offended by this comment, but respectfully replied to the elder monk, Wan Sing [永星和尚] that he had never witnessed his martial arts [武術], so how could he give his opinion if he was being overpraised or not.

The elder monk, Wan Sing [永星和尚], looked at Leung Kwan [梁坤] and told him that when someone was learning such a skill, there would always be difficulties and hardships that a person would have to conquer. These should not be feared, because with hard training over a long period of time, they would eventually overcome all obstacles. But, because Leung Kwan [梁坤] was still young and had an arrogant attitude, Wan Sing [永星和尚] concluded that his bridge hand / Kiu Sau [橋手] had not yet achieved the final level of achievement. Therefore, if he was to contest a skilled master [功夫大師], he would be defeated. Unfortunately, Leung Kwan [梁坤] was not convinced by Wan Sing's [永星和尚] words of wisdom and experience. He therefore politely requested his older uncle / Si-Baak [師伯] to test him, and stated that if Wan Sing [永星和尚] was able to force down his bridge hand / Kiu Sau [橋手], he would openly admit defeat.

At this, Gwok Yan [覺因] asked his older brother / Sihing [師兄] if he would give his student some instruction, as this would help him to alter his proud attitude and realise that there were others more skilled than him. Elder monk Wan Sing [永星和尚] nodded in agreement and turned to face the young Leung Kwan [梁坤]. Leung Kwan [梁坤] adopted a bow stance [弓步] [131b] and stretched out his right forearm. As he applied all his power into this right arm, his muscles tensed and it was clear to see that from his form, he was highly skilled in the bridge hand / Kiu Sau [橋手]. The elder monk Wan Sing [永星和尚] then asked Leung Kwan [梁坤] if he was ready. At this, Wan Sing [永星和尚] stepped forward and placed his left hand on Leung Kwan's [梁坤] right arm. Wan Sing [永星和尚] then applied his force against Leung Kwan's [梁坤] bridge hand / Kiu Sau [橋手] and slowly pressed it down. [150a] [150b] Unfortunately, the article finishes at this point. I can only assume that after this instruction, Leung Kwan [梁坤] realised his errors and altered his attitude.

Gung Bu translates as "bow stance", and can also be known as "Deng Shan Bu" (mountain-climbing stance) or "Gong Jian Bu" (bow and arrow stance). The lead leg is slightly bent and the foot points straight forward. The back leg can be either straight or slightly bent with the foot angled outward at 45 degrees and the heel in line with the heel of the front foot. This results in a "lunging" pose. The weight distribution is 70% on the front foot and 30% on the back foot.

This stance is often used for attacking as the leg postion partly protects the groin and the stance allows the practitioner to punch with more power by driving the back leg into the floor. The back leg can also be drawn forward quickly for kicking attacks. [131b]

When Leung Kwan [梁坤] was still a young man, he performed an amazing feat during a Buddhist [佛教徒] celebration. To demonstrate his skill, and the power of his bridge hands / Kiu Sau [橋手], he stood on a stone platform and stretched out his arms. Four people then held onto his arms, as he lifted them off the ground so that their feet were dangling in the air. They pulled as hard as they could but were unable to move his bridge hands / Kiu Sau [橋手]. While standing firm, Leung Kwan [梁坤] was also able to concentrate all his power into his legs so that no one was able to move him. It is stated that even with his legs tied with a rope, he could be pulled by 20 people and they still could not move him. [150a]

During these years at the temple, under the guidance of the venerable Gwok Yan [覺因], Leung [梁坤] gained a respect for the Buddhist [佛教徒] practices and became a follower of many Buddhist [佛教徒] customs. He did this as a layman / Or Hong Yan [外行人] without taking the monastic vows or becoming a monk. It is believed that Leung [梁坤] was an "ordained novice", which is a layman / Or Hong Yan [外行人] attached to the temple who followed Buddhist [佛教徒] teachings, but did not follow the monastic vows of the monks. Although he had a great love of Buddhism [佛教] and many of its practices, Leung [梁坤] would continue to eat meat and drink alcohol from time to time. Because he lived at the temple, he cared little for earning money, and would perform various duties within the temple to earn his keep. Unfortunately, in his seventh year of training at the temple under Gwok Yan [覺因], the monk passed away at the grand old age of 110 years. It is believed that this was in the mid 1830s, when Leung [梁坤] was aged 21 years. I can therefore conclude that this would be between 1834 to 1836. Leung Kwan [梁坤] was deeply saddened by the loss of his teacher [功夫老師] and decided to leave the temple. [66] [152] [154b]

The story of how Leung Kwan acquired his nickname, "Tit Kiu Sam / Iron Bridge Three [鐵橋三]"

After many years of Kung Fu [少林功夫] training, Leung [梁坤] wanted to test his own strength and abilities. While travelling around, he came across a place known as Long Bridge. It is understood that many martial artists [武術家] came to this place, to either demonstrate or test their skills. Due to his Buddhist [佛教徒] beliefs, instead of fighting, he decided on another way to test himself. He therefore decided to demonstrate his power and the strength of his bridges, in a peaceful way. He asked for six volunteers to hold onto his outstretched arms and told them to try to not move. Leung Kwan [梁坤] then dragged these six men one hundred steps with his arms extended, while they held on. All the people gathered there, were astounded by this incredible feat and enquired how he had achieved such strength. These people then started to call him Tit Kiu Sam [鐵橋三], which translates to mean Iron Bridge Three. This was because he had demonstrated that his bridges were as strong as iron, and three represented that he was the third child in his family. [151] [154b] [156]

The term Kiu / Bridge means forearm. There are twelve basic techniques for forearm-bridges. These techniques were inherited from the Southern Shaolin Temple. They are also called the "Twelve Hung's bridges". Blows with the bridges / forearms, is a feature of the Southern Shaolin School. [84]

Wing Lam states that around this period, Leung [梁坤] was a member of Hung Hei-Kwun's [洪熙官], Lok-Sin-San Fong School [武術學校] and trained under both Hung [洪熙官] and Luk Ah-Choi / Lu A Cai [陸阿采]. It is possible that Gwok Yan [覺因] may have introduced the young Leung Kwan [梁坤], during the years he had been tutoring him, to Hung Hei-Kwun [洪熙官]. While at this school [武術學校], he became friends with Wong Kei-Ying [黃麒英] who was a fellow Hung Kuen [洪拳] practitioner and student under Luk [陸阿采], which made them Kung Fu brothers [師兄弟]. A story from Wong Lam's Hung Gar history, tells of a lion dance that this school [武術學校] performed, with Luk Ah-Choi [陸阿采] and Wong Kei-Ying [黃麒英] ending up in a fierce battle fighting for their lives. Leung Kwan [梁坤], with several other masters [功夫大師] from this school [武術學校], came to their aid and fought off the overwhelming crowd of opponents, until none stood against them. This battle was the start of the reputation that Leung [梁坤] would build over the next few decades. This same source also states that the other prominent future masters [功夫大師] affiliated to this school, [武術學校] besides Wong Kei-Ying [黃麒英], were So Hak Fu [蘇黑虎] and Lai Yan-Chiu [黎仁超]. (This could explain how these masters [功夫大師] became friends and in time would exchange ideas and training methods.)

Story of the fight at the dinner party

Leung Kwan [梁坤] had been invited to a dinner party where several of the guests had enquired about his Kung Fu [功夫] skills. At this time, Leung [梁坤] was still reasonably young and hadn't yet acquired his reputation as a renowned Kung Fu master [功夫大師]. The other guests at the party encouraged Leung [梁坤] to display his skills and show his strength, but he was reluctant to demonstrate as he did not wish to boast or show off. Unfortunately, his reluctance only made several of the other guests more persistent in their requests for a display. One of the other guests at the party was a Kung Fu master [功夫大師] by the name of Hu Hai [胡海]. As time passed, the other guests began neglecting him for the young Leung [梁坤], and the attention given to this reasonably unknown young man, made him jealous. He became upset and his resentment grew towards Leung Kwan [梁坤].

As Leung [梁坤] was pleading with the guests around him to let the matter drop and move on, Hu Hai [胡海] suddenly let the jealousy overcome him, and stood up, challenging the young Leung [梁坤]. Because Leung Kwan [梁坤] was a follower of Buddhism [佛教], he courteously declined the challenge, stating that he wished for no trouble and didn't want to upset the host of the party. Hu Hai [胡海] moved forward, insisting that the issue be resolved. Leung [梁坤] then stated that Hu Hai [胡海] was a renowned Sifu [師父] and that he was only an ordinary student. If he was defeated, it only meant that he needed more training to improve his skills, but the matter had a much greater significance to a respected Sifu [師父]. He then went on to point out that defeat for such a teacher [功夫老師] would have a detrimental effect on his reputation, which would be more harmful than defeat would be to the novice. Leung Kwan [梁坤] therefore respectfully urged Hu Hai [胡海] to reconsider the challenge. Hu Hai [胡海] declined the request, and started to attack Leung [梁坤]. Leung [梁坤] countered, with his first strike demolishing Hu Hai's [胡海] guard, and his second strike leaving Hu Hai [胡海] unable to counterattack. The third strike was a feint, which made Hu Hai [胡海] collapse to the floor in anticipation of what the blow might achieve. In a show of mercy, Leung [梁坤] ceased and Hu Hai [胡海] hurriedly left the party.

Unfortunately, Hu Hai [胡海] didn't appreciate Leung's [梁坤] decency. Due to his anger and resentment, he conspired against Leung [梁坤]. He told one of his friends who was another Sifu [師父], called Ma Nam [馬南], that Leung Kwan [梁坤] had no respect for other Kung Fu teachers [功夫老師] and had made several insulting comments about him. Hu Hai [胡海] then lied even further, by saying that Leung [梁坤] had even miscalled Ma Nam [馬南]. Ma Nam [馬南] was taken in by the lies of Hu Hai [胡海] and become very angry at this show of disrespect. Ma Nam [馬南] was so enraged by Hu Hai's [胡海] story, that he sent one of his students to Leung Kwan [梁坤], declaring that he meet with him for a challenge match. The student told Leung [梁坤] that this meeting was to take place next to the nearby Pearl River [珠江]. Leung Kwan [梁坤] was surprised to receive this challenge for no apparent reason. He believed that if he declined this public challenge, it would bring shame and disgrace on the names of his teachers [功夫老師] and the school of Siu Lum / Shaolin [少林]. Realising that he had little choice, he accepted.

When Leung [梁坤] arrived at the appointed place on the bank of the Pearl River [珠江], Ma Nam [馬南] was waiting for him on a junk [船] in the middle of the river. Ma Nam [馬南] sent one of his students in a small boat, to bring Leung [梁坤] across to the junk [船]. Leung [梁坤] was not a good swimmer, and believing that there might be some sort of trap on the junk [船], he came up with an idea to try and intimidate Ma Nam [馬南]. When the boat landed at the bank, Leung [梁坤] placed one foot on the front and slowly pushed down, pretending that he was stepping on board. Using his strength and power, he started to make the front end of the boat sink, and Ma Nam's [馬南] student shouted out. Leung [梁坤] replied that he was very heavy and would make the boat sink if he got in it. He therefore suggested to Ma Nam's [馬南] student, that he rowed back to the junk [船] and brought his Sifu [師父] to the bank, while he waited there for him. Ma Nam [馬南] had been watching this incident from his junk [船], and he realised that Leung's [梁坤] skill was superior to his own. Ma Nam [馬南] understood that he could not contend with Leung Kwan [梁坤] and so decided to sail away instead of fighting him. [84] [115] [151] [154b] [158] *(However, one source* [154b] *states that Ma Nam [馬南] and Hu Hai [胡海] apologised to Leung Kwan [梁坤], inviting him to a nearby hotel where they hosted a dinner in his honour.)*

News of these incidents soon spread around Canton [廣州], which started to enhance Leung Kwan's [梁坤] reputation. As his fame spread, several other prominent adversaries also challenged Leung [梁坤], (who was now more commonly known by his nickname of Tit Kiu Sam [鐵橋三]). This was done to either test Leung Kwan [梁坤], or to defeat him and therefore enhance their own reputations. Leung [梁坤] won all of these challenge matches and came to be regarded as a prominent master [功夫大師] himself. It is stated that during some of his challenge matches, he would crush an opponent using his forearms targeted at various pressure points.

Leung Kwan [梁坤] would wander around the region searching for other masters [功夫大師] to learn from, to enhance his skills and knowledge. Wong Kiew Kit states that Leung Kwan [梁坤] went to the West Zen Temple / Sai Sim Ji / Xi Chan Si [西禪寺] located outside the city walls of Canton [廣州], not far from the old city's west gate. Sam Dak / San De [三德] was the abbot [方丈] of this temple, and one of his monks and students was the Venerable Cheng Choe. Wong Kiew Kit states it was this monk, the Venerable Cheng Choe, who taught the Great Majestic Kuen / Tai Hung Kuen [大雄拳] (Triple Stretch) to Leung Kwan / Liang Kun [梁坤] (Tit Kiu Sam [鐵橋三]). *(Therefore this could either be a different monk altogether, or another possibility is that it was an alias used by Gwok Yan [覺因] and this happened some years before. I could not find any other sources that even mentioned a monk by the name of Cheng Choe in this period.)* [83a]

It is believed that about this time, he perfected a unique form [套路] (routine) called the Tit Sin Kuen (Iron Wire Fist / Tie Xian Quan [鐵線拳]) from his experiences of the Kung Fu [功夫] he had trained in. [109] [109c] [109d] [109e] Leung Kwan [梁坤] arranged the choreography of this routine [套路] from the skills taught to him by Gwok Yan [覺因], and his experiences and knowledge gained from his other teachers [功夫老師], including Hung Hei-Kwun [洪熙官]. This form [套路] (routine) is a combination of meditative breathing, with isometric exercises of predominately dynamic tension, to increase the practitioner's muscular strength, internally as well as externally, while encouraging a firm and secure stance. The movements of this routine [套路] are carefully synchronised with qigong breathing to cultivate internal power. After this form [套路] (routine) has been completed at the initial stages, it can then be enhanced by the use of weights on the forearms, in the shape if iron rings. His Siu Lum / Shaolin training [少林], combined with his dedicated practising of these forms [套路] (routines), had developed Leung's [梁坤] stances to be very strong and stable, which in time he would become famous for. It is stated that the constant practising of this form [套路] (routine), aided Leung [梁坤] to develop substantial physical strength for his stature. *(One source states that Leung Kwan / Liang Kun [梁坤] was not a big man and that he only weighed about 120lbs).* [159]

Because Leung Kwan [梁坤] lived at the temples much of the time, where he would perform various tasks to cover his keep, he very rarely needed money. But, when he required some money to buy anything, he would go down to the banks of the Pearl River [珠江] and arrange bets with various people around this vicinity. The usual bet was that he would get into a low stance on the river bank, and they had to try and push him off the bank into the water. Because Leung Kwan [梁坤] was a slim, small man, countless men would accept the bet, believing he would be weak and easy to move. But due to his skill, they could not move him. This would then be seen by much bigger men, who were obviously stronger and more powerful. They believed that this was a staged trick, so they would take up the bet. Leung [梁坤] would then reposition himself, ensuring he had a good, strong, rooted stance, and the new challenger would start to push. They would continue pushing until they were all sweaty, red faced, and worn out with exhaustion. These bets would also encourage a large crowd of spectators, who would witness Leung's [梁坤] skilful abilities, noting that he was never moved.

It is stated that on one occasion, several strong men assumed this was a staged prank and so decided to place a substantially large bet that they could as a group, move Leung [梁坤]. This was for a considerable sum of 500 coins. Again, Leung [梁坤] assumed his low horse stance [馬步] [131a] [131b] and rooted himself so firmly, that they were also unable to dislodge him. It was performing these amazing feats which captivated the spectators and challengers alike, which reaffirmed Leung Kwan's [梁坤] nickname of Tit Kiu Sam [鐵橋三]. [84]

During the late 1840s and early 1850s, Leung Kwan [梁坤] would spend time wandering around Guangdong [廣東] and its neighbouring provinces. During one of these journeys, he came across and befriended another martial artist [武術家] called So Chan [蘇燦], who would later be known by the nickname of Beggar So / So Hut Yee / Su Qi'er [蘇乞兒]. Leung [梁坤] travelled with So Chan [蘇燦] as far north as the city of Cheng Sha / Changsha [長沙] in Hunan Province [湖南省]. During this journey, he supported and encouraged So Chan [蘇燦] who was struggling to deal with the death of his parents and girlfriend. They had been killed because of So Chan's [蘇燦] previous reckless lifestyle, which had led to this tragic incident. So Chan [蘇燦] had tried to escape the memories of these events. He had turned to drink and wandered around living the perilous Jianghu lifestyle [江湖]. At Changsha [長沙], Leung's [梁坤]

support and encouragement at last helped So Chan [蘇燦] to regain his spirits. While they travelled together, they would exchange ideas and methods regarding their Kung Fu [功夫] skills. [115]

Leung Kwan [梁坤] (Tit Kiu Sam [鐵橋三]) had by now become well known for helping people; in particular, he would help and work with other martial artists [武術家]. For these actions, he had become very well respected by many people. One source uses the term, in the Mo Lum / Wulin [武林] (martial arts forest), to represent the help he gave to other martial artists [武術家]. [156]

A story of Leung Kwan's travels when he was educated in the Buddhist Secrets

A monk called Jing Ming [澄明], from the Fuzhou [福州], Xichan temple [西禪寺], in Fukien / Fujian Province [福建省], would travel around southern China collecting donations for his temple. Jing Ming [澄明] was a large, powerful man who was also a skilled practitioner of the martial arts [武術]. During his stay in Canton [廣州], he had heard stories about Leung Kwan's [梁坤] amazing skills and decided he should meet such a renowned master [功夫大師]. He therefore sent a messenger to Leung [梁坤], inviting him to meet. Leung [梁坤] took up this invitation, and returned with the messenger to the temple where Jing Ming [澄明] was staying. (This was one of the Buddhist temples [佛寺] in Canton [廣州], possibly the Guangxiao Temple [光孝寺].) When they met, Jing Ming [澄明] explained that he had heard many stories about these amazing feats that Leung [梁坤] performed, and asked if he could possibly test his strength. Leung Kwan [梁坤] agreed to the test and proved that the stories were true, as Jing Ming [澄明] was unable to move him out of his stance or move his arms.

Jing Ming [澄明] praised Leung Kwan [梁坤] for his skill and then asked if he would like to accompany him on his travels, collecting donations for the restoration of a large statue of Buddha at his temple. Leung [梁坤] replied that he had lived within the Buddhist temples [佛教徒寺] most of his life, and that although he hadn't taken the vows to become a monk himself, his heart belonged to Buddha, so that it would bring him joy to be of service. Jing Ming [澄明] understood that he had much in common with Leung Kwan [梁坤], and he requested that Leung [梁坤] stay with him at the temple until they were ready to travel.

After a short stay at this temple, preparing for the trip, both men then set off travelling in the direction of Fukien / Fujian Province [福建省]. They were always treated with respect in the many towns and villages, as they collected donations for the restoration of the statue of Buddha. After leaving one village in Fukien / Fujian Province [福建省], they became lost and wandered about, until they sighted a temple [寺] in the distance. This temple [寺] was all on its own in a wood with no villages or any others buildings nearby. They knocked on the main temple gate and were answered by a middle aged lady who greeted them with a Buddhist salute [禮佛]. When the travellers realised the temple [寺] was a nunnery, they both returned the Buddhist salute [禮佛] and requested to be forgiven for disturbing her. As they turned to leave, the nun [尼姑] replied that as they were all Buddhists [佛教徒], therefore such strict normal procedures should be relaxed. She then invited them in, which they graciously accepted.

As the nun [尼姑] led them through the temple [寺], Leung Kwan [梁坤], being an experienced Kung Fu master [功夫大師], had a keen eye and sensed that from the way this nun [尼姑] held herself and moved, that she was not just a normal lady. He surmised that for a person to conduct themselves and move the way this nun [尼姑] did, could only be attained with extensive and committed training. The two travellers were then shown to a room where they could stay for the night, and a little later, were given some food. Leung [梁坤] thanked the nun [尼姑] for her hospitality and enquired after her name, to which she replied that she was known as Yun Shen [雲深]. After they had eaten, both men then settled down for the night. During the night they were woken up by a noise. When they listened a little harder, they noticed that the sound which woke them was being repeated, and this intrigued the two travellers. They both arose and being curious, quietly traced this noise to the main hall where they observed Yun Shen [雲深] sat at a chair, while other nuns [尼姑] were training. As both the travellers studied martial arts [武術], the training techniques practised by the nuns [尼姑] intrigued them.

As they continued to watch this training from their hiding place in the shadows, they were suddenly surprised when Yun Shen [雲深] called out to them, asking why they were watching them train. They were both amazed that they had been noticed, and wondered how Yun Shen [雲深] had come to realise that they were there. The two travellers apologised and explained that they had been woken up by the sounds of their training. They then went on to ask how she could possibly have known they were there watching from the shadows. Yun Shen [雲深] replied that, due to her training, her eyes and ears were much more acute than a normal person's. She then suggested that by the way they both moved and had watched, taking such a keen interest, they were also martial arts [武術] practitioners. She then continued by politely requesting that they demonstrate their styles. Both men had realised that Yun Shen [雲深] must be an exceptional martial artist [武術家], and replied that their skills were low, therefore they felt any demonstration they performed would be worthless. Yun Shen [雲深] didn't take any notice of their reply and asked again, insisting that, as her guests, they give some display of their style. At this request, Leung Kwan [梁坤] felt it only courteous and respectful to perform a demonstration [武術表演] for the nuns [尼姑]. He therefore saluted before dropping into a stance, and performed a section of his Tit Sin Kuen (Iron Wire Fist / Tie Xian Quan [鐵線拳]) form. During this perforamce, he demonstrated a high level of chi which resulted in producing cracks in the dirt floor where he had stood.

Yun Shen [雲深] applauded his skill and commented that his level of mastery was very good, making him a credit to the school of Siu Lum / Shaolin [少林]. She then went on to say that if he wished to reach perfection, he needed to incorporate the secret Siu Lum / Shaolin techniques of the "Tiger's roar / Fu How [虎吼]" and the "Dragon's hissing / Lung Yam [龍吟]". Leung [梁坤] replied that his teachers [功夫老師] had not shown him these methods and so he was unaware of them. Yun Shen [雲深] stated that her nuns [尼姑] were educated in these methods, and that words without facts were hard to believe, therefore a practical demonstration would prove more enlightening. She instructed one of the young nuns [尼姑] to contend against Leung [梁坤], to which he replied that he was honoured to be educated in these methods. Buddhist salutes [禮佛] were exchanged between Leung [梁坤] and the young nun [尼姑] before adopting their stances, with leading arms touching. Leung [梁坤] was surprised at the force applied against his arm by this young nun [尼姑] and therefore appreciated her level of skill straight away. He then delivered a series of strikes at the nun [尼姑] which were all countered and quashed. After this exchange, Yun Shen [雲深] intervened, stopping the fight and asked Leung [梁坤] if her points had been proven.

Leung Kwan [梁坤] responded by acknowledging Yun Shen's [雲深] superior methods, stating that he had been totally unaware that his training had been incomplete, regarding such skills. Yun Shen [雲深] then stated that she was willing to teach Leung [梁坤] the methods and techniques, so that he would be able to achieve these skills. While teaching Leung [梁坤], she told him that as a Buddhist [佛教徒], training should not be about aggression and overcoming an opponent, but about virtue and achieving enlightenment. For Buddhist [佛教徒] Kung Fu [功夫] practitioners, training the body is only the initial step, it is the mind that needs to be trained to achieve the "Three Treasures" and therefore attain complete mastery of oneself and one's abilities. Leung Kwan [梁坤] realised the truth in Yun Shen's [雲深] words and teachings, and was forever grateful. [84]

Leung Kwan [梁坤] eventually returned to Canton [廣州], and once again resided at the various Buddhist temples [佛教徒寺] there. During the 1840s to 1860s, when Leung [梁坤] was not travelling around and in Canton [廣州], he was mainly living at the Honam Temple [河南寺] (known as Haitong, Hoi Tong, Hoy Tung, Haichung or Sea Monastery [海幢寺]). While at the Honam Temple [河南寺], he had become very good friends with several of the monks at this monastery, including Chan Yee / Chen Yi [塵異和尚], Chi Yuen / Zhi Yuan [智圓和尚] and Sou Ki / Xiu Yi Ji [修己和尚]. During this period, he would exchange methods with some of these monks. He taught them his Iron Thread method, and in return, he was taught a routine [套路] called the Rat Tail Staff [鼠尾棍法]. [154b] It is stated that Sou Ki / Xiu Yi Ji [修己和尚] was a very competent practitioner of martial arts [武術], and this common interest in Kung Fu [功夫] brought the two closer, discussing methods and ideas, as well as training together. While with Sou Ki / Xiu Yi Ji [修己], he met other monks from the Baozhi Temple [寶莊嚴寺], [84]

(this is an old name for the Temple of the Six Banyan Trees [六榕寺]. [55]) and he would also spend a lot of time at this temple.

The story of the jealous monk

While at the Baozhi temple [寶莊嚴寺] (Temple of the Six Banyan Trees [六榕寺]), Leung [梁坤] noticed a man by the name of Li Cong (Lee Chung) [李忠] who rented a small room there. Li Cong (Lee Chung) [李忠] was a school teacher, but unfortunately, was very poor. He was a sad and sickly-looking man, who Leung [梁坤] took pity on. He therefore taught him a few exercises to improve his health and also make him stronger. But this was under the proviso that he had to commit to practice on a regular basis. These exercises were small methods from his Iron Wire Fist / Tit Sin Kuen / Tie Xian Quan [鐵線拳]. Li Cong [李忠] accepted his advice, and within a short space of time, started to feel better. After one year of consistent hard training, he was not only back to full, normal health, but also stronger and fitter than he'd ever been. *(The school teacher Li Cong / Lee Chung [李忠] is generally acknowledged as being the first disciple [武術弟子] of Leung Kwan [梁坤] Tit Kiu Sam [鐵橋三].)*

At the nearby Lingfeng Temple [靈峰寺], *(Lingfeng [靈峰寺] was another name used by locals for the West Zen Temple / Sai Sim Ji / Xi Chan Si [西禪寺] because of the turtle shaped rock within its grounds),* one of the monks known as Hui Ci [許慈], had a bad reputation for being impetuous, rash, and generally a disagreeable sort of a person, which is totally un-Buddhist [非佛教徒]. Not only was Hui Ci [許慈] a big, strong man, but he was also a practitioner of martial arts [武術] and was renowned for his power. As the two temples were reasonably close to each other, he would often visit the Baozhi Temple [寶莊嚴寺] in his spare time. One day, when he was at the Baozhi Temple [寶莊嚴寺], he noticed how well and strong Li Cong [李忠] looked from when he last had seen him. Being inquisitive, Hui Ci [許慈] approached Li Cong [李忠] and asked him how he had achieved this. Li Cong [李忠] told him that he had recently started to practice martial arts [武術], and in particular, the Tit Sin Kuen [鐵線拳]. Hui Ci [許慈] commended him for being an educated man (a school teacher), who had still studied the martial arts [武術]. He then went on to say that he respected Li Cong's [李忠] school [武術學校] if it could achieve these results, and requested that he would like to be given a demonstration. Li Cong [李忠] politely declined, but Hui Ci [許慈] attacked regardless. He struck with a doubled fist punch to both sides of the body, which Li Cong [李忠] blocked. Hui Ci [許慈] then followed this up with a finger tip strike to the eyes, which Li Cong [李忠] avoided. Li Cong [李忠] was astounded and shocked at Hui Ci's [許慈] vicious attacks and decided to teach this bully a lesson. He therefore retaliated with a strong kick to the shin which sent Hui Ci [許慈] crashing to the ground.

After this, Hui Ci [許慈] held up his palms, thanking Li Cong [李忠] for the lesson, and then asked to be forgiven for his rudeness. Li Cong [李忠] in return, stated his regret for his retaliation. He then brought some medicine for Hui Ci's [許慈] injured leg and applied it. Hui Ci [許慈] praised Li Cong [李忠] for his skill and enquired who his master [功夫大師] was. When he was told, he was surprised that such a great master [功夫大師] was living in that very temple and he hadn't noticed. He then asked Li Cong [李忠] if he could visit Tit Kiu Sin Sam [鐵橋三] (Leung Kwan [梁坤]), to which Li Cong [李忠] agreed. When Li Cong [李忠] approached Leung Kwan [梁坤] with Hui Ci [許慈], he explained what had happened and Leung [梁坤] started to rebuke his student for the fight. At that moment, Hui Ci [許慈] interrupted and explained it was entirely his fault, but then added that, due to this incident, he had now been able to meet such a great teacher [功夫老師]. After saying these words, he then showed his respect by kowtowing / Kau tau [磕頭] to Leung [梁坤], requesting that Leung [梁坤] take him as his student.

After this, Leung [梁坤] started to instruct Hui Ci [許慈] in various exercises, but these didn't include any fighting techniques. After a month of training, Hui Ci [許慈] started to become dismayed at this and wondered if Leung Kwan [梁坤] was treating him as a fool. Hui Ci's [許慈] feelings of regret and disappointment soon turned to resentment and anger, and he decided to avenge himself by inciting his previous Sifu [師父] to challenge Leung Kwan [梁坤]. This man was called Li Er Gong [李義幹], and Hui Ci [許慈] provoked him into challenging Leung Kwan [梁坤] through various lies. He followed Hui Ci [許慈] to the temple to duel [決鬥] with Leung Kwan [梁坤]. Leung [梁坤] was totally unaware of Hui Ci's [許慈] feelings, and had been teaching his normal methods, as he believed that skills and exercises were needed to strengthen a student first, before any fighting techniques were taught. So when Hui Ci [許慈] with Li Er Gong [李義幹] approached, Leung [梁坤] greeted these gentlemen as normal, unaware of any bad feelings or there motives. Li Er Gong [李義幹] was a big strapping man, and when he saw how thin and skinny Leung Kwan [梁坤] looked, he thought him too feeble to bother with. He spat at the floor in front of him, then turned and walked away. Leung [梁坤] was bewildered by this behaviour, and asked Hui Ci [許慈] why this gentleman had done that, without saying anything, and then left. Hui Ci [許慈] revealed that Li Er Gong [李義幹] had come to challenge him, but after seeing how small and weak Leung [梁坤] was, compared to him, he believed there would be no honour in such a match.

Leung [梁坤] realised what the situation was, and requested Hui Ci [許慈] to ask Li Er Gong [李義幹] to return, so they could test skills. Hui Ci [許慈] ran after his former teacher [功夫老師] and after several words, persuaded him to return to Leung Kwan [梁坤]. Li Er Gong [李義幹] looked determined and struck out at Leung [梁坤] who dodged this blow by moving back and stooping down. He then suddenly thrust forward, grabbing Li Er Gong [李義幹] and lifted him up, before then throwing him to the floor. Li Er Gong [李義幹] was a skilled practitioner who quickly recovered and retaliated, delivering several strikes. Leung [梁坤] countered these strikes with a series of blocking moves before delivering a palm strike to Li Er Gong's [李義幹] ribs. This was a powerful strike which dropped Li Er Gong [李義幹], and caused him a great deal of pain. Li Er Gong [李義幹], feeling embarrassed and humiliated, stumbled away in defeat. Leung Kwan [梁坤] then turned to Hui Ci [許慈] and told him that he was no longer his teacher [功夫老師], and that he should leave straight away. Hui Ci [許慈] left in disgrace. [84]

During this period, Leung Kwan [梁坤] was challenged several times, and won all these matches, which enhanced his reputation even further. He became very well known in and around the city of Canton [廣州]. In the mid to late 1850s, because of his outstanding Kung Fu [功夫] skills and fighting abilities, he was honoured as one of the Ten Tigers of Guangdong / Kwong Tung Sap Fu [廣東十虎]. This enhanced his already high reputation even further, and encouraged more people to study under such a renowned master [功夫大師]. Due to this, he found employment as a Kung Fu instructor [功夫老師] at a Canton dye-works called the Kwong Cheong Leung Textile Factory [廣昌梁布廠].) [154] [154a] This was located at Rainbow Bridge / Choi Hung Qui [彩虹橋] in the West Gate (Sai Kwan / Xiguan [西關]) area of Canton / Guangzhou [廣州市彩虹橋].

廣昌梁布廠
Canton dye-works called the Kwong Cheong Leung Textile Factory
廣州市彩虹橋
Rainbow Bridge, Canton

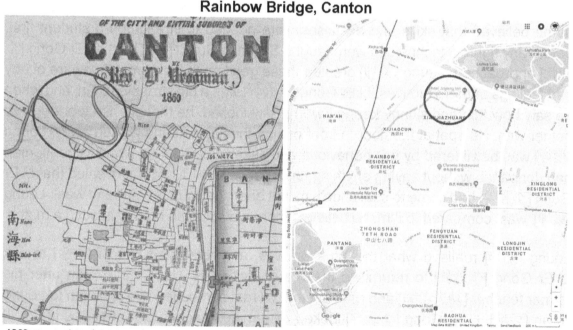

1860 map and modern map showing the approximate location of the Canton dye-works called the Kwong Cheong Leung Textile Factory at Rainbow Bridge would have been.

Rainbow Bridge / Choi Hung Qui [彩虹橋] was an old stone bridge which was built during the Southern Han Dynasty (917–971AD) to cross the See Ma Chung / Sima

Chung [駟馬涌] waterway. Due to the river narrowing because of silt build up, it was replaced by a reinforced concrete structure in 1930. Its present day location is in the Liwan District [荔灣區], at West China Road / Wai See Lou / Xihua Lu [西华路] where it crosses the See Ma Chung / Sima Chung [駟馬涌], near Litchi Bay Road / Lai Waan Lou / Liwan Lu [荔湾路].[154d] Before 1950, Liwan Road [荔湾路] was called Trinity Lane [三聖巷]) [154c] In the History of the nearby Guangzhou City 4th Secondary Middle School [西華路太保直街廣州市第四中学] (which was originally the site of the West Zen Temple / Sai Sim Ji / Xi Chan Si [西禪寺]), it states that during the 1800s, the surrounding agricultural land experienced rapid development to cater for the textile and weaving industry. [52]

After Leung's [梁坤] first disciple [武術弟子], who was the school teacher called Li Cong / Lee Chung [李忠], his next disciples [武術弟子] included Coi Chan / Choi Jaan / Choy Jan [蔡進], Ng Hei-Kwan / Ng Hei Gun / Ng Hei Kwoon / Ng Hei Goon [吳喜勤], Ngau Chu / Ngau Gi [魏智], Ma Gee-Tiem / Ma Ji Tim [馬志添](known as six fingered Tiem [六指添]), Blackfaced Sing [黑面星] and Lam Fook Sing / Lam Fook Shing / Lam Fuk-sing [林福成]. Lam Fuk-Sing [林福成] would in time teach the Tit Sin Kuen (Iron Wire Fist / Tie Xian Quan [鐵線拳]) to Wong Kei Ying [黃麒英] and Wong Fei Hung [黃飛鴻], after they had helped him following an incident at one of his performances [武術表演]. Ng Hei Kwan had originally taken part in the classes at the dye works under Leung [梁坤], and later became one of his disciples [武術弟子], being taught the more advanced skills and methods of Tit Sin Kuen (Iron Wire Fist / Tie Xian Quan [鐵線拳]). *(Out of respect for the different sources, I have included all variations of the spelling of these people's names.)* [84] [152] [155] [156]

Due to his skill and power, as well as his kind nature, Leung [梁坤] became very well respected with many other prominent martial artists [武術家]. These wished to train with him, which gave him the opportunity to share various skills and techniques. Leung Kwan / Liang Kun [梁坤] continued to improve his core style of Hung Kuen [洪拳] by incorporating the other skills and styles that had influenced him during his training, exchanging ideas and methods with other skilled masters [功夫大師]. His major contribution to the Hung Kuen [洪拳] system was his Tit Sin Kuen [鐵線拳], which other famous masters [功夫大師] were enthusiastic to learn. Many Hung Kuen [洪拳] practitioners were also anti-Ch'ing / anti-Qing [反清清朝] sympathisers, wishing the demise of this regime and Leung Kwan [梁坤] was no exception. He was renowned for fighting crime, and would often take on the corrupt gangs that plagued the city. Leung [梁坤] was also appreciated for helping and accepting poorer students, who could not afford to pay the normal training fees. [151]

Sometime around the mid 1870s, Leung [梁坤] attempted to retire, wishing for a quieter, more peaceful Buddhist [佛教徒] way of life. He regretted all the fighting and the people he had hurt in his younger days. He therefore decided to retreat from his public life in Canton [廣州] (Guangzhou [廣州]) city and settled in a small village (in the area now called the Baiyun District [白雲區]) near White Cloud Mountain / Baak Waan Mountain / Baiyun Shan [白雲山]. He had a great fondness for this peaceful and beautiful area just outside the city. Unfortunately, this simple way of life didn't last long, as potential students tracked him down, seeking instruction from him because of his fame and renown as a great Kung Fu master [功夫大師].

The story of Leung Kwan's Bridge Hand

A business man called Choi Jiang / Cai Zan [蔡赞], was one person that had tracked Leung Kwan [梁坤] down. He attempted to entice him back to Canton [廣州] so that he could study under him. On the third attempt, he finally persuaded Leung [梁坤] to leave his peaceful life at Bak Wan and return with him to his home in Canton [廣州]. One source [154b] states that Choi Jiang / Cai Zan [蔡赞] was living on Honam Island [河南島] (which is now the Haizhu District [海珠區]). He was a prosperous businessman who lived an affluent lifestyle. Leung Kwan [梁坤] stated that for him to teach him, he had to curb his lavish habits to ensure that he was strong and determined, to endure the rigors of arduous Kung Fu [功夫] training that he would be put through. Choi Jiang / Cai Zan [蔡赞] agreed to these demands stating that he was prepared and determined to commit to the regime that Leung [梁坤] thought best. After these conditions had been agreed, Leung [梁坤] was invited to live at Choi Jiang's / Cai Zan's [蔡赞] home while his training continued. Besides living in Choi Jiang's / Cai Zan's [蔡赞] home, he was also paid a generous amount of money for teaching his martial arts [武術].

Choi Jiang / Cai Zan [蔡赞] started his initial training in the horse stance [馬步] (sometimes also called riding horse stance [131a] [131b]) to build up the strength in his legs and back. Leung [梁坤] then taught him other methods of training which incorporated techniques to improve speed and power, using a sandbag to strike against. After several months, Choi Jiang / Cai Zan [蔡赞] began to notice how he had improved, which encouraged him to train even harder and more frequently.

The Horse Stance mǎbù / 馬步 (sometimes also called the Horse Riding Stance) is an significant posture in Chinese martial arts and its name comes from the position of a person riding on a horse.

In Southern Shaolin / Southern Chinese martial arts, a wider horse riding stance is assumed to enable the practitioner to be more stable while fighting on boats and barges. The horse stance in southern Chinese systems is commonly done with the thighs parallel to the ground and the toes pointing forward or angled slightly out. [131a]

Ma Bu, known as "horse stance" or "horse-riding stance," is an elementary stance used in most styles of Kung Fu. The feet are parallel, facing forward and usually shoulder-width apart with the knees bent at 90 degrees. The body is sunk down to create a grounding effect with equal weighting on each foot, making for a very secure stance. This stance is often used in conditioning and building up knee strength exercises and drills. Historically many kung fu masters expected students to be able to maintain Ma Bu stance for at least five minutes before learning the routines of a style. [131b]

A good martial artist [武術家] had recently arrived in Canton [廣州] from the north. This martial artist [武術家] was known as Cha [查], and he had studied since he was young. When he became aware of Leung's [梁坤] arrangement as Choi Jiang's / Cai Zan's [蔡贊] live-in teacher [功夫老師], he became envious. He believed that this would be a suitable position for him and so decided to challenge Leung Kwan [梁坤], hoping to take his place as Choi Jiang's / Cai Zan's [蔡贊] new teacher [功夫老師]. Cha [查] went to Choi Jiang's / Cai Zan's [蔡贊] house and introduced himself to Leung [梁坤], stating his intentions. Both men saluted each other before adopting their fighting stances. Cha [查] attacked straight away, charging forward and throwing a barrage of punches which Leung [梁坤] countered, using a circular bridge hand block in a continuous motion. Cha [查] then changed his tactics, moving to the side of Leung [梁坤], attacking from another angle, aiming high then low. Leung [梁坤] adjusted to face this new attack and just continued to block defensively without any counter attacks. After some time, when Cha [查] had attacked with a considerable amount of strikes, he then suddenly stepped back and bowed to Leung [梁坤], before turning away and leaving Choi Jiang's / Cai Zan's [蔡贊] home.

Choi Jiang / Cai Zan [蔡贊] was amazed by the fight he had just witnessed, but was puzzled as to why, as in his opinion, Cha [查] had just left in defeat, and Leung [梁坤] hadn't even hit him back. Leung [梁坤] explained that, as two highly experienced practitioners, they both knew that all Cha's [查] attacks were easily countered by Leung's [梁坤] bridge hand blocks, so there was no need for him to counterattack. Cha [查] had become aware of this in his mind, and so appreciating Leung's [梁坤] higher skill, accepted defeat. Leung [梁坤] then went on to say that as he was a devout Buddhist [佛教徒], there was no need to attack or injure Cha [查] unnecessarily. Choi Jiang / Cai Zan [蔡贊] realised not only the skill but the wisdom of his Sifu [師父], and continued to be his loyal disciple [武術弟子] thereafter. [64] [84]

Shortly after, another rich person requested that Leung [梁坤] taught him his style of Kung Fu [功夫]. This man was called Wu Shi Guan [伍熙官], and Leung [梁坤] would go to his home to teach him. Another disciple [武術弟子] that Leung Kwan [梁坤] accepted during this period, was a doctor called Shi Yu Liang [施雨良] (Si Yu Lueng / Si Yu-Luen). This doctor had two twin sons, called Zhi Tien [志添] and Cui Zhu [區珠] who both became students of Leung [梁坤]. It is understood that not all of Leung's [梁坤] students were educated in the Tit Sin Kuen [鐵線拳], but only his most trusted disciples [武術弟子], who regarded the method of this form [套路] (routine) as a treasured technique. Leung [梁坤] or his disciples [武術弟子] guarded this routine [套路] with a passion that was not openly or freely given, and so when taught, it was valued as a cherished reward. [154c] [155] [156]

During this latter part of Leung's [梁坤] life, he started to find himself in a prosperous position. He was earning good money from teaching his wealthy disciples [武術弟子] and was living with his student, the wealthy businessman, Choi Jiang / Cai Zan [蔡贊]. Leung [梁坤] wanted for nothing, but he found that he had many hours of spare time in the day when his student was at work. During these hours, he had got into the habit of smoking opium [鴉片煙], and by the time he was in his early seventies, was addicted. Through this addiction, he had gradually become ill which also caused him to lose weight. Realising that he needed to break this habit, he sought advice from a Buddhist monk [和尚]. The best part of his life was spent residing at different temples in the company of Buddhist monks [和尚]. It would appear that the majority of these monks were also like-minded, and shared a common interest, as Kung Fu [功夫] practitioners themselves. Leung [梁坤] believed that in order to break this addiction, he needed to change his daily routine. He therefore decided to return to his former simplistic Buddhist [佛教徒] way of life living back at the temple, and to focus on martial arts [武術].

Leung Kwan [梁坤] (Tit Kiu Sam [鐵橋三] / Iron Bridge Three) was never satisfied with his level of martial arts [武術], and was therefore always searching to enhance his skills and understanding. This practice continued even during his later years. Around the age of 70, he heard of a monk at the Kau Ham [茶寇庵寺] Temple of Oversea Village [海外鄉寺] in Xinhui [新會], who was called Yee Shing / Yi Sing [意誠和尚]. (Xinhui [新會], also known as Sun Wui City, is a district of the city of Jiangman [江門]. Jiangman [江門] is located approximately 65 kms south west of Canton / Guangzhou [廣州].) Yee Shing was renowned for his expertise at the Five-Point Plum Blossom Staff / Ng Dim Mui Fa Gwan [五點梅花棍]. Leung Kwan [梁坤] disregarded his age and travelled straight to Kau Ham (Chang Ngum) Temple [茶寇庵寺] to find the monk Yee Shing [意誠和尚], and learn this routine [套路]. Once he had completed all the routine [套路], he came back to the Honam Temple [河南寺] (Hoi Tung Temple [海幢寺]) in Canton [廣州]. [84] [150] [151] [152] [154b] [156]

In the Iron Thread book [84], it states that Leung Kwan [梁坤] went to the Chang Temple / Chang Ngum, which was located near the village of Oi Hoi / Wai Hai [外海], to study a staff / Gwun [棍] method called Five Petals of Mume-Plume Blossom / Ng Dim Mui Fa Gwan / Wudien Mei Hua Chun [五點梅花棍]. This was with a monk called Yee Chee / Yi Jie [易捷] and it was this routine that made Leung Kwan [梁坤], ill so that shortly after, he passed away. *(These two accounts are so similar that I can only assume that it is the same story but some details have been confused over the years.)*

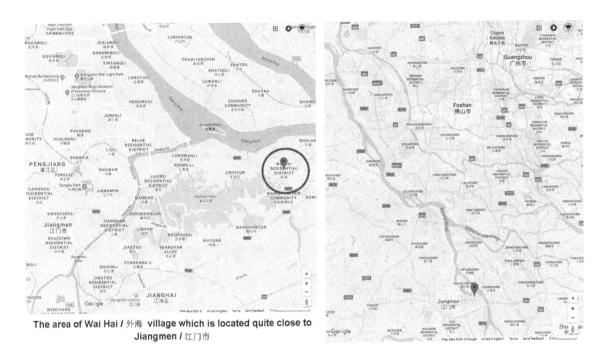

The area of Wai Hai / 外海 village which is located quite close to Jiangmen / 江门市

Back at The Honam Temple [河南寺], Leung Kwan [梁坤] decided to continue his education with a different staff / Gwun [棍] method called the 36 Point Copper Ring Pole [三十六點銅環棍], under a monk called Yu Kwong / Yuan Guang [宇光和尚]. Initially the monk [宇光和尚] was unwilling to teach Leung [梁坤] because of his poor health, but Leung [梁坤] was adamant about the issue and persisted in his request. Eventually, the monk Yu Kwong / Yuan Guang [宇光和尚] was unable to refuse any longer, and so conceded to Leung's [梁坤] demands on the condition that he gave up smoking opium [鴉片煙]. In a real attempt to break his addiction, Leung [梁坤] committed himself to intense training to distract him from his opium smoking [鴉片煙]. Due to the previous several years of smoking opium [鴉片煙], which had taken a toll on his body, and also due to his age, he was unable to withstand the strenuous training that he had been used to before. Leung [梁坤] fell ill, as the strain was too much for his weakened body to take. Unfortunately about ten days later, he passed away at the age of 73 years. Sources are again split in the year being either 1886 or 1888, depending which date of birth they state. [107] [151] [154] [154a]

Leung Kwan's [梁坤] body was taken by his disciples [武術弟子] and buried near Baiyan Shan / White Cloud Mountain [白雲山]. His students then made a monument and planted some trees at this site, as a memorial to their celebrated master [功夫大師]. [84]

Baiyun Shan, Baiyun Mountain, or Mount Baiyun is a mountain next to Canton / Guangzhou. The mountain's name came from the white clouds that cover its peaks in late Spring or when the sky clears after rain. Historically, Baiyun Mountain is covered with numerous scenic spots and historical sites, but unfortunately very few of them have survived to present day.[160]

The hill rises approximately 1200 feet above the Pear River with sparse vegetation and few trees. These hills serve as the cemetery of the vast city of Canton [廣州] and are covered for several miles with graves and tombs. [12c] This is also mentioned in the Presbyterian Archives Research Centre, "A Tour of Old Canton", page 3, and has a photo of a traditional style grave. Although this is probably not Leung Kwan's [梁坤] grave, I have included it to show that this was a common practice, and to give an idea of what it could possibly look like. [63]

Up until around the time of the reign of the Kuang-hsu Emperor / Guangxu Emperor [光緒帝] (14th August 1871 – 14th November 1908), Leung Kwan [梁坤] (more commonly known as Tit Kiu Saam / Tie Qiao San [鐵橋三]) was regarded as one of the most famous martial art experts in southern China and was named as one of the Ten Tigers of Canton / Kwong Tung Sap Fu [廣東十虎]. [151] It is stated that Leung Kwan [梁坤] was a very well respected person. The main reason for this, is that even with all his skill and fame, he had a humble character, understanding that there was always something to learn or improve on. All through his life and even in his old age, he sought out other great masters [功夫大師] to train with them, exchanging ideas and methods. Due to his humble beliefs, he would also often seek the company of Buddhist monks [和尚] who he felt more comfortable and at home with.

Chan Cheung-Tai [陳長泰]

(traditional Chinese: 陳長泰; simplified Chinese: 陈长泰; pinyin: Chen Changtai, known as Iron Finger Chan / Tit Ji Chan / traditional Chinese: 鐵指陳; simplified Chinese 铁指陈; pinyin: Tie Zhi Chen)

The town of Taishan / 台山 shown on a modern map

According to the Taiping Institute, Chan Cheung-Tai / Chen Changtai [陳長泰] was born in the town of Tou Shan / Taishan [台山] which is located approximately 110 kms south-west of Guangzhou [廣州]. [14] *(Before 1914, Tou Shan / Taishan [台山] was called Sunning / Xinning [新寧])*. It is believed that Chan Cheung-Tai [陳長泰] was born sometime around 1820, during the reign of either the Emperor Kar Hing Dai / Jiaqing [嘉慶帝] (9th February 1796 – 2nd September 1820) or the Tao Kuang Ti Emperor / Daoguang [道光帝] who came to power on the 3rd October 1820. He was from a poor family, and when he was a young man, it is stated he was sometimes a little foolish and reckless. Due to his nature at this time, he believed that through being strong and powerful, he could make his fortune. In order to accomplish this, he therefore decided to study the Siu Lum / Shaolin [少林] style of Eagle Claw / Jing Jar [鷹爪] Kung Fu [功夫]. He believed this style would help him achieve his goal of becoming a tougher and skilful fighter. [109d] [109e] [115a] [161]

The style of Eagle Claw / Jing Jar [鷹爪] is renowned for its gripping techniques, joint locks, takedowns and pressure points strikes. This style is characterised by its long, graceful movements to simulate both the wings and claws of the eagle. It is a close range fighting style with fast footwork, to enable the practitioner to get into their opponent quickly to deliver either fast, powerful strikes, or grabbing them to manipulate and control them using Chin Na [擒拿] techniques of joint locks and takedowns. The eagle claw / Jing Jar [鷹爪] hand formation is used to either grab, then manipulate an opponent, or to attack pressure points, penetrating vulnerable areas such as the neck, jaw or face. Other hand techniques include punches and palms which are combined with aggressive kicks. These methods are characteristic of the Chinese grappling system known as Chin Na [擒拿] which is part of the Eagle Claw / Jing Jar [鷹爪] style. [162]

Chin Na or Qinna (擒拿) is the Chinese word to describe joint locking techniques used in Kung Fu to control an opponent.

Chin Na techniques are used by various martial arts styles around the world, but certain Chinese martial arts styles are renowned for specialisation in these techniques.

Eagle Claw (Yīng zhua quán 鷹爪拳), is one such style which includes 108 Chin Na techniques, Praying Mantis (Tánglángquán 螳螂拳), the Tiger Claw methods of Hung Gar (洪家), and Shuai Jiao are also other styles which feature numerous Chin Na applications.

Chin Na can normally be grouped as follows:
1. *"Fen jin" or "zhua jin" means to divide the muscle or tendon, and grabbing the muscle or tendon. These are techniques which rip apart an opponent's muscles or tendons.*
2. *"Cuo gu" translates to misplacing the bone. These are usually joint techniques which puts the bones in wrong positions.*
3. *"Bi qi" means sealing the breath. Bi qi are various techniques to prevent an opponent from inhaling. This is not strangulation but methods which besides using the windpipe, also affect the muscles surrounding the lungs, to shock the body into contraction which will impair breathing.*
4. *"Dian mai" or "dian xue" means sealing the vein / artery or acupressure cavity. Akin to dim mak, these are techniques for sealing or striking the blood vessels and chi points.*
5. *"Rou dao" or "rou shu dao" means soft technique) which are safe and so can be used for sparring and / or training purposes.*

The southern Chinese martial arts have more Chin Na techniques than the northern systems. The southern styles are more dependent on using hand techniques which cause closer range fighting. [163]

The Taiping Institute state that Chan Cheung-Tai [陳長泰] (also known by his nickname of Iron Finger Chan / Chen Tiezhi / [鐵指陳]) was renowned for his locking techniques. [14] This obviously reflects his skill at the Chin Na / [擒拿] side of the style. They also state that Chan Cheung-Tai [陳長泰] was a practitioner of the Hung Kuen [洪拳] style. My assumption is that he possibly studied both, the Eagle Claw / Jing Jar [鷹爪] and the Hung Kuen [洪拳] styles during the course of his life.

Little is known of Chan Cheung-Tai's [陳長泰] early life and from whom he studied martial arts [武術]. It is generally believed that he was a disciple of a Siu Lum / Shaolin monk [少林僧] and studied under him somewhere within Guangdong. [109a] He was also renowned for his skill of the Siu Lum / Shaolin [少林] method of Diamond Finger / Yi Zhi Jin Gang Fa (Siu Lum Kam Kung Chee [少林金剛指] or Yak Chee Sim Kung Fu [一指禪功夫]). Due to this expertise, he acquired the nickname of Iron Finger Chan / Tit Ji Chan / Tie Zhi Chen [鐵指陳], [109] [109b] [109c] [164] (sometimes also spelt as Tit Chee Chan or Tit Chi Chan). This art requires constant daily practice, striking with the forefinger at a hard object such as a wall or tree. At first, the level of force used to strike the wall is only slight, and is then gradually increased over a period of time. Initially the skin on the finger tears as the muscles and sinews swell. Although this causes much pain, relentless and diligent practice must be continued. The finger and skin will become much tougher and after a period of three years dedicated practice, it is stated that the finger is able to make a hole in wood or break a stone. [114] One source [109a] states that Chan Cheung-Tai [陳長泰] (Iron Finger Chan / Tit Ji Chan / Tie Zhi Chen [鐵指陳]) was able to do a one finger stand with his index finger, and could also use this finger as a weapon to poke into an opponent's heart.

It is stated that Chan Cheung-Tai [陳長泰] was a very fast and highly skilled martial artist [武術家], whose body was as hard as steel. He was that highly skilled in the Siu Lum / Shaolin [少林] method of Diamond Finger / Yi Zhi Jin Gang Fa (Siu Lum Kam Kung Chee [少林金剛指] or Yak Chee Sim Kung Fu [一指禪功夫]), that he could punch a hole in a brick wall with any one of his fingers. When he became of age, possibly sometime in the 1840s, he decided to travel to the provincial capital city [省會城市] of Canton [廣州] to seek a better life. Unfortunately, during this early part of his life, he was a mercenary type of person and would earn money by bullying and threatening people. Chan [陳長泰] got involved with a group of wealthy businessmen, who would use him to do certain jobs which involved him intimidating people. However, during this time he would often do things without thoroughly planning them out and after several bad incidents he decided to change his ways. [115] [161]

Chan Cheung-Tai [陳長泰] (Iron Finger Chan [鐵指陳]) became a totally changed man and sometime later, opened up a shop selling bean curd / Tofu [豆腐店]. His shop [豆腐店] was located close to the main East Gate / Dongguan [東關]) of Canton [廣州 大東門外]. [115] This area is now in the Yuexiu District / Yud Seo Keu [越秀區]. During the period of the Ten Tigers [廣東十虎], this was part of Panyu [番禺] County. *(Panyu [蕃禺] was the original name for the walled city of Canton [廣州] and when this name was changed to Canton / Guangzhou [廣州], the name of Panyu [番禺] was still used for the surrounding area until the end of Ch'ing Dynasty / Qing [清朝].* [166b] [166c])

East Gate (Dongguan / 東關) of Canton

Chan Cheung-tai / Iron Finger Chan's Tofu (Bean curd) shop located close to the East Gate of Canton.
廣州大東門外開了一間豆腐店

Story of the bad Lama Monk

One day, a big burly Tibetan Lama Monk with big bushy eyebrows, came wandering [遊方和尚，身穿黃色喇嘛僧袍，濃眉大眼、身材魁梧] along the street towards Chan's [陳鐵志-鐵指陳] Tofu shop [豆腐店]. This monk was wearing yellow robes [身穿黃色喇嘛僧袍] and carrying a huge iron tripod [巨大鐵鼎] in his right hand, that weighed more than two hundred catty (jin [斤] [165]). As he came along to each shop in the street, the Lama Monk [身穿黃色喇嘛僧袍] would place this large, heavy, iron tripod [巨大鐵鼎] across the front entrance. He would stand there with the iron tripod [巨大鐵鼎], blocking the opening of the stores and would not remove it until the different shop owners or merchants had given him some money. This method of intimidation had worked well for the monk [喇嘛] so far, because the different store owners and merchants could not move the heavy iron tripod [巨大鐵鼎] and so had no choice but to pay him or lose business.

Eventually, the Lama Monk [身穿黃色喇嘛僧袍] arrived at Chan Cheung-Tai's [陳長泰] tofu shop [豆腐店] and repeated his usual practice, placing the heavy iron tripod [巨大鐵鼎] across the shop [豆腐店] entrance. Chan [陳鐵志-鐵指陳] took no notice of the monk [喇嘛] and just ignored him. After a while, the monk [喇嘛] became frustrated with Chan's [陈铁志-鐵指陳] lack of interest, so he lifted up his tripod [巨大鐵鼎] and dropped it on the main counter. Due to the very heavy weight of this iron tripod [巨大鐵鼎], the wooden shop counter was damaged. At this, Chan [陈铁志-鐵指陳] politely requested that the Monk [喇嘛], as a religious and honourable person, should reimburse him the money to pay for the damage he had caused. Unfortunately, the Lama Monk [喇嘛] was not an honourable person and he just returned a sneer at Chan's [陳鐵志-鐵指陳] civil request. The monk's [喇嘛] wicked behaviour and then the sneer, made Iron Finger Chan [鐵指陳] angry. Chan [鐵指陳] struck the iron tripod [巨大鐵鼎] with his fingers, which penetrated it putting five holes in the tripod. He then grabbed it and with a wave of his arm, the tripod [巨大鐵鼎] was flung far into the air. The heavy iron tripod [巨大鐵鼎] landed with a loud thumping sound over twenty feet away. Due to the weight, the iron tripod [巨大鐵鼎] sank nearly two feet deep into the mud. The Lama Monk [喇嘛] paled at the power and skill demonstrated by Iron Finger Chan [鐵指陳]. He realised that Chan's [鐵指陳] power and Kung Fu [功夫] skills were far too great for him to contend with and quickly left.

All the local merchants and store keepers who had witnessed this, cheered and came to Chan Cheung-Tai's [陳長泰] tofu shop [豆腐店] to congratulate him for teaching the bad Lama Monk [喇嘛] a lesson. This monk [喇嘛] never came back to this street or made trouble for these merchants in this area again. [115] News of this incident soon spread around the provincial capital city [省會城市] of Canton [廣州], and many of the citizens came to regard Chan Cheung-Tai [陳長泰] as a hero due to this incident. Other stories of his good deeds, as well as him being a skilled Kung Fu [功夫] fighter, enhanced his reputation with the local community and fellow martial artists [武術家] alike. During the mid to late 1850s, Chan Cheung-Tai [陳長泰] (Iron Finger Chan / Tit Ji Chan / Tie Zhi Chen [鐵指陳]) was chosen as one of the Ten Tigers of Canton / Kwong Tung Sap Fu [廣東十虎]. This was due not only to his skills as a Kung Fu master [功夫大師] and his now reformed character, but also for his good deeds helping the poor, the deprived and the needy. Unfortunately, out of the members of the Ten Tigers of Canton / Kwong Tung Sap Fu [廣東十虎], there seems to be the least information about Chan Cheung-Tai [陳長泰]. A more detailed account of Chan Cheung-Tai [陳長泰] remains elusive and I have no information about his later life or when he passed away.

Tam Chai-Kwan [譚濟筠]

(traditional Chinese: 譚濟筠; simplified Chinese: 谭济筠; pinyin: *Tan Jijun*)
(sometimes spelt as Tam Chai Hok / Tan Ji He / 三脚譚 or Tam Chai Wen)

Tam Chai-Kwan's [譚濟筠] original name was Tam So Shek / Tan Shi Wo [潭石窩], but he changed it to Tam Chai-Kwan [譚濟筠] later in his life when he started to become well known. [115] [115a] [166] It is believed that Tam Chai-Kwan [譚濟筠] was born sometime before the 1820s, during the reign of the Emperor Kar Hing Dai / Jiaqing [嘉慶帝] (9th February 1796 – 2nd September 1820). According to the Taiping Institute, this was in the town of Sui Kia / Suixi [遂溪] which is located approximately 15 kms north-west of the city of Zhanjiang [湛江] and approximately 370 kms south-west of the provincial capital city [省會城市] of Canton [廣州] (Guangzhou [廣州]). [14]

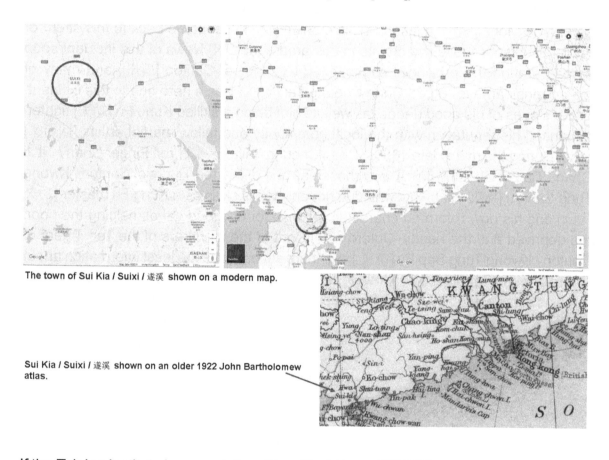

The town of Sui Kia / Suixi / 遂溪 shown on a modern map.

Sui Kia / Suixi / 遂溪 shown on an older 1922 John Bartholomew atlas.

If the Taiping Institute is correct, then Tam Chai-Kwan [譚濟筠] must have moved from Sui Kia / Suixi [遂溪] to Huadu [花都區] sometime in his childhood, although, another source states that Tam Chai-Kwan [譚濟筠] was from the Red Sand Pond Village / Chep Lai Sha Tong Tsuen / Shatang Cun [赤坭沙塘村] of Far Dou / Hua County / Huaxian [花縣]. [166a] Another possible option is that Tam Chai-Kwan [譚濟筠] was actually born in the town of Sui Kia / Suixi [遂溪], but he moved to the Red Sand Pond

Village / Chep Lai Sha Tong Tsuen / Shatang Cun [赤坭沙塘村] at such a young age that some sources believe the Sui Kia / Suixi [遂溪] connection is irrellevent. The Red Sand Pond Village / Chep Lai Sha Tong Tsuen / Shatang Cun [赤坭沙塘村] is located approximately 10 kms south west of Chong She Yuen Tsuen / Cang Shu Yuan Cun [藏書院村]. This is where the Taiping Institute states that the Kung Fu master [功夫大師] Hung Hei-Kwun [洪熙官], had settled down to live. This was sometime around the 1780s, and while here, Hung Hei-Kwun [洪熙官] had started to teach his style of Hung Kuen [洪拳]. From this period, one of his more notable disciples was a man called Tam Min / Tan Min [譚敏]. (During this period, the Huadu District [花都區] was called Hua County / Huaxian [花縣].) This same source [166a] states that Tam Min / Tan Min [譚敏] was also from the Red Sand Pond Village / Chep Lai Sha Tong Tsuen / Shatang Cun [赤坭沙塘村].

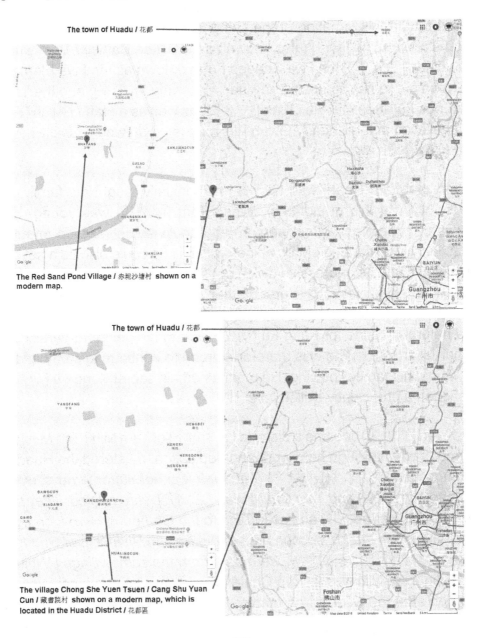

The Red Sand Pond Village / 赤坭沙塘村 shown on a modern map.

The village Chong She Yuen Tsuen / Cang Shu Yuan Cun / 藏書院村 shown on a modern map, which is located in the Huadu District / 花都區

It is understood that Tam Min / Tan Min [譚敏] later continued to teach Kung Fu [功夫] in the Huadu [花都] area after Hung Hei-Kwun [洪熙官] had moved on. It is not stated if he continued at Hung Hei-Kwun's [洪熙官] martial arts school [武術學校] in Chong She Yuen Tsuen / Cang Shu Yuan Cun [藏書院村], or if Tam Min / Tan Min [譚敏] established a new school [武術學校]. I have assumed that he may have opened a new school [武術學校] in his home village of Red Sand Pond Village / Chep Lai Sha Tong Tsuen / Shatang Cun [赤坭沙塘村] from the information stated by the Gathering Hero Lion Dance and Martial Arts Gym from the Zhuliaocun area of the Baiyun District in Guangzhou [廣州市白雲區竹料聚英獅藝武術館]. [166a]

Tam Min / Tan Min [譚敏] later blended his own family style of Kung Fu [功夫] with the Hung kuen [洪拳] style that Hung Hei-Kwun [洪熙官] had taught him. This style became known as the Huadu branch style of Hung Kuen [花都洪拳]. Tam Chai-Kwan [譚濟筠] was taught this variation of the Hung Kuen [洪拳] style which included the Three Extensions routine [套路] (also known as the Three Battles / Sam Chein Kuen / San Zhan Quan [三展拳]), the Five Shapes Form (known as the Five Elements Fist / Ng Yihng Kuen or the Ng Hong Lei Lun Kuen / Wu Xing [五形拳]) and the Taming the Tiger Fist (Fook Fu Kuen / Fu Hu Quan [伏虎拳]) as well as a staff / Gwun [棍] routine [套路]. It is believed that this staff / Gwun [棍] routine [套路] was possibly the Tam Ga Long Staff [譚家長棍]. [14]

It is believed that Tam Chai-Kwan [譚濟筠] was initially taught his family's style of martial arts [武術] by his grandfather. When Tam [譚濟筠] was young, he was a straightforward, honest and direct person who could sometimes be impulsive and therefore act hastily. Unfortunately, combined with this he could also be a hot-tempered young man who could be aggressive which caused problems. This eventually led to a disagreement between him and his grandfather who decided not to continue teaching him. This was a huge set back for Tam [譚濟筠] as it is stated that he was talented and had a natural aptitude for Kung Fu [功夫]. Due to his desire to persist and keep learning martial arts [武術] he was therefore forced to continue to study and practice in secret without his family knowing. He maintained his secret Kung Fu [功夫] training until he reached a proficiently skilled level. [109c]

Tam Chai-Kwan [譚濟筠] became a disciple [武術弟子] of Tam Min / Tan Min [譚敏] and over a period of time, through hard work and dedication, mastered the Huadu branch style of Hung Kuen [花都洪拳]. [14] [172a] *(Although it is not stated, I have wondered if Tam Min / Tan Min [譚敏] and Tam Chai-Kwan [譚濟筠] were related. They both have the same surname of Tam [譚] and according to the Gathering Hero Lion Dance and Martial Arts Gym from the Zhuliaocun area of the Baiyun District in of Guangzhou [廣州市白雲區竹料聚英獅藝武術館] [166a], were both from the same village.)* While training under Tam Min / Tan Min [譚敏], Tam Chai-Kwan [譚濟筠] met a local lady whom he married. Soon after the wedding ceremony, Tam Chai-Kwan's [譚濟筠] wife became pregnant and they had a son whom they named Tam Aun / Tan An [譚雁]. It is believed that during the following years, Tam Chai-Kwan's [譚濟筠] wife and son [譚雁] stayed at Red Sand Pond Village / Chep Lai Sha Tong Tsuen / Shatang Cun [赤坭沙塘村] in the Huadu [花都] area while he travelled around living the Jianghu [江湖] lifestyle.

It is stated that Tam Chai-Kwan [譚濟筠] was often underestimated as a competent fighter which was generally due to his short stature. During these years he had many fights and challenge matches where he gained the nickname of Three Leg Tam / Sam Kuk Tam [三脚譚]. [115] [166] This nickname was due to Tam's [譚濟筠] mastery of three particular kicking techniques he used while fighting. [109] There is a slight difference of opinion between the sources as to the type of kicks that Tam Chai-Kwan [譚濟筠] used. They agree with two of the types of kicks but differ in opinion about the third kick.

These three kicks are :-
1. Tiger Tail kick / Fu Mei Gerk [虎尾脚] : which can be performed several ways such as a rearward kick to a person attacking from behind or by spinning / turning to deliver a kick to an opponent attacking from the front.

2. Organ Seeking kick known as the Nail Kick / Dink Gerk [釘腿] : a kick striking to the opponent's groin. [168]

3. Wikipedia and Wong Kiew Kit state that the third kick was a Sweeping Floor kick / So Tong Tau [掃堂腿] :- a low spinning sweeping kick to take the opponent's legs away. [109a] [85] However, some other sources state that the third kick was a Shadowless kick / Mo Ying Gerk [無影脚] : which consists of a simultaneous grapple or distraction with the hands and a low kick. The upper body movement caused by the hands draws the attention of the target up and away from the feet which lash out at a target between the stomach and the knee. The combination of the close range low target area of the kick at speed and the use of diversionary technique, lends it the appearance of an unseen kick for which the technique has become famous, and therefore given the name of the Shadowless kick / Mo Ying Gerk [無影脚]. [164] [169]

Tam Chai-Kwan [譚濟筠] was also an idealist and through his Kung Fu [功夫], encountered people who were involved in anti-Ch'ing / anti-Qing [反清清朝] activities. Because he also believed in this cause, he would on occasions became involved with members of the revolutionary party. At times, Tam [譚濟筠] would be fully engaged in the movement and take part in their activities. Although no details are stated of what any of these activities were, it is recorded that through his involvement, he would at times put himself in dangerous situations. [115] [166]

Sometime during the early 1850s, Tam Chai-Kwan [譚濟筠] travelled to the provincial capital city [省會城市] of Canton [廣州]. Unfortunately, I have been unable to find the exact lacation of where he was staying in the city of Canton [廣州] during this period. One source [115a] states that he was good friends with Wong Ching-Hoh / Huang Chengke [黃澄可] who lived on Benevolence and Love Street / Wai Oi Street [惠愛街] in the old walled city of Canton [廣州]. It may be possible that he was visiting Wong Ching-Hoh [黃澄可], and he may have stayed with him at his home or at lodgings located nearby. Now that Tam Chai-Kwan [譚濟筠] was a bit older and more mature, he had lost some of the bad character traits he had in his youth.

The story of Tam Chai-Kwan and the ferry.

One day, Tam Chai-Kwan [譚濟筠] was in the West Gate / Sai Kwan / Xiguan [西關] area of Canton [廣州] and wanted to cross the Pearl River [珠江] to Honam Island [河南島]. He was in a hurry because he was running late and eager to get to Honam Island [河南島] where he had an important meeting. Unfortunately, when he arrived at the Wong Sa / Huangsha Ferry Pier [黃沙碼頭], the ferryman had just cast off and the boat was leaving. Tam [譚濟筠] shouted out to the ferryman, asking him to wait for him. The ferryman looked back at Tam [譚濟筠] and seeing that he was a small man, ignored his request and continued to cast off. Tam [譚濟筠] appealed to him again but this time the ferryman responded with a dirty look and some abusive language. Because Tam [譚濟筠] was desperate to get to his meeting, he had no choice but to run and jump for the ferryboat.

By now, the ferryboat was a good distance from the pier [黃沙碼頭], but Tam [譚濟筠] ran as fast as he could and leapt for the boat, managing to land on it. Due to the distance and effort he had put into his jump, the impact of his landing shook the ferry and frightened the passengers. Tam [譚濟筠] at once apologised to all of the worried passengers for this reckless act. However, the ferryman was not happy and attacked Tam [譚濟筠] by swinging his long bamboo barge pole [竹篙] in an attempt to hit him. Fortunately Tam [譚濟筠] saw this attack coming and was able to easily block it. The bamboo barge pole [竹篙] cracked against Tam's [譚濟筠] blocking arm and broke into two pieces. The force of his block vibrated down the remaining bamboo barge pole [竹篙] that the ferryman still held, and made him stagger and nearly fall into the Pearl River [珠江]. Tam [譚濟筠] rushed forward and steadied the shocked ferrymen so that he did not fall into the water. At first the ferryman thought that he was going to be attacked, but he was supprised when Tam [譚濟筠] then reassured him that that was not his intention. As Tam [譚濟筠] continued to talk with the ferryman, he soon became comforted by his calming kind words. After this incident, the ferryman gained a lot of respect for Tam Chai-Kwan [譚濟筠] and the two became friends. [115]

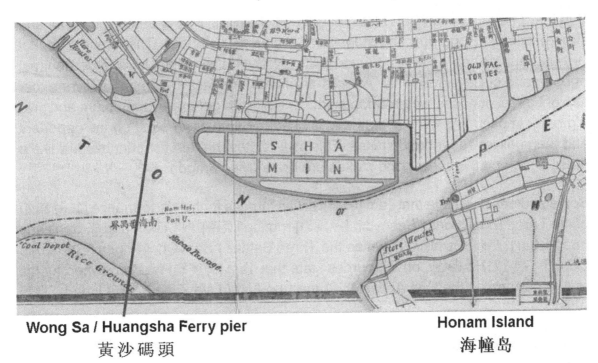

Wong Sa / Huangsha Ferry pier
黃沙碼頭

Honam Island
海幢島

Some sources state that Tam Chai-Kwan [譚濟筠] also followed a Wing Chun [詠春拳] master [功夫大師] called Leung Jan [梁贊] ([梁贊], aka Leung Tsan / Liang Zan), with whom he had made good progress in this style, improving his technique. [115] [115a] [166] Leung Jan's [梁贊] teacher had been Leung Yee-Tai / Liang Erti [梁二娣] and had been a poler on the Red Opera boats [紅船粵劇團]. He had originally been taught by the renowned Siu Lum / Shaolin abbot [少林方丈] Gee Seen Sim See [至善禪師], when he had been in hiding. Tam's [譚濟筠] Wing Chun [詠春拳] training would possibly have been sometime in the early to mid 1850s or later, as Leung Jan [梁贊] had only started studying Wing Chun [詠春拳] himself, in the 1840s. It is not stated where Tam Chai-Kwan [譚濟筠] studied under Leung Jan [梁贊]. It is known that from the mid 1850s, Leung Jan [梁贊] was in Fat Shan / Foshan [佛山], because he took over the family pharmacy after his father died. Sources claim that this pharmacy and martial arts school [武術學校] was located in Fai Jee Street [輝捷街], Fat Shan / Foshan [佛山]. This pharmacy was called Mr Jan's Hall / Jan Sang Tong [佛山贊先生]. (ie His name is Leung Jan [梁贊], nickname [佛山贊先生], Mr Jan's Hall / Jan Sang Tong [贊生堂] is his school teaching martial arts [武術]). I have been unable to find out where Leung Jan [梁贊] was living or teaching before this, but he was originally from Gu Lao Village / Kao Lo Tsuen / Gulaocun [古勞村] and later returned to this village when he retired. [70a] [167] [168] Gu Lao Village / Kao Lo Tsuen / Gulaocun [古勞村] is located in the district of Hok Shan / Heshan [鶴山] located inbetween the towns of Hok Shan / Heshan [鶴山] and Fat Shan / Foshan [佛山].

After training under Leung Jan [梁贊], Tam Chai-Kwan [譚濟筠] merged the Hung Kuen [洪拳] and Wing Chun [詠春拳] to create his own style which he called Crane

275

Sun Fist / Honk Yeung Kuen / He Yang Quan [鶴陽拳]. This is a very powerful and strong style with long arm and stepping movements / stances. The Crane Sun Fist / Honk Yeung Kuen / He Yang Quan [鶴陽拳] style also displays a large contrast of open and close movements. Attacks are fierce and fast, which can deliver either straight direct punches, or throw long circular strikes to generate momentum and give a greater impact. The palm of the hand is used to rotate or rebound off the opponent and then deliver spear-hand strikes. This style states that the fist punches are like a fierce tiger, and the spear hand strikes are like a flying dragon. [109d] [109e] [115] [115a] [166]

Some sources also state that Tam [譚濟筠] was famous for his performance [武術表演] of the Three Extensions / Saam Jin [三展拳] routine [套路]. [164] The Three Extensions / Saam Jin [三展拳] is also known as the Three Battles / Sam Chein Kuen / San Zhan Quan [三展拳]. However, other sources state that Tam [譚濟筠] was renowned for his skill at performing the Five Ancestor Crane Sun Fist / Five Zuhe Yang Quan [五祖鶴陽拳]. [115] [166]

Five Ancestors Fist *(Wuzuquan or Ngo-cho Kun) is a southern Chinese Kung Fu style that has techniques from five styles:*
1. *breathing methods and iron body of Bodhidharma (達尊拳)*
2. *posture and dynamic power of Luohan (羅漢拳)*
3. *precision and efficient movement of Emperor Taizu (太祖拳)*
4. *hand techniques and the softness and hardness of Fujian White Crane (白鶴拳)*
5. *agility and footwork of Monkey (猴拳)*

A blend of these five styles was consolidated with a sixth style called Xuan Nu (also known as Hian Loo / 玄女拳).

There are two accounts of Wuzuquan's history. One dates back to around 1300 AD, founded by Bái Yùfeng, who was 13th century monk from the Henan Shaolin Temple (in the north of China) to whom Five Animals style and Hóngquán (洪拳) have also been credited; the other to Chua Giok Beng / Cài Yùmíng / 蔡玉明 -or- 蔡玉鳴 who was from Jinjiang near Quanzhou in Fujian Province, in the latter half of the 19th century. Most of the history and principles are associated with the Bai branch.

The Cai / Chua branch (also known as He Yang Pai / 鶴阳派 which is a tribute to Cai's Teacher).

A principal feature of Five Ancestors is its dependence on the Three Battles / Sam Chien / :三戰 stance and also the hand routine / form of the same name, which was acquired from Fujian White Crane. The "three battles" refers mainly to the three stages of Wuzu that practitioners achieve: combat preparation, combat tactic and combat strategy. To attain a good level of skill, all three need to be mastered. The Three Battles can also mean conceptual, physical, and spiritual.

Sam Chien is the most important routine / form in the style because it develops the eight principles of Five Ancestor. This is the first form taught to students so they are able to learn and practice the fundamental points of the Five Ancestors from the beginning of their training.

Five Ancestors is renowned for its large range of power generational techniques. Depending on the character of each ancestor and on the power required these techniques change. Some branches focus on tension routines / forms that develop power, while others focus on a relaxed body, instead seeking maximum transmission of power known as jin. [170]

This Wikipedia article ties in the connection between the Three Extensions / Saam Jin routine [套路] (also known as the Three Battles / Sam Chein Kuen / San Zhan Quan [三展拳]) and the Five Ancestor Crane Sun Fist / Five Zuhe Yang Quan [五祖鶴陽拳] stated by the different sources. The Three Extensions / Saam Jin routine [套路] (Three Battles / Sam Chein Kuen / San Zhan Quan [三展拳]) has been adopted by many styles since. A detailed account of the Three Battles / Sam Chein Kuen / San Zhan Quan [三展拳] can be found in the 2009 December issue of Inside Kung Fu magazine, pages 66-69. This article was titled, "Kung Fu's Power Form", and was written by Alex Co. [170a]

Sometime around the mid 1850s, Tam Chai-Kwan / Tan Jiyun [譚濟筠] set up his own school [武術學校] to teach and promote his new style of Crane Sun Fist / Honk Yeung Kuen / He Yang Quan [鶴陽拳]. It is not stated whether this school was in Canton [廣州] or somewhere else. During these years, he had built up a reputation for being a skilled Kung Fu master [功夫大師] who had proved himself as a formidable fighter, and for which he had been given the nickname of "Three Legged Tam / Sam Kuk Tam [三脚譚]". This status, combined with his anti-Ch'ing / anti-Qing [反清朝] beliefs and activities, were the reasons he was chosen as one of the Ten Tigers of Canton / Kwong Tung Sap Fu [廣東十虎]. [109] [109a] [109b] [109c] [109d] 115] [166] It is believed that Tam Chai-Kwan [譚濟筠] exchanged ideas with some of the other Tigers at this time, including his good friend Wong Ching-Hoh / Huang Chengke [黃澄可].

Sometime later, Tam Chai-Kwan [譚濟筠] returned to the Red Sand Pond Village / Chep Lai Sha Tong Tsuen / Shatang Cun [赤坭沙塘村] in the Huadu [花都] area, and set up a martial arts school [武術學校]. I think it is reasonable to assume that Tam Chai-Kwan [譚濟筠] inherited Tam Min's / Tan Min's [譚敏] school [武術學校] from the information stated by the Gathering Hero Lion Dance and Martial Arts Gym from the Zhuliaocun area of the Baiyun District in of Guangzhou [廣州市白雲區竹料聚英獅藝武術館]. [166a]

When Tam's [譚濟筠] son, Tam Aun / Tan An [譚雁] was old enough to learn, he taught him his style of Kung Fu [功夫]. In time, Tam Aun / Tan An [譚雁] took over the running of the martial arts school [武術學校] from his father, and he became known as the King of the Staff at Northern Poon Yue [禺北棍王]. *(During this period, this area was part of Panyu [番禺] County. Panyu [番禺] was the original name for the walled city of Canton [廣州] and when this name was changed to Canton / Guangzhou [廣州], the name of Panyu [番禺] was still used for the surrounding area until the end of Ch'ing Dynasty / Qing [清朝]. This area was ceded to Guangzhou [廣州] which now consists of the areas of Yuexiu [越秀區], parts of Liwan [荔灣區], Haizhu [海珠區], Tianhe [天河區], most of Baiyun [白雲區] and most of Huangpu [黃埔區].* [166b] [166c]) When Tam Aun / Tan An [譚雁] retired, one of his students called Cheung Kou / Zhang Gong [張拱] from Lee Stream Village of Far Dou / Far Doo Lee Kay Tsuen / Lixicun [花都李溪村], inherited the school. Lee Stream Village / Far Doo Lee Kay Tsuen / Lixicun [花都李溪村] is located approximately 38 kms north-west of the Red Sand Pond Village / Chep Lai Sha Tong Tsuen / Shatang Cun [赤坭沙塘村] and only approximately 12 kms east of the town of Huadu [花都]. Cheung Kou / Zhang Gong [張拱] was also skilled with the staff and was known as the King of Staff at Northern Countryside [北郊棍王]. [166a]

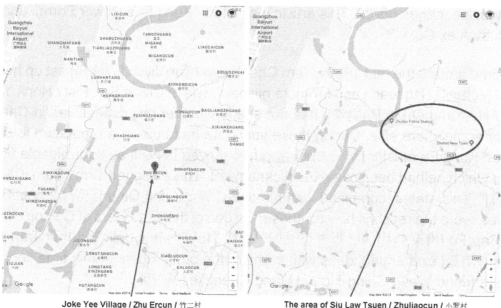

Joke Yee Village / Zhu Ercun / 竹二村   The area of Siu Law Tsuen / Zhuliaocun / 小罗村

The Gathering Hero Lion Dance and Martial Arts Gym [廣州市白雲區竹料聚英獅藝武術館] states that the next successor of the style was a man called Fung Yak Sing / Feng Risheng [馮日勝], who was from Joke Yee Village / Zhu Ercun [竹二村]. This village is located approximately 5 kms south of Lee Stream Village / Far Doo Lee Kay Tsuen / Lixicun [花都李溪村]. [166a] Fung Yak Sing / Feng Risheng [馮日勝] continued the style before then passing it on to his son who was called Fung Yue Sun / Feng YuXin [馮裕新]. Another source [172] confirms that he was from the Siu Law Tsuen / Zhuliao [Z虎寮] area of the Baiyun District [白雲區] of Guangdong [廣東省].

278

Fung Yue Sun / Feng YuXin [馮裕新] and his son, Fung Yeh Wai / Feng YiHui [馮亦慧] expanded the style's syllabus further by incorporating more routines [套路]. Many years earlier, Tam Min's / Tan Min's [譚敏] younger sister had married a man from the Zhuliao [小羅村] area and the local inhabitants had invited Tam Min / Tan Min [譚敏] to open a school [武術學校] there. Some of the routines [套路] practiced included the Twelve Bridge Hand Boxing / Sap Yi Ji Kiu Sau [十二橋手] (*Gong, Yau, Bik, Jik, Fan, Ding, Chyun, Tai, Lau, Wan, Jai, Ding*) [171], Battle of the Five Forms and Single Arm Boxing / Du Bi Quan [獨臂拳]. [14] [172] [172a]

The Twelve Bridge Hand Boxing / Sap Yi Ji Kiu Sau [十二橋手] consists of the following :

Hard (*Gong*): *Striking hard with "Heavy Hand" to end the confrontation as fast as possible.*
Soft (*Yau*): *If an opponent is stronger, "Use" their strength against them.*
Press (*Bik*): *Press the opponent back and so forcing them to retreat and defend.*
Straight (*Jik*): *If you lose contact, continue like a spring with straight attacks.*
Separate (*Fan*): *To separate and break contact if necessary.*
Fix (*Ding*): *To control and fix an opponent so as to use close range attacks with elbows or finger pokes etc,.*
Inch (*Chyun*): *Controlling an opponent so they can't evade so as to attack the vital points such as throat and eyes.*
Lift (*Tai*): *Lift an opponent up.*
Keep (*Lau*): *"Receive what comes", allowing the opponent to come in close with their attacks so as to enable you to capture them.*
Send (*Wan*): *If an opponent presses forward, using their strength and pull them forward.*
Control (*Jai*): *To subdue the opponent and control them.*
Adapt (*Ding*): *Adapting to an opponent's actions.* [171]

This school [武術學校] continues today in the Baiyun District [白雲區] of Guangdong [廣東省] under the name of Tam Ga Kuen / Tan Jia Quan [譚家洪拳]. [14] [166a] [172] The Huadu style of Hung Kuen [花都洪拳] has a relatively small number of routines compared with other Hung Kuen [洪拳] styles. Their emphasis is on thoroughly training the basics with a view to mastering the few techniques incorporated within the style.

洪熙官祖師嫡傳---花縣赤坭譚敏(嶺南奇人)宗師系第七代傳人
Tam Man, the lineal of Grand Master Hung Hei Kwun was born in Far Dou (Flower Country) of Canton. He nickname is 'Strange man of Lingnam', and is the successor of seventh generation.

廣州花都譚家老洪拳
Tam's old Hung Gar Fist of Far Dou (Flower Country) of Guangzhou

廣州市白雲區竹料聚英獅藝武術館
Gathering Hero Lion Dance and Martial Arts Gym.

傳承體系: *The inheritance order*
祖師洪熙官 *Founder: Hung Hei Kwun*
→譚濟筠（廣東十虎之一）花都赤坭沙塘村人 *Tam Chai-Kwan (One of the Canton Ten Tigers) from Red Sand Pond Village of Far Dou*
→譚　敏（嶺南奇人）花都赤坭沙塘村人 *Tam Man (Strange Man of Lingnam) from Red Sand Pond Village of Far Dou*
→譚　安（禺北棍王）花都赤坭沙塘村人 *Tam On (King of Staff at Northern Poon Yue) from Red Sand Pond Village of Far Dou*
→張　拱（北郊棍王）花都李溪村人 *Cheung Kou (King of Staff at Northern Countryside) from Lee Stream Village of Far Dou*
→馮日勝（竹二村人）*Fung Yak Sing from Joke Yee Village*
→馮裕新（竹二村人）*Fung Yue Sun from Joke Yee Village*
→馮亦慧(竹二村人)*Fung Yeh Wai from Joke Yee Village*
→馮國鑫、馮偉鎮 *Fung Kok Yum, Fung Wai Chun*
[166a]

A more detailed account of Tam On [譚　安] (King of Staff at Northern Poon Yue [禺北棍王]) can be found in the 1976 edition of Real Kung Fu magazine, pages 28 to 33. [50d] This article states that the two pillars of Tam Ga Kuen / Tan Jia Quan [譚家洪拳] are the Three Battles / Sam Chein Kuen / San Zhan Quan [三展拳] and the Tam Ga Long Staff [譚家長棍] routine called the Eight Diagram Long Pole / Ng Long Baat Gwa Gwan [五郎八卦棍].

Chau Tai / Zou Tai [鄒泰]

(sometimes spelt Chow Thye, traditional Chinese: 鄒
泰; simplified Chinese: 邹泰; pinyin: Zhou Tai.)

Chau Tai [鄒泰] was born in 1828 at his family home which was located on Yao Zi ridge (hill) / Yiu Tse Ling [耀子嶺], in the village of Guanyao / Kwun Yiu Tsuen [官窰村], in Nam Hoi Yuen / Nanhai county [南海縣] of Guangdong Province [廣東省]. This was during the reign of the Tao Kuang Ti Emperor / Daoguang [道光帝], who had come to power on the 3rd, October, 1820 and reigned until 25th, February, 1850. The village of Guanyaocun / Kwun Yiu Tsuen [官窰村], is located approximately 22 kms north-westly of Canton / Guangzhou [廣州市] and 21 kms north-eastly of the town of Samshui / Sanshui [三水]

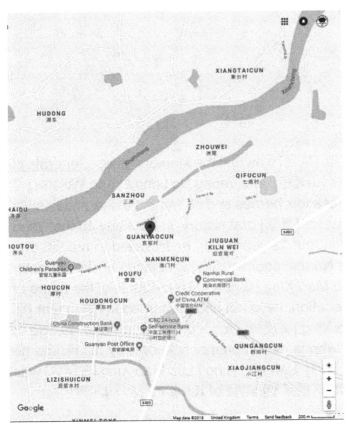

Nanhai County is named after the South China Sea, and was previously a county in Guangdong Province.

This area now makes up Nanhai District in Foshan and Liwan District in Guangzhou. [183]

The first map shows the location of Guanyaocun [官窰村].

The second map below, shows Guanyaocun's [官窑村] location in relation to Canton and Sanshui.

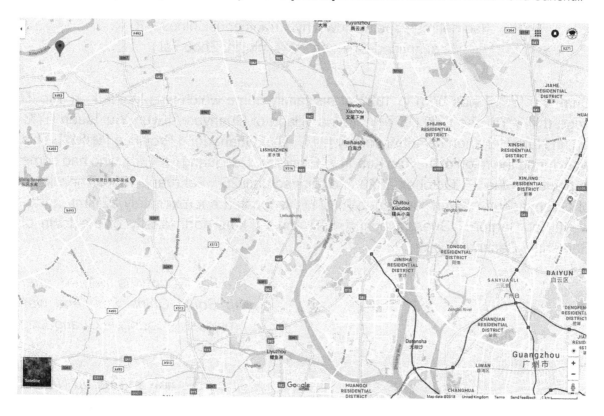

It is understood that as a boy, Chau Tai [鄒泰] was told the stories of the, "Generals of the Yang Family", and of Yang Yande's [楊延德] (aka Yeung Ng Long / Yang Wulang [楊五郎]) exploits. He greatly admired these folk heroes and so wanted to learn their style of Kung Fu [功夫]. According to Chau Gar [鄒家] oral history, in the early 1840s when Chau Tai [鄒泰] became a teenager (about 13 years old), he travelled to martial arts school [武術學校] in Nam Hoi Yuen / Nanhai county [南海縣] to study under a master [功夫大師] called Law Mui Hing / Luo Mao Xing [羅茂興]. (Unfortunately, the name of this school [武術學校] and its exact location, have not been recorded in Chau Gar [鄒家] history.) Law Mui Hing / Luo Mao Xing [羅茂興] was a disciple from the lineage of Yang Yande [楊延德] (official name) who is more commonly known by his nickname of Yeung Ng Long / Yang Wulang [楊五郎]. Law Mui Hing / Luo Mao Xing [羅茂興] was a master [功夫大師] of the Yang Family [楊家拳] style of Kung Fu [功夫]. [181]

I have used Wikipedia to give some background information of the Yang Family and Yang Yande [楊延德].

Yang Yande (楊延德) was the fifth son of Yang Ye who was a Song Dynasty general in the Generals of the Yang Family legends. In these legends, he survived the battle against the Liao Dynasty army that killed his father, and so left the army to become a Buddhist monk.

*Yang Yande is more commonly known by his nickname of **Yang Wulang** (楊五郎) which means "5ᵗʰ son,". He was born into a military family and so was taught martial arts from an early age. He was highly skilled and renowned for his family's style of spear fighting.*

General Yang Ye's army was surrounded during the battle of Mount Twin Wolves. Yang Yande's three elder brothers had died and his fourth older brother was missing. Yang Yande had lost contact with his family, and realising they had lost the day, he left the battle and went to the Buddhist monastery at Mt Wutai (Ng Toi in Cantonese) where he became a monk. He removed the head of his spear, because as a monk, he was no longer able to use lethal weapons. Yang Yande converted the spear techniques to staff ones, and created a new method called the Fifth Brother Eight Diagram Pole / Ng Lung Ba Gwa Gwan / 五郎八卦棍.[181a]

During the Song Dynasty in August 986AD, their army was commanded by General Yang Ye [楊業]. At this time, he was fighting against the Liao Dynasty and was forced by his superior, Wang Shen [王侁], to take a battle against the far numerically bigger Liao force, which he knew would only result in his defeat. The Liao general, Yelu Xiezhen [耶律斜軫], was warned of Yang Ye's [楊業] approach and so ambushed him. Yang Ye [楊業] fought a desperate battle from noon till dusk before he retreated to Chenjiagu [陳家谷]. One of his sons called Yang Yanyu [楊延玉], was killed, and it is believed that this was the battle that Yang Yande [楊延德] / Yang Wulang [楊五郎] escaped from before going to Mt Wutai. [181b]

Mount Wutai [五台山] (meaning "Five Plateau Mountain"), is also known as Qingliang Shan. This is a Buddhist holy spot located in the north-eastern Chinese province of Shanxi, near the source of the river Qingshui. [182][182a]

After being ambushed by the Liaos and losing a major battle, Yang Yande [楊延德] / Yang Wulang [楊五郎] escaped to a Buddhist temple on Wutai Mountain / Ng Toi Shan [五台山] where he became a Buddhist monk [和尚]. He continued to practice his spear every day, but in line with Buddhist principles of no killing, he removed the sharp bladed spear-head. Although Buddhist monks [和尚] believe in forgiveness and the sanctity of life, they also needed to protect themselves from thiefs, bandits and wild animals. Yeung Ng Long / Yang Wulang [楊五郎] trained the other monks [和尚] at the temple in the Yang Family Spear / Yeung Ka Cheong / Yang Jia Qiang [楊家槍] using a long staff, and so adapted these spear techniques to the staff. Due to the spear influence, this is considered a "single end" pole routine / form [套路] as techniques are delivered primarily with one end. Yang Wulang's [楊五郎] practice has passed down to posterity as the Yang Family Spear / Yeung Ka Cheong / Yang Jia Qiang [楊家槍], or if using a staff, as the adapted routine [套路] which over the generations became known as the Fifth Brother Eight Diagram (Octagonal) Staff / Ng Lung Ba Gwa Kwun

[五郎八卦棍]. The title of Fifth Brother represents the fact that he was the fifth in his family. [181e] [181f] [181j]

The Xiantong Temple [顯通寺] state that Yeung Ng Long / Yang Wulang [楊五郎] came here and they display an iron pole which the temple state is the one used by him. [181c] [182d] The Xiantong Temple [顯通寺] is located at the foot of the Bodhisattva Summit, and is the biggest and oldest among the five famous temples in Wutai Mountain [五台山]. [182b] [182c] [182d] It can be difficult to establish fact from fiction as Yeung Ng Long / Yang Wulang [楊五郎] has become immortalised in Chinese folklore and the novels entitled "Generals of the Yang Family". These stories recount the unflinching loyalty and the remarkable bravery of the Yangs as they sacrificed themselves to defend their country from foreign military powers, namely the Khitan –ruled Liao Dynasty (907–1125) and Tangut-ruled Western Xia (1038–1227). [181c] This story is also told in the 1983 Shaw Brothers film entitled, "The Eight Diagram Pole Fighter" [五郎八卦棍], with Gordan Liu playing the role of Yang Yande [楊延德] (Yeung Ng Long / Yang Wulang [楊五郎]). [181d] I have found references stating that the Yang Family Spear / Yeung Ka Cheong / Yang Jia Qiang [楊家槍] is still being practiced by Buddhist monks [和尚] at Mount Wutai / Wutai Shan [五台山]. [181g [181h] [181i]] Over the centuries, Buddhist monks [和尚] and their unshaved lay disciples [俗家弟子] have circulated around China teaching at the various temples that they settled at.

After introductions, Chau Tai [鄒泰] was accepted by Law Mui Hing / Luo Mao Xing [羅茂興] and his training began. During these years at the school [武術學校], his training regime was long and arduous. Chau Tai's [鄒泰] Kung Fu [功夫] training consisted of various aspects of the Yang Family martial arts [楊家拳] including the famed Yang Family Spear / Yeung Ka Cheong / Yang Jia Qiang [楊家槍]. This comprised a variety of Yang [陽] training methods focusing on the external, hard physical style of the art to improve speed and strength. In contrast to this style, but to also compliment it, he was taught a range of Yin [陰] techniques. His Yin [陰] training focused on the internal side of the art with slower, softer, yielding movements, with the emphasis of synchronizing the hands with the waist to generate powerful techniques. Techniques are practised slowly so as to refine each movement to perfection. The ultimate goal is to achieve controlled, effortless strikes while continually moving, with the ability to redirect an opponent's force or attacks with smooth alterations in either hand or foot movements.

Chau Tai's [鄒泰] education also included Traditional Chinese Medicine [中醫]. Besides being taught about herbal medicine, he was also taught how to prepare anti-inflammatory plaster, the art of cupping [拔罐], bone-setting [整骨 or 正骨] as well as sinew and ligament treatments. In traditional Chinese herbal medicine, many parts of plants, such as the leaves, roots, stems, flowers and seeds are used. Also, some minerals and animal products are mixed into various formulas and given as teas or tablets to be consumed, or liquids or powders to be massaged into the skin. [125] [181]

Anti-inflammatory plaster is a piece of paper or cloth which is covered in a medicinal paste (various herbs etc) and this is applied to the skin over an area of pain. [125a] [125b]

Cupping / báguàn [拔罐] is a style of Chinese massage. A match is lit and placed inside a glass cup, before then removing and placing the cup against the skin. The air expands as it is heated, to create lower pressure in the glass cup which then by suction, sticks to the skin. The part of the body to be treated is covered with massage oil and then several cups placed on the skin. The oil allows the glass cups to slide around creating reverse-pressure massage.

Bone-setting / Diē-dá [跌打] is a procedure often conducted by martial artists who are skilled in Chinese medicine. This treatment is for bone fractures, sprains, trauma and and bruises. [125]

During my research, I found some references stating that Chau Tai [鄒泰] was also known by the nickname of Iron Head Chau / Tee Tau Chau / Zhou Tie Tou [周鐵頭]. He had gained this nickname after mastering the art of Siu Lum / Shaolin Iron Head skill. After discussing this with (Michael) Chau Sui / Zhou Shou [鄒穗] (4th generation, great grandson), he informed me that this is not correct. [109d] [109e] [181]

It is stated that Chau Tai [鄒泰] mastered the Yang Family Spear / Yeung Ka Cheong / Yang Jia Qiang [楊家枪] so well, that when he left the temple, he was requested to become a sheriff / Po Tau / Bu Tou [捕頭] for the Ch'ing / Qing [清朝] authorities. This position covered an area of Nam Hoi Yuen / Nanhai county [南海縣]. Due to his excellent martial arts skills, Chau Tai [鄒泰] quickly became very prominent within this field. Before long, due to his renown, he was able to become the chief guard on an escort convoy transporting valuable goods around southern China. Chau Tai [鄒泰] mainly covered the provinces of Szechuan / Sichuan [四川省], Yunnan [雲南省] and Kweichau (sometimes spelt Kweichow) / Guizhou [貴州省]. At this time, Chau Tai [鄒泰] used a great spear which was twelve feet and two inches long (3.7metres). On one occasion, bandits ambushed his convoy in a forest and due to the narrowness of the path, Chau Tai [鄒泰] was forced to dismount from his horse and fight on foot so that he could manoeuvre with more flexibility. The length of his great spear became a hindrance in the confined area of the forest path, and Chau Tai [鄒泰] was unable to use his spear correctly. Unfortunately, this impediment led to the bandits overcoming him and robbing the convoy.

Chau Tai [鄒泰] realised that the great spear he used was not suitable for fighting in southern China, due to the terrain. Frustrated by this incident, he went to Eight Row Mountain / Pak Pai Mountain / Bapaishan [八排山] in Kwangsi / Guangxi Province [廣西省] where he became a recluse. Due to Kwangsi's / Guangxi's [廣西省] location on the border, in the far south of China and its mountainous terrain, it was accustomed to constant unrest. Even the Ch'ing / Qing [清朝] authorities had left the region alone until 1726, but throughout the 1800s it was an area of frequent trouble. Chau Tai [鄒泰] had chosen this area because of its dangerous, but beautiful and remote, mountainous terrain. Here he knew he would have no distractions, but it would be challenging for him to train and perfect his techniques.

In Chau Gar [鄒家] oral history, it is recorded that Chau Tai [鄒泰] went to the Eight Row Mountain / Pak Pai Mountain / Bapaishan [八排山] in Kwangsi / Guangxi Province [廣西省]. It is believed that this is referring to the Eight Row Mountain / Pak Pai Mountain / Bapaishan [八排山] which is actualy located approximately 3 kms over the Kwangsi / Guangxi Province [廣西省] border in Pingtang County [平塘鎮], of Kweichow / Guizhou Province [貴州省]. This mountain is part of the Nanling mountain [南嶺] range. It is assumed that Chau Tai [鄒泰] knew this area from his days as chief guard on an escort convoy. *(In some versions of Choy Li Fut history, it is stated that the Green Grass Monk / Ching Cho [青草] resided at the Eight Row Mountain / Pak Pai Mountain / Bapaishan [八排山] in Kwangsi / Guangxi Province [廣西省] after the destruction of the Southern Siu Lum / Shaolin Temple [南少林寺].)* [36]

Pingtang County / Xiàn / Píngtáng [平塘鎮]) is a is a high mountain valley in the county in Guizhou, in southwest China. This area is inhabited mainly by members of the Buyei and Miao ethnic minorities, who together make up 55% of the county's population. [185]

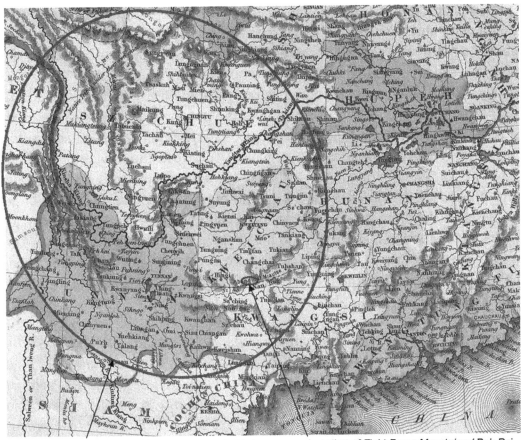

Szechuan / Sichuan [四川省], Yunnan [雲南省] &
Kweichau / Guizhou [貴州省] Provinces, covered by
Chau Tai [鄒泰] as the chief guard for the escort convoy.

Location of Eight Rows Mountains / Pak Pai
Mountain / Bapaishan [八排山]

Above, shows the location of the Eight Row Mountain /
Pak Pai Mountain / Bapaishan 八排山 in relation to
Canton / Guangzhou / 廣州.

Below, shows the location of the Eight Row Mountain / Pak
Pai Mountain / Bapaishan 八排山 in relation to the Guizhou
and Guangxi border.

It is stated that Chau Tai [鄒泰] was a confident and courageous man with an unconstrained character. Unfortunately, sometimes these character traits made him arrogant and proud. For some time, he became trapped in a cycle of constantly drilling his techniques in an effort to try and further improve them. Fortunately, this cycle was eventually broken when an unrecorded skilled master [功夫大師] suggested to Chau Tai [鄒泰] that he would greatly improve if he did not restrict himself to the studying of his family's style of Kung Fu [功夫], but to be more open with his thinking for the methods when applying the techniques. Chau [鄒泰] took the advice offered by this master [功夫大師] and expanded his studies. He altered his ideas about movement and the application of Yin and Yang [陽陰] through his technique. These changes enable him to make dramatic improvements, and from this he created his own unique style. It is understood that some refer to this style as the Soft Cotton Palm / Yun Min Cheung / ruan mian zhang [軟綿掌]. This style mainly uses soft movements to control hard and powerful attacks. The name of Soft Cotton Palm [軟綿掌] was derived from soft continuous non-stopping palm movements of this style. [115] [115a]

"Cotton Palm" Strikes These soft strikes depend on the strength and penetrating power of the practitioner's internal chi. The strikes use a minimal amount of physical force such as one would use to stroke a newborn baby's hair. The penetration of the chi, can cause mild discomfort, severe temporary pain with no after effect, internal haemorrhaging, or death to an opponent. An extremely high level of expertise and excellent control over one's chi is required to perform this syle of strikes. This technique is common in all advanced levels of all internal martial arts. [175]

After adapting his open hand style, Chau Tai [鄒泰] continued this process with the Yang Family Spear / Yeung Ka Cheong / Yang Jia Qiang [楊家槍]. He realised that he needed to reduce the length of the spear so as to make it more manageable, and therefore more practical for the landscape of southern China. During the next several years, using his skill and experience as a practitioner of the staff / Gwun [棍], he created various staff / Gwun [棍] techniques until he finaly developed the Zhou Family Bagua Staff / Chau Gar Ba Gua Gwun [周家八卦棍]. The reduction in length made it lighter, faster and easier to control. The new type of staff / Gwun [棍] now used by Chau Tai [鄒泰], was a seven foot two inch (218.44cm) long rat-tail (tapered end). Foot techniques include movements such as eight sections with four flatsteps, three angles (triangle) steps, side steps in four directions, and a stationary position known as the war horse step. These steps were combined with a lot of jumping movements which are the fundamental component. These movements were combined with six and a half hand techniques which include steal, bounce (rebound), cutting chop, kill, circle, tap and strike. (Tapping is considered as the half movement.) A performance routine [套路] of this style is made up of five sets of movements, which are known as the "Five Tigers descend on Szechuan / Ng Fu Ha Sze Chuen / Wu Hu Xia Sichuan [五虎下四川]." [181]

The characteristics of the Zhou Family Bagua Staff / Chau Gar Ba Gua Gwun [周家八卦棍] are based on principles of Yin and Yang [陽陰] with both hard and soft movements. Initially practice focuses on power which is generated from the waist, and the staff / Gwun [棍] is held with the hands close together. Once this has been achieved, attention moves on to soft staff / Gwun [棍] movements, with concentration on maintaining a calm spirit. This is achieved with circular and continuous staff movements which are synchronised with the body. Training can be done unaccompanied or with a partner, and includes opposing practice, fixed step, moving step, moving in two sides steps and four directions steps, three sliding spears, passing four gates (four directions) and waving staff / Gwun [棍]. Chau Tai [鄒泰] devised a poem to help his students understand the fundementals of the Zhou Family Bagua Staff / Chau Gar Ba Gua Gwun [周家八卦棍]. [181]

The poem for practice is :

心法為: 陰陽善拆無情棍, 八卦形圈要認真, 混青槍放麒麟步, 平山子干曉知蹤, 標龍出手如風箭, 三槍下馬不能容, 提欄擋力身如柱, 馬退連環吞吐槍, 鎖喉槍法前師訓, 棍法長門習短方, 遇到適時應退步, 剛柔收縮是陰陽

Yin and Yang easy to break ruthless staff, Gossip form the circle severely. Mixing up the block and attack in unicorn step. Flat and triangular step know where to go. Fast dragon attack like arrow, three spears to push the enemy fall down from horse. Body like a column when taking staff for blocking. Stepping back continuously with block and attack spear. Locking throat spear method following the technique of teacher. Method of using the staff is combined with long and short movement and stepping back when necessary. Appropriate use of soft and hard with hold and release are the key points. [181]

Chau Tai [鄒泰] had spent nearly eight years in his self-imposed exile living on the Eight Row Mountain / Pak Pai Mountain / Bapaishan [八排山] in Kwongsi / Guangxi Province [廣西省]. After creating these improvements, he decided to give up his life of solitude and returned to Guangdong Province [廣東省]. He had spent several years previously as a sheriff/ Po Tau / Bu Tou [捕頭], then as the chief guard on an escort convoy living the Jianghu [江湖] lifestyle. He once again returned to the Jianghu [江湖] lifestyle after leaving the Eight Row Mountain / Pak Pai Mountain / Bapaishan [八排山]. During the mid to late 1850s, Chau Tai [鄒泰] would spend much of his time in and around the provincial capital city [省會城市] of Canton [廣州]. It was during this period that several incidents occurred that would enhance his reputation and so make him more prominent with the local population of Canton [廣州].

A story about Chau Tai and the Taoist priest

During the mid 1850s, a Taoist priest [道士] called Mui Fat / Miaofa [妙法] would trick ordinary people into becoming his students with acts of Chi Gung / Qigong [氣功].

He deceived would-be followers who believed that his Chi Gung / Qigong [氣功] was actually magic. Mui Fat [妙法] was from the Chun Tei Temple / Zhun ti guan [準提觀] which was located in the village of Sam Yuen Li / San Yuan Li [三元里], just outside the old city walls of Canton [廣州] (Guangzhou [廣州]) at that time.

The area of the village of San Yuan Li / 三元里

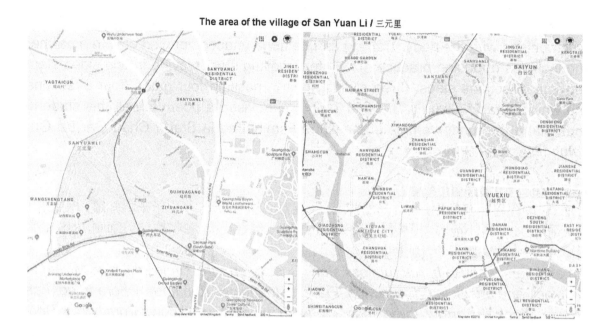

(Sam Yuen Li / San Yuan Li [三元里] was a small traditional village located approximately 2 kms outside the old city wall of old Canton [廣州]. Today this village has been consumed by the urban expansion of Guangzhou [廣州] and is now surrounded by skyscrapers.) This area is now located in the Baiyun District [白雲區], and is named after the Baiyun Mountain (the "White Cloud Mountain"). Much of Baiyun was formerly part of northern Panyu County after the establishment of the PRC in October, 1951, Baiyun was ceded to the City of Guangzhou and formally established as a suburban district north and east of the city. [174] [174a]

Chau Tai [鄒泰] didn't like Mui Fat's [妙法] methods because he understood that Mui Fat [妙法] was deceiving the local residents, using his 'Chi Gung / Qigong [氣功]' to accomplish this enticement. He therefore went to the Chun Tei Temple [準提觀] to talk with Mui Fat [妙法] about this. When Chau [鄒泰] found Mui Fat [妙法] at the temple [準提觀], he was with a crowd of people. Chau [鄒泰] wanted to talk with him in private, but Mui Fat [妙法] told him to say what he had to say openly in front of these people. Chau [鄒泰] therefore spoke to him openly and tried to convince him to stop cheating the people. Mui Fat [妙法] didn't listen to what Chau [鄒泰] had to say, but instead he became angry, believing that Chau [鄒泰] had shamed him in front of the people who were present.

As Mui Fat [妙法] judged that he had lost face in front of the people at the temple, he demanded that Chau Tai [鄒泰] fight him as a matter of honour. Chau [鄒泰] tried to calm him down insisting that this was not his intention, but unfortunately no reassurances he gave were even acknowledged by the Taoist priest [道士]. In fact, Mui Fat [妙法] took these as a sign of weakness and started to ridicule Chau Tai [鄒泰] for being a coward. After this, Chau [鄒泰] realised that he had no choice but to fight Mui Fat [妙法]. He understood that the Taoist priest [道士] was a skilled master [功夫大師] who would also rely on his Chi Gung / Qigong [氣功] capabilities, but he believed in his own skills and so accepted the challenge. Many of the onlookers were worried for Chau Tai's [鄒泰] safety and advised him not to fight, while others were shouting that he deserved the consequences for provoking Mui Fat [妙法].

Mui Fat [妙法] started to show off, swaggering around, confident that he would beat Chau Tai [鄒泰]. He then faced Chau [鄒泰] and attacked using his powerful Chi Gung / Qigong [氣功]. During this attack, Chau [鄒泰] managed to evade Mui Fat's [妙法] strikes until he was able to counterstrike back. His retaliatory head strike caught the Taoist priest [道士] full on in the body. The force of Chau's [鄒泰] head strike sent Mui Fat [妙法] hurtling backwards, crashing to the floor over ten feet (three metres) away. Mui Fat [妙法], the Taoist priest [道士] was defeated and the news of this incident soon spread around the provincial capital [省會城市] which helped to enhance Chau Tai's [鄒泰] reputation with the citizens of Canton [廣州]. [115]

Wong Kiew Kit and Wikipedia state that Chau Tai [鄒泰] became famous after fighting a French International boxing champion. [85] [109a] [109b]

(While researching Chau Tai [鄒泰] in 2012, I found a foreign language web site that told the story of this match with the French International boxing champion. Unfortunately at the time I only saved the details of the story and did not record the web site address. In 2017, while writing the detailed history of Chau Tai [鄒泰], I was unable to find this site again so I could reference it as a source. I can therefore only conclude that the site has either expired or been taken down. However, the Wikipedia talk section does mention that Chau Tai [鄒泰] achieved fame after he defeated an international boxing champion from France, [109a] and the Thai wikipedia site [109c] mentions that he defeated the bodyguard or bodyguards of a Western opium trader using his staff / Gwun [棍].) (Michael) Chau Sui / Zhou Shou [鄒穗] (4ᵗʰ generation) confirms this story, but states that the match was with bare hands and no weapons involved. [181]

The Story of Chau Tai fighting the French International Boxing Champion

Chau Tai [鄒泰] gained great prominence and recognition after a match with a French International boxing champion. This French boxer was a bodyguard to a rich French merchant who imported opium [鴉片]. He used opium [鴉片] as a commodity to trade for various Chinese goods, which he would then export to Europe. It is understood that this event took place sometime in the mid 1850s, just before the Second Opium War which started on the 8th, October, 1856. [9] Some of the more educated of the local population of Canton [廣州] understood that opium [鴉片] was a drug which was no good. Chau Tai [鄒泰] knew that foreign merchants were taking advantage of the Chinese people by getting them addicted to opium [鴉片]. Chau [鄒泰] was also known to oppose the use of opium [鴉片] as he felt it was a foreign habit used to weaken his countrymen. It was generally the Han Chinese [漢族] population who suffered most through the use and addiction to opium [鴉片]. Many Ch'ing / Qing [清朝] officials were easily bribed and would become rich through their corrupt dealings with foreign merchants, which was one of the many reasons why Chau [鄒泰] had very strong anti-Ch'ing / anti-Qing [反清朝] beliefs.

During some incident, the rich French merchant trader was threatened about his business of importing opium [鴉片] by several local Han Chinese [漢族] businessmen. To silience these critics and avoid any future problems, the rich merchant decided to use his bodyguard to resolve this issue. The merchant had been prudent in his choice of the bodyguard, as he had employed a French International boxing champion, and was therefore a man of proven fighting abilities. The French merchant stated that he did not respect any of the local martial artists [武術], and that to prove that Chinese boxing (Kung Fu [功夫]) was inferior to western boxing he made an open challenge to the martial arts community in the Canton [廣州] region. A boxing ring was set up at a venue in the Shameen Island [沙面島] (now known as Shamian) area of Canton [廣州], and his bodyguard would fight any local fighters.

(Although it is stated that the French bodyguard was an International boxing champion, it did not state if he was either a bare knuckle boxer or a French style Savate boxer.)

Savate can also be known as Boxe Française, French boxing, French kickboxing or French foot-fighting, and is a French style of martial arts. It combines aspects of western boxing with various kicks. Savate's name comes from the French for "old boot", which was a heavy type of footwear that was worn during fights).

The modern form of Savate is largely a combination of French street fighting techniques from the early 1800s, which at that time, was a common type of street fighting in Paris and northern France. In the south of France and particularly in the port of Marseille, sailors created a style of fighting with high kicks and open-handed slaps. It is believed that kicks and slaps were used on land to evade legal penalties for using a closed fist, which was considered a deadly weapon under French law. Savate or Chausson was also at this time developing in the ports of north-western Italy and north-eastern Spain.[176]

Many Kung Fu [功夫] fighters took up the challenge, but were all beaten by the big, strong Frenchman. Several local Kung Fu masters [功夫大師] approached Chau Tai [鄒泰], and requested that he defend the honour of the Chinese people by taking up this challenge.

The general opinion was that Chau Tai [鄒泰] was not expected to do well against the bigger Frenchman. The French bodyguard had a good reputation, with a proven fighting record behind him as a champion. It was only the poorer local Han Chinese [漢族] that were hoping Chau [鄒泰], as one of their own, could defeat the bigger foreign barbarian. During this period, Western foreigners were considered as barbarians by most Chinese. [129] [177]

China believed that the Chinese Empire was the Celestial Dynasty and so the centre of world civilization, which made the Emperor the head of the civilized world. All other countries were deemed under the sovereign rule of China.

China therefore took the view that all other countries were deprived and backward with little to offer them. [178]

A barbarian is a person who is thought to be uncultured. The word is often used either as a common reference to a member of a country or Ethnic group, who is considered by a civilised people to be inferior.

Historically, the Chinese people used various words for foreigners which included words such as [夷] Yi, which is commonly translated as "barbarians." [179]

Even though the French bodyguard was a very big, strong man, he was surprisingly fast and it is stated that this fight was a very tough match, with Chau Tai [鄒泰] suffering several facial injuries during the furious exchanges. The fight was brought to a conclusive end after Chau Tai [鄒泰] dodged several head shots and countered with a low leg kick. The French bodyguard fell to the floor, screaming with a broken leg and the match was over. Due to the opium [鴉片] trade and incursions made by the western powers, foreigners were generally feared and hated by most Chinese. Therefore to beat a foreigner who was regarded as an international boxing champion, gained Chau Tai [鄒泰] great renown, and enhanced his reputation as an exceptional fighter. [181]

Not long after this match, Chau Tai [鄒泰] was chosen as one of the Ten Tigers of Canton / Kwong Tung Sap Fu [廣東十虎]. Chau [鄒泰] was so dedicated to the studying and practising of martial arts [武術], that he was regarded as being obsessed. He was therefore considered the keenest and most devoted practitioner of the Ten Tigers of Canton / Kwong Tung Sap Fu [廣東十虎]. It is stated that Chau Tai [鄒泰] was a very skilled practitioner with the staff / Gwun [棍]. The Thai Wikipedia [109c] and Wong Kiew Kit state that his skill with the staff / Gwun [棍] was due to his expertise performing the Tai Cho Chooi Wan Khun / Soul-Chasing Staff of the First Emperor [始皇追魂棍]. [85] I asked (Michael) Chau Sui / Zhou Shou [鄒穗] about this staff routine, and he stated that to his knowledge, this is not correct and that his great grandfather did not perform this routine [套路].

Chau Tai [鄒泰] had used his skill and experience as a practitioner of the staff / Gwun [棍] to create his own routine [套路] which he had called the Zhou Family Bagua Staff / Chau Gar Ba Gua Gwun [周家八卦棍]. [109] [109d] [109e] [164] This had been redeveloped from the Yang Family Spear / Yeung Ka Cheong / Yang Jia Qiang [楊家槍], (or if using a staff as the adapted routine [套路] known as the Fifth Brother Eight Diagram (Octagonal) Staff / Ng Lung Ba Gwa Kwun [五郎八卦棍]) while he had been on the Eight Row Mountain / Pak Pai Mountain / Bapaishan [八排山] for eight years, during the late 1840s untill some time into the early 1850s. It is reputed that due to Chau Tai's [鄒泰] skill with the staff / Gwun [棍] he was given the title of the Lingnan (Southern China) King of the staff / Lingnam Gwun Wong di Ching Ho / Lingnan gun wang de chenghao [嶺南棍王的稱號]. [115]

Lingnan or Lĩnh Nam [嶺南] is an area in the south of China's "Five Ranges" (Tayu, Qitian, Dupang, Mengzhu, and Yuecheng) which covers the modern Chinese provinces of Jiangxi, Hunan, Guangdong, Guangxi, and Hainan as well as northern Vietnam. [183a]

It is known that besides Chau Tai [鄒泰] being highly skilled with the staff / Gwun [棍], several of the other Ten Tigers [廣東十虎] were also renowned for their skills with this weapon. These were Wong Kei-Ying / Huang Qiying [黃麒英], (who also taught his son Wong Fei-Hung / Huang Feihong [黃飛鴻]), So Chan / Su Can [蘇燦] who was more commonly known by his nickname of So Huk Yee [蘇乞兒] and Tam Chai-Kwan / Tan Jiyun [譚濟筠] who was also known by the nickname of Three Leg Tam / Sam Kuk Tam [三脚譚]. Out of these three, two of them have passed on Fifth Brother Eight Diagram (Octagonal) Staff / Ng Lung Ba Gwa Kwun [五郎八卦棍] routine [套路] down through their lineages. [50d] [184] It is known that Chau Tai [鄒泰] changed this routine [套路] and renamed it Zhou Family Bagua Staff / Chau Gar Ba Gua Gwun [周家八卦棍]. (Michael) Chau Sui / Zhou Shou [鄒穗] stated that he didn't know if Chau Tai [鄒泰] was friends with any of the orther Tigers [廣東十虎]. But I think it is fair to assume that these masters [功夫大師], who were all highly skilled with the staff / Gwun [棍], could have shared their ideas and methods regarding this weapon, especially as Chau Tai [鄒泰], Wong Kei-Ying [黃麒英] and Tam Chai-Kwan [譚濟筠] all knew the Fifth Brother Eight Diagram (Octagonal) Staff / Ng Lung Ba Gwa Kwun [五郎八卦棍] routine [套路], which was to become a pillar of their future syllabuses.

During the 1860s, Chau Tai [鄒泰] was married and his wife would lived at the family home in the village of Guanyao / Kwun Yiu Tsuen [官窑村]. In 1868, they had a son whom they called Chau Kam Choi / Jian Cai Zhou [鄒監才]. It is understood that after the birth of his son, Chau Tai [鄒泰] started to settle down and leave the Jianghu [江湖] lifestyle behind. He started to teach his son, Chau Kam Choi / Jian Cai Zhou [鄒監才], from the age of five years, his style of Kung Fu [功夫]. Now in his late forties, he also taught Kung Fu [功夫] to his extended family which included his nieces and nephews. Around 1878, he started to teach his family on a more formal basis at the local village ancestral hall; Chau Tai's [鄒泰] main disciples being Chau Hor Chuen / Zhou Ke Quan [鄒 可全], Chau Yun Tin / Zhou Ren Tian [鄒潤田], Chau Chung / Zhou Zhong [鄒忠], Chau Sing / Zhou Seng [鄒勝] and Tse Sire / Xie She [謝蛇], besides his own son. Tse Sire / Xie She [謝蛇] was the only non-family member to be taught by Chau Tai [鄒泰].

It is stated that Chau Tai [鄒泰] incorporated the various experiences during his life to formulate his own style, which is known as Chau Gar Kuen [周家拳]. Initially, basic techniques are taught with narrow hand and leg movements with a concentration of power which is directed from the waist. Once this has been achieved, the emphasis is then on gentle, flowing movements with the power applied swiftly and smoothly. Attitude is also important and it is taught that the practitioner must be controlled with an orderly, fast manner. They must be tolerant, patient and undeterred in defence, but also have the humility to withdraw at the opportune moment so as not to be defeated unnecessarily.

Tse Sire / Xie She [謝蛇] was keen to study under Chau Tai [鄒泰], and so had moved to the village of Guanyao / Kwun Yiu Tsuen [官窑村], getting a job as a cowherd. When he realised that Chau Tai [鄒泰] would only teach family members, he secretly watched them train in the village ancestral hall and would then practice on his own. This secret learning continued for more than half a year before Chau Tai [鄒泰] found out. He had found Tse Sire / Xie She [謝蛇] an earnest young man, who had a deep passionate desire to learn the Zhou Family Bagua Staff / Chau Gar Ba Gua Gwun [周家八卦棍]. Chau Tai [鄒泰] therefore decided to make an exception to his rule and accept him as a disciple. It is understood that Tse Sire / Xie She [謝蛇] continued to study the Zhou Family Bagua Staff / Chau Gar Ba Gua Gwun [周家八卦棍] until 1896, when Chau Tai [鄒泰] passed away at the age of sixty eight. [181]

Sometime later, Tse Sire / Xie She [謝蛇] became very good friends with Tam Sam [譚三] who founded the Buk Sing Choy Li Fut [北勝蔡李佛] style at the village of Little North / Siu Buk / Xiaobei [小北]. It is understood that Tse Sire / Xie She [謝蛇] and Tam Sam [譚三] exchanged ideas and techniques. Tse Sire / Xie She [謝蛇] took on students teaching them the Zhou Family Bagua Staff / Chau Gar Ba Gua Gwun [周家八卦棍] and Buk Sing Choy Li Fut [北勝蔡李佛]. Tse Sire's / Xie She [謝蛇] successor was a man called Tse Tim / Xie Tian [謝添] who, in time passed it onto Tse Ki / Xie Ji [謝基]. [181]

In 1912 at the age of forty four, Chau Kam Choi / Jian Cai Zhou [鄒監才] had a son whom he called Chau Hung / Zhou Xiong [鄒雄] (3rd generation). Chau Kam Choi / Jian Cai Zhou [鄒監才] taught his son the family style from the age of four, but unfortunately, Jian Cai Zhou [鄒監才] died in 1924 when Chau Hung / Zhou Xiong [鄒雄] was only twelve years old. The twelve year old Chau Hung / Zhou Xiong [鄒雄] continued his education of Chau Gar Kuen [周家拳] under the tutelage of his uncles.

(Michael) Chau Sui / Zhou Shou [鄒穗] (4th generation) was born in Canton / Guangzhou [廣州市] in 1957. Michael [鄒穗] was taught his family style from the age of five years old by his father, and was himself teaching from the age of twelve. Under the recommendation of his father, Michael [鄒穗] also studied Buk Sing Choi Li Fut [北勝蔡李佛] under Master Tse Ki / Xie Ji [謝基]. (Descended from Tse Sire / Xie She [謝蛇] who had originally studied the Zhou Family Bagua Staff / Chau Gar Ba Gua Gwun [周家八卦棍] under Michael's great grandfather, Chau Tai [鄒泰]). Michael [鄒穗] began his training with Master Tse Ki / Xie Ji [謝基] at the age of five and studied under him for seven years. Michael [鄒穗] continued to develop his own skills and was regarded as a master [功夫大師] by the age of thirty.

Michael [鄒穗] states that in 1973, at the age of sixteen, his uncle and cousins came together to put the entire Chau Gar Kuen [周家拳] system together. Previously, Chau Tai [鄒泰] had only taught his family members various aspects of the system, so that they only knew a quarter each. (Michael) Chau Sui / Zhou Shou [鄒穗] became the first person to know and master the entire Chau Gar Kuen [周家拳] system.

Chau Hung / Zhou Xiong [鄒雄] and (Michael) Chau Sui / Zhou Shou [鄒穗] emigrated from Canton to San Francisco in the USA, in 1987. Michael [鄒穗] would teach martial arts after work, until he was finally able to open up his own martial arts school [武術學校] in 1992. This was located at 5070 Mission Street, in the Mission District of San Francisco. In 1998, he relocated his martial arts school [武術學校] called the Chau Gah Kung Fu Academy, to Judah Street in the Sunset District of San Francisco. [186]

The traditional Chinese medicine [中醫] techniques have been handed down through the family for generations. (Michael) Chau Sui [鄒穗] currently treats patients from all over the world that travel to him in San Francisco. Besides being a herbalist, Michael is skilled in various other practices which include, preparing anti-inflammatory plaster, cupping [拔罐] sinew & ligament treatments and bone-setting [整骨 or 正骨]. Traditionally, some Kung Fu masters [功夫大師] besides being expert fighters, were also doctors. This principle stems back to the Siu Lum / Shaolin Temple [少林寺] and (Michael) Chau Sui [鄒穗] believes that the two go hand in hand. [181]

(Michael) Chau Sui [鄒穗] told me that within the Chau Gar [鄒家] system, the five internal Yang sets are called the Five Tigers descend on Szechuan / Ng Fu Ha Sze Chuen / Wu Hu Xia Sichuan [五虎下四川]. I have since found out that this is a common martial phrase used to describe particularly ferocious and brutal methods or techniques. (This is not the same as what Grandmaster Wang Desheng is famed for.) He stated that these Yang sets are to help a student train and develop a solid foundation with power. The five internal Yin sets are referred to as Tai Chi Staff / Taiji Gun [太极棍] within the Chau Gar [鄒家] system. (Michael) Chau Sui [鄒穗] informed me that these internal sets are to help a student train to improve their technique.

(Michael) Chau Sui / Zhou Shou [鄒穗] performing the Zhou
Family Bagua Staff / Chau Gar Ba Gua Gwun
[周家八卦棍], 1992.

Many thanks to (Michael) Chau Sui / Zhou Shou [鄒穗] for helping to provide information and photos for my research into his great grandfather, Chau Tai [鄒泰].

Chau Gah Kung Fu Academy, Judah Street in the Sunset District of San Francisco.

(Michael) Chau Sui / Zhou Shou [鄒穗] & Chau Hung / Zhou Xiong [鄒雄] (105yrs old) 2017.

Conclusions & Assumptions

Through the individual histories many of the Ten Tigers of Canton / Kwong Tung Sap Fu [廣東十虎] moved around living the Jianghu [江湖] lifestyle. But, during the 1850s, when the Ten Tigers of Canton / Kwong Tung Sap Fu [廣東十虎] (Guangdong) were elected, it is believed that they were all living within the provincial capital city [省會城市] of Canton [廣州] or its surrounding suburbs and villages. The map below shows the areas where the Tigers lived or had their schools [武術學校] during this period.

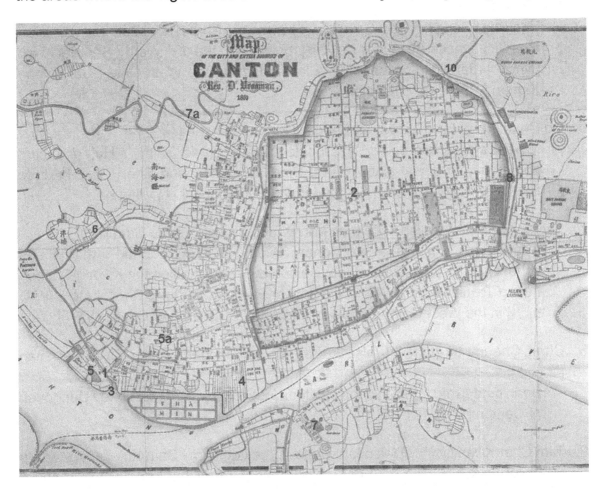

1. Wong Yan-Lam [王隱林]
   Martial arts school [武術學校] and bone setting clinic / Tip Da Yee Kwun [跌打醫館], practising Tibetan medicine [藏傳醫術], in Kim Sin Street / Jianshan Jie [兼善街] just off Wong Sa Road [黃沙大道], which was located in the West Gate / Sai Kwan / Xiguan [西關] of Canton [廣州].

2. Wong Ching-Hoh [黃澄可]
   Living in Benevolence and Love Street / Wai Oi Street [惠愛街] which was located in the middle of the old walled city of Canton [廣州].

299

3. So [蘇] (known as So the Black Tiger / So Hak Fu [蘇黑虎])
   Martial arts school [武術學校] located in Wong Sa Road / Huangsha Avenue [黃沙大道], in the West Gate / Sai Kwan / Xiguan [西關] area of Canton [廣州] close to the Wong Sa / Huangsha Ferry Pier [黃沙碼頭].

4. Wong Kei-Ying [黃麒英]
   Po Chi Lam Clinic / Bao Zhi Lin [宝芝林] and martial arts school [武術學校], located in Jingyan Street / Chan Yun Street [靖遠街] of Canton [廣州].

5. Lai Yan-Chiu [黎仁超]
   The Chao Feng [朝奉] of Shun Hang Pawnshop [信亨押店] located in Wong Sai Road/Huangsha Avenue [黃沙大道], but lived in the 10th Ward / Sap Sai Kwan [西第十] (5a). Both of these were located within the West Gate / Sai Kwan / Xiguan [西關] area of Canton [廣州].

6. So Chan [蘇燦] (also known as Beggar So / So Hut Yee [蘇乞兒])
   Martial arts school [武術學校] located at the Three Saints / Holy / Sacred community or social club / Saam Sing Se / Sansheng She [三聖社], Three Saints Street [三聖社大街] located in the Pun Tong [泮塘] village.

7. Leung Kwan [梁坤] (also known as Iron Bridge Three / Tit Kiu Sam [鐵橋三])
   Spent much of his life at the Honam Temple [河南寺], but had a martial arts school [武術學校] located at the Canton dye-works called the Kwong Cheong Leung Textile Factory [廣昌梁布廠], near Rainbow Bridge / Choi Hung Qui [彩虹橋] in the West Gate / Sai Kwan / Xiguan [西關] area of Canton [廣州] (7a).

8. Chan Cheung-tai [陳長泰] (also known as Iron Finger Chen / Tit Chee Chan [鐵指陳])
   Bean curd / Tofu [豆腐店] shop located close to the main East Gate / Dongguan of Canton [廣州大東門外].

9. Tam Chai-Kwan [譚濟筠] (also known as Three Leg Tam / Sam Kuk Tam [三脚譚])
   Unfortunately I have not been able to find if Tam Chai-Kwan [譚濟筠] had a martial arts school [武術學校] in Canton [廣州], but it is recorded that he had a school [武術學校] near Red Sand Pond Village / Chep Lai Sha Tong Tsuen / Shatang Cun [赤坭沙塘村] of Far Dou / Hua County / Huaxian [花县], located approximately 27 kms north-west of Canton [廣州]. What is recorded is that he spent some time in Canton [廣州] during this period, but again I have been unable to find this location. An assumption is that it may have been with, or somewhere close to, his good friend Wong Ching-Hoh [黃澄可], who lived in Benevolence and Love Street / Wai Oi Street [惠愛街] in the old walled city of Canton [廣州].

10. Chau Tai [鄒泰]

It is understood that as he was living the Jianghu [江湖] lifestyle during this period he didn't stay at one address for too long. But it is understood that at one stage, he was staying somewhere in the area of village of the Sam Yuen Li / San Yuan Li [三元里], just outside the old city walls of Canton [廣州].

Through the individual histories of the Ten Tigers [廣東十虎], we know there was definitely some connections and interactions between several of them. How deep this interaction was, is hard to say, but it is known that certain ideas, methods and routines [套路] were definitely exchanged. Also, through some of the individual histories, I can state that besides a mutual respect for each other, several of these masters [功夫大師] actually regarded each other as good friends. Hak Fu Mun [黑虎門] history (and several independent sources) states that So Hak Fu [蘇黑虎] was friends with Wong Yan-Lam / Wang Yinlin [王隱林], Wong Kei-Ying / Huang Qiying [黃麒英], Lai Yan-Chiu / Li Renchao [黎仁超] and So Chan / Su Can [蘇燦] (who was more commonly known by his nickname of So Hat-Yee [蘇乞兒] which means Beggar So), with whom he exchanged ideas and methods. He may well have been friends with the other members of the Ten Tigers of Guangdong / Kwong Tung Sap Fu [廣東十虎], but this has not been recorded. I believe the reason for this, is that only the names with whom So Hak Fu [蘇黑虎] exchanged methods, have been recorded in Hak Fu Mun oral history. I would therefore think it is fair to assume that all the Ten Tigers of Guangdong / Kwong Tung Sap Fu [廣東十虎] actually knew each other, and were on friendly terms. This was also confirmed by David Rogers, who was told by his Sifu [師父], Master Deng Jan Gong [鄧鎮江], that at the time of the Ten Tigers [廣東十虎], all of the masters [功夫大師] would meet up for Yum Cha [飲茶] at the tea houses, where they would freely exchange techniques. *(Sifu David Rogers of the Rising Crane Centre located in Bedford, UK.)*

It is recorded that the Ten Tigers of Guangdong / Kwong Tung Sap Fu [廣東十虎] were also chosen for their anti-Ch'ing / anti-Qing [反清清朝] beliefs and deeds. It is therefore possible that some of these masters [功夫大師] may have worked together in their anti-Ch'ing / anti-Qing [反清清朝] activities. There are no specific details or records regarding any deeds or activities. This is because these activities were treasonous, and so could be used as evidence which would lead to their execution by beheading.

The 1979 Hong Kong film, the "Ten Tigers of Kwangtung" [廣東十虎] and several books including "The Ten Tigers of Kwangtung-Trouble at the Sai Shaan Monastery" [十虎大鬧西山寺], and "Ten Tigers of Guangdong: Blood, Battle at the West Cannon Fortress" / Ngo Sze Shan Yan's Guangdong Shihu Xuezhan Xipaotai [廣東十虎血戰西炮台], all depict these ten renowned masters [功夫大師] as a group, who helped each other and worked together, at certain times. The Lama Pai [喇嘛派] poem states, "A lot of fighting in the city, the Ten Tigers of Guangdong made the earth tremble", [90] which in my opinion, this statement sounds as if they worked as a group of sorts. I can only assume that these stories are based on some facts, and after all my research, I believe it is a possibility that the Ten Tigers of Canton / Kwong Tung Sap Fu [廣東十虎] may have worked together as a group of friends, at some point during their history.

Sources

[1]   http://en.wikipedia.org/wiki/Cantonese

[1a]   http://en.wikipedia.org/wiki/Pinyin

[1c]   https://en.wikipedia.org/wiki/Qianlong_Emperor

[2]   https://en.wikipedia.org/wiki/Kung_fu_(term)

[2a]   https://en.wikipedia.org/wiki/Chinese_martial_arts

[3]   http://en.wikipedia.org/wiki/Hanfu

[4]   http://en.wikipedia.org/wiki/Queue_(hairstyle)

[5]   http://en.wikipedia.org/wiki/Manchu_people

[6]   http://en.wikipedia.org/wiki/First_Opium_War

[7]   http://en.wikipedia.org/wiki/Taiping_Rebellion

[8]   http://taipingrebellion.com/

[9]   http://webs.bcp.org/sites/vcleary/ModernWorldHistoryTextbook/Imperialism/section_5/secondopiumwar.html

[10]   http://www.archives.presbyterian.org.nz/photogallery9/page1.htm

[11]   http://en.wikipedia.org/wiki/Panthay_Rebellion

[11a]   http://en.wikipedia.org/wiki/Dungan_Revolt_(1862–77)

[12]   http://en.wikipedia.org/wiki/Liangguang

[12a]   http://en.wikipedia.org/wiki/Viceroy_of_Liangguang

[12b]   http://ocw.mit.edu/ans7870/21f/21f.027/rise_fall_canton_03/cw_essay01.html

[12c]   http://www.1902encyclopedia.com/C/CAN/canton.html

[12cc] http://en.wikipedia.org/wiki/Tael

[12d]   http://www.pbenyon.plus.com/Hurrah/Chap_05.htm

[12e]   http://www.pdavis.nl/China2.htm

[12f]   http://en.wikipedia.org/wiki/Battle_of_Canton_(1857)

[12g]   China: Being "The Times" Special Correspondence from China in the Years 1857-58 by George Wingrove Cooke **ISBN-13:** 978-1241161996

[12h]   http http://en.wikipedia.org/wiki/Sacred_Heart_Cathedral_(Guangzhou)

[12i]   http://en.wikipedia.org/wiki/Shamian_Island

[12j]   The Treaty Ports of China and Japan: A Complete Guide to the Open Ports of those Countries, together with Peking, Yedo, Hongkong and Macao. **ISBN-13:** 978-1108045902

[12]   The Royal Navy: A History from the Earliest Times to 1900" written by Sir William Laird Clowes **ISBN-13:** 978-1861760166

[13]   http://www.black-tiger association.org/History/TenTigersOfCanton/tabid/59/Default.aspx

[14]   http://www.taipinginstitute.com/courses/lingnan/hung-kuen

[15]   http://en.wikipedia.org/wiki/Lei_tai

[16]   The Shaolin Grandmasters' Text. **ISBN** 0-9755009-0-2

[17]   The Art of Shaolin Kung Fu by Wong Kiew Kit. **ISBN**-10 0804834393

[18]   http://www.kungfu-taichi.com/servlet/kungfoo/Action/Resource/ResourceKey/1961

[19]   http://www.bgtent.com/naturalcma/CMAarticle13.htm

[20]   http://www.chinagamerguy.com/2014/02/the-riddle-of-southern-shaolin/ (Translated from Shaolin Fang Gu, by Wen Yu Chen ISBN:7-5306-2830-5 by Chris Toepker)

[21]   http://www.whatsonxiamen.com/travel_msg.php?titleid=120&traveltype=Travel in Xiamen

[21a]   https://www.facebook.com/notes/benny-meng/the-holy-land-of-martial-arts-southern-shaolin- temple/268354163176512
        article written by Benny Meng, Ving Tsun Museum, 5717 Brandt Pike, Dayton, USA.

[21b]   http://ptnsl.cn/?p=1152

[22]   http://www.kungfumagazine.com/ezine/article.php?article=1181 / 1175 / 1176
[22a] http://www.wle.com/kungfu/node/20
[22b] http://www.amoymagic.com/Kungfu.htm
[23]   http://en.wikipedia.org/wiki/Guangzhou
[24]   Comprehensive Asian Fighting Arts By Draeger & Smith. **ISBN**-10: 0870114360
[25]   http://www.bgtent.com/naturalcma/CMAarticle21.htm
[25a] http://www.bgtent.com/naturalcma/CMAarticle24.htm
[26]   http://en.wikipedia.org/wiki/Shaolin_Monastery
[27]   http://www.shaolin-gongfu.de/cms/de/node/1002#
[28]   http://shaolin-wahnam.fi/shaolin/39-the-venerable-zhi-zhan
[29]   http://en.wikipedia.org/wiki/Jee_Sin_Sim_See
[30]   http://en.wikipedia.org/wiki/Southern_Shaolin_Monastery
[30a] http://guangmingzhicheng.blog.163.com/blog/static/16471803201343195644113/
       (A record of the Southern Shaolin Legend produced by the Quanzhou Evening newspaper
       for the Quanzhou World Southern Fujian Cultural Festival, 31st May 2013.)
[31]   http://yeeskf.com/jee-sin-sim-see/
[31a] https://en.wikipedia.org/wiki/Five_Elders
[32]   http://en.wikipedia.org/wiki/Bak_Mei
[32a] http://www.peimeikungfu.com/home.php?lang=en&page=&rub=7
[32b] http://sifuochwingchun.com/wing-chun-kung-fu-history/legendary-five-elders-of-the-sil-
       lum- temple-creators-of-wing-chun/
[33]   http://yeeshungga.com/our-style/history/
[33a] http://www.pakmeipai.nl/history1.html
[33b] http://shaolinhouse.com/products-page/wooden-dummy-history/
[33c] https://www.shaolinarts.com/history_and_philosophy
[33d] http://ussd.com/history-of-shaolin-kempo/
[34]   http://www.hlk.zoomshare.com/13.html
[35]   http://www.hungsing.com/founder.htm
[36]   https://en.wikipedia.org/wiki/Jeong_Yim
[36a] https://en.wikipedia.org/wiki/Tiandihui
[36b] http://www.hungsing.com/fongDaiHung.htm
[36c] The Origins of the Tiandihui by Dian H. Murray In Collaboration with Qin Baoqi.
       ISBN-13: 978-0804723244
[37]   http://www.kungfulibrary.com/shaolin-shouthern-she-zu-quan.htm (from the book - SHE ZU
       QUAN: Pugilistic Art of the SHE Nationality)
[37a] http://taipinginstitute.com/menu-styles/zy/yanqing-quan
[38]   http://special.lifeofguangzhou.com/2008/node_771/120599495435801.shtml
[39]   http://www.chinaholiday.com/scenic-of-guangzhou/guangzhou-sea-temple-at-guangzhou/
[40]   http://zh.wikipedia.org/wiki/海幢寺   (Chinese)
[41]   http://en.wikipedia.org/wiki/John_Thomson_(photographer)
[42]   http://en.wikisource.org/wiki/Illustrations_of_China_and_Its_People/Volume_1
[43]   http://www.heatons-of-tisbury.co.uk/allom.htm
[44]   http://www.chinese-outpost.com/history/thomas-allom-china-illustrated/
[45]   http://www.chinatravelsavvy.com/destinations/guangzhou/attractions/hualin-temple/
[46]   http://zh.wikipedia.org/wiki/华林寺(广州)   (Chinese)
[47]   http://www.powerhousemuseum.com/imageservices/page/81/
[48]   http://digital.nls.uk/thomson/china.html
[48a] https://en.wikipedia.org/wiki/John_Thomson_(photographer)
[49]   http://chingcho.webs.com/history.htm
[50]   http://ykwcaa.com/

[50a]   Hak Fu Mun oral history (passed down through the generations)

[50b]   The Qianlong Emperor Inspects Southern China / Kin Loong har Kwong Nam / Qianlong Xia Jiangnan [乾隆下江南]. *(This book is in Chinese and has no ISBN number)*

[50c]   Paper Swordsmen Jin Yong And the Modern Chinese Martial Arts Novel by John Christopher Hamm **ISBN-13:** 978-0824828950

[50d]   Real Kung Fu, 1976 (pgs 5-7)

[51]   http://www.black-tiger-association.org/History/Origins/tabid/61/Default.aspx

[51a]   http://www.black-tiger-association.org/History/TenTigersOfCanton/tabid/59/Default.aspx

[52]   http://www.douban.com/group/topic/6709792/

[53]   http://en.wikipedia.org/wiki/Guangxiao_Temple_(Guangzhou)

[53a]   http://zh.wikipedia.org/wiki/光孝寺(广州)   *(Chinese)*

[53b]   https://en.wikipedia.org/wiki/Lingnan

[53c]   https://en.wikipedia.org/wiki/Qing_conquest_of_the_Ming

[54]   http://www.travelchinaguide.com/attraction/guangdong/guangzhou/bright_filial.htm

[55]   http://en.wikipedia.org/wiki/Temple_of_the_Six_Banyan_Trees

[55a]   http://zh.wikipedia.org/wiki/六榕寺   *(Chinese)*

[56]   http://www.travelchinaguide.com/attraction/guangdong/guangzhou/six_tree.htm

[57]   http://gocn.southcn.com/english/localculture/200804080008.htm

[57a]   http://travelcathay.com/2014/03/05/travel-guangzhou-temple/

[58]   https://zh.wikipedia.org/zh/大佛寺(广州)   *(Chinese)*

[59]   http://www.southern5.com/Fut.html

[60]   http://en.wikipedia.org/wiki/Guangdong

[60a]   http://en.wikipedia.org/wiki/Pearl_River_(China)

[61]   Black Belt magazine issue August 1965 pages 20-23

[61a]   Black Belt magazine issue September 1965 pages 32-38

[61b]   Black Belt magazine issue October 1965 pages 34-39

[61c]   Black Belt magazine issue November 1965 pages 16-21

[61d]   Black Belt magazine issue December 1965 pages 28-29 & 24-31

[61e]   Black Belt magazine issues January 1966 pages 15-21 & 52-53

[61f]   Black Belt magazine issues February 1966 pages 30-35

[62]   Chambers's Concise Gazetteer Of The World.

[63]   http://www.archives.presbyterian.org.nz/photogallery9/page1.htm

[64]   Southern Shaolin Kung Fu Ling Nam Hung Gar. **ISBN-10:** 1586573616

[65]   http://www.shaolin.org/answers/ans99b/nov99-1.html

[66]   http://www.bgtent.com/naturalcma/CMAarticle14.htm

[67]   http://www.cityu.edu.hk/lib/about/event/cantonese_opera/origins.htm

[68]   http://everything2.com/title/Wing+Chun

[69]   http://www.londonwingchun.co.uk/red-junk-opera-company

[70]   http://practicalhungkyun.com/history/legendary-founders/

[70a]   http://en.wikipedia.org/wiki/Leung_Yee-tai

[71]   http://en.wikipedia.org/wiki/History_of_Wing_Chun

[72]   http://www.shaolinarts.com/historyAndPhilosophy

[73]   http://tunglungkungfu.page.tl/

[74]   http://goldenwillowgungfu.com/history/hung-hei-gun/

[75]   http://www.shaolin.org/answers/ans05a/mar05-1.html

[75a]   http://en.wikipedia.org/wiki/Duel

[76]   http://en.wikipedia.org/wiki/San_Te

[76a]   http://www.lifeofguangzhou.com/node_10/node_228/node_232/2009/04/27/1240813125636 76.shtml

[77]   http://practicalhungkyun.com/2013/11/hung-kyuns-four-fingers-supporting-heaven-poem/

[78]   http://www.shaolin.org/general-2/iron-wire/iron-wire08.html
[78a]   http://www.shaolin.org/general-2/kungfu-sets/triple-stretch.html
[78b]   http://www.shaolin.org/answers/ans10b/dec10-2.html
[78c]   http://www.shaolin.org/answers/ans06a/may06-1.html
[78d]   http://practicalhungkyun.com/2013/01/six-and-half-point-long-pole-luk-dim-bun-gwan/
[79]   http://en.wikipedia.org/wiki/Duan_Quan
[80]   http://www.wongkiewkit.com/forum/archive/index.php/t-5285.html
[80a]   http://en.wikipedia.org/wiki/Alms
[80b]   http://en.wikipedia.org/wiki/Showdown_at_the_Cotton_Mill
[81]   http://www.shaolinchamber36.com/buddhist-blog/the-genesis-of-shaolin/
[81a]   http://www.dvdbeaver.com/film/dvdcompare/36thchamber.htm
[81b]   http://thehkneo.com/olderfilms/T3COS.htm
[81c]   https://en.wikipedia.org/wiki/The_36th_Chamber_of_Shaolin
[81d]   http://practicalhungkyun.com/wp-content/uploads/2015/01/36ᵗʰ-chamber-of-shaolin.pdf
[82]   Monk San De's Three Visits to the Xichan Monastery" written by Woshi Shanren
[83]   http://www.shaolin.org/answers/ans07b/dec07-1.html
[83a]   http://www.shaolin.org/general-2/iron-wire/iron-wire05.html
[84]   Iron Thread. Southern Shaolin Hung Gar Kung Fu Classis Series **ISBN 13:** 9781847991928
[85]   http://www.shaolin.org/answers/ans99b/nov99-2.html
[85a]   http://www.shaolin.org/shaolin/four-gates.html
[85b]   http://www.shaolin.org/general-2/dragon-strength/dragon-strength05.html
[85c]   http://www.shaolin.org/answers/ans05a/mar05-2.html
[85d]   http://www.shaolin.org/general-2/dragon-strength/dragon-strength01.html
[85e]   http://www.shaolin.org/answers/ans98b/dec98-2.html
[86]   http://www.angelfire.com/extreme5/fit2fightclub/lamakungfuhistory.html
[87]   http://en.wikipedia.org/wiki/Lama_(martial_art)
[88]   http://www.xiaquan.com/html/history.html
[88a]   http://www.zwbk.org/MyLemmaShow.aspx?zh=zh-tw&lid=127634   (Chinese)
[88b]   http://www.risingcrane.co.uk
[88c]   https://en.wikipedia.org/wiki/Yum_cha
[89]   http://en.wikipedia.org/wiki/Sing_Lung
[89a]   http://www.zhfgwh.com/a/shansifengjing/72927.html   (Chinese)
[89b]   http://zh.wikipedia.org/wiki/庆云寺_(肇庆)   (Chinese)
[90]   Authentic Lama Pai Kung-Fu **ISBN-13**: 978-1500432829
[91]   http://www.plumpub.com/kaimen/2006/hop-gar-kung-fu/
[92]   http://www.usadojo.com/styles/history-hop-gar.htm
[93]   History of the pirates who infested the China Sea from 1807-1810 by Charles F Neumann
        ISBN : 9781163500132
[93a]   http://www.thewayofthepirates.com/famous-pirates/cheung-po-tsai/
[93b]   https://en.wikipedia.org/wiki/Cheung_Po_Tsai
[94]   http://en.wikipedia.org/wiki/Dinghu_Mountain
[95]   http://en.wikipedia.org/wiki/Wuxia
[95a]   http://wenku.baidu.com/view/4bb3af8984868762caaed5c9
[96]   http://taipinginstitute.com/menu-styles/ln/gumgong-kuen
[96a]   http://www.usadojo.com/articles/gene-ching/keeping-secrets.htm
[96b]   https://zh.wikipedia.org/wiki/王隐林   (Chinese)
[97]   http://en.wikipedia.org/wiki/Hung_Hei-gun
[97a]   http://www.fuhok.com/history-hung-gar
[97b]   https://en.wikipedia.org/wiki/Luohan_(martial_arts)
[97c]   http://www.chinese-culture.pl/?page_id=1223

[98]   http://practicalhungkyun.com/2013/03/why-is-hung-kyun-called-hung-kyun/
[99]   http://hunggaruk.com/history-of-hung-gar/
[100]   http://www.intermartialarts.com/legends/hung-gar-kung-fu
[100a]   http://www.fuhok.com/history-tiger-crane
[100b]   http://ensomartialarts.com/shaolin-kung-fu/
[101]   http://5animalkungfu.com/hung-ga-history.htm
[102]   http://yeeshungga.com/our-style/lineage/lukahchoi.html
[102a]   http://www.shaolinwushucenter.com/lineage/
[102b]   https://zh.wikipedia.org/wiki/洪拳
[103]   http://www.hunggar.pl/en/hung-gar-kung-fu/masters-of-hung-gar-kuen.html
[104]   http://www.fuhok.com/history-teaching-dynasty
[105]   http://en.wikipedia.org/wiki/Wong_Kei-ying
[105a]   https://zh.wikipedia.org/wiki/黃麒英   (Chinese)
[106]   http://www.tony-nampaikungfu.com/english_site/en_historia_03_hong_quan.html
[106a]   http://www.tony-nampaikungfu.com/english_site/en_frames_genealogia_01.html
[106b]   http://practicalhungkyun.com/wp-content/wi8x8va/legendary-grand-masters-of-hung-kyun-
         part-01.pdf
[107]   http://clonmelhunggar.tripod.com/id15.html
[108]   http://www.southern5.com/Hung.html
[108a]   http://www.hunggarkuen.com/early-history-of-hung-kuen/
[108b]   https://prezi.com/4jrbnz9xacqz/time-line-of-china-growth-of-people-and-communism/
[109]   http://en.wikipedia.org/wiki/Ten_Tigers_of_Canton
[109a]   http://en.wikipedia.org/wiki/Talk:Ten_Tigers_of_Canton
[109b]   https://zh.wikipedia.org/wiki/廣東十虎   (Chinese)
[109c]   https://th.wikipedia.org/wiki/สืบพยัคฆ์กวางตุ้ง   (Thai)
[109d]   http://www.china-expats.com/Foshan_KungFu.htm
[109e]   http://www.xklsv.org/viewwiki.php?title= Guangdong Sahp Fu
[110]   http://bodhimonastery.org/becoming-a-buddhist-lay-disciple.html
[111]   http://en.wikipedia.org/wiki/Prātimokṣa
[111a]   https://en.wikipedia.org/wiki/Chinese_Buddhism
[112]   https://en.wikipedia.org/wiki/Hung_Ga
[112a]   Five Pattern Hung Kuen. **ISBN-13:** 978-9627284093
[113]   http://www.zwbk.org/MyLemmaShow.aspx?zh=zh-tw&lid=127636   (Chinese)
[114]   Training Methods of 72 Arts of Shaolin. **ISBN-13:** 978-1847284068
[114a]   http://lotoblanco.com/2012/06/   (Spanish)
[115]   http://bac-wongfeihong.blogspot.co.uk/   (Chinese)
[115a]   https://zh.wikipedia.org/wiki/英雄之廣東十虎   (Chinese)
[115b]   https://en.wikipedia.org/wiki/Zhongshan
[115c]   https://zh.wikipedia.org/wiki/中山路_(广州)   (Chinese)
[116]   http://en.wikipedia.org/wiki/Dit_da_jow
[116a]   https://en.wikipedia.org/wiki/Marten
[116b]   https://en.wikipedia.org/wiki/Yellow-throated_marten
[117]   http://zh.wikipedia.org/wiki/醉拳   (Chinese)
[117a]   https://en.wikipedia.org/wiki/Fu_Zhensong
[117b]   https://en.wikipedia.org/wiki/Fu_Style_Baguazhang
[118]   http://www.fujowpai.com/history.html
[118a]   https://en.wikipedia.org/wiki/Fu_Jow_Pai
[118b]   http://fongskungfu.com/Images_files/History/Fu-Jow_Pai.html
[118c]   Wushu Kung Fu Qigong magazine, September 1998, pgs 38-40.
[119]   http://www.yhachina.com/topic.php?channelID=13&topicID=114

[120]   New Martial Hero, issue 303 (GM Wong Cheung interview by Hui Yet Chiu, 1973)

[121]   Martial Arts Weekly (GM Wong Cheung interview, 1973)

[122]   http://blog.xuite.net/chongchan922/hkblog/186043044Chung+Wai+Ming,+the'King+of+Radio+Broadcasting +播音皇帝+-+鍾偉明

[122a]   The Ten Tigers of Kwangtung-Trouble at the Sai Shaan Monastery [十虎大鬧西山寺]*(Chinese)*

[122b]   http://www.hkmemory.org/chung/text/listen-audio-zh.php?pageNum_audio=0   *(Chinese)*

[122c]   Ngo Sze Shan Yan's Guangdong Shihu Xuezhan Xipaotai (Ten Tigers of Guangdong: Blood Battle at the West Cannon Fortress) [廣東十虎血戰西炮台]

[123]   http://www.kungfulibrary.com/hunggar.htm GUNG GEE FOOK FU KUEN by Lam Sai Wing

[124]   http://www.fuhok.com/history-piece-wong-tai-life

[125]   http://en.wikipedia.org/wiki/Traditional_Chinese_medicine

[125a]   http://www.theworldofchinese.com/2013/10/time-to-get-patched-up/

[125b]   膏药（膏药）_百度百科

[126]   http://www.hunggar.pl/en/yin-yang/15-linia-przekazu-hung-gar-kuen.html

[127]   http://en.wikipedia.org/wiki/Lion_dance

[128]   http://www.fuhok.com/history-great-in-his-own-right

[129]   http://en.wikipedia.org/wiki/Wong_Fei-hung

[129a]   https://zh.wikipedia.org/wiki/黃飛鴻   *(Chinese)*

[129b]   http://baike.baidu.com/view/7450.htm   *(Chinese)*

[130]   http://www.zwbk.org/MyLemmaShow.aspx?zh=zh-tw&lid=127666   *(Chinese)*

[131]   http://naamkyun.com/2012/01/the-shadowless-kick-of-hung-ga-wong-keiying/

[131a]   https://en.wikipedia.org/wiki/Horse_stance

[131b]   https://en.wikipedia.org/wiki/Wushu_stances

[131c]   http://practicalhungkyun.com/2014/04/faq-april-2014-hung-ga-kyun-umbrella/

[132]   http://practicalhungkyun.com/history/wong-family/#sthash.fg7NaRLd.dpuf

[133]   http://yeeshungga.com/our-style/lineage/wongfeihung.html

[134]   http://www.hunggar.pl/en/hung-gar-kung-fu/masters-of-hung-gar-kuen.html

[135]   https://en.wikipedia.org/wiki/Thirteen_Factories

[136]   http://www.topchinatravel.com/china-attractions/wong-fei-hung-memorial-hall.htm

[136a]   https://en.wikipedia.org/wiki/Wong_Fei-hung_Memorial_Hall

[136b]   www.china-expats.com/TouristGuides_Foshan_CityDistricts.htm - China

[137]   http://www.lifeofguangzhou.com/node_10/node_228/node_233/node_235/2006/04/27/1146 1245882518.shtml

[137a]   https://en.wikipedia.org/wiki/Canton_Merchant_Volunteers_Corps_Uprising

[137b]   https://zh.wikipedia.org/wiki/广州商团事变   *(Chinese)*

[138]   https://en.wikipedia.org/wiki/Shantou

[138a]   http://en.wikipedia.org/wiki/Southern_Praying_Mantis

[138b]   https://en.wikipedia.org/wiki/Kowtow

[139]   http://www.bgtent.com/naturalcma/CMAarticle31-hakka.htm

[140]   http://en.wikipedia.org/wiki/Xiguan

[141]   http://www.zwbk.org/MyLemmaShow.aspx?zh=zh-tw&lid=127684   *(Chinese)*

[142]   http://www.zwbk.org/MyLemmaShow.aspx?zh=zh-tw&lid=127698   *(Chinese)*

[143]   http://en.wikipedia.org/wiki/Guan_Yu

[144]   http://en.wikipedia.org/wiki/Litter_(vehicle)

[144a]   https://zh.wikipedia.org/wiki/喜轎   *(Chinese)*

[145]   https://zh.wikipedia.org/zh-hant/蘇燦   *(Chinese)*

[145a]   http://practicalhungkyun.com/2013/09/hung-kyun-faq-september-2013-wong-fei-hung-and-drunken-boxing/

[145b]   https://en.wikipedia.org/wiki/Hung_Fut

[146]   http://www.hkcinemagic.com/en/page.asp?aid=186&page=1

[146a] https://zh.wikipedia.org/wiki/龙津路 *(Chinese)*
[147] http://www.shaolin.org/answers/ans10b/dec10-1.html
[147a] http://www.shaolin.org/answers/ans09a/may09-2.html
[148] http://en.wikipedia.org/wiki/Comprador
[149] http://en.wikipedia.org/wiki/Zui_quan
[150] http://practicalhungkyun.com/history/lineage-of-tit-kiu-saam/
[150a] https://fankwoen.wordpress.com/2014/02/02/tit-kiu-saams-bridge-hands-defeat-enemies/
[150b] https://fankwoen.wordpress.com/2014/02/15/part-2-tit-kiu-saams-bridge-hands-defeat-enemies/
[151] http://www.zwbk.org/MyLemmaShow.aspx?zh=zh-tw&lid=127606 *(Chinese)*
[152] http://www.fuhok.com/history-three-iron-bridges
[153] http://zh.wikipedia.org/wiki/能仁寺_(九江) *(Chinese)*
[154] http://en.wikipedia.org/wiki/Leung_Kwan
[154a] https://zh.wikipedia.org/wiki/梁坤 *(Chinese)*
[154b] http://baike.baidu.com/view/99751.htm *(Chinese)*
[154c] https://zh.wikipedia.org/wiki/荔湾路 *(Chinese)*
[154d] https://zh.wikipedia.org/wiki/彩虹桥_(广州) *(Chinese)*
[155] http://www.weito.org/history.html
[156] http://yeeshungga.com/our-style/lineage/tietkiusaam.html
[157] http://www.shaolin.org/general-2/kungfu-sets/iron-wire.html
[158] http://www.goldenlion.com.au/kung-fu/classes/traditional-training/
[159] http://www.hunggarkuen.com/hung-gar-kuen-kung-fu-style-2/
[160] http://en.wikipedia.org/wiki/Baiyun_Mountain_(Guangzhou)
[161] http://www.zwbk.org/MyLemmaShow.aspx?zh=zh-tw&lid=127687 *(Chinese)*
[162] http://en.wikipedia.org/wiki/Eagle_Claw
[163] http://en.wikipedia.org/wiki/Chin_Na
[164] http://practicalhungkyun.com/history/ten-tigers-of-gwong-dung/
[165] http://en.wikipedia.org/wiki/Catty
[166] http://www.zwbk.org/MyLemmaShow.aspx?zh=zh-tw&lid=127674 *(Chinese)*
[166a] https://www.youtube.com/watch?v=wsSuYvkXftw *(Chinese)*
[166b] https://en.wikipedia.org/wiki/Panyu_District
[166c] https://en.wikipedia.org/wiki/Guangzhou
[167] http://en.wikipedia.org/wiki/Leung_Jan
[168] Complete Wing Chun: The Definitive Guide to Wing Chun's History and Traditions **ISBN-13:** 978-0804831413
[169] http://en.wikipedia.org/wiki/Shadowless_Kick
[170] http://en.wikipedia.org/wiki/Five_Ancestors
[170a] http://www.bengkiam.com/bengkiam/archive/Kung Fu's Power Form - Alex Co.pdf
[171] http://practicalhungkyun.com/2014/08/hung-kyun-faq-august-2014-hung-gas-twelve-bridges- explained-in-twelve-lines-practical-plain-simple/#more-2972
[172] https://www.youtube.com/watch?v=A9-70NJXdC0 (Baiyun district Tam Ga)
[172a] http://www.chinahunggar.com/p/blog-page_2.html *(Chinese)*
[173] https://www.youtube.com/watch?v=IMnKzFfJ9To
[173a] https://www.youtube.com/watch?v=wxqh1sREiBs
[174] https://en.wikipedia.org/wiki/San_Yuan_Li
[174a] https://en.wikipedia.org/wiki/Baiyun_District,_Guangzhou
[175] The Power of Internal Martial Arts: Combat Secrets of Ba Gua, Tai Chi and Hsing-I **ISBN-13:** 978-1556432538
[176] http://en.wikipedia.org/wiki/Savate

[177] Western Civilization: A Global and Comparative Approach, Since 1600 (Volume 2) By Kenneth L. Campbell **ISBN-13:** 978-0765622549

[178] http://en.wikipedia.org/wiki/Foreign_relations_of_imperial_China

[179] http://en.wikipedia.org/wiki/Barbarian

[181] Michael, Chau Sui / Zhou Shou [鄒穗], Chau Gar oral history.

[181a] https://en.wikipedia.org/wiki/Yang_Yande

[181b] https://en.wikipedia.org/wiki/Yang_Ye

[181c] https://en.wikipedia.org/wiki/Generals_of_the_Yang_Family

[181d] https://en.wikipedia.org/wiki/The_Eight_Diagram_Pole_Fighter

[181e] https://www.wongkiewkit.com/forum/showthread.php?11700-Legacy-of-Wong-Fei-Hung-Q-A-Series-by-Sifu/page8

[181f] http://www.angelfire.com/rpg/hoardian/carlstadt/forms.htm

[181g] https://en.wikipedia.org/wiki/Shaolin_Kung_Fu

[181h] The Shaolin Monastery: History, Religion, and the Chinese Martial Arts, by Meir Shahar **ISBN-13:** 978-0824833497

[181i] http://www.singaporekungfu.com/single-end-staff-kung-fu.html

[181j] http://plumblossom.net/Articles/Inside_Kung-Fu/March2003/

[182] https://en.wikipedia.org/wiki/Mount_Wutai

[182a] https://zh.wikipedia.org/wiki/五台山   (Chinese)

[182b] http://www.cits.net/china-travel-guide/Wutaishan/xiantong-temple.html

[182c] http://www.chinadaily.com.cn/m/shanxi/wutaishan/2014-10/20/content_18810063.htm

[182d] https://zh.wikipedia.org/zh-hans/显通寺   (Chinese)

[183] https://en.wikipedia.org/wiki/Nanhai_County

[183a] http://en.wikipedia.org/wiki/Lingnan

[184] http://practicalhungkyun.com/2013/12/hung-ga-kyuns-eight-trigrams-long-pole-ng-long-baat-gwa-gwan/

[185] https://en.wikipedia.org/wiki/Pingtang_County

[186] http://www.manta.com/c/mmp79tz/chau-gah-king-fu-academy

Printed in the United States
by Baker & Taylor Publisher Services